Eastern Europe in 1968

Kevin McDermott · Matthew Stibbe
Editors

Eastern Europe in 1968

Responses to the Prague Spring and Warsaw Pact Invasion

palgrave
macmillan

943.7042

Editors
Kevin McDermott
Sheffield Hallam University
Sheffield, UK

Matthew Stibbe
Sheffield Hallam University
Sheffield, UK

ISBN 978-3-319-77068-0   ISBN 978-3-319-77069-7 (eBook)
https://doi.org/10.1007/978-3-319-77069-7

Library of Congress Control Number: 2018934657

© The Editor(s) (if applicable) and The Author(s) 2018
This work is subject to copyright. All rights are solely and exclusively licensed by the Publisher, whether the whole or part of the material is concerned, specifically the rights of translation, reprinting, reuse of illustrations, recitation, broadcasting, reproduction on microfilms or in any other physical way, and transmission or information storage and retrieval, electronic adaptation, computer software, or by similar or dissimilar methodology now known or hereafter developed.
The use of general descriptive names, registered names, trademarks, service marks, etc. in this publication does not imply, even in the absence of a specific statement, that such names are exempt from the relevant protective laws and regulations and therefore free for general use.
The publisher, the authors and the editors are safe to assume that the advice and information in this book are believed to be true and accurate at the date of publication. Neither the publisher nor the authors or the editors give a warranty, express or implied, with respect to the material contained herein or for any errors or omissions that may have been made. The publisher remains neutral with regard to jurisdictional claims in published maps and institutional affiliations.

Cover illustration: Young Czechs demonstrate their support for Dubček and the Prague Spring, Wenceslas Square (probably late August 1968).
© Photo by Bill Ray/The LIFE Picture Collection/Getty Images

Printed on acid-free paper

This Palgrave Macmillan imprint is published by the registered company Springer International Publishing AG part of Springer Nature
The registered company address is: Gewerbestrasse 11, 6330 Cham, Switzerland

Acknowledgements

This volume is the product of an international workshop held at Sheffield Hallam University in July 2017. The organisers, Kevin McDermott and Matthew Stibbe, wish to acknowledge the generous financial support of the Humanities Research Centre, Sheffield Hallam University, and the kind assistance of Professor Chris Hopkins and Professor Clare Midgley.

Kevin McDermott would like to thank Susie Reid, Frankie and Alex, Daryl and Jeremy Agnew, John Morison and all his colleagues and friends in the Czech and Slovak Republics.

Matthew Stibbe wishes to thank Sam, Nicholas and Hannah, to remember the constant help and encouragement of his late father, Paul Stibbe (4 January 1924–6 March 2017), and to express his gratitude for the past and on-going support of his step-mother, Hazel, and his sisters, Alex and Emily.

Contents

The Prague Spring and Warsaw Pact Invasion Through
the Soviet and East European Lens   1
Kevin McDermott and Matthew Stibbe

For a Civic Socialism and the Rule of Law: The Interplay
of Jurisprudence, Public Opinion and Dissent
in Czechoslovakia, 1960s–1980s   23
Kieran Williams and James Krapfl

The 'Anti-Prague Spring': Neo-Stalinist and Ultra-Leftist
Extremism in Czechoslovakia, 1968–70   45
Kevin McDermott and Vítězslav Sommer

The Impact of the Prague Spring on the USSR   71
Zbigniew Wojnowski

Ideological Offensive: The East German Leadership,
the Prague Spring and the Warsaw Pact Invasion
of August 1968   97
Matthew Stibbe

'To Hell with Sovereignty!': Poland and the Prague Spring   125
Tony Kemp-Welch

Hungary 1968: Reform and the Challenge of the Prague Spring 147
Csaba Békés

1968: A Bulgarian Perspective 169
Jordan Baev

Ceauşescu's Finest Hour? Memorialising Romanian Responses to the Warsaw Pact Invasion of Czechoslovakia 193
Calin Goina

The 'June Events': The 1968 Student Protests in Yugoslavia 215
Kenneth Morrison

1968: The Prague Spring and the Albanian 'Castle' 235
Ana Lalaj

Echoes of the Prague Spring in the Soviet Baltic Republics 257
Irēna Saleniece and Iveta Šķiņķe

'Down with Revisionism and Irredentism': Soviet Moldavia and the Prague Spring, 1968–72 279
Igor Caşu

Index 299

Notes on Contributors

Jordan Baev is Professor of International History and Senior Research Fellow of Security Studies at the Rakovski National Defense College, Sofia, Bulgaria. He has written approximately 300 publications in thirteen languages, among them nine monographs and thirteen documentary volumes, on Cold War political, diplomatic, military and intelligence history, international terrorism, peace-keeping and civil–military relations. He is also editor-in-chief of the forthcoming two-volume *History of the Bulgarian Intelligence Services*.

Csaba Békés holds a Research Chair at the Institute of Political Science, Hungarian Academy of Sciences, is Professor of History at Corvinus University, Budapest, and founding director of the Cold War History Research Centre, Budapest, Hungary. He is also a recurrent visiting professor at Columbia University, New York. His main fields of research are Hungarian foreign policy after World War II and the role of the East-Central European states in the Cold War. His latest co-edited book is *Soviet Occupation of Romania, Hungary, and Austria 1944/45–1948/49* (2015).

Igor Caşu is Lecturer and Director of the Centre for the Study of Totalitarianism, State University of Moldova, Chișinău. His recent publications include 'The Fate of Stalinist Victims in Soviet Moldavia after 1953', in K. McDermott and M. Stibbe (eds), *De-Stalinising Eastern Europe* (Palgrave, 2015) and *The Class Enemy: Political Repressions, Violence and Resistance in Moldavian (A)SSR, 1924–1956* (2015). He is currently researching a monograph on the famine in Soviet Moldavia, 1946–47.

Calin Goina is Associate Professor in the Department of Sociology and Social Work at Babes-Bolyai University, Cluj-Napoca, Romania. His doctorate, from the Sociology Department at the University of California, Los Angeles, was on the social history of a Romanian rural settlement before, during and after state socialism. He has published on collectivisation, rural social history and the history of Romanian communism.

Tony Kemp-Welch is Reader Emeritus in History, University of East Anglia, UK. He has held research posts at the Universities of Oxford, Harvard, Moscow and Cambridge. His books on Poland include *Poland under Communism: A Cold War History* (2008). He is now returning to the study of Soviet politics under Lenin, Trotsky and Stalin.

James Krapfl teaches modern European history at McGill University, Montreal, Canada. His award-winning book *Revolution with a Human Face* (2013) explains how Czechoslovak citizens struggled to establish a democratic political culture between 1989 and 1992. He has also written on Macedonian nationalism, Czech and Slovak memories of the Great War and 'revolution envy' in Poland and Hungary after 1989.

Ana Lalaj is Professor at the Institute of History, Tirana, Albania. Her books include *The Files of War* (2014) and *The False Spring of '56* (2015). She has also published several articles on the Cold War based on recently declassified archival records. She is currently working on a monograph entitled *Albania in the Cold War*.

Kevin McDermott is Professor of Modern East European History at Sheffield Hallam University, UK and author of numerous works on Soviet, Comintern and Czechoslovak history, most recently *Communist Czechoslovakia, 1945–89: A Political and Social History* (Palgrave, 2015). He has co-edited four previous volumes with Matthew Stibbe on various aspects of post-war East European history.

Kenneth Morrison is Professor of Modern Southeast European History at De Montfort University, Leicester, UK. He is the author of several books on the region, including *Nationalism, Statehood and Identity in Post-Yugoslav Montenegro* (2017), *Sarajevo's Holiday Inn: On the Frontline of Politics and War* (Palgrave, 2016) and (with Elizabeth Roberts) *The Sandžak: A History* (2013).

Irēna Saleniece is Professor of History and Head of the Oral History Centre at Daugavpils University, Latvia. She is the author of two monographs and over eighty scholarly publications devoted to Latvian history. Her research interests include school policy in twentieth-century Latvia, Sovietisation, the history of the teaching profession, historical source study and oral history.

Iveta Šķiņķe is Head of the Foreign Service History and Diplomatic Documents Division at the Ministry of Foreign Affairs of the Republic of Latvia. Previously she worked as a staff member of the Latvian State Archives and collected materials for the virtual exhibition 'The Aftermath of the Prague Spring and Charter 77 in Latvia/the Baltics'.

Vítězslav Sommer is Research Fellow at the Institute for Contemporary History, Academy of Sciences of the Czech Republic, and head of 'The Road to Technocratic Socialism: Concepts of Governance in Socialist Czechoslovakia (1953–1975)' research project funded by the Czech Science Foundation. His dissertation, published in 2011, explored the origins of Communist Party historiography in Czechoslovakia and its development in the Stalinist, post-Stalinist and reform communist periods. His recent research is on the history of expertise in late socialism and post-socialism.

Matthew Stibbe is Professor of Modern European History at Sheffield Hallam University, UK. He has published widely in the field of twentieth-century German, Austrian and international history, including four previous collections of essays on Eastern Europe since 1945, co-edited with Kevin McDermott. He is currently working on a global history of civilian internment during World War I.

Kieran Williams teaches politics at Drake University, Des Moines, Iowa, USA. His biography *Václav Havel* was published in 2016. Previous books include *The Prague Spring and Its Aftermath* (1997) and (with Dennis Deletant) *Security Intelligence Services in New Democracies* (Palgrave, 2000). He is currently working on a comparison of gun laws and political reactions to mass shootings in Europe.

Zbigniew Wojnowski is Senior Lecturer in Modern History at the University of Roehampton, UK. His first monograph, *The Near Abroad. Socialist Eastern Europe and Soviet Patriotism in Ukraine, 1956–1985* (2017) explores how Soviet encounters with the outside world shaped politics, society and culture in the post-Stalinist USSR. He is currently working on the history of popular music and *perestroika* in the USSR and socialist Eastern Europe.

Abbreviations and Glossary of Terms

aktiv/aktyw	Meeting or group of party activists
apparatchik	Communist party-state official or bureaucrat
Balfour Declaration	Public declaration made by British Foreign Secretary Arthur James Balfour on 2 November 1917 in favour of establishing a 'nation home for the Jewish people' in Palestine
BCP	Bulgarian Communist Party
Bezirk	East German administrative district
Biafran War	War been the Nigerian military government and the would-be secessionist state of Biafra, lasting from 6 July 1967 to 15 January 1970 and involving large-scale famine among Biafran civilians
CC	Central Committee (of Communist Party)
CDSP	Current Digest of the Soviet Press
Cominform	Communist Information Bureau
Comintern	Communist International
CPCC	Central Party Control Commission
CPM	Communist Party of Moldavia
CPSU	Communist Party of the Soviet Union
ČSSR	Czechoslovak Socialist Republic (formal name and acronym adopted for the communist state in Czechoslovakia under the July 1960 constitution)
Cultural Revolution	Movement launched in China from 1966 to 1976 under Communist Party leader Mao Zedong,

	involving large-scale purges, particularly of older party members, and the ruthless reinforcement of 'Maoist' ideology
ECP	Estonian Communist Party
Euro-communism	Revisionist movement in West European Communist Parties in the 1970s and 1980s
FDJ	Free German Youth (GDR)
FRG	Federal Republic of Germany (West Germany)
GDR	German Democratic Republic (East Germany)
glasnost	Gorbachev's policy of 'openness'
Gulag	Main Administration of Camps (USSR)
HSWP	Hungarian Socialist Workers' Party
K-231	Club of Former Political Prisoners (Czechoslovakia)
KAN	Club of Committed Non-Party Members (Czechoslovakia)
KGB	Committee for State Security (USSR)
KhTS	Chronicle of Current Events (USSR)
kolkhoz	Collective farm (USSR)
Komsomol	Young Communist League (USSR)
KSČ	Communist Party of Czechoslovakia
kulak	Better-off peasant
LCP	Latvian Communist Party
LSSR	Latvian Soviet Socialist Republic
NATO	North Atlantic Treaty Organisation, western military alliance founded in 1949
NEM	New Economic Mechanism (Hungary)
Neues Deutschland	'New Germany', SED daily newspaper
nomenklatura	List of key appointments approved by the party
'normalisation'	Term referring to hard-line system in Czechoslovakia, 1969–89
NPF	National Patriotic Front (Soviet Moldavia)
NVA	National People's Army (GDR)
'Operation Danube'	Code-name for the Warsaw Pact military invasion of Czechoslovakia
Ostpolitik	West German policy of détente towards Eastern Europe, mid-1960s onwards
PCC	Political Consultative Committee (of Warsaw Pact)
perestroika	Gorbachev's policy of 'reconstruction'
Petőfi Circle	Intellectual discussion group founded in Budapest in 1956 and often regarded as the spiritual cornerstone of the Hungarian Revolution of October–November
Politburo (or Presidium)	Highest decision-making body of communist party

ABBREVIATIONS AND GLOSSARY OF TERMS xv

PPSH	Labour Party of Albania
Pravda	'Truth', CPSU daily newspaper
PZPR	Polish United Workers' Party
RCP	Romanian Communist Party
Rudé právo	'Red Right', KSČ daily newspaper
samizdat	'Self-publishing' in the USSR and Eastern Europe
SDP	Social Democratic Party (Czechoslovakia)
SDS	Collected *Samizdat* Documents (USSR)
Securitate	Romanian secret police
SED	Socialist Unity Party of Germany (GDR)
Sejm	Lower house of the Polish parliament
SFRJ	Socialist Federal Republic of Yugoslavia (*Socijalistička federativna republika Jugoslavija*)
Sino-Soviet split	Ideological split between the Soviet bloc and the People's Republic of China which began in the late 1950s and became open after 1960
Six Day War	War between Israel and its Arab neighbours (Egypt, Jordan and Syria) from 5 to 10 June 1967, ending in Israeli victory and military occupation of the Golan Heights, the West Bank, Arab East Jerusalem, the Gaza strip and the whole of the Sinai Peninsula
SKH	Croatian League of Communists
SKJ	Yugoslav League of Communists
Solidarity	Independent (non-communist) Polish trade union, founded in 1980
SPD	Social Democratic Party (West Germany)
Stasi	East German secret police
StB	State Security (Czechoslovakia)
'Šumava'	Code-name for large-scale military exercises in Czechoslovakia, June–July 1968
TASS	Soviet news agency
UDBA	State Security (Yugoslavia)
UN	United Nations
USSR	Union of Soviet Socialist Republics
Volkspolizei	People's Police (GDR)
Warsaw Pact	Soviet-led military organisation founded in 1955

Archival Abbreviations

AAN	Archive of Modern Records (Poland)
ABS	Archive of the Security Services (Czech Republic)
AČR	Czech Radio Archive
AJ	Yugoslav Archive
AMPJ	Archive of the Ministry of Foreign Affairs (Albania)
ANIC	Central Historical National Archive (Romania)
AOSPRM	Archive of Social-Political Organisations of the Republic of Moldova
AQSH	Central State Archive (Albania)
AÚSD	Archive of the Institute of Contemporary History (Czech Republic)
BStU	The Federal Commissioner for the Records of the State Security Service of the Former German Democratic Republic (Stasi Records Agency)
COMDOS	Central Archive of the Bulgarian State Security and Military Intelligence Services (Bulgaria)
DA	Diplomatic Archive of the Ministry of Foreign Affairs (Bulgaria)
DALO	State Archive of the Lviv Region (Ukraine)
DAOO	State Archive of the Odessa Region (Ukraine)
DVIA	State Military History Archive (Bulgaria)
ERA	Estonian National Archive
LSA	Lithuanian Special Archive
MNL-OL	Hungarian National Archive
NA	National Archive (Czech Republic)
RGANI	Russian State Archive of Contemporary History

SAPMO-BArch	Foundation for the Archive of the Parties and Mass Organisations of the Former GDR (Germany)
TsDA	Central State Archive (Bulgaria)
TsDAHO	Central State Archive of Mass Organisations (Ukraine)

Chronology of Main Events, 1968–69

1968

5 January	Central Committee plenum of the Communist Party of Czechoslovakia (KSČ) elects Alexander Dubček as First Secretary.
4 March	KSČ Presidium starts process of abolishing censorship with almost immediate effect.
8 March	'March Events' begin in Poland with large-scale student protests in Warsaw and other cities.
23 March	Leaders of the USSR, Czechoslovakia, GDR, Poland, Hungary and Bulgaria meet in Dresden to discuss the situation in Czechoslovakia.
5 April	KSČ Central Committee plenum adopts the reformist Action Programme.
4–5 May	Leaders of the USSR and Czechoslovakia meet in Moscow.
8 May	Secret meeting in Moscow of leaders of the USSR, GDR, Poland, Hungary and Bulgaria ('the Five').
2 June	Major student strikes and occupations ('June Events') begin in Yugoslavia.
20 June–11 July	Extended military exercises ('Šumava') on Czechoslovak territory involving mainly Soviet, but also Polish, Hungarian, East German and Czechoslovak forces.
26 June	Czechoslovak National Assembly formally adopts a law abolishing censorship.

xix

27 June	Publication of Ludvík Vaculík's 'Two Thousand Words' manifesto.
14–15 July	Leaders of 'the Five' meet in Warsaw and send 'Warsaw Letter' to the Czechoslovak Central Committee, the KSČ Presidium having declined to attend.
28 July–6 August	Ninth World Youth and Student Festival held in Sofia.
29 July–1 August	Bilateral meeting of Soviet and Czechoslovak leaders at Čierna nad Tisou.
3 August	Meeting of leaders of the USSR, Czechoslovakia, GDR, Poland, Hungary and Bulgaria in Bratislava issues joint proclamation. Draft 'Letter of Invitation' is handed to Petro Shelest, head of Ukrainian party.
17 August	Soviet Politburo decides unanimously to intervene militarily in Czechoslovakia.
18 August	Leaders of Poland, GDR, Hungary and Bulgaria agree with Soviet decision.
20–21 August	Soviet-led military invasion of Czechoslovakia ('Operation Danube'). KSČ Presidium votes seven to four to condemn the intervention.
21 August	Dubček and other KSČ leaders are arrested by Soviet officers. Mass passive resistance to invasion begins throughout Czechoslovakia.
21 August	Nicolae Ceaușescu, the Romanian leader, condemns the Soviet invasion in a speech in Bucharest.
22 August	Fourteenth Extraordinary Congress of KSČ is held clandestinely in a Prague factory.
23–26 August	Arrested Czechoslovak leaders meet their Soviet counterparts in the Kremlin and reluctantly agree the top secret 'Moscow Protocol'.
September–November	Demotion and resignation of several leading Prague Spring reformers.
18 October	Czechoslovak National Assembly ratifies treaty on the 'Temporary Presence of Soviet Troops in the ČSSR'.
1969	
16 January	Self-immolation of Jan Palach in Prague. He dies three days later.
28 March	Large-scale demonstrations throughout the country after Czechoslovak ice hockey team defeats the USSR at the world championships in Stockholm.

17 April	KSČ Central Committee votes to remove Dubček as First Secretary and replace him with Gustáv Husák. 'Normalisation' of the country begins in earnest.
19–21 August	Mass protests in thirty-one Czechoslovak towns and cities mark the first anniversary of the invasion. They are met with considerable police brutality.

East European Communist Party Leaders at the Time of the Prague Spring

Albania—Enver Hoxha
Bulgaria—Todor Zhivkov
Czechoslovakia—Alexander Dubček
East Germany—Walter Ulbricht
Hungary—János Kádár
Poland—Władysław Gomułka
Romania—Nicolae Ceauşescu
Soviet Union—Leonid Brezhnev
Yugoslavia—Josip Broz Tito
Soviet Estonia—Johannes Käbin
Soviet Latvia—Augusts Voss
Soviet Lithuania—Antanas Sniečkus
Soviet Moldavia—Ivan Bodiul
Soviet Ukraine—Petro Shelest

The Prague Spring and Warsaw Pact Invasion Through the Soviet and East European Lens

Kevin McDermott and Matthew Stibbe

The year 1968 has often been portrayed as a pivotal moment in post-1945 history, characterised by the emergence of a globalised, or at least transnational, youth protest movement that crossed land borders and continents, and was transmitted, via television, radio and newspapers, to audiences in all parts of the world. In South-East Asia it was marked by the Tet Offensive, one of the largest military operations launched by Viet Cong fighters against the US army in Vietnam, and on the US home front by the assassinations of Martin Luther King and Robert Kennedy, and large-scale urban civil unrest, not least during the Democratic National Convention in Chicago. In China, the Cultural Revolution, a violent campaign which had already begun in 1966, reached its apogee. In West Africa, the Biafran War, waged since 1967 to wrest regional independence from Nigeria, entered into a period of gruesome stalemate

K. McDermott (✉) · M. Stibbe
Sheffield Hallam University, Sheffield, UK
e-mail: k.f.mcdermott@shu.ac.uk

M. Stibbe
e-mail: m.stibbe@shu.ac.uk

© The Author(s) 2018
K. McDermott and M. Stibbe (eds.), *Eastern Europe in 1968*,
https://doi.org/10.1007/978-3-319-77069-7_1

amid widespread famine among the local population. In the Middle East, the Palestine Liberation Organisation issued its National Charter, which called for continuous popular armed struggle to end what it referred to as the 'Zionist occupation' not only of Arab lands captured by the Israeli Defence Force in the Six Day War, but of all territory that had constituted the state of Israel since its foundation in 1948, on the grounds that the Balfour Declaration of 1917 and the UN's planned partition of Palestine in 1947 were both 'contrary to the will of the Palestinian people and to their natural right in their homeland'. In Western Europe, university campus sit-ins and street demonstrations were common in West Berlin, West Germany, Italy, the Netherlands, Belgium and even in London. The highpoint of the student protest movement, however, came with the 'May events' in Paris, the consequences of which—as Chinese Premier Zhou Enlai reputedly said in 1971—were still 'too early' to predict. In Albania in 1968 there was a final, and in Romania a partial, break with the Soviet bloc, with lasting repercussions for both countries. In Poland, student groups rebelled in March 1968, prompting a nationalist and anti-Semitic backlash from the governing party and security services. In June, large-scale student unrest also rocked Yugoslavia. And in Eastern Europe as a whole, the Prague Spring and its elimination through the five-power Warsaw Pact invasion in August signalled both the beginning and the end of what was seen as the most ambitious and far-reaching attempt to humanise communism since 1917.[1]

Over the last twenty years or so, there has been a tendency among experts to view 1968 in Eastern Europe through the lens of what happened subsequently, in 1989.[2] According to this narrative, shared by contemporary eye-witnesses and participants ranging from the KGB foreign intelligence officer turned defector Vasili Mitrokhin to erudite Czechoslovak dissidents such as Václav Havel, the crushing of the Prague Spring provided a necessary stepping stone towards the overthrow of communism in the negative sense that it demonstrated that the system could never be reformed or rendered humane from within.[3] Or as the German historian and GDR specialist Ilko-Sascha Kowalczuk, paraphrasing the psychologist Annette Simon, neatly puts it, while student rebels in Western Europe 'dreamt' of revolution in 1968, and afterwards had to put up with a handful of democratic reforms as a consolation for failure, the advocates of 'socialism with a human face' in Eastern Europe pushed for modest change and instead got the ultimate prize: (peaceful) revolution leading to the overthrow of communist rule, albeit some twenty years later.[4]

The contributors to this volume of essays take divergent approaches to understanding the Prague Spring and the Warsaw Pact intervention that took place in its wake. Some adopt a top-down framework, examining the decision in favour of military action from the standpoint of high politics and relations between different Soviet bloc leaders. Here they continue in the path set by the international project led by the Austrian historian Stefan Karner in 2008, which—by selecting, and reproducing for scholarly use, hundreds of files from the archive of the Central Committee of the Communist Party of the Soviet Union and other newly available material—was able to revise substantially previous assumptions about elite decision-making in Moscow.[5] Other contributors are more interested in questions about public opinion and popular reactions, and others still in ideological responses and state propaganda, expressions of opposition and dissent, the sudden re-surfacing of what were thought to be long-buried national and ethnic tensions, or the place of 1968 in local, national and regional memory.

What we have in common, however, is a determination to look beyond 1989 when considering the causes and consequences of the events in Czechoslovakia in 1968. Indeed, the fiftieth anniversary of the Prague Spring seems like an opportune moment for new perspectives. On the one hand, the rise of right-wing populist movements, particularly in Poland and Hungary, but also elsewhere in Eastern Europe (and beyond), has significantly undermined previous narratives concerning the inevitability and lasting victory of liberal democracy, pluralism and the 'open society' after 1989.[6] On the other hand, the death of the last of the twentieth-century pro-Soviet dictators, the hard-line Cuban leader Fidel Castro (who overtly supported the Warsaw Pact invasion in 1968), and the simultaneous emergence of new forms of grass-roots leftism, whether *Syriza* in Greece, *Podemos* in Spain or Jeremy Corbyn's new-look Labour Party in the UK, have also raised the possibility of a renewal of the relationship between socialism, democracy and human rights.[7] For all of these reasons, 'socialism with a human face' may be worth re-investigating on its own terms rather than simply being cast as the 'failure' that prefigures, and partly explains, the 'success' of the East European and global '1989'.[8]

The Prague Spring: 'Socialism with a Human Face'

On 5 January 1968, the forty-six-year-old Slovak, Alexander Dubček, was elected First Secretary of the Communist Party of Czechoslovakia (KSČ) replacing the discredited hard-liner Antonín Novotný, who had led the party since 1953. In light of Moscow's refusal to back Novotný against opposition in the KSČ Central Committee, Dubček appeared to be the best compromise candidate. He had spent his childhood and early youth in the Soviet Union, had been head of the Slovak party since 1963, had only modest reformist credentials before 1968 and was thus initially regarded as a trusted friend of the USSR—'our Sasha'. And yet, in the course of the next eight months under Dubček's tutelage the KSČ initiated a series of reforms, collectively known as 'socialism with a human face', which shook the communist world.[9] It was a bold peaceful project that attracted global attention and its fundamental task was to overcome the deep-seated crises that had afflicted Czechoslovak politics, economics, society and culture since the Stalinist 1950s. The Prague Spring is historically compelling because the vision of a democratised and humanised socialism—or 'third way' between Soviet state socialism and Western liberal capitalism—appealed not only to disillusioned East European Marxists, but, more pertinently, strongly influenced Mikhail Gorbachev's path-breaking policies of *glasnost* ('openness') and *perestroika* ('reconstruction') in the USSR after 1985.[10] The ramifications of the Czechoslovak reforms, both at home and abroad, were profound not least because a new and to some extent spontaneous actor entered the fray—popular opinion and a nascent civil society. The elusive notion of 'freedom' proved intoxicating for a population that had hitherto been silenced, cowed and repressed. At this basic level, the Prague Spring was a breath of fresh air. However, for leading KSČ progressives the innovations had their limits—they represented precisely a 'democratisation' of the existing communist regime, not a conscious route to a fully fledged pluralistic democracy. Their architects, after all, were Marxist communists, not social democrats or parliamentary liberals.

The concept of 'socialism with a human face' was, perhaps intentionally, left vague and meant different things to different people, but its potentialities were explosive. As Kieran Williams and James Krapfl demonstrate in their chapter on Michal Lakatoš, the prominent legal theorist, ideas to refashion the political, economic and judicial spheres had a long pedigree in Czechoslovakia going back to the late 1950s and early 1960s. In essence, the goal of such Marxist reformers was to forge a humane, civilised and modernised socialism in tune with Czechoslovak political culture and contemporary conditions, and moreover one which was, tacitly at least, to be an improvement on the Soviet prototype. This new polity would be achieved by democratising the relationship between state and society, by reconciling individual liberty, reason and social justice, by permitting broader public input in regional and national affairs and by eliminating the openly authoritarian aspects of the system. In this way, it also had a more immediate and pressing practical aim: to re-legitimise communist rule in the eyes of millions of 'ordinary' Czechs and Slovaks. Nonetheless, the reforms remained restricted and highly contradictory, the crucial dilemma being how to reactivate public life and involve citizens in the management of the state *without* jeopardising the party's monopoly of power and how, in the absence of coercion, to maintain control over a popular opinion that threatened to go well beyond Dubček's 'centrism'. In addition, 'socialism with a human face' strongly implied that the existing regimes in the Soviet bloc were somehow 'inhuman'. As Soviet party boss Leonid Brezhnev tetchily asked Dubček in May 1968: 'What's with this human face? What kind of faces do you think we have in Moscow?'[11] But the truly radical latency of the slogan was that no one knew precisely where it would lead—to a revitalised socialism that would strengthen KSČ authority or a multi-party democracy that would end it and remove Czechoslovakia from the Soviet orbit. The geopolitical stakes were thus extremely high in 1968.

The Action Programme, ratified by the KSČ Central Committee on 5 April 1968, encapsulated both the hopes and limitations of the Prague Spring. This eclectic document was riddled with ambiguities and compromises, but endeavoured to institutionalise a division of power in the communist system, projected economic de-centralisation, safeguarded democratic civil liberties, including the freedom of press, assembly, association and foreign travel, posited, uniquely for a communist government, full political and civil rehabilitation of victims of Stalinist illegalities, and recognised the autonomy of artistic and cultural organisations. As such, the Programme was broadly welcomed by the Czechoslovak public, but it did not go down well in the Kremlin, Brezhnev ominously describing it as an example of 'petty-bourgeois spontaneity' and 'a bad program that opens up the possibility of the restoration of capitalism'.[12] This somewhat exaggerated assertion must be seen in the context of developments in Prague since March. The one initiative that really did strike at the heart of orthodox communist rule was the end of preliminary censorship of the media. The KSČ Presidium's intensely controversial decision in early March effectively curtailing censorship was a brave and massively popular notion, but one that within weeks brought about an unprecedented situation bordering on the complete freedom of expression in the press, television and radio. This was a veritable landmine as it offered the potential for unrestrained debate, a clash of views, even oppositional currents; in short, a nascent civil society. By the early summer, it was clear that the party monopoly on ideas and history had collapsed.

To make matters worse, key conservatives were being dismissed from their posts. In late March, Novotný was replaced by Ludvík Svoboda as President of the republic while the prime portfolios of Minister of the Interior and Foreign Affairs and the party secretary for ideology all fell to notable reformers. Czechoslovak television and radio were headed by leading radicals. High-ranking staffing changes also affected the Czechoslovak People's Army raising concerns about the latter's willingness and ability to defend the borders with West Germany. This personnel turnover endangered long-standing channels of Soviet influence and communication in the KSČ, the security services and military, compelling Brezhnev to lament that 'so many "good and sincere friends of the Soviet Union" had been forced to step down'.[13] In these circumstances an internal backlash against mounting 'counter-revolution' was not slow in coming and by summer 1968 the reactionary Slovak party leader, Vasil Bil'ak, and several other hard-liners formed an insidious pro-Moscow 'fifth column' inside the KSČ upper echelons. Furthermore, as Kevin McDermott and Vítězslav Sommer argue in their chapter, unreconstructed 'neo-Stalinists' at all levels of the party were attempting, with a measure of success, to popularise anti-intellectual and anti-Semitic bombast, reassert Leninist ideological 'norms' and convince Soviet officials that the country faced a burgeoning crisis, in this way undermining faith in the entire renewal process.

The 'ultra-leftist' onslaught on the creative intelligentsia reflected the reality that they were indeed the spearhead of innovation during the Prague Spring. In early April, 150 intellectuals established the Club of Committed Non-Party Members (KAN) as a pressure group to ensure that the KSČ fulfilled its reform pledges and democratic potential. Despite its loose administrative structure and relatively small membership, estimated at 15,000 in July, KAN, by its very existence as an independent body of non-communists, aroused profound concern among conservatives both at home and abroad. As did two other controversial bodies: K-231 and the steering committee of the Social Democratic Party (SDP). The former, numbering as many as 130,000, was founded by ex-political prisoners and sought full judicial, political and moral rehabilitation for its members. The reactivation of an autonomous SDP also signalled a threat to the KSČ and therefore its steering committee operated on the margins of legality. The prime importance of these associations and of the actions of radical intellectuals is that they created severe difficulties for the Czechoslovak leaders in negotiating with their Soviet counterparts, who could claim with a degree of validity that Dubček was tolerating the formation of rival 'anti-communist' organisations. The pinnacle of this 'counter-revolutionary' activity was the famous 'Two Thousand Words' manifesto written by the novelist Ludvík Vaculík and published on 27 June. The manifesto provocatively called for 'public criticism, resolutions, demonstrations… strikes, and picketing' to induce the resignation of corrupt and dishonest communist functionaries. Although Vaculík shunned all 'illegal, indecent, or boorish methods', his appeal for grass-roots activism was bound to raise alarm, and fear, among domestic and foreign hard-liners, and even among many moderates.[14]

'Night Frost in Prague': Soviet Intervention

As we have seen, the Soviet Politburo's concerns over developments in Czechoslovakia were manifold and became evident as early as March 1968. Most specialists—including many of the contributors to this volume—conclude that issues of geopolitics and national security were paramount in the decision to suppress the Prague Spring. But other factors must be considered, in addition to the crucial issues of the end of censorship and the demotion of pro-Soviet dignitaries. Ideological 'deviations' from classical Marxism-Leninism, the reduction in powers of the secret police and the espousal of genuine legality, the notion of 'market socialism' and workers' councils, limited autonomy in foreign and military affairs, and the exposure of Soviet involvement in the judicial crimes of the 1950s all provoked much consternation in Moscow and other Warsaw Pact capitals. Fed by contentious reports from the KGB and the Soviet embassy in Prague, the Kremlin did not so much fear the collapse of socialism and a return to capitalism in Czechoslovakia, as a thoroughly reformed socialist system based on democratic norms, cultural and civic freedoms and popular participation, a polity that would almost certainly prove highly attractive to the peoples of other East European countries. Hence, regardless of Dubček's insistent pleas of fidelity to the Soviet Union, by the summer of 1968 the Brezhnevite Politburo had lost political trust in the Czechoslovak reformers and concluded that only military action would 'normalise' the situation in its erstwhile ally.

It should be emphasised, however, that recourse to armed intervention was very much a final hurdle. Several other forms of pressure had been put on Prague since the early spring of 1968, including hints of economic sanctions, extended Warsaw Pact manoeuvres (code-named 'Šumava') on Czechoslovak territory in late June and early July, a propaganda campaign in the Soviet mass media, bilateral and multilateral meetings, ultimately inconclusive, of communist party leaders at Dresden (March), Moscow (May), Warsaw (July), Čierna nad Tisou (July–August) and Bratislava (August), and private communications between Brezhnev and Dubček. As far as the Kremlin was concerned none had worked by August 1968. As for the precise timing of the invasion, the Soviet Politburo wished to pre-empt the convocation of the Fourteenth Extraordinary Congress of the KSČ, scheduled for early September, which would have formally ratified the reformist course undertaken since January and undoubtedly removed many conservative stalwarts from the party's leading organs. Speculation about divisions in the Soviet elites between 'doves' and 'hawks' has not been confirmed by recent archival discoveries, but this does not mean that differences did not exist among individuals and relevant bureaucracies.[15]

It is almost universally agreed that three core elements shaped the Kremlin's decision to invade: military-strategic considerations; the perceived threat to the Soviet model of socialism in Czechoslovakia; and the 'spill-over' effect to other East European states. It appears that a pivotal factor was security, both of the USSR and the bloc as a whole. Moscow was fearful that Czechoslovak foreign policy and defence reforms would weaken the unity and military capability of the Warsaw Pact, delay the stationing of Soviet nuclear missiles on Czechoslovak soil and thereby expose the 'socialist commonwealth' to American 'imperialism' and West German 'revanchism'. Moreover, the possibility of the Czechoslovak contagion spreading to Poland, Hungary, East Germany and the USSR itself, via Ukraine, raised the spectre of a general loosening of bloc relations. Indeed, for Brezhnev post-war Soviet territorial gains in Eastern Europe were inviolable, 'even at the cost of risking a new war'.[16]

On the ideological front, which should never be under-estimated, Czechoslovak attempts to re-envisage deeply entrenched Leninist principles such as 'democratic centralism' and in particular the party's 'leading role' were viewed as a negation of the very essence of socialism. One expert concluded that 'perhaps the final Soviet judgment... was that only an invasion could consolidate Soviet hegemony and avert the danger of eventual loss of control of the Communist Party and of its policy in Czechoslovakia, and, ultimately, over the entire area of Eastern Europe'.[17]

According to another eminent scholar, Kieran Williams, the Czechoslovak reformers stood accused of breaking the Soviet operational code of correct political behaviour in three ways: they were reluctant to meet their Soviet counterparts; they did not unequivocally ally themselves to the pro-Moscow faction in the KSČ; and they refused to carry out their promises to reassert authority over the direction of reform. Hence, the signals emanating from Prague were mixed and were interpreted in the Kremlin as indications of 'dithering, if not outright deceit'. By August 1968 the Soviet Politburo had come to the decision that Dubček had failed to fulfil his obligations to restore 'order' in Czechoslovakia, in turn 'betraying fraternal relations' with the Soviet party. For Williams, it was this erosion of trust that drove the Politburo to use armed might.[18] The invasion itself was launched on the night of 20–21 August. The vast bulk of troops and tanks were Soviet, the other Warsaw Pact countries—with the exception of Romania who was not invited to participate—contributing relatively small numbers. The intervention can be considered a military success, but a political disaster. In the hectic early hours of 21 August, hard-line conservatives in the KSČ Presidium were outvoted seven to four and were thus unable to establish a Moscow-friendly 'revolutionary government of workers and peasants'. In these unforeseen circumstances, the Soviets were forced to negotiate with the incumbent leaders. As mass passive resistance raged at home, Dubček and the entire Czechoslovak executive were transported to the Kremlin and more or less compelled to sign the top secret 'Moscow Protocol'. Under its terms, nearly all the reforms of the Prague Spring were gradually renounced: between late 1968 and 1971 the media was brought under strict party control, unrepentant radicals were sacked, demoted or resigned, and recalcitrant intellectuals were silenced. Dubček himself condoned many of these measures, but this acquiescence did not prevent his removal from office in April 1969. He was replaced by the pro-Soviet Gustáv Husák and the twenty years of 'normalisation' associated with his name began.

East European Responses to the Prague Spring and Warsaw Pact Invasion

Reactions to Czechoslovak developments in communist Eastern Europe were not uniform. In terms of elite responses, as discussed in some detail by Matthew Stibbe, Tony Kemp-Welch and Jordan Baev, the Polish party leader, Władysław Gomułka, the East German First Secretary, Walter Ulbricht, and to a lesser extent the Bulgarian supremo, Todor Zhivkov, were, from as early as February–March onwards, deeply alarmed at the potentialities of the Prague Spring and were staunch advocates of 'all necessary steps' in the face of creeping 'counter-revolution'. By way of contrast, Csaba Békés's contribution vividly demonstrates that the Hungarian First Secretary, János Kádár, adopted a more cautious, differentiated approach and sought, with the Kremlin's backing, to mediate between Dubček and his East European 'colleagues'. Nevertheless, by August Kádár felt constrained to uphold the Soviet decision to provide armed 'fraternal assistance'. In short, most Warsaw Pact members not only readily fell into line but helped to frame the increasingly shrill invective against the Czechoslovak 'heretics'. The glaring exception was Romania. Here, Nicolae Ceaușescu, party head since 1965, was intent on staking out a measure of autonomy from Moscow and, although he had scant sympathy with the Dubčekites' reformist agenda, on 21 August he publicly condemned the Soviet-led invasion and even took steps to defend 'the Romanian land', as he patriotically called it, from a feared attack by the Red Army. In Albania, which since the early 1960s had distanced itself from the USSR and charted a distinctly pro-Chinese path, the party leader Enver Hoxha used the Czechoslovak imbroglio, as Ana Lalaj's essay shows, to formally extract his country from the Warsaw Pact. In the Soviet Union itself, republican parties, like the Latvian and Moldavian described by Irēna Saleniece and Iveta Šķiņķe and by Igor Cașu respectively, dutifully followed Moscow's interpretation, albeit with the occasional marginalised voice of dissent.

Beyond the gilded corridors of power, the reactions of Soviet and East European citizens to the Prague Spring and its military suppression were multifarious, as evidenced by several of our contributors. It is notoriously difficult to decipher 'popular opinion' in non-pluralistic authoritarian systems, not least because 'ordinary people' were often reluctant to reveal their 'true' beliefs in case of official reprisal. But, using an array of party and state security archival records and oral historical methodologies scholars have been able, however approximately, to reconstruct public moods and attitudes at this time of crisis in the Soviet bloc. Hence, we can conclude with some surety that there was comparatively scarce overt, let alone organised, mass opposition to the Warsaw Pact invasion of Czechoslovakia. For the most part East Europeans kept their thoughts to themselves, in effect silently endorsing the actions of their rulers. In the USSR, as Zbigniew Wojnowski indicates in his contribution, responses ranged from fervent support for the intervention—and not only from party members—to outright rejection, as evinced by the public demonstration of a small band of dissidents in Moscow's Red Square on 25 August. By far the most extreme examples of protest were the self-immolation of two individuals in Latvia in April and May 1969. It should also be noted that, according to Soviet Defence Ministry statistics, five Red Army personnel (one sergeant and four soldiers) committed suicide in Czechoslovakia between 21 August and 20 September, although the immediate circumstances of their deaths are opaque. What is known is that some, perhaps many, Soviet troops did not realise that they were being deployed in Czechoslovakia. Some thought, apparently, that they were combatting 'counter-revolution' on 'the territory of Germany' and were therefore psychologically shaken when confronted with irate Czechs and Slovaks—brother and sister Slavs—who harangued them in perfectly decent Russian.[19]

Similar reactions can be adduced in the other Warsaw Pact states that participated in the military operations against Czechoslovakia—Poland, Hungary, Bulgaria and the GDR.[20] Here, as in the Soviet Union, the vast majority of people displayed no outward signs of dissent, but anti-invasion and pro-Dubček inscriptions, slogans and leaflets were produced, a handful of students were kicked out of university, a few of their professors were expelled from the party, and even a number of arrests were made. Over and above this, isolated acts of opposition were mainly, though not exclusively, the preserve of the youth, including a surprising amount of young workers and apprentices who possibly felt that they had even less to lose than students, and parts of the 'new' intelligentsia, especially those employed in the media, scientific research and the creative industries.[21] In Romania, it is generally argued that Ceauşescu's vocal condemnation of Soviet aggression represented his 'finest hour', garnering him widespread approbation. However, this interpretation is challenged by Calin Goina, who contends, on the basis of a series of in-depth interviews with elderly inhabitants, that the scale of popular legitimacy for Ceauşescu's regime has probably been exaggerated in the existing historiography.

In Yugoslavia, as Kenneth Morrison elucidates, the student demonstrations of June 1968 were influenced as much by Western 'New Left' ideas as events happening in Prague and elsewhere in Eastern Europe as evidenced by their attacks on the so-called 'red bourgeoisie', a reference to the 'new class' of privileged party bureaucrats; their radical protests against the Vietnam War and, by implication, their questioning of Belgrade's over-reliance on US economic aid; and their demand for more rather than less socialism. Nevertheless, Yugoslav leader Josip Broz Tito's manner of appeasing the students by acknowledging the legitimacy of their complaints showed that internal Yugoslav developments were equally important both in provoking the demonstrations and ensuring that, in the end, though they shook the authority of the one-party state, they did not seriously threaten it. The official Yugoslav and Romanian responses to the challenges of 1968, while hardly compatible with each other, thus shared one thing in common: they were both entirely at odds with the attitude of communist hard-liners in Prague and across the Soviet bloc, who really did believe that their particular version of the Leninist one-party state was facing an existential challenge at the hands of reformists in the KSČ, a challenge that could only be solved by outside military intervention.

THE CONSEQUENCES AND LEGACIES OF THE WARSAW PACT INVASION

Among the immediate consequences of the Warsaw Pact invasion, the most fundamental was the so-called 'Brezhnev Doctrine', propounded by Soviet theorists as a means of justifying the use of armed force against Czechoslovakia. The doctrine, first enunciated in the official party newspaper *Pravda* in September 1968 and formally in operation through to the Gorbachev era, restricted the sovereignty of communist states by asserting the duty of the USSR to intervene in any socialist country if events there threatened the existing order or the common interests of the Soviet bloc as a whole. In a truly disingenuous feat of sophistry, it was denied that this 'limited sovereignty' contradicted the concept of national self-determination. By promulgating the doctrine, the Brezhnev leadership made it abundantly clear that in the final resort the Soviet Politburo reserved the exclusive prerogative to decide when socialism was in jeopardy and to overcome that danger by force of arms if necessary. It was not a happy omen for the peoples of Eastern Europe.[22]

Further afield, the crushing of the Prague Spring accentuated the shift to a divisive 'polycentrism' in world communism. Originating with the Soviet–Yugoslav split in 1948 and the Sino–Soviet rift in the early 1960s, 'polycentrism' signified a gradual, but palpable, decline in Moscow's hegemony over the international communist movement. As we have seen, the Cuban regime backed the invasion, but several communist countries inside and outside the Warsaw Pact, including Romania, Albania and China, did not. Criticism also came from high-ranking non-aligned states. While Egyptian leader Colonel Gamal Abdel Nasser preferred to remain quiet, Tito's Yugoslavia and Indira Gandhi's India both publicly condemned the Kremlin's blatant disregard of Czechoslovak national sovereignty, with Tito in particular departing from what had looked like an increasingly pro-Moscow position during and immediately after the 1967 Middle East crisis.[23] Among many West European communist parties, the Italian, Spanish and French most explicitly, the Czechoslovak reforms and their untimely demise underlay the emergence of 'Euro-communism'. This significant trend of the 1970s and 1980s sought to re-define the theoretical and practical grounds for a transition to socialism more in tune with pluralist indigenous conditions and less beholden to the Soviet model. It took some of its ideas from the April 1968 Action Programme of the KSČ, especially the desirability of 'a more active European policy aimed at the promotion of mutually advantageous relations with all states ... safeguarding the collective security of the European continent'.[24] Needless to say, like communism in general, 'Euro-communism' and the parties that advocated it fell victim to the collapse of the Soviet bloc and the USSR itself in 1989–91.

Hence, in the 1990s and beyond the consensual view among West and East European scholars was that the consequences of the Prague Spring and Warsaw Pact invasion did not add up to very much. For the celebrated British historian of post-war Europe Tony Judt, for instance, the 'thwarted hopes of 1968' were superseded in November 1989 by the much more 'expeditious' (and defiantly anti-KSČ) phenomenon of the peaceful 'Velvet Revolution'. The point for him was underlined by the tragi-comic nature of Dubček's attempted political come-back 'from two decades of obscurity' at the turn of 1989–90:

> as soon as he began to make public speeches it became embarrassingly clear that poor Dubček was an anachronism. His vocabulary, his style, even his gestures were those of the reform Communists of the Sixties. He had learned nothing, it seemed, from his bitter experiences, but spoke still of resurrecting a kindler, gentler, Czechoslovak path to Socialism. To the tens of thousands of young people in the streets of Prague, or Brno, or Bratislava he was at first a historical curiosity; soon he became an irritating irrelevance.[25]

While Judt's uncompromising comments come from a Western social democratic perspective, a more straightforwardly conservative line—popular with much of the right and centre-right in the Czech Republic after 1993—simply postulated that Czechoslovakia had been under the grip of hard-line Marxists for the whole period from 1948, and had only managed to free itself and achieve true national liberation in 1989. The brief interlude marked by the Prague Spring had merely represented another variant of the same coercive, Soviet-imposed and Soviet-maintained dictatorship. Indeed, in July 1993 parliamentarians in the newly created Czech Republic unequivocally rejected the communist past, adopting a law which declared: 'the regime based on Communist ideology, which determined the direction of the state and the fate of its citizens in Czechoslovakia from 24 February 1948 to 17 November 1989, was criminal, illegitimate and deserves condemnation'.[26] The parliament of the Slovak Republic passed very similar legislation in March 1996.[27]

Two decades on from the 1990s, however, the anti-communist narratives that bracketed the entire communist era as one long, dreary dead end have themselves been overtaken by more authoritarian discourses which—since they also affect how Eastern Europeans today see their past and understand their present—must count among the important consequences and legacies of the Prague Spring and Warsaw Pact invasion. As several of our contributors show, above all Zbigniew Wojnowski, as a moment of crisis 1968 brought forth a reassertion of state patriotism in some of the countries under review. In the case of the USSR, including in particular the national republics in the western borderlands, as well as in Poland and the GDR, much of this was directed against West Germany which was denounced as an imperialist power representing the same dark phenomena that the Red Army had fought against in World War II. In more extreme anti-Semitic versions of this discourse, West Germany was also linked to Israel, the Jews and the USA, who together were supposedly striving for a Zionist-inflected bid for world hegemony in opposition to all peace-loving, patriotic anti-imperialist forces in the Soviet bloc, the Arab Middle East, the Caribbean and communist South-East Asia.[28] On the other hand, in Albania, Yugoslavia and for a shorter period of time Romania, state patriotism was mobilised against the Soviet Union as well as the West. This expressed itself in an anti-imperialist agenda aimed at Moscow and Washington simultaneously, one that combined support for 'national sovereignty' with extremely harsh internal repression. The biggest change took place in East Germany, where, in the aftermath of the Prague Spring and Erich Honecker's takeover as party First Secretary in 1971, attempts were made to construct a new form of state patriotism, which for the first time clearly demarcated the GDR as a nation in its own right, with its own progressive traditions and its own selective, class-based relationship to the political and cultural heritage of the past.[29] This GDR-specific concept of statehood, which projected the survival of German communism and the Berlin Wall for decades ahead, enjoyed some success in the 1970s and early 1980s, before collapsing ignominiously in the late 1980s, along with the Honecker regime itself.

The strengthening of official state patriotism above or alongside commitment to proletarian internationalism, however, was not the only response to the Warsaw Pact invasion. The neo-Nazi hooligan arrested for disrupting a party meeting at a factory in Staßfurt, East Germany, on 30 August 1968 and for having the words 'Rather dead than red' (*Lieber tot statt rot*) tattooed on his left upper arm[30]; the extreme neo-Stalinists in the KSČ who rejected party-sponsored rehabilitation of those purged in the Stalin era and called for a return to 1950s-style 'true communism'; the hard-line critics of Brezhnev's supposedly 'too soft' approach towards Czechoslovakia and Romania in 1968–69, who often came from or claimed to represent Russophile/anti-irredentist elements living in the south-western borderlands of the USSR and who deployed a new-found politics of geographical or ethnic identity as opposed to conventional 'socialist-internationalist' or 'anti-capitalist' arguments to support their demand for an even greater assertion of Soviet military might in the region; and minority national groups in Romania who refused to remember Ceaușescu's proud stand against the Kremlin in 1968 or to become emotionally invested in it, all in their own way challenged official variants of what it meant to be a 'patriotic' citizen in late 1960s Eastern Europe. What these admittedly very different and diverse groups had in common was a sense of victimhood and equally a belief that they alone represented the authentic voice of the people (and of their sacrifices during World War II). Often, they came from those sections of society who had not benefitted greatly either from the region-wide growth in specialist jobs in agriculture and industry or from the upward social mobility and expansion of higher education of the early to mid-1960s associated with the 'scientific and technological revolution'.[31]

The dominant sentiment animating these disaffected strata was that the party-state no longer belonged to, or spoke for, them but only for the corrupt and unpatriotic Brezhnevite communists who had organised the military overthrow of the Prague Spring, but then inexplicably kept Dubček (and some of his 'elitist' or 'centrist' precepts) in power even after August 1968. A parallel 'victim discourse' developed in non-aligned Yugoslavia, where some of the student radicals of 1968, notably the future Bosnian Serb leader Radovan Karadžić, became disillusioned with promises of political reform made by Tito and turned in later years to ethno-nationalism, thereby rejecting the delicately balanced supra-national foundations of the post-1945 Yugoslav federal state.[32] It is indeed not too much of a stretch to see links between these discourses and attitudes and the nationalist anti-democratic/anti-pluralist views expressed by left- and right-wing populists in Eastern and Western Europe, and across the wider world, in the 2010s.[33]

Finally, Dubček's vision of a 'kinder, gentler, Czechoslovak path to Socialism' and its crushing by Warsaw Pact forces did not simply provoke a backlash against 'reform communism' and a search for authoritarian alternatives, but rather enlivened debates about the meaning of leftist or progressive internationalism and its ties with social justice and human rights. While few of Dubček's Eastern European admirers outside Czechoslovakia thought that his version of 'socialism with a human face' could be directly transferred to the situation in their own societies, their enthusiasm for the reforms of the Prague Spring often reflected much more than mere support for the notion of 'national sovereignty' against the kind of military intervention legitimised by the Brezhnev Doctrine. Take, for example, the Polish opponents of state censorship who also championed Israel's right to defend itself in 1967 against the threat of invasion by its Arab neighbours, both in conscious opposition to the 'anti-Zionist' rhetoric of the official media *and* with thoughtful reference to Poland's own struggles for national survival and legally recognised existence in a hostile, insecure world.[34] Or the students on the chemistry course at the Technical High School in Merseburg, East Germany, who not only condemned the Warsaw Pact assault on Czechoslovakia but also linked their critique to other instances of 'inhumane' Soviet foreign policy which failed to live up to the standards they expected of socialist countries, among them the USSR's refusal to provide aid to the starving people of Biafra and its backing (alongside Britain) of the corrupt Nigerian military government in Lagos.[35]

A third example, coming from Czechoslovakia itself, is the stance taken by what Williams and Krapfl call the 'jurists of the Prague Spring'. Their perceptions on law and legalism were rooted in a specific national and ideological (Stalinist and, in the 1960s, post-Stalinist) context, as were Dubček's ideas on reform communism. But after 21 August 1968, as Williams and Krapfl maintain, there was a shift. The Brezhnev Doctrine, which justified the Warsaw Pact's intervention in Czechoslovakia and the systemic violence that went with it, was not deemed to be 'normal' even in socialist-legal terms. Rather, there was now an expectation that invading armies and international organisations, as well as domestic political actors and private citizens, not only should but also could be subject to the rule of law and the liberties and responsibilities that stemmed from it.

In the face of the unexpected crisis of democratic representation in much of the Western world in the 2010s, the sudden rise of populist and racist movements across Europe, and the turn towards obscurantist political and judicial retrenchment, notably in Hungary and Poland, the need to uphold legal and constitutional safeguards protecting the right to be different, to live differently, and—following Rosa Luxemburg—to think differently, is more pressing than ever. In this sense, the most important legacy of the Prague Spring can be found in those parts of the KSČ's Action Programme that called for 'a more explicit guarantee of freedom of speech for minority opinions and interests' and for 'better [preservation] ... of the personal rights and property of citizens', while simultaneously maintaining the socialist commitment to state involvement in economic planning and the provision of universal social needs.[36] While populists, authoritarian rightists and anti-socialists today might dismiss such freedoms as 'fake', 'cosmopolitan', 'elitist' and/or 'anti-national', we could do a lot worse than hope for their proper defence and ultimate vindication in years to come.

Notes

1. For sources that seek to place 1968 in a global, or at least European-wide, context, see: C. Fink et al. (eds), *1968: The World Transformed* (Cambridge, 1998); G. Eley, *Forging Democracy: The History of the Left in Europe, 1850–2000* (Oxford, 2002), pp. 341–65; M. Kurlansky, *1968: The Year that Rocked the World* (London, 2004); J. Suri, *The Global Revolutions of 1968* (New York, 2007); N. Frei, *1968: Jugendrevolte und globaler Protest* (Munich, 2008) [new and updated edn, Munich, 2018]; M. Klimke and J. Scharloth (eds), *1968 in Europe: A History of Protest and Activism, 1956–1977* (Basingstoke, 2008); V. Tismaneanu (ed.), *Promises of 1968: Crisis, Illusion, and Utopia* (Budapest, 2011); M. Klimke et al. (eds), *Between Prague Spring and French May: Opposition and Revolt in Europe, 1960–1980* (New York and Oxford, 2011); R. Gildea et al. (eds), *Europe's 1968: Voices of Revolt* (Oxford, 2013); T.S. Brown, *West Germany and the Global Sixties: The Anti-Authoritarian Revolt, 1962–1978* (Cambridge, 2013); P. Gassert and M. Klimke (eds), *1968: On the Edge of World Revolution*, 2nd edn (Montreal, 2018); G. Katsiaficas, *The Global Imagination of 1968: Revolution and Counterrevolution* (London, 2018). On the Palestinian National Charter of 1–17 July 1968, see G.S. Mahler and A.R.W. Mahler (eds), *The Arab–Israeli Conflict: An Introduction and Documentary Reader* (London, 2010), pp. 134–8. On Zhou Enlai's comment, supposedly made in response to a question posed by US Secretary of State Henry Kissinger during his visit to China in 1971, and often mistakenly interpreted as a reference to the 1789 French Revolution, see R. Callick, *The Party Forever: Inside China's Modern Communist Elite* (New York, 2013), p. 232.
2. For a broader historical comparative perspective, see G.-R. Horn and P. Kenney (eds), *Transnational Moments of Change: Europe 1945, 1968, 1989* (Lanham, MD, 2004).
3. On Mitrokhin, see C. Andrew, 'Introduction' to *The Mitrokhin Archive: The KGB in Europe and the West* (London, 1999), p. 8. The 'unreformability' of the communist system is implicit in Havel's account of the Prague Spring in V. Havel, *Disturbing the Peace: A Conversation with Karel Hvížďala* (London, 1990), pp. 93–115. See also A. Tucker, *The Philosophy and Politics of Czech Dissidence from Patočka to Havel* (Pittsburgh, PA, 2000), pp. 125–6. Many scholars since 1989 have also shared this somewhat unfavourable interpretation of the historical meaning of the Prague Spring. See, for example, A. Ebbinghaus (ed.), *Die letzte Chance? 1968 in Osteuropa: Analysen und Berichte über ein Schlüsseljahr* (Hamburg, 2008), esp. p. 25: 'The year 1968 demonstrated the inability of communism to reform itself'; O. Tůma, 'Conspicuous Connections,

1968 and 1989', in M. Kramer and V. Smetana (eds), *Imposing, Maintaining, and Tearing Open the Iron Curtain: The Cold War and East-Central Europe, 1945–1989* (Lanham, MD, 2014), pp. 501–14 (here p. 512): 'The repeated lesson of the events of Czechoslovakia in 1968 was that Communism cannot be reformed'; and S. Moyn, *The Last Utopia: Human Rights in History* (Cambridge, MA, 2010), pp. 135–6: 'dissidence of any kind only made significant inroads in the communist world, and became highly visible to the West, as a result of the implausibility of reform communism that the events of the summer of 1968 made so clear'.
4. I.-S. Kowalczuk, *DDR: Die 101 wichtigsten Fragen* (Munich, 2009), p. 124.
5. S. Karner et al. (eds), *Prager Frühling: Das internationale Krisenjahr 1968*, vol. 1: *Beiträge* and vol. 2: *Dokumente* (Cologne, Weimar and Vienna, 2008). For a useful summary of the overall findings of this project, see S. Karner, 'Der kurze Traum des "Prager Frühlings" und Moskaus Entscheid zu seinem Ende', in Ebbinghaus (ed.), *Die letzte Chance?*, pp. 28–44 (here esp. p. 44).
6. For a critical analysis of the rise of far right and extreme left variants of populism across the world since 2010, which convincingly stresses rejection of pluralism and an 'anti-elitist' sense of victimhood as the main common denominators linking together all manifestations of this global phenomenon, see J.-W. Müller, *Was ist Populismus? Ein Essay* (Berlin, 2016).
7. On Castro's support for the military suppression of the Prague Spring, see R. Gott, *Cuba: A New History* (New Haven, CT, 2004), p. 237; also T.S. Brown, '"1968" East and West: Divided Germany as a Case Study in Transnational History', *American Historical Review*, vol. 114, no. 1 (2009), pp. 69–96 (here p. 93).
8. For the East European '1968' as 'failure', see also W. Outhwaite, 'What Is Left After 1989?', in G. Lawson, C. Armbruster and M. Cox (eds), *The Global 1989: Continuity and Change in World Politics* (Cambridge, 2010), pp. 76–93 (here pp. 90–1).
9. The classic English-language works on the Prague Spring are: G. Golan, *Reform Rule in Czechoslovakia: The Dubček Era, 1968–1969* (Cambridge, 1973); H.G. Skilling, *Czechoslovakia's Interrupted Revolution* (Princeton, NJ, 1976); K. Dawisha, *The Kremlin and the Prague Spring* (Berkeley, CA, 1984); and K. Williams, *The Prague Spring and Its Aftermath: Czechoslovak Politics 1968–1970* (Cambridge, 1997). More recent studies include: M.M. Stolarik (ed.), *The Prague Spring and the Warsaw Pact Invasion of Czechoslovakia, 1968: Forty Years Later* (Mundelein, IL, 2010); and G. Bischof et al. (eds), *The Prague Spring and the Warsaw Pact Invasion of Czechoslovakia in 1968* (Lanham, MD, 2010). For a valuable collection of documents, see J. Navrátil et al. (eds), *The Prague Spring 1968: A National Security Archive Documents Reader* (Budapest,

1998). For an overview, see K. McDermott, *Communist Czechoslovakia, 1945–89: A Political and Social History* (London, 2015), pp. 121–51. Major German-language works include: L. Prieß et al., *Die SED und der 'Prager Frühling' 1968: Politik gegen einen 'Sozialismus mit menschlichem Antlitz'* (Berlin, 1996); and Karner et al. (eds), *Prager Frühling* (as note 5 above). For a Slovak-Czech anthology, see M. Londák, S. Sikora and coll., *Rok 1968 a jeho miesta v našich dejinách* (Bratislava, 2009). By far the most comprehensive set of published primary sources is the massive twenty-two volume *Prameny k dějinám československé krize v letech 1967–1970* (Prague and Brno, 1993–2011).

10. When asked in the late 1980s what was the difference between the Prague Spring and *glasnost* and *perestroika*, Gennadii Gerasimov, Gorbachev's foreign policy spokesman, quipped 'twenty years'. See A. Brown, *The Rise and Fall of Communism* (New York, 2009), p. 593. In some sources, Gerasimov's answer is given as 'nineteen years'. See, for instance, T. Garton Ash, *In Europe's Name: Germany and the Divided Continent* (London, 1993), p. 124.
11. Cited in M. Kramer, 'The Prague Spring and the Soviet Invasion in Historical Perspective', in Bischof et al. (eds), *The Prague Spring*, p. 53.
12. R.G. Pikhoia, 'Czechoslovakia in 1968: A View from Moscow According to Central Committee Documents', *Russian Studies in History*, vol. 44, no. 3 (2005–06), pp. 35–80 (here p. 50).
13. M. Kramer, 'The Czechoslovak Crisis and the Brezhnev Doctrine', in Fink et al. (eds), *1968: The World Transformed*, pp. 124–5.
14. Cited in Navrátil et al. (eds), *The Prague Spring 1968*, pp. 177–81 (here p. 180).
15. The Soviet Politburo resolution of 17 August ratifying military action was passed 'unanimously' (*edinodushno*—'united in spirit', though not *edinoglasno*—'unanimous by vote'). See Navrátil et al. (eds), *The Prague Spring 1968*, pp. 376–7, n. 69.
16. Cited in Z. Mlynář, *Night Frost in Prague: The End of Humane Socialism* (London, 1980), p. 241.
17. Skilling, *Czechoslovakia's Interrupted Revolution*, p. 729.
18. Williams, *The Prague Spring*, pp. 35–8 and 111.
19. For details on Soviet fatalities—ninety-eight in all—see http://www.radio.cz/ru/rubrika/progulki/sovetskie-poteri-1968-go (last accessed 10 November 2017). Also G. Krivosheev, *Rossiia i SSSR v voinakh XX veka: Poteri vooruzhennykh sil. Statisticheskoe issledovanie* (Moscow, 2001). We wish to thank Kieran Williams and Jordan Baev for bringing these sources to our attention.
20. As noted by several of our contributors, the GDR afforded crucial logistical support to Soviet troops on the East German side of the border with

Czechoslovakia, but did not in the end provide boots on the ground in Czechoslovakia itself after a last-minute directive from Moscow.
21. Frei, *1968: Jugendrevolte und globaler Protest*, pp. 189–207.
22. On the Brezhnev Doctrine, see M.J. Ouimet, *The Rise and Fall of the Brezhnev Doctrine in Soviet Foreign Policy* (Chapel Hill, NC, 2003); and R.A. Jones, *The Soviet Concept of 'Limited Sovereignty' from Lenin to Gorbachev: The Brezhnev Doctrine* (Basingstoke, 1990).
23. See L. Lüthi, 'The Non-Aligned: Apart From and Still Within the Cold War', in N. Mišković et al. (eds), *Delhi—Bandung—Belgrade: Non-Alignment between Afro-Asian Solidarity and the Cold War* (London and New York, 2014), pp. 97–113 (here pp. 101–2). Also T. Jakovina, 'Tito, the Bloc-Free Movement, and the Prague Spring', in Bischof et al. (eds), *The Prague Spring*, pp. 397–418.
24. The KSČ's 'Action Programme', April 1968, excerpts reproduced in Navrátil et al. (eds), *The Prague Spring 1968*, pp. 92–5 (here p. 95). On Euro-communism, see M. Bracke, *Which Socialism, Whose Detente? West European Communism and the Czechoslovak Crisis of 1968* (Budapest, 2007).
25. T. Judt, *Postwar: A History of Europe since 1945* (London, 2005), p. 620. In reality, Dubček's popular reception, at least in November and December 1989, was not as dismissive as Judt suggests. See J. Krapfl, *Revolution with a Human Face: Politics, Culture, and Community in Czechoslovakia, 1989–1992* (Ithaca, NY, 2013), pp. 145–6.
26. 'Law Concerning the Illegitimacy of the Communist Regime', cited in V. Tismaneanu, *Fantasies of Salvation: Democracy, Nationalism, and Myth in Post-Communist Europe* (Princeton, NJ, 1998), p. 119. See also Ebbinghaus (ed.), *Die letzte Chance?* p. 25. It should be noted, however, that the Lustration Law of 1991 had carved out an exception for officials who occupied positions during 1968—they would not be barred from holding office after 1989.
27. J. Přibáň, *Legal Symbolism: On Law, Time and European Identity* (London, 2007), p. 166.
28. See, for instance, J. Herf, *Undeclared Wars with Israel: East Germany and the West German Far Left, 1967–1989* (Cambridge, 2016). Also R.S. Wistrich, *From Ambivalence to Betrayal: The Left, the Jews, and Israel* (Lincoln, NA and London, 2012), pp. 433–42.
29. Useful here is A. Saunders, *Honecker's Children: Youth and Patriotism in East(ern) Germany, 1979–2002* (Manchester, 2007), esp. pp. 30–1.
30. See 'Inhaftierungen', n.d., in Der Bundesbeauftragte für die Unterlagen des Staatssicherheitsdienstes der ehemaligen Deutschen Demokratischen Republik (BStU), MfS, Bezirksverwaltung Magdeburg, AS 7/73, Bd. 7, Bl. 3–11 (here Bl. 9).

31. On the East European use of the term 'scientific and technological revolution', and academic explorations in 1960s Czechoslovakia of its impact on post-1956 communist society, see A. Jamison, 'Science and Technology in Postwar Europe', in D. Stone (ed.), *The Oxford Handbook of Postwar European History* (Oxford, 2012), pp. 630–48 (here p. 637). For more details, see J. Krejčí and P. Machonin, *Czechoslovakia, 1918–92: A Laboratory for Social Change* (Basingstoke, 1996), pp. 168–99. For the official Brezhnevite position on the supposedly harmonious link between scientific advances and human progress in the Soviet bloc, a discourse that those who experienced little or no social mobility in the 1960s and 1970s were far less likely to buy into, see M.P. Gapochka and S.N. Smirnov, *The Unity of Social and Scientific Progress under Socialism: 250th Anniversary of the USSR Academy of Sciences* (Moscow, 1979).
32. On Karadžić and one or two other leading figures in the 1968 Sarajevo student protests who turned to extreme Serb ethno-nationalism two decades later—including Slavko Leovac and Milorad Ekmečić—see R.J. Donia, *Radovan Karadžić: Architect of the Bosnian Genocide* (Cambridge, 2015), pp. 31–2.
33. Müller, *Was ist Populismus?* pp. 68 and passim. Some recent sociological studies have drawn connections between the West European '1968' and the tactics used by authoritarian populist movements in 2016–17. See notably T. Wagner, *Die Angstmacher: 1968 und die Neuen Rechte* (Berlin, 2017); also, the British journalist and author Nick Cohen's assertion that 'the alt-right is as much a satirical as a political movement… [it] wants to provoke liberals into showing they are repressive, so that it can cast itself in the role of the transgressive rebel'—N. Cohen, 'Censorship Wins No Arguments and Just Helps the Right', *The Observer*, 14 January 2018. However, while there is undoubtedly a transgressive and rebellious streak in 'new right' and populist thinking, the sense of victimhood and claim to represent the 'true' will of the people also suggests possible parallels and continuities with the lesser-known East European '1968', and more particularly with the diverse and often quite nationalist, inward-looking or authoritarian/anti-Western response across the communist states to the Warsaw Pact invasion of Czechoslovakia.
34. See D. Stola, 'Anti-Zionism as a Multipurpose Policy Instrument: The Anti-Zionist Campaign in Poland, 1967–1968', in *Journal of Israeli History*, vol. 25, no. 1 (2006), pp. 175–201 (here esp. p. 182).
35. 'Information zur politisch-ideologischen Situation unter den Studenten', 28 January 1969, in BStU, MfS, Archiv der Zentralstelle, SED-KL, 828, Bl. 40–56 (here Bl. 53).
36. The KSČ's 'Action Programme', April 1968 (as note 24 above), p. 93.

For a Civic Socialism and the Rule of Law: The Interplay of Jurisprudence, Public Opinion and Dissent in Czechoslovakia, 1960s–1980s

Kieran Williams and James Krapfl

For legal theory, like philosophy and literature, to transcend the times in which it was written and leave 'an insight of lasting validity', the times themselves must 'bring forth with particular intensity a recurring social theme and problem'.[1] The law professors who jointly authored this observation applied it to Germany's Weimar period (1919–33), and found the necessary intensity present in three ways. First, the foreign and domestic dimensions were tightly intertwined, as the threat of civil war trod fast on the heels of world war. Second, the country was undergoing a total crisis that challenged the fundamentals of constitution, culture and commerce. Third, that crisis put the state 'up for grabs', its very identity contestable. As important as these three conditions was

K. Williams (✉)
Drake University, Des Moines, IA, USA
e-mail: kieran.williams@drake.edu

J. Krapfl
McGill University, Montreal, Canada

the duration of the period itself, for 'a struggle over methods and aims requires a certain amount of time'—long enough to allow for the crisis to find reflection in theory, but not too long for stability to be achieved and the crisis to pass.[2] Should the times fail to rise to the requisite level, the theories they produce disappear instead into *Ungeistesgeschichte*, the history of failed ideas.[3]

The Prague Spring, although the exhilarating climax to a decade of quiet crisis in Czechoslovakia, was no match for Weimar in its intensity. Perhaps it did not last long enough, snuffed out too soon by 'normalisation' after the Soviet-led invasion; perhaps the crisis was never acute enough to throw all assumptions into doubt. In any event, the legal and philosophical product of the time has vanished into *Ungeistesgeschichte*. Without making any exaggerated claims for their quality or impact, we want to retrieve the writings of reform socialist jurisprudence for several reasons. First, the only survey of legal theorising in the 1960s, by Zdeněk Jičínský, does not do justice to the intricacies of his own development or that of his colleagues.[4] Second, turning to these writings reminds us that we should commemorate not just the year 1968 but also the years that came before and after; symbolically, the Prague Spring starts with the conference on Franz Kafka and the abandonment of multi-year economic planning in 1963 and ends in late 1971 with the stage-managing of bogus parliamentary elections on a reported turnout of 99.45%.[5] While 1968 was the year for essays, manifestos and speeches, the preceding years were the calmer ones in which more elaborate arguments were developed. Third, we can locate these writings in a still longer story of the return to law in Czechoslovakia after two decades of high authoritarianism (1939–59); in these jurists' works we find conceptions of law, the state and civil society that this chapter will show briefly flourished in public sentiment and grass-roots demands, lived on among the disbarred or demoted lawyers of the dissident world, and reappeared in the revolutionary demands of 1989.[6] In this respect, at least, the jurists of the Prague Spring did touch on recurring social themes and problems in a way that transcended their time.

The Velvet De-Stalinisation of Michal Lakatoš

The drift to legalism is well illustrated by the career and output of Michal Lakatoš. His *Considerations on the Values of Democracy* (*Úvahy o hodnotách demokracie*) was one of the few books that could appear during 1968 and speak directly to what was happening. Sent to press in September, one month after the invasion but before the shutdown of free speech in the following spring, the book is thoroughly representative of the ideas driving the reform movement while transcending the political switchbacks of Alexander Dubček's sixteen months in power. Lakatoš and his work are also worth retrieving to answer the question of how the Prague Spring was ever possible, starting out as an inner-party struggle by men and women who, two decades before, had been ardent Stalinists. Born in 1925 in Bracovce (eastern Slovakia), Lakatoš studied law at Charles University in Prague after World War II, and taught there from 1950 until 1957, when he moved to the Academy of Sciences' new Institute of State and Law founded by Ivan Bystřina, who seems to have been his mentor and patron. Employment in that institute granted Lakatoš proximity to the seminars and teams that would feed ideas into the policy networks of the Communist Party (of which he had been a member since 1945), although he never became a Central Committee functionary like his colleague Zdeněk Mlynář.[7] After 1968 he left the party and was fired from the Institute, working for the next twenty years as a company attorney. He was among the first signatories of Charter 77, the landmark dissident appeal to the state to honour its commitments under the constitution and international law, and after 1989 he was readmitted to the Institute.[8]

While there is an undeniable world of difference between the early works of Lakatoš on 'people's democracy', written in 1953–54, and his *Considerations* of 1968, there is nothing of the 'bonfire of the self' that members of his generation ignited in other fields, such as literature.[9] Lakatoš moved through roughly the same set of phases, from Stalinist to Khrushchevian neo-Leninist to footloose socialist, but did so without ever disavowing any previous statement or position from his own past, without denouncing any fellow jurists or Soviet counterparts on whom he once relied as authorities, and without conceding any ground to the targets of his youthful polemics.[10] It is this smoother evolution that makes Lakatoš's writings in 1968 especially intriguing: if he did not undergo the wrenching, self-critical rupture that would accompany a crisis of belief, how did he arrive at the unquestionably reformist position he takes in *Considerations*? We will show that it was possible for him to get there by a series of relatively small steps, qualifications and adjustments, and that in his earlier writings there was enough of a germ of his later views that it was not necessary to disown them.

Lakatoš came to the law at a time of radical transition in Czechoslovakia, from pre-war normativism to the materialist view imported from the Soviet Union. His early writings rebuked fellow Marxists for being too timid in developing a distinctly socialist legal science,[11] but his own understanding of law was largely that of the leading Soviet jurist (and show trial prosecutor) Andrei Vyshinsky: as the sum of rules of behaviour and norms reflecting the will of the ruling class and trying to modify social relations and conduct in the interests of that class. Law was said to originate in the consciousness and will of a class's individual members, as a reflection (*odraz*) of the objective facts of their lives' material conditions, especially means and relations of production. Since all norms, including morals, could be said to arise in this way, Lakatoš distinguished legal ones by their enjoyment of state sanction.[12]

The young Lakatoš dutifully provided a myth of the new socialist state, one acting through law and strengthening itself through *zákonnost* (lawfulness, legality, law and order). Law-making he reserved to the highest body of state power, the National Assembly, to ensure uniformity and coherent responsiveness to the will of the ruling working class. Citing Czechoslovakia's Stalinist leader, Klement Gottwald as well as Vyshinsky, Lakatoš summed up socialist rule as 'dictatorial' only in that it strictly upheld normative acts, issued them only through the established legislative process and expected them to be respected, including by employees of the state, who should enjoy no special derogations or use technical rule-making to distort the purpose of primary legislation[13] (Lakatoš was later critical of Stalinists who equated *zákonnost* with severity and insensitivity to the rights conferred by socialist law[14]). While courts played an important pedagogical role, in Lakatoš's view they merely applied legal norms and did not interpret them, and their decisions were restricted to the instant case; once courts started to make law by power of precedent, he warned, they could easily become a conservative brake on revolutionary change.[15]

It is noteworthy that we can already detect in the brash young Lakatoš threads that would run from his initial works to the immanently critical ones of the later 1960s. One lay in his defence of the 'managed democracy' of 1945–48, going against the official party line that did not regard the post-war government's Košice programme as truly revolutionary or socialist because it had left much property in private hands and allowed multi-party competition within certain bounds.[16] Lakatoš instead saw 1945 as the first phase of the revolution, and what followed the communist seizure of power in February 1948 was simply the next instalment. It was also a view of socialist politics as participatory, interest-driven and quasi-pluralistic. Owing to the gatekeeping function of the National Front, into which several other parties were corralled with the communists, Lakatoš could already portray Czechoslovakia's politics from 1945 as 'defending the interests of all working layers of our people', and even before 1948 the tendency was to try to 'make possible the greatest involvement of toilers, led by the working class, in the government'.[17] The implication of this take on history was to vindicate a distinctly Czechoslovak path, 'not the Soviet form of revolution, but a new form of socialist revolution':

> History confirmed what was foreseen by V. I. Lenin, that all nations will move to socialism but the forms of approach to socialist revolutions will vary in different conditions. Marxism-Leninism was enriched by new knowledge and revolutionary experience. To the Soviet form of socialist revolution was added the new form of approach to socialist revolution—a revolution nationalist and democratic.[18]

This passage is just the first hint of what would soon burst through in the maturing Lakatoš's work, especially in collaboration with Ivan Bystřina: an open recognition of the limits of Soviet experience and teaching, and a bold claim to be making a substantial contribution to filling the gaps.

In the wake of the revelations in 1956 about the lawlessness of the actual state under Stalinism, Lakatoš undertook some unsurprising revisions. His new works dropped the abundant references to Stalin and Gottwald, but they suffered from no crisis of confidence or orientation. Lakatoš continued to look eastward for inspiration: Mao Zedong briefly featured as a major new authority, until the Sino–Soviet split in 1960, whereupon he was replaced by greater reference to Lenin, especially to his *State and Revolution* (1917), and to Soviet jurists such as Dzhangir Kerimov (although Vyshinsky still got the odd quotation).[19] Beneath these cosmetic changes, Lakatoš was only refining—not discarding— his materialist understanding of the law as the expression of the factual interests of a dominant class. At this point, Lakatoš seems to have been bothered not by Stalinism's crimes so much as by the messy proliferation of secondary rules, decrees and directives from the mysterious bowels of ministries, and by gaps in the law exposed through court cases.

His path to reformism thus started from a technical desire for a legislative process that would be more consistent, open and timely, rather than for a state that would respect human rights. And his notion of law remained teleological: 'The ultimate goal of law-making is the legal regulation of social relations to ensure the building of a communist society'.[20]

The solution, it seemed at first, would lie in keeping with Nikita Khrushchev's announcement at the Soviet Communist Party's Twenty-First Congress in early 1959 that as a country approached communism its state would shed its functions onto social organisations. Lakatoš accordingly strove to embed interest groups in the science of socialist law-making as essential intermediaries between the will of the individual and that of the collective. This involvement could take the form either of ensuring mass organisations a right to be consulted in the drafting of bills (which, he pointed out, was supposed to happen under standing orders from 1949), or delegating to them and to commissions of experts the power to propose and write those bills, or putting major bills to a referendum. He also endorsed the experiment in judging minor offences by lay magistrates at 156 'comrades' courts' (*soudružské soudy*) in the late 1950s and then seventy-two 'local people's courts' (*místní lidové soudy*) under the new 1960 Constitution as a 'significant element of the future communist self-administration' (trade unions were also given certain dispute resolution powers at the time).[21] The expected results would be a legal superstructure more in touch with the reality of the economic base, a procedure for harmonising the non-antagonistic differences of group interests, and a plebiscitary participation superior to that found in the bourgeois West.[22]

THE CIVIC SOCIALISM OF *CONSIDERATIONS ON THE VALUES OF DEMOCRACY*

The Khrushchevian *élan* that had buoyed Lakatoš's writings began to wane in 1962 and in the following year the Czechoslovak Communist Party grudgingly revisited the crimes of Stalinism while admitting that the economy was in recession.[23] The terms of public discussion broadened and fellow jurists, such as Zdeněk Mlynář in his important book *State and Man* (*Stát a člověk*, 1964), applied rediscovered classics of Western political theory and recent American critiques of the leisured, but alienating consumer lifestyle to (as his sub-title put it) 'considerations on political management under socialism'.[24] Lakatoš followed suit two years later with a work that was similarly aimed at the general public: *The Citizen, Law and Democracy* (*Občan, právo a demokracie*).[25] Like Mlynář, and drawing perhaps on the journalism skills he had acquired at the party's political school in 1950, Lakatoš shifted to a more personal style and a focus on the welfare of the individual, which he admitted, although not self-critically, had been overlooked in previous research.[26] As the book's title signalled, there was a pronounced sensitivity to the person as a citizen, bearing rights conferred, defined and limited by law in a discrete social context. Using social contract imagery with a Marxist twist, Lakatoš assumed that the state rests on the consent of individuals who have elected to organise themselves into a society of free producers seeking protection from exploitation; the socialist state and its law exist to protect and preserve the interests of such an individual and the aggregate interests of workers, and if it loses sight of that function, it becomes a criminal enterprise. Acknowledging, at last, the 'personality cult' of Stalinism while adhering to his long-held wish that the law be clear, consistent and knowable, Lakatoš advocated more opportunities for ordinary citizens to use the law, such as through the courts, whose independence Lakatoš now valued more highly than in previous writings, and recall of legislators, who should be chosen in multi-candidate elections.[27] Citing reform economists such as Ota Šik, Lakatoš was contributing to what would become the guiding narrative (or myth) of the Prague Spring: individuals have their own interests arising from their objective material situations, and they will pursue them, but those interests can be happily harmonised with a common 'essence' or general 'heading' without duress or violence.[28]

As in his earlier writings, Lakatoš wanted this harmonisation to be broadly participatory, which he admitted it had not been because socialism suffered from its own forms of mass manipulation (like Mlynář, he borrowed from critics of Western messaging and media, such as William Lederer's 1961 book, *A Nation of Sheep*). His tone, however, remained optimistic, confident that unlike Western governments, socialist ones acknowledged their guilt in this regard, had resorted to it mostly under the extraordinary conditions of the 'personality cult', and now sought to correct it by the 'maximum involvement of citizens in the management of society'.[29] He wanted to hold the Communist Party to the commitment made on several occasions, most recently in May 1964, that it would ensure expert input into law-making through the National Assembly's committee structure.

The works cited in the notes confirm that despite Khrushchev's ouster in October 1964, this book was still very much in the spirit of his time as leader of the Soviet Union. Institutionally, it remained focused on the national legislature and on the Leninist ambition of someday slimming the state and consolidating decision-making and implementation into the hands of one representative body. Whereas Mlynář was rediscovering the Western models of separation of powers and checks and balances, Lakatoš preferred to think of a dual *kontrola* (control or oversight)—an external one exerted by engaged citizens via legislators on assertive parliamentary committees, and an internal one exercised by independent courts and the Communist Party. Like Mlynář, Lakatoš was intrigued by Yugoslavia's new type of legislature with multiple functional chambers and multi-tiered selection of delegates, but not yet certain that they should be emulated.[30]

This gentle evolution of small shifts continued over the next two years into the writing of *Considerations on the Values of Democracy*. The most conspicuous change was in Lakatoš's use of the term 'civil society' (*občanská společnost*). In earlier writings, he had mentioned it but always put it in inverted commas to keep his distance from a phrase Marxists regarded as a euphemism for exploitative social relations under capitalism.[31] By the time of *The Citizen, Law and Democracy* he had dropped the commas, but still refrained from embracing it as an ideal under socialism.[32] In the interval before his next book, he published two articles on the front pages of widely read literary weeklies, in which he enthusiastically employed the phrase as an extension of his view of the individual as a citizen (*občan*) rooted in society (*společnost*)—it might be more accurately, if clumsily, translated as 'society of citizens'.[33] In *Considerations*, Lakatoš defines civil society as the 'subject of social movement', that is the sum of all relations between people when capital has been taken out of private ownership.[34] The central question of the book is where might guarantees be found that representative government under socialism could be re-grounded in civil society and new abuses of power prevented. In seeking an answer, Lakatoš announced that he was returning to 'the alpha and omega of all practical problems of political management [*řízení*]'.[35]

The values to which the book's title refers are likewise rooted in those actual human relations, being the behavioural norms that human consciousness produces and internalises through a process both evolutionary and revolutionary: crises kill off obsolete values, but some survive, adapt and co-exist alongside new ones. 'Bourgeois' values of civil and political rights can, in modified form, find their place next to socialist values of socio-economic rights. Lakatoš takes pains to stress that values cannot be easily changed at the whim of a leader, and they cling within broad civilisational boundaries; he implies that the Soviet Union represents an Asiatic value set alien to that of Czechoslovakia. Politics, to be effective and humane, must match these values and institutionalise the dominant ones through law; if the match is made, a dynamic equilibrium results, with leaders staying responsive and the led not feeling alienated or manipulated. The question, then, is how to make the match occur and endure.

In reply, in chapter two the conjoined themes of responsibility and accountability are pursued. In Czech, as in most languages, both concepts are covered by one word, *odpovědnost*; the English distinction turns on the possibility of delegation and sanction. On one definition, accountability is 'a relationship between an actor and a forum, in which the actor has an obligation to explain and to justify his or her conduct, the forum can pose questions and pass judgement, and the actor may face consequences'.[36] So, in Lakatoš's terms, government will be *accountable* if each law-maker is liable to scrutiny and sanction (recall, defeat) by the voters, and executive departments to oversight by legislative committees and courts. Responsibility is more removed, less susceptible of punishment and may have to be traced back through authorised representatives; so, as Lakatoš asserts, it is civil society that is *responsible* for the overall direction of society by articulating its driving values and electing legislators to convert those values into law. Both aspects of *odpovědnost* entail mediation, through organisations representing particular interests or sectors, or through journalists and public opinion. Most of Lakatoš's effort goes into a sketch of a legislative process driven by interest articulation (groups propose or draft new bills, enlist expert input, pressure legislators to pass the bill and then monitor its implementation) and enforced by an impartial judiciary. The Communist Party enjoys a prominent place in this sketch, but it is conditional on the independence of other social organisations, which have to enjoy direct access to law-making bodies.[37] It is this direct input that would distinguish the reformed Czechoslovak system not only from its Stalinist predecessor, but also from the parliamentary democracies of Western Europe.

In chapter three, Lakatoš follows pro-market economic reformers of the day in committing the political system to greater freedom of individual choice. In doing so he fills in the anthropology animating the book's civic socialism. Man, he asserts, yearns for realisation as a personality and society needs to accord each person a guaranteed space in which to pursue fulfilment. Out of that space will come innovation and 'fruitful activity'; denying it leads to individual degradation, social stagnation and dictatorship. Later, he adds that man yearns for self-government not out of nostalgia for some fabled state of nature, but simply out of aversion to being unfree to make his own decisions. Values come into play as guiding factors in decision-making, which Lakatoš presents as an exercise of free will within limits—a person when choosing must actively undertake conscious mental steps, but does so in conditions not of his making. Lakatoš assumes that people can prioritise and act on the prioritised value(s). He applies this faculty to elections, allowing at first for low-brow preferences,[38] but holding that as a nation evolves to higher levels of 'socio-political consciousness' the criteria for representation will become ever more demanding. The ideal candidate for office would possess a combination of virtues: he (the language of the original text is completely masculine, so 'he' would be more faithful to it, even if to us now it is extremely gendered) would be descriptively typical of the group nominating him (say, the metalworkers' union); he would be well trained or educated or possess expertise; he would be skilled in politics as a vocation; and he would be able to see how to reconcile sectoral interests to a general societal interest.

Having set the stage for competition on non-antagonistic differences, in chapter four Lakatoš finds a place for opposition under socialism. As his preferred political system would still differ in every vital respect from Western parliamentary democracy, this socialist opposition would not be formally recognised as such or seek to replace the ruling group. It would consist instead of the right to disagree in public, either through the media or on the floor of the legislature or within the Communist Party, and would always have to be constructive (he allows later for censorship of disloyal anti-socialist views).[39] He reminds his reader of the situation in 1945–48, when the country had multiple parties jostling with each other within the National Front coalition but technically no opposition—an arrangement he had defended in his earliest writings.

By this point, half-way through *Considerations*, Lakatoš has sketched out a model of value articulation and representation, at the centre of which is a black box inhabited by the Communist Party and independent social organisations, out of which flow laws and policies harmonising particular interests with those of society as a whole. It resembled no previous political arrangement in Czechoslovak or Soviet history, nor the adversarial systems of the English-speaking world (in which two parties alternated in governing alone, to the left or right of the median voter), nor the consociational systems of Western Europe (in which all major interests were ensured parity or proportional chunks of the state and not dialectically integrated). Despite his birth in Slovakia, he showed no interest in the constitutional balancing of the country's two nations through federalisation or in the collective rights of its Hungarian, Rusyn or Roma minorities.

The second half of the book explores the political model's environmental elements, starting with public opinion. Like the values and interests previously noted, and, later in chapter nine, morals, opinions originate in concrete daily experience, encounters with phenomena that cause people to form notions of justice and of the justice system and its inadequacies. The emotions aroused by everyday life mingle with the voices of modern mass media, but the latter have limited effect and cannot contradict what people feel to be true based on their experience. Lakatoš thus has little fear under post-Stalin socialism of the 'hidden persuaders' who manipulate America from Madison Avenue. The question is not whether public opinion is distorted, but whether it is allowed to feed into law- and policy-making. The contingency of trust is the subject of chapter six, and like the earlier discussion of choice and opinion it relies on market imagery. The citizen is directly, and positively, compared to the consumer, who in the age of division of labour must trust the seller to provide a reliable product. Likewise, since modern democracy is perforce representative rather than direct, we have to be able to trust the people we deputise to make law for us. Lakatoš expresses a grudging respect for bourgeois practices such as the vote of no-confidence, but insists that socialist democracy must find its own ways of imparting and withdrawing trust.

Rather than specify those ways, Lakatoš moves in chapter seven to further elaboration of civil society, viewed now in terms of the citizen's opportunity to participate. He urges his country to take the lead in reversing the worldwide decline in civic involvement, which he admits will be difficult when ordinary people are drained by the demands of daily life. *Considerations* in places departs from abstraction to paint critical vignettes of daily life under socialism, acknowledging the grind of commuting and work followed by the easy distractions of light entertainment. His tone here is sympathetic and probably reflects his own experience of living on the edge of Prague.[40] The challenge is thus to encourage the devotion of a portion of precious leisure time to civic activity; this requires not just institutional reform, but also a revolution in lifestyle that will overcome strong disincentives to collective action, including the intimidating need for expertise. As previous attempts to offload some state duties onto social groups and to empower local government foundered on the persistent centralisation of politics within the Communist Party, Lakatoš scales back his expectations with citizens assigned primarily an oversight function (*kontrola*)—of the sort dissidents would later claim with regard to the state's record on human rights.

As the book winds down, Lakatoš indicates that his reforms would work largely within existing institutions. While on the one hand taking a free-market view of group formation (groups should be allowed to organise on the basis of any existing social interest and in all likelihood could not survive if not so grounded), he sees a future for the National Front as the 'integrating platform' on which all these groups, overseen but not dominated by the Communist Party, would be reconciled and harmonised. Yugoslav-style additions, such as self-managing councils in enterprises, are recommended not for replication but as inspiration for forms tailored to Czechoslovak conditions. Chapter eleven draws together several threads in the concept of 'legal certainty' as a natural extension of man's striving for his bare existence, for assurance of his social and political position, possessions, values and human relations. In these final pages, Lakatoš avers that strict 'legality' (*zákonnost*) is not enough; strenuous enforcement is worthless if the written law conflicts with prevailing values, especially folk conceptions of justice.

Reform Socialist Jurisprudence in the Public Sphere

Several themes that Lakatoš developed in *Considerations* featured in public debate in 1968–69, though probably more because he shared in the *Zeitgeist* than directly influenced it. A survey of district and enterprise newspapers selected from Bohemia, Moravia and Slovakia suggests that the term 'civil society' was entirely absent, yet the notion of a society of *citizens*, defined independently of class, enjoyed a renaissance, linked with the idea of *kontrola* on state offices and party functionaries.[41] For example, student participants in the Strahov demonstration in late October 1967 and local eyewitnesses responded vociferously to a party functionary who praised police suppression of the protest, arguing that 'in a decent state, a citizen should be able to speak critically'.[42] Adopting a legalistic stance, they pointed out that 'the constitution guarantees citizens a voice... Democracy and freedom of criticism alone can ensure feedback, once and for all preventing the party's policies from becoming the affair of a few "irresponsible comrades"'.[43] Local newspapers took it upon themselves to become watchdogs of the public interest, often exposing misdemeanours on the part of state, party, enterprise or union officials.[44] As votes of 'distrust' in secretaries and directors became more and more common in local political and economic organisations, they reported on these as well.[45] The idea of *kontrola*, whether by citizens directly or through organisations to which citizens would have access, was common.

Echoing Lakatoš's concern with citizen involvement in public affairs, there was considerable public discussion in 1968–69 about how to improve communication between citizens and the state formally and institutionally. The action programmes of district national committees (local councils), for example, often promised more localised administration through the creation of geographically smaller administrative units or by having staff members divide their time among a district's towns; both measures would purportedly help democratise the work of national committees and make it easier for citizens to avail themselves of 'socialist legality'.[46] Such proposals placed emphasis on the accountability of state organisations, while others emphasised the responsibility of the party with respect to society as a whole. As a plenary meeting of the Třebíč district party committee acknowledged, 'Considerable unclarity can be seen in how the party's role is understood, especially its mission and standing, particularly at a time when serious errors have been uncovered in the violation of socialist legality, suppression of criticism and shifting responsibility onto the shoulders of others'.[47] The solution, in this case, was 'comradely *kontrola*' of individual units in the party organisation.[48] Both state and party bodies at local levels often created further opportunities for *kontrola* by opening their meetings to the public.[49]

In contrast to Lakatoš's view of public opinion as objectively rooted in practical experience, making it somehow stable and infallible, public discussion of popular opinion in 1968–69 repeatedly emphasised its mutability by taking for granted that it had to be 'formed'. It could be formed through free debate, but power to mould public opinion was also attributed to newspapers and similar media.[50] Newly founded interest groups, like the 'Peace Council' established in Třebíč in November 1968, also pledged 'to help form public opinion'.[51] However it came about, there was general agreement with Lakatoš that state organs' policies should be in harmony with public opinion, rather than the other way around, and that public opinion should actively, and scientifically, be consulted in order to shape policy, rather than being used cynically to inform repression or manipulation.[52]

While public opinion was generally acknowledged in 1968–69 to be changeable, *values* were popularly viewed as innate and deeply rooted in national history. Teachers in Poděbrady defended the Strahov student demonstrators because of 'their innate sense of justice and for criticism of incompetence', values they assumed were above question.[53] The Slovak National Uprising of 1944 was 'rehabilitated' in 1968 as 'an expression of Slovaks' deep feeling for truth, justice and progress'.[54] After the invasion, the fiftieth anniversary of Czechoslovakia's founding in 1918 provided the opportunity—in both parts of the federalising state—to celebrate 'Czechoslovak values of humane justice, freedom and a longing for world peace'.[55] Even the Czechoslovak workers' movement, 'in its beginning after World War I', was depicted as motivated by an innate sense of justice: 'it sought socialism with a human face, not the deformations of the 1950s'.[56] While a self-affirming mythology was clearly being articulated in these and countless similar examples, they demonstrate that Lakatoš was not alone in seeing values as civilisational, and in holding that they should find expression in law.

Something we *do not* find in Lakatoš, but do find in the public debate of 1968–69, was invocation of *rights*. Following on the April 1968 foundation of the grassroots 'Organisation for the Defence of Human Rights' in Bratislava, a participant in a May meeting of the Třebíč district's school directors likewise invoked the 1948 Universal Declaration of Human Rights—which Czechoslovakia had recently signed—to point out 'violations of socialist legality in the period of deformation [the Stalinist period]'.[57] The district national committee responded in July by enshrining the protection of rights in its Action Programme: 'as a fundamental principle of its own Action Programme, [the committee] regards rectification of errors and incorrect decisions caused in past years by the violation of socialist legality in the conduct of administration, and the strengthening of the protective rights and justified interests of citizens in the execution of state administration'.[58] *Matica slovenská*, the custodian of Slovak culture, likewise vowed to support human rights, arguing that their protection was necessary to guarantee the nation's future.[59] Further research will be necessary to determine exactly how and when this emphasis on human rights entered Czechoslovak political discourse and how common it was in 1968–69, but certainly it predated the initiatives of the mid—to late-1970s with which it is more commonly associated.[60]

The term 'legality' usually appeared before 21 August 1968 in the phrase 'socialist legality'. This did not change after the invasion, but the emphasis shifted. The Prague Spring was characterised by a growing expectation that the 'renewed' party and state would be law-abiding, and so public discussion generally focused on what the *socialist* part of the equation meant. After 21 August, there was a collective, tacit agreement that that question was now secondary to whether the state—and international actors—would indeed adhere to the rule of law, whatever that might be. The Presidium of the Communist Party immediately protested the Soviet-led invasion as a violation of international law, and this became a refrain in popular discussion of 'the current situation' in subsequent weeks.[61] As hope of ending the occupation receded, citizens took refuge in domestic law. 'From the very beginning it was clear to us', said the district prosecutor in Třebíč, 'that in all cases we will respect our applicable laws, and we will demand rigorous obedience to them not just from all our citizens, but from the members of foreign armies as well'.[62] Public condemnation of the illegality of Stalinism, and of subsequent disregard in official quarters for valid laws, continued well into 1969 in connection with the rehabilitation of those repressed under Stalinism, which was expanded to compensate not just victims of court verdicts and national committee criminal commissions, but 'everyone who in past years was wronged by violations of socialist legality… by any administrative act'.[63] Though the term was still 'socialist legality', the emphasis was clearly on 'legality' rather than 'socialism', which was increasingly left undefined. Rehabilitation, moreover, was 'a matter not just for legal experts, but for all state and public organs, the press, and the whole public—which can facilitate its speedy realisation'.[64]

After the April 1969 plenum of the party's Central Committee, when Husákian normalisation began in earnest, the regime co-opted the new emphasis on legality for its own 'realist' purposes. Laws were turned against citizens who had supported reforms or who protested on the first anniversary of the invasion, whether by reinterpreting existing laws or passing new ones.[65] Acceptance of this state of affairs was presented as a necessary precondition for a peaceful life: 'We need full concentration and absolute calm [*klid*]. Let us therefore not tolerate any disruption of work discipline or violation of legality, especially by provoking crisis situations, defaming our political and government representatives, distributing illegal printed matter and flyers, insults and attacks on other socialist states and their representatives'.[66] 'Rigorous adherence to socialist legality' was part of a package of normalisation policies, including the restored authority of 'leading workers' and national committees as well as 'fraternisation' with other socialist countries, above all the USSR.[67] The term 'socialist legality' was now used to denote the constitutional system as such, as if to say 'this is the system we have; accept it'.[68] Emphasis on the legal side of the equation continued, even if it was a focus on form rather than content, but even this was progress, of a sort, indicative that there would be no reversal of the Weberian transition from charismatic to legal authority that the Prague Spring had affected. At the same time, the new inflection of 'socialist legality' definitively squelched reformist debates on the meaning of *socialism*, precluding any positive consensus about the signifier's content.

The Prague Spring's Impact on Legal Thinking in Dissent and Revolution

The reverse side of the coin was, of course, the development of a new opposition, which emphasised a less cynical approach to legality. Initially this was still a self-consciously socialist opposition, though it took to heart the lesson of 1968 that socialism of any desirable sort was impossible without first ensuring the rule of law. The authors of the 'Ten-Point Manifesto', issued on 21 August 1969, upheld the inviolability of international law, castigated 'the disbanding of voluntary organisations which have in no way contravened the law', lamented the weakening of legal sanctions against powerholders who had broken the law, insisted on the legality of the Communist Party's Vysočany Congress (held, despite the invasion, on 22 August 1968) and pledged to oppose 'by legal means anything that goes against our reason and our human conscience'.[69] Authors of the 1972 Workers' Proclamation likewise urged workers to insist on adherence to internal party and union rules, particularly with regard to elections, and to demand compliance with safety regulations and the Labour Code.[70] Gradually this socialist opposition of the early 1970s grew into the more politically diverse group of dissidents clustered around Charter 77, which if anything made the principle of legality, without qualifying adjectives, and citizens' *kontrola* even more central to its programme.

The revolution of 1989 was in part a revolution for the rule of law; Civic Forum, a statewide revolutionary association modelled on Charter 77, put 'law' (*právo*) at the top of its list of demands on 26 November.[71] There were also brief popular attempts to realise the legal programme of 1968. Law students in particular disseminated guidelines on how citizens could take advantage of hitherto untested laws that gave them the right to recall delegates to representative assemblies and to dismiss workplace directors through votes of no confidence. Together with legal experts active in Civic Forum and the specifically Slovak network Public against Violence, these students established free legal advice centres. In December 1989 and January 1990, these grassroots efforts enjoyed notable success. The civic initiatives became, at local as well as national and federal levels, means through which citizens could exercise *kontrola* over state and economic organs, to ensure that they acted in accordance with the law and to propose measures stemming from the popular will. The students even echoed Lakatoš's views on the relationship between law and values, positing that 'law is a form of social consensus regarding certain forms of behaviour. As long as there is social consensus (agreement), one can never speak of the violation of valid law'.[72]

In early 1990, however, this Prague Spring-inspired vision of what could still, perhaps, be called 'socialist legality' came into conflict with another vision, articulated by such former communist jurists as Petr Pithart and Zdeněk Jičinský, who preferred a more 'legalistic' interpretation of 'valid law' than what the students proposed, even if it should go against social consensus. Thus it was Jičinský who proposed cancelling the by-elections that had been set in motion by popular recall initiatives, recommending instead the method of co-optation that the Husák regime had used (technically in accordance with the law) to purge representative assemblies after 1969.[73] Thus it was Pithart who urged workers to desist from firing directors who had lost their trust, promising new laws that would allow ministries and national committees to address the situation from above.[74] Pithart in particular praised the Czechoslovak transition, which he was loath to call *revolution*, for maintaining legal continuity, but if we recall the legal theory of the Prague Spring we must acknowledge that the form of legal continuity chosen was not the only one possible. As a result, perhaps, Czechs and Slovaks since 1990 have more than once confronted the question of whether operative laws are at variance with societal values—and what should be done about it if so.

Notes

1. A.J. Jacobson and B. Schlink, 'Constitutional Crisis: The German and the American Experience', in A.J. Jacobson & B. Schlink (eds), *Weimar: A Jurisprudence of Crisis* (Berkeley, CA, 2000), p. 19.
2. Jacobson and Schlink, 'Constitutional Crisis', p. 20.
3. As used by the jurist Rudolf Smend, 'Constitution and Constitutional Law (1928)', in Jacobson & Schlink (eds), *Weimar*, p. 234.
4. Z. Jičínský, *Právní myšlení v 60. letech a za normalizace* (Prague, 1992).
5. 'Konečné výsledky voleb', *Rudé právo*, 29 November 1971.
6. On the place of rights in the longer narrative, see M. Kopeček, 'Human Rights between Political Identity and Historical Category', *Czech Journal of Contemporary History*, no. 4 (2016), pp. 5–18.
7. Mlynář's story is told in A. Catalano, 'Zdeněk Mlynář and the Search for Socialist Opposition', *Czech Journal of Contemporary History*, vol. 3 (2015), pp. 90–156.
8. We draw on Lakatoš's entry in *Kdo je kdo v České republice 94/95* (Prague, 1994), p. 318.
9. M. Shore, 'Engineering in the Age of Innocence: A Genealogy of Discourse Inside the Czechoslovak Writers' Union, 1949–1967', *East European Politics and Societies*, vol. 12, no. 3 (1998), pp. 397–441.
10. Economists went through a similar development of sidestepping rather than openly renouncing their pasts. See J. Suk, *Veřejné záchodky ze zlata: Rozprava o novém modelu socialismu v československé politické ekonomii šedesátých let* (Prague, 2016). For an analogous case of a leading social theorist, see V. Sommer, 'Scientists of the World, Unite! Radovan Richta's Theory of Scientific and Technological Revolution', in E. Aronova and S. Turchetti (eds), *Science Studies during the Cold War and Beyond* (New York, 2016), pp. 177–204. The economists and Richta achieved greater international renown owing to translations of their works, which were not made for the jurists' output.
11. M. Lakatoš, *Formy československého práva* (Prague, 1956), p. 10.
12. Lakatoš, *Formy československého práva*, p. 8.
13. M. Lakatoš, *Otázky lidové demokracie v Československu* (Prague, 1957), pp. 128–9.
14. I. Bystřina and M. Lakatoš, *Některé otázky teorie práva* (Prague, 1960), pp. 198–200.
15. Lakatoš, *Formy československého práva*, pp. 64–6.
16. H. Gordon Skilling outlines the official view and Bystřina's departure from it in 'People's Democracy and the Socialist Revolution: A Case Study in Communist Scholarship, Part I', *Soviet Studies*, vol. 12, no. 3 (1961), pp. 253–8.

17. Lakatoš, *Otázky lidové demokracie*, pp. 98, 102.
18. Lakatoš, *Otázky lidové demokracie*, p. 90.
19. In *Otázky tvorby práva v socialistické společnosti* (Prague, 1963), Lakatoš quotes Vyshinsky approvingly (p. 113) that the task of the law-maker is to be able to grasp in a timely fashion the needs and demands of a given phase of socialist development.
20. Lakatoš, *Otázky tvorby práva*, p. 155.
21. J. Tolar, G. Přenosil and M. Lakatoš, *Místní lidové soudy* (Prague, 1965), pp. 7–49. Lakatoš was responsible for Chapter 1 of this work, completed in October 1963. He did not endorse another innovation from 1957: the direct election of district judges.
22. Bystřina and Lakatoš, *Některé otázky teorie práva*, pp. 150–68, 204–9; Lakatoš, *Otázky tvorby práva*, pp. 25–7, 112–21, 161–79.
23. K. McDermott, *Communist Czechoslovakia, 1945–89: A Political and Social History* (London, 2015), pp. 101–7.
24. Z. Mlynář, *Stát a člověk: Úvahy o politickém řízení za socialismu* (Prague, 1964).
25. H.G. Skilling, *Czechoslovakia's Interrupted Revolution* (Princeton, NJ, 1976), p. 146 reports that Lakatoš had finished the text in 1964, but could not get it published for two years.
26. M. Lakatoš, *Občan, právo a demokracie* (Prague, 1966), p. 10.
27. Lakatoš, *Občan, právo a demokracie*, pp. 16, 20–1, 23–7, 63, 149–59.
28. Lakatoš, *Občan, právo a demokracie*, pp. 58–9.
29. Lakatoš, *Občan, právo a demokracie*, p. 160.
30. Lakatoš, *Občan, právo a demokracie*, pp. 116–19, 140–3.
31. For example, in Lakatoš, *Otázky tvorby práva*, p. 106.
32. Lakatoš, *Občan, právo a demokracie*, p. 20.
33. M. Lakatoš, 'Břemeno odpovědnosti', *Literární noviny*, no. 28 (1967), pp. 1, 3; 'Občanská společnost hledá své místo', *Kulturní noviny*, no. 8 (1968), pp. 1, 8.
34. M. Lakatoš, *Úvahy o hodnotách demokracie* (Prague, 1968), p. 10.
35. Lakatoš, *Úvahy*, p. 8.
36. M. Bovens, 'Analysing and Assessing Accountability: A Conceptual Framework', *European Law Journal*, vol. 13, no. 4 (2007), p. 450.
37. In his article 'Občanská společnost hledá své místo' (p. 8), Lakatoš bluntly complained that the party in effect supplanted civil society and left the latter dysfunctional as a result.
38. Lakatoš, *Úvahy*, p. 65 wonders how most young Czechs would vote if pop idol Karel Gott stood for office against a less famous politician, and notes that a film actor—presumably, Ronald Reagan—had recently won the governorship of an American state.
39. Lakatoš, *Úvahy*, p. 100.

40. Lakatoš lived in Černošice, a village on the western bank of the Berounka river that marks the capital's southern fringe.
41. The districts of Topoľčany (Slovakia), Třebíč (Moravia) and Nymburk (Bohemia) were selected since they were the birthplaces of prominent figures of the Prague Spring (Dubček, Svoboda and Smrkovský, respectively), giving journalists and supervisory bodies there extra reason to embrace liberalisation.
42. 'Bajka o prázdném sudu', *Nymbursko*, 9 April 1968.
43. 'Bajka o prázdném sudu'.
44. See, for example, 'Pol roka mlčania', *Socialistický dnešok* (Topoľčany), 3 April 1968; 'Mohli, alebo nemohli', *Socialistický dnešok*, 10 April 1968; 'Opäť pol roka mlčania?' *Socialistický dnešok*, 22 May 1968; and 'Dočkám sa odpovede?' *Socialistický dnešok*, 29 May 1968.
45. See, for example, Z. Šebková, 'Zčeřená hladina se uklidnila', *Nymbursko*, 4 June 1968; 'Stanovisko redakce k článku', *Nymbursko*, 30 October 1968.
46. 'Súhlas s Programom ONV', *Socialistický dnešok*, 7 August 1968.
47. 'O dalším postupu strany rozhoduje ideologická a organizátórska práce', *Jiskra* (Třebíč), 29 May 1968.
48. 'Situace vyžaduje iniciativu celé strany', *Jiskra*, 22 May 1969.
49. A. Krumpár, 'Umenie odísť', *Socialistický dnešok*, 10 April 1968; 'Právo občana', *Socialistický dnešok*, 22 May 1968.
50. 'Svěží vítr zavál v "Národním domě",' *Nymbursko*, 19 March 1968; J. Procházka, 'Moje setkání s životem', *Nymbursko*, 2 July 1968.
51. 'Akční program Okresní mírové rády', *Jiskra*, 6 November 1968.
52. A. Rezníkov, 'Po klidu—vzrušení…', *Nymbursko*, 19 March 1968; 'Znát názory občanů', *Jiskra*, 5 February 1969; 'Počítače a politika', *Jiskra*, 30 April 1969.
53. Učitelé ZDŠ Poděbrady, 'Otevřený dopis pracujícím závodu ZPA Pečky', *Nymbursko*, 9 April 1968.
54. *Socialistický dnešok*, 21 August 1968. Slovak historians had begun de-Stalinising interpretations of the Uprising in 1961, but the process of publicly reclaiming the Uprising as a broadly based, Slovak-led phenomenon (rather than a principally Communist movement led by Soviets and Czechs) culminated only in 1968. See J.L. Ryder, 'Slovak Society, the Second World War, and the Search for Slovak "Stateness"' (PhD diss., McGill University, 2017), pp. 226–33.
55. J. Fiala, 'Škola života', *Nymbursko*, 26 November 1968.
56. A. Mareš, 'Vzpomínání', *Jiskra*, 17 January 1969.
57. Skilling, *Czechoslovakia's Interrupted Revolution*, p. 202; 'Učitelé a dnešek', *Jiskra*, 8 May 1968. Societies for the defence of human rights were set up in other parts of Czechoslovakia as well. See Ľ. Čakajda, 'Dôsledne za prekonanie problémov', *Socialistický dnešok*, 2 July 1969.

58. 'Akční program Okresního národního výboru v Třebíči', *Jiskra*, 17 July 1968; 'Stanovisko redakce k článku', *Nymbursko*, 30 October 1968.
59. 'Ohlas k slovenskému národu', *Smer* (Banská Bystrica), 11 August 1968.
60. See, for instance, S. Moyn, *The Last Utopia: Human Rights in History* (Cambridge, MA, 2010), esp. pp. 120–2, 161–6.
61. Proclamation by the Central Committee Presidium on 21 August 1968, in J. Pelikán (ed.), *The Secret Vysočany Congress* (London, 1971), pp. 15–16; J. Gális, 'Pedagogika na rázcestí' and 'V ktorej krajine sa nachadzám?' *Úderník* (Partizánske), 6 September 1968.
62. 'Zákony platí nejen pro naše občany', *Jiskra*, 16 October 1968.
63. 'O rehabilitační poradně v Třebíči', *Jiskra*, 29 January 1969.
64. 'O rehabilitační poradně'.
65. 'Akční směrnice...', *Nymbursko*, 3 July 1969; 'Nad paragraphy', *Jiskra*, 17 September 1969.
66. 'Prohlášení vedoucích hospodářských pracovníků n. p. Závody oborové mechanizace Nymburk', *Nymbursko*, 28 September 1969.
67. 'První okresní konference národních výborů', *Jiskra*, 17 December 1969.
68. 'Snemovanie poľnohospodárov', *Socialistický dnešok*, 2 June 1969.
69. 'The Ten Point Manifesto', 21 August 1969, in J. Pelikán, *Socialist Opposition in Eastern Europe: The Czechoslovak Example* (London, 1976), pp. 117–24.
70. 'The Workers' Proclamation', January 1972, in Pelikán (ed.), *Socialist Opposition*, pp. 160–3.
71. 'Co chceme: Programové zásady Občanského fóra', in J. Suk (ed.), *Občanské forum: Listopad-prosinec 1989*, vol. 2 (Brno, 1998), p. 28.
72. Studenti PF UK, 'Pracovně právní důsledky případného přerušení práce', Prague, 25 November 1989, quoted in J. Krapfl, *Revolution with a Human Face: Politics, Culture, and Community in Czechoslovakia, 1989–1992* (Ithaca, NY, 2013), p. 156.
73. J. Suk, *Labyrintem revoluce: Aktéři, zápletky a křižovatky jedné politické krize (od listopadu 1989 do června 1990)* (Prague, 2003), p. 283.
74. 'Projev P. Pitharta v čs. tevizi [*sic*]', *InForum*, no. 11, 23 January 1990, translated in Krapfl, *Revolution with a Human Face*, pp. 178–81.

The 'Anti-Prague Spring': Neo-Stalinist and Ultra-Leftist Extremism in Czechoslovakia, 1968–70

Kevin McDermott and Vítězslav Sommer

The Prague Spring has attracted much scholarly attention in the past 50 years. Historians have exhaustively documented the policies, strategies and tactics of what might be termed the Czechoslovak political mainstream in 1968–69: the 'centrist' and 'progressive' reformers in the Communist Party of Czechoslovakia (*Komunistická strana Československa*—KSČ) and their 'conservative' adversaries who sought to curtail any substantive change.[1] A fair amount has also been written about an embryonic 'civil society' based on the emergence of diverse social and cultural movements and pluralistic socio-political attitudes.[2] But little is known about the extremes of political life during the Prague Spring. That is, on the one hand, the ultra-reactionary 'neo-Stalinists', who categorically rejected the vision of 'socialism with a human face' as an attempt

K. McDermott (✉)
Sheffield Hallam University, Sheffield, UK
e-mail: k.f.mcdermott@shu.ac.uk

V. Sommer
Institute of Contemporary History, Czech Academy of Sciences, Prague, Czech Republic
e-mail: sommer@usd.cas.cz

© The Author(s) 2018
K. McDermott and M. Stibbe (eds.), *Eastern Europe in 1968*,
https://doi.org/10.1007/978-3-319-77069-7_3

to restore capitalism in Czechoslovakia, and, on the other, those rather nebulous 'anti-communist forces', who had never reconciled themselves to the existence of the communist system. The symbiotic relationship between these two poles of opinion is historically important because it indicates a darker 'uncivil' side of the Prague Spring reminding us that Czechoslovak political culture is more heterogeneous and composite than the standard Masarykian 'democratic-humanist-pluralist' mythology.[3]

Our focus here is squarely on neo-Stalinist extremism in the KSČ, an approach which we believe affords a fresh angle on developments in 1968–70. The conventional narrative portrays the party as essentially united around reformist politics with merely a handful of conservatives and old Stalinists conspiring with Moscow against Alexander Dubček's leadership. Moreover, the traditional, and to some extent nationalist, interpretation of the Prague Spring as a whole is informed by the image of the nation solidly behind reform, aside from a tiny band of 'traitors' who acted clandestinely against the will of the vast majority of the population. In this chapter, we suggest that reality was somewhat more complicated than this sharp unequal binary. Although the bulk of party activists were, in varying degrees, convinced of the necessity of a 'renewal process', there was a tenacious core of rank-and-file sectarians vocally airing their grievances from February onwards and promoting the thesis that 'counter-revolution' was stalking Czechoslovakia; there were powerful like-minded ultra-conservative officials connected with Soviet diplomatic and, possibly, security circles; and, significantly, there were swathes of regional *apparatchiks*, party members and industrial workers, who were alarmed by the potentialities of the Dubčekite project, confused by 'intellectual' reformist politics and concerned that the party could lose control and, as a consequence, its capacity to follow the socialist path of development. In short, influential anti-reformist networks, tendencies and anxieties existed at all levels of the party in 1968. From this we conclude that it was precisely these diffuse undercurrents that were gradually mobilised in the fraught months after the Warsaw Pact invasion to affect the relatively smooth, though calamitous, transition from the Prague Spring to 'normalisation'.

Who Were the Neo-Stalinists?

The use of binding labels is problematic in 1968 conditions, not least because individuals could and did adopt shifting and mediating stances making them difficult to pigeon-hole. Conventional categorisations such as 'left', 'right', 'centre', 'radical', 'conservative' or 'progressive' obscure as much as they illuminate given the dynamic allegiances and nuanced ideological positions. That said, it is vital to demarcate as clearly as possible between factions and trends. On the 'left'—by which we mean the substantial anti-reformist wing of the KSČ—it is hard to discern strict dividing lines between a neo-Stalinist extremist like Josef Jodas and strident reactionaries like Vasil Bil'ak and Alois Indra, two of the signatories of the notorious 'Letter of Invitation' requesting Soviet intervention and subsequent arch-normalisers. To be sure, much united them. We do not, however, include Bil'ak, Indra and company among the ultra-leftists because before the invasion they largely upheld party discipline and unity, expressed support, albeit often lukewarm, for at least some of the post-January changes and refrained from publicly attacking the Dubčekite leadership, of which they were members. In contrast, the non-elite 'ultras' considered the reform package overwhelmingly a counter-revolutionary abomination, felt free to lambast prominent reformers by name and used vituperative terminology more in tune with the 1930s than the 1960s; hence the designation 'neo-Stalinist'. Who were these dogmatic sectarians and what motivated them?

In an article published in 2006, Pavel Urbášek identified several ideologically coherent, though distinct, neo-Stalinist groupings and cliques operating in Czechoslovakia in the years 1968–70. These included the so-called 'Jodasovci', 'Famírovci', the Left Front (*Levá fronta*) and the Leninist Youth Union (*Leninský svaz mladých*), among others.[4] In our estimation, it is important to add three other strands of ultra-leftism. First, high-ranking *nomenklatura* functionaries, some of whom were adherents of Antonín Novotný, Dubček's discredited predecessor as KSČ First Secretary, and others who would play a conspicuous role in Gustáv Husák's 'normalisation' regime after 1969—Pavel Auersperg, Bohuslav Chňoupek, Michal Chudík, Karel Hoffmann, Květoslav Innemann, Antonín Kapek, Bohumír Lomský, Karel Mestek, Vilém Nový, Otakar Rytíř and Viliam Šalgovič. Second, hovering in the shadows were lesser lights such as František Havlíček, Jan Šimek, Jan Svoboda, Josef Valenta, Jan Kladiva and Jan Němec, all of whom were deeply sceptical about the post-January changes and maintained personal links with Soviet diplomats resident in Prague. And third were individual regional party officials, for example Jaromír Brovják in Ostrava and Josef Kalenda in Hradec Králové, and writers like Rudolf Černý and Antonín Černý (unrelated), who were closely associated with neo-Stalinist positions.[5]

Their professional, generational and status backgrounds were diverse. Some were elderly rank-and-file founders of the party who had suffered under the First Republic and in Nazi concentration camps (Jodas, Ladislav Morávek, Karel Šmidrkal); others were acting, or former, dignitaries in the party, government or security elites (Kapek, Lomský, Šalgovič); others still were middle-aged *apparatchiks* in the party machine (Havlíček, Šimek, Svoboda). The 'ultras' also had representatives on the editorial boards of prestigious journals (Valenta), in higher education (Kladiva, Jaromír Hrbek) and in influential bodies like the Union of Czechoslovak–Soviet Friendship (Němec) and the People's Militia. In terms of their stature and clout, it was obvious to ardent reformers, such as the journalist Jiří Kantůrek, that it was 'the forty somethings like Kapek' rather than 'old Jodas' who presented 'the greatest danger'.[6] The neo-Stalinists did not form a tight knit organisational force, let alone a clearly defined inner-party faction. Indeed, generally they seem to have operated independently of each other and some were more overtly and virulently Stalinist than others. Neither do they appear to have established links with like-minded hard-liners in other Soviet bloc states.[7] Nevertheless, they were broadly united by their fervent ideological beliefs based on their irrevocable faith in the leading role of the party and in the 'eternal' Soviet alliance.

It would be all too easy to mock the views of the neo-Stalinists, as some pro-reformers evidently did at the time.[8] However much 'progressives' found them crass, offensive or plain stupid, they need to be taken seriously given that their impact on the party, and arguably beyond, was not inconsiderable. We have identified three underlying and mutually reinforcing sets of values, or mentalities, that bound the disparate 'ultras' together. First was their implacable suspicion, bordering on an innate antipathy, of 'intellectuals', often accompanied by implicit, sometimes explicit, anti-Semitism. Second was their embedded fear that reform threatened not only the 'holy of holies'—the unity and leading role of the Communist Party—but ultimately the very existence of socialism, the epitome of which was the Soviet model imported into Czechoslovakia after the 'Victorious February' of 1948. Third was their conviction that 'anti-communism' was rife in society and, crucially, was beginning to infect the party itself in the guise of 'elitist' reformers, journalists and writers who were by definition divorced from the mass of upright communists and citizens. In its worst form, as in the Hungarian Revolution of October–November 1956, 'anti-communism' was perceived by party diehards as a violent, even murderous, opposition, which in turn fostered an elemental leftist backlash.

A brief survey of the discourse and rhetoric of the 'ultras' is instructive as it clearly reveals their Stalinist lineage. The terms 'honest' (*poctivý*), 'honourable' (*čestný*) and 'patriot' (*vlastenec*) appeared quite regularly, suggesting that their self-image was one of genuine hardworking Czechs and Slovaks defending their country in the name of the common people. By contrast, the 'enemy' was construed as alien, a 'fifth column' associated with foreign powers, somehow un-Czech or unpatriotic, thus insinuating a kind of 'rootless cosmopolitanism'. In classical Stalinist manner, these covert traitors had to be 'exposed' and overcome. In addition, the 'ultras' exuded a sustained commitment to society's 'collective needs', while the 'self-interested' petit-bourgeois intellectuals merely pursued their narrow 'individualistic' or sectional goals. To this extent, the neo-Stalinists endeavoured to appeal, partially successfully, to the myth of majoritarian 'national unity' and 'proletarian internationalism'. This emphasis on class antagonism, 'socialist patriotism' and international solidarity, actively encouraged for years by the Novotný regime, helps us understand why the 'ultras'' criticisms of post-January developments struck a chord with relatively large numbers of workers, party members and lower-level functionaries, without necessarily gaining firm and consistent popular backing for their extremist doctrinal tenets.

THE JODASITES' FEBRUARY INTERVENTION

The neo-Stalinists first entered the fray as early as February 1968, when, in the wake of Novotný's ouster and replacement by the compromise candidate Dubček at a stormy Central Committee plenum on 3–5 January,[9] a group of five 'old communists' from the Prague working-class district of Libeň—Jodas, Morávek, Karel Pospíšil, Šmidrkal and Václav Svoboda—dispatched a fractious letter to various regional, district and factory KSČ organisations. The idea of sending a missive emerged from an *aktiv* (meeting) of eighty party stalwarts in the U Zábranských pub on 17 February to mark the twentieth anniversary of the communist takeover and it is possible that the authors conceived it as part of an on-going pro-Novotnýite campaign to seek support among party loyalists, lower-ranking officials and industrial workers. It was believed, apparently, that in the flux following Novotný's 'temporary defeat' pressure from below might influence Dubček in a broadly conservative direction.[10]

It is worth examining the twenty-page letter in some depth because it encapsulates many of the central concerns of the neo-Stalinists and lays bare their intolerant dogmatism and fanaticism.[11]

Characterising themselves as 'ordinary' (*řadoví*) party members, the Jodasites started by bemoaning the distinct lack of information provided by the new KSČ executive about the January changeover, a state of affairs that was interpreted as a conscious ploy to keep comrades in the dark. The malcontents then came to the crux. For several years 'dual power' had persisted in the party: on one side stood the Central Committee with whose decisions they 'fully agree', and on the other 'the apparat', which 'advocates a different ideology, dictates, intimidates, intrigues and limits the rights of party members'. In the past decade this internal 'fifth column', composed of the offspring of former factory owners, lawyers, businessmen and 'social fascists', all directed by western émigrés like 'the traitor' Hubert Ripka,[12] had wormed their way into the party machine, the KSČ daily organ *Rudé právo* ('Red Right'), the Higher Party School, the Institute of Party History, and Czechoslovak Television and Radio. The prime aims of these 'revisionist and liquidationist cliques' were to 'eliminate the leading role of the communist party' and working class; 'to slander and ridicule (*zesměšňovat*) the socialist order' and the Soviet Union; 'to enforce bourgeois democracy from liberalism to anarchy'; 'to enforce coexistence with the capitalist West [and] to propagate bourgeois life-style, its decadent and degenerate culture'. In this depiction of relentless 'revisionist' infiltration and 'internal subversion' of the party, the Jodasites were remarkably prescient: this was precisely the justification—'the quiet counter-revolution' from within—that the Soviets would put forward from July onwards for their military preparations.[13]

The authors of the letter went on to assert that inner-party hierarchies had emerged pitting 'bosses' (*pány*) against 'commoners' (*kmány*). In this situation, 'workers were only good for paying membership dues' and, it was inferred, were rarely consulted, informed or valued. Neither did the neo-Stalinists shy away from *ad hominem* barbs against the numerous 'fractionalist' communists and intellectuals blamed for this 'de-politicisation' and 'ideological ... deadening' of party organisations. They included, among many others, Jaroslav Šabata, Ota Šik, František Kriegel, Josef Smrkovský, Radoslav Selucký, Eduard Goldstücker and Milan Hübl, most of whom were of Jewish origin and all firm adherents of reform. Dark and symbolic references to 'Zionism' made the

Jodasites' thinly veiled, yet underlying, anti-Semitism palpable. Their conclusion was unequivocal: the January change of guard was nothing other than a 'putsch of the bourgeois and neo-bourgeois elements in the party' with the aim of transforming the intellectuals' 'elite of influence' into an 'elite of power'. The diatribe ended with a rousing sectarian call to arms: 'Down with the breakers of party unity! Careerists, bourgeois liquidators and imperialist agents—out of the party!'

The letter was a crude and ugly intervention, prompting a measured rebuttal from the Prague KSČ City Committee on 14 March 1968: 'all communists are equal in the party and no individual has the right to call another communist a splitter, fractionalist, revisionist, provocateur or liquidator'. Eight other pre-war communists from Prague-Libeň went further, denouncing the missive's 'pogromistic phrases about a fifth column in the party ... lack of patriotism, Zionism [and] social fascism'.[14] These totally justified attacks notwithstanding, several important aspects of the neo-Stalinists' critique did find resonance among relatively wide segments of the party faithful. For instance, their professed defence of grassroots 'open politics' against shady behind-the-scenes 'cabinet politics' and their accusation of a virtual informational 'cover-up' about the January events mirrored the views of many functionaries and members and were construed as a plea for greater inner-party democracy and workers' rights.[15] No less a figure than Oldřich Černík, the new 'centrist' Prime Minister, disparaged 'cabinet politics' and advocated a 'politics of the masses' at a Presidium meeting on 7 May.[16] In addition, it could be argued—basically in line with the Jodasites—that by the mid-1960s vital sections of the party's internal organs had indeed become heavily influenced, if not controlled outright, by reformist 'technocrats' (Šik, Radovan Richta, Zdeněk Mlynář, etc.) and the hard-line ideologists were fighting a losing battle.[17]

There is also evidence that the neo-Stalinists' anti-Semitic proclivities reflected a wider social malaise from which communists, even luminaries, were not immune. For example, Oldřich Švestka, the arch-conservative chief editor of *Rudé právo*, decried the impact of 'so-called Jordan Slavs' on his newspaper and other mass media outlets.[18] Věra Šťovíčková, a top broadcaster, received more than a few intimidating letters and postcards, generally anonymous, assailing her alleged pro-Israeli attitudes. One read: 'Communists condemn you and consider you an agent of a Zionist-revisionist centre'.[19] The most obscene instance was a spiteful letter addressed in mid-June to that 'Zionist hyena bastard' Goldstücker, a survivor of the Stalinist trials of the early 1950s and chair of the Czechoslovak Writers' Union. Ostensibly from 'honest members of the KSČ', Goldstücker attributed the outrage to disaffected Stalinist operatives in the secret services.[20] The flood of anti-Jewish and anti-democratic invective, which was particularly evident in May and June, appears to have been loosely coordinated and was sufficiently vicious for one television editor to speak of a 'moral crisis' at the heart of Czechoslovak society.[21]

More relevant for our purposes, many party cadres and workers, judging from communications sent to Dubček and reports on the regional KSČ conferences held in March and April, were almost as fearful of the potential consequences of reform as the Jodasites. One notification from the Český Dub town committee in northern Bohemia spoke of an emerging 'atmosphere of unhealthy psychosis', of 'extremes' and 'demagogic attacks against the party, communists and socialism'. These were partly engendered by radio and television programmes and press articles, which 'unobjectively' and 'tendentiously' exaggerate 'certain negative phenomena'. Another memorandum warned of 'the tragedy in Hungary' in 1956 which could be repeated in Czechoslovakia if the party hierarchy continues to display 'indecisiveness'. 'Several authors' were worried that 'democratisation' might induce 'anarchy'.[22] It was also emphasised that since the second half of February, party officials and rank-and-file were adopting more 'critical positions' towards the January plenum as the future direction of the party was thrown into question. Disorientation, doubt, confusion and scepticism were on the rise and there were signs of 'conservative' opposition to 'anti-working class' policies, the 'retreat from Marxism–Leninism', 'misgivings' about possible worsening relations with the Soviet Union and 'excesses' in the mass media. In western Bohemia a 'majority ... expressed concerns about party unity' and a dispatch from northern Moravia warned ominously that if the 'new leadership' does not 'solve this serious situation it will gradually lose the support of party members and workers'.[23] Such files landing on Dubček's desk must, at a minimum, have inclined him and his colleagues to tread carefully in their mooted reforms.

Internal KSČ sources indicate that the widespread fears and vacillations of early spring had not noticeably waned by mid-summer in the tense period following the publication of Ludvík Vaculík's highly controversial '2000 Words' manifesto on 27 June. An evaluation of the extraordinary district and regional conferences that took place in June and July concluded starkly that 'the party is not united' with 'many members' being 'on the defensive and unable to orientate themselves to fresh circumstances'. In addition, 'sections of the party are still not convinced of the correctness of the new course', there continued to exist 'a lack of faith in the intelligentsia' and 'a number of basic organisations and communists ... are insufficiently prepared for dialogue with other components of our society'. Although only a 'minority of delegates' regarded the state of affairs inside the KSČ 'very pessimistically', it was nevertheless affirmed that 'self-confidence is in decline [and] the party suffers from low levels of political initiative ... and ideological activity'. At the same time, it was recorded that a 'majority of conferences' believed the 'main danger' came not from right-wing anti-socialists, but from outdated 'conservative and bureaucratic forces', itself a telling indication of the perceived pervasiveness of anti-reformist tendencies in the KSČ.[24] In sum, we can say that throughout the eight months of the Prague Spring the entire Czechoslovak party was internally fractured and the irrevocable Leninist principle of democratic centralism was coming under severe strain.[25] A majority of functionaries embraced, to a greater or lesser extent, the winds of change, but a small minority utterly rejected them and, just as significantly, a hefty proportion adopted what might be called intermediate moods and positions characterised by indecision, passivity, pessimism and concern for the future.

'Anti-Communist Terror'

Symbiotically linked to leftist currents in the KSČ was the conviction, seemingly seared into the soul of the neo-Stalinists, that loyal party comrades were increasingly confronted with the spectre of 'anti-communist terror'. And like all entrenched mentalities, there was more than a measure of validity to this 'myth' of 'reactionary' violence: the security services archive and other sources are replete with this trope, frequently cataloguing verbal and physical abuse against party notables and secret police operatives. The following cases will suffice. In late April 1968, Karol Bacílek, the Minister of National Security at the time of the notorious Stalinist show trials in the early 1950s, reported that he had received several anonymous letters sent from Bratislava and elsewhere in Slovakia. Two in particular were noteworthy—both deemed him a 'murderer' (*vrah*) and 'monster' (*netvor*), threatened to kill him and have 'his grave ... adorned with human excrement'. Bacílek's windows had been smashed and he had been verbally abused in the street, all of which had depressed him and harmed his family life.[26] Prime Minister Černík likewise received a menacing letter: you 'will be hung'.[27] In late May, Bil'ak asserted to the hard-line Ukrainian party leader, Petro Shelest, that: 'Among the [Czechoslovak] party activists and state security [StB] agents there have been many instances of suicide induced by threats from rightists ... "Soon the time will come when we will hang all Communists, stringing them up by their feet"'.[28] Indeed, Ministry of Interior documents confirm that several StB officials had committed suicide for 'political reasons', often as a result of anonymous psychological and occasionally even physical assaults probably related to media revelations about police brutality during the Stalinist purges.[29] In similar vein, Indra informed the Presidium on 7 May that there had been recent 'attempts to steal weapons from arms depots' and 'many cases of attacks on civil militiamen'.[30] There were also reports that the names and addresses of party members and functionaries were being collated on a so-called 'index'.[31]

As late as autumn 1988, communists looking back on their experiences in 1968 vividly recalled the 'psychological terror' unleashed against 'friends of the USSR'—'it was horrific' (*to byla hrůza*). Bohumír Beránek, an engineer from Prague's third district, wrote: 'In a number of places ... counter-revolutionary forces had prepared lists of inconvenient (*nepohodlných*) persons who were slated for physical liquidation'. In Týniště nad Orlicí, forty 'old communists' were to be disposed of and fourteen workers in Roztoky nad Vltavou were to share the same fate. In total, he estimated that 60,000 people were to be 'physically eliminated' in the event of a 'counter-revolutionary triumph'.[32] These are, without doubt, gross over-exaggerations, but they reveal a recurrent historic dread among party stalwarts, dating at least from the lynch mobs of Budapest in October 1956, of elemental anti-communist violence lurking just below the surface.[33] As the leading reformist Mlynář succinctly put it: 'we Communists were quite simply afraid'.[34] This fear was corroborated by a female communist-worker from Brno, who recollected that in 1957 eleven labourers in her factory had been earmarked for 'physical liquidation' by a self-styled 'Revolutionary Resistance Movement'.[35] By 1968, such *angst* was bound up with the emergence of 'anti-socialist' groups like K-231 (the club of former political prisoners) and the Club of Committed Non-Party Members (KAN), both of which were accused by the 'ultras' of harbouring reactionary extremists and criminal elements.[36] This charge was again massively distorted, but regardless of the 'facts' these beliefs found a ready audience among sections of the party and security police for whom the rising scourge of 'anti-communist terror' was an everyday, albeit largely imagined, reality.

THE LEADING ROLE OF THE PARTY AND SOVIET CONNECTIONS

In many ways the conviction that the sacrosanct 'leading role of the party' was in mortal danger formed the cornerstone of the neo-Stalinists' critique of the Dubčekite innovations. In mid-February, Jan Šimek, the hard-line deputy head of the Ideological Department, informed his Soviet interlocutor, the diplomat Igor Cherkasov, that the party's political hegemony was no longer guaranteed because, according to the 'simply revisionist' draft Action Programme, a revamped KSČ would in future play an 'equal role' in the National Front with the other legal non-communist parties, the Socialist Party and People's Party. From this it was but a short step to the creation of an 'opposition party'. It was thus clear to Šimek that 'the authority of the KSČ in society is lower now than before'.[37] The embattled Novotný weighed in with the same concerns at a Presidium meeting on 14 March.[38] Vilém Nový, an ultra-conservative Central Committee member and National Assembly delegate, put it another way in a private letter to the Presidium in mid-July. Closely echoing Soviet concerns, he asked: 'who is really running the party? Is it the CC [Central Committee] headed by Dubček ... or some second centre in the party, which possesses far more powerful weapons in the press and mass media? Not just me, but thousands of cadres and ordinary party members are posing this question'.[39] Kapek, the highest ranking neo-Stalinist, also bitterly complained at a Presidium session in late April that the party was 'losing its working-class character' in favour of the 'intelligentsia'.[40] But it was not only dignitaries who bemoaned the fading 'leading role'—such fears were mirrored in the party apparatus and wider membership. In early May, internal memoranda detailed the apprehensions of local communists about the 'disparagement of the leading role' and in July the chair of the Plzeň National Committee, Gustav Rada, asserted that the 'chaotic' situation, and by implication the weakening of the party, would aid those who wished to return to 'bourgeois democracy'.[41] In June, 'serious concerns' were expressed in People's Militia units about the 'fate of the party's leading role' which could be exploited by 'anti-communist forces'.[42]

Even in the confusing days immediately following the Warsaw Pact invasion, the issue refused to go away. On 29 August, the north Moravian security services discovered leaflets in Frýdek Místek which claimed that after January the party had lost its guiding function.[43] In early September, in the midst of nationwide passive resistance to the Soviet occupation, a survey of KSČ activists in Litoměřice in northern Bohemia revealed that 32.6% of respondents believed either fully or 'partially' that the post-January changes had 'threatened the leading role of the party' and 21.3% that they had 'endangered the development of socialism' in the country.[44] And the anti-reformists' worst nightmares were not entirely unfounded. In late May 1968, it had been revealed that two local *party* resolutions had recommended deleting the 'leading role' from Article 41 of the Czechoslovak Constitution.[45] Was this not the very 'liquidationist' platform that the Jodasites had railed against in their February letter?

A fascinating question is: how far did the neo-Stalinists have the ear of the Soviets? Did they in any way influence thinking in the Kremlin? It is not easy to tackle this conundrum, not least because conclusive archival evidence is lacking. That said, we can document numerous instances of contact. The principal channel of communication between Czechoslovak 'ultras' and the Moscow hierarchy came via officials in the Soviet embassy in Prague, who held regular conclaves with KSČ anti-reformers. A prime example of these furtive gatherings is that on 4 March between the Soviet diplomat, Marat Kuznetsov, and Jan Svoboda, head of the party's Youth Department, and Josef Valenta, editor-in-chief of the organisational journal *Život strany* ['Life of the Party']. Svoboda and Valenta depicted events since January as a 'broadly based attack by right-wing opportunists' with a view to 'weakening the unity of the party ... and revising [its] general line'. Svoboda and Valenta claimed that 'no-one in the KSČ Central Committee controls the mass media ... censorship has been abolished' and 'overtly anti-socialist groups' are emerging. Closely emulating the Jodasites' argument, they maintained that the 'revisionists' were especially strong in the press, radio and television, a situation which had 'in essence paralysed the activity of healthy forces and honest communists'. This takeover of the means of communication had been prepared 'over several years', but now the culprits 'have torn off their masks'—a stereotypical Stalinist 'double-dealing' metaphor—and have begun to act 'self-assuredly and arrogantly'.[46] In similar fashion, Havlíček, the deposed head of the party's Ideological Department, met Sergei Prasolov, another

Soviet plenipotentiary, on at least three occasions in April 1968 and was scathing in his onslaught on the 'Zionists, pro-bourgeois elements' and 'reactionary swine' who 'for more than ten years' have been preparing a 'counter-revolution' in Czechoslovakia with the aim of 'restoring capitalist relations'.[47]

The most striking case, however, of Soviet acknowledgement of the neo-Stalinists was Leonid Brezhnev's reference to Jodas by name at the high-powered bilateral Soviet–Czechoslovak talks in Čierna nad Tisou on 29 July. Calling him an 'old communist who worked for years in illegality', the Soviet General Secretary cited with enthusiasm an interview that Jodas had recently given in the Czechoslovak army newspaper *Obrana lidu* ['Defence of the People'] in which he had assailed the 'rightist anti-socialist forces' in the KSČ who 'held in their hands all the means of mass information'.[48] The outcome, Jodas contended, was that communists were now 'outlaws' (*mimo zákon*), excluded from the media and hence effectively disempowered.[49] It is hard to imagine that such accusations, combined with regular contact at a semi-diplomatic level, had no effect on the decision makers in Moscow. Indeed, it is commonly accepted that the Soviet ambassador to Czechoslovakia, Stepan Chervonenko, and lower-ranking diplomats like Kuznetzov, Prasolov and Ivan Udaltsov dispatched one-sided and contentious reports to their superiors, some of which ended up directly in Brezhnev's secretariat. Furthermore, on at least one occasion in 1968 Chervonenko participated in a Soviet Politburo session dedicated to Czechoslovak affairs and we now know from Brezhnev's recently published diary notes that he was in regular telephone contact with his ambassador in Prague, although the exact nature of their conversations remains unclear.[50]

Neo-Stalinists from the Warsaw Pact Invasion to Normalisation

We have argued that before August 1968, Czechoslovak neo-Stalinists represented an extremist, though far from uninfluential, response to the establishment of a new reformist political mainstream. Their meetings and statements seemed to be obsolete voices from the Stalinist past, the over-hysterical reactions of disgruntled retired party 'dinosaurs' who yearned nostalgically for the 'glorious' revolutionary past and who were reluctant to accept the inevitable development towards a more advanced, and more democratic, version of socialism. However, after

21 August the neo-Stalinists in the KSČ gained momentum and became an extraordinarily aggressive pressure group, albeit essentially informal and lacking in coherence. They vigorously attacked 'revisionists' in order to change Czechoslovak political discourse towards anti-reformist and pro-Soviet positions. More important, the activities of Jodas and others were part of a much broader transition as party members and functionaries began to reassess the causes and outcomes of the Prague Spring. With only a measure of exaggeration, the neo-Stalinist assault on reformism after the invasion can be considered the tip of an iceberg, the most visceral and overt negation of the Prague Spring. But significant sectors of the party faithful were afflicted by other more or less negative attitudes: dissatisfaction, wavering, disillusionment and, most relevant, resignation. All these phenomena, from furious calls for violent revenge, anti-Semitism and conspiracy theories to conformism, pragmatism, doubt and apathy, mirrored the transformation of the party from a reformist institution to a political body increasingly amenable to 'consolidation' mentalities and practices. It thus seems analytically feasible to discuss the politics of the neo-Stalinist reaction after August 1968 in the wider context of the gradual de-composition of the fragile reformist consensus among party members. In short, we tend to see ultra-leftist extremism after August 1968 not simply as an ideological excess restricted to old habitual Stalinists, but rather as a symptom of a much more fundamental shift in the structure of party politics.

It is worth emphasising that mass approbation for reformist policies was conditional even during the weeks and months when the Prague Spring euphoria was at its peak. To be sure, immediately after the invasion enthusiastic backing for the party leaders and anti-Soviet resistance were almost universal in the country.[51] According to public opinion surveys from September 1968, reform politics remained deeply rooted, especially among young people. More troubling for the progressives was the fact that there began to emerge the first signs of resignation, disillusionment and mistrust among both party elites and ordinary communists, many of whom raised serious questions about the future development of the reform project. In addition, many Czechoslovak citizens were beginning to express grave concerns about the lack of information on current developments in the country.[52] Fairly rapidly, initial national unity exhausted itself as did reformist zeal. Party memoranda noted that the general sense of uncertainty fostered 'a differentiation of views' in the KSČ rank-and-file. Older members, predominantly inter-war communists, inclined even to sporadic public acts of support for the Soviet occupation, as was the case in two industrial enterprises, Transporta Chrudim and Gumotex Břeclav, in early September 1968.[53]

Granted, such manifestations of post-invasion anti-reformist sentiment did not become mass political phenomena and attracted strictly limited popular endorsement, but public denunciation of reform and positive reactions to the military intervention did begin to alarm the authorities. Indeed, the stubbornness and belligerence of the 'ultras' seemed to threaten the reformist majority in the party. The very existence of neo-Stalinist tendencies was welcomed by the Soviets who used their presence in Czechoslovak politics as a source for legitimising the 'fraternal assistance' and exerting pressure on the renewed Dubčekite executive. Moreover, the neo-Stalinists were eager to collaborate with the invading armies, from inviting Soviet officers to public meetings to coordinating actions against proponents of reformist policies. Although lacking centralised and national leadership in the autumn of 1968, the emergence of neo-Stalinist cliques in specific local and regional contexts had the potential to sway popular attitudes as well as influence the manner in which 'consolidation' measures were introduced.

In this section, we will examine two eminent groups of neo-Stalinists. Both collectives were composed largely of 'old communists' and gained a degree of political clout, including the attention of the highest party elites. The first operated in Ostrava, the key industrial and coal-mining centre with an impressive party organisation of more than 50,000 members. In this mass body, a cohort of approximately 100–200 active 'old communists' around Jaromír Brovják, the director of the Elektrosvit enterprise, carried the flag of radical pro-Soviet and anti-reformist politics.[54] Already before the intervention, the Brovják clique had established contact with the Red Army when delegates of the Ostrava ultra-leftists met secretly with Soviet officers in the Polish border town of Cieszyn in late July 1968. The Ostrava 'ultras' were dismayed by the fact that Soviet troops had left Czechoslovakia when the Warsaw Pact military exercises under the code name 'Šumava' were completed. They requested Soviet military representatives not to abandon Czechoslovakia to the 'counter-revolutionary elements'. After the invasion, Brovják and his peers immediately started to collaborate with the foreign military authorities and, simultaneously, to pressurise the regional party bosses. On 2 September 1968, an '*aktiv*' of inter-war communists' took place in Ostrava–Vítkovice under the direction of the Brovjákites.[55] The outcome of this tumultuous meeting of around 125 participants was a brief statement declaring that Soviet soldiers were not occupiers, but 'class brothers' and 'bearers of genuine Marxism–Leninism'. The 'Vltava' radio station run by the Warsaw Pact forces broadcast this resolution and it was also printed in the Soviet daily *Pravda* on 5 September.

The collaboration of this group with the Soviets was not limited to symbolic support or anti-reformist propaganda. For example, activists around Brovják helped the Red Army to intern two prominent Ostrava reformists who were kidnapped and transported to the Slovak town Trenčín, where they faced interrogation by Soviet officials. The neo-Stalinists from Ostrava also diligently denounced local reform communists and repeatedly warned the arch-conservative party secretary Biľak that they were prepared to launch an inner-party putsch and proclaim Ostrava as a 'Czechoslovak Petrograd', surely a conscious reference to the Bolshevik Revolution of October 1917.[56] This cabal was not a large and well-organised faction, but its close cooperation with the Soviets and willingness to openly attack the reformist 'elites' meant that their activities were scrutinised by the party leadership and vocally opposed by local progressives. Indeed, in late 1968 and early 1969 as the 'temporary' military presence continued and reformist fervour gradually dissipated, the marginal neo-Stalinist groups became ever more aggressive and hence more threatening for the champions of reform-oriented policies and ideas.

Similarly, the occupation of Czechoslovakia energised the collective around Jodas based in the Prague working-class neighbourhoods of Karlín and Libeň. As in the case of the Ostrava neo-Stalinists, these notorious Prague hard-liners recognised the new political milieu as favourable for their agenda. Thus, on 9 October 1968 a meeting of 'old communists' initiated by Jodas was convened in the Čechie hall in Libeň.[57] The keynote speaker was Antonín Kapek, a member of the KSČ Central Committee and one of the five signatories of the infamous 'Letter of Invitation' to the Soviet authorities. It was not surprising that Red Army officers were welcomed as celebrated participants at this rally. According to available reports, the atmosphere was remarkably confrontational. The audience of approximately 300 or 400 was loud and angry, speakers mocked reform-oriented politicians, journalists and intellectuals, the Soviet army was praised and Emanuel Famíra introduced himself to the enraged throng proudly asserting: 'I am a conservative, collaborator and high traitor!'[58] The resolution approved at the gathering designated the situation in the country after January 1968 as the heyday of counter-revolution and anti-communism, bordering on 'white terror'. Jodas read out a letter to the prosecutor's office demanding the indictment of the perpetrators of alleged crimes committed by the Czechoslovak media after January 1968 and of those who had purportedly pursued and attacked supporters of the Warsaw Pact armies and organised strikes, undertaken sabotage and other activities targeted against allied troops.

A second meeting was held in Čechie on 22 January 1969.[59] This time the crowd of almost 500 participants listened to the main speech delivered by Vilém Nový. Shortly before this event the organisers had distributed a pamphlet entitled 'The Truth about Jan Palach's Death', a conspiracy theory that construed the self-immolation of Palach as a carefully prepared provocation and was thus condemned as the 'action of extreme right-wing anti-socialist forces'. The party leadership expressed concern about these conclaves of 'old comrades' and local radical anti-reformists which were attended by august party *apparatchiks* such as Kapek, Nový and Innemann. For instance, in the discussion at the Presidium session on 8 November 1968 the Čechie assembly was identified as a 'dangerous' and 'harmful' phenomenon which aimed to revive 'the style of the 1950s'.[60]

The ultra-leftist current of the party also endeavoured to cement itself on a more permanent and centralised basis. The most visible result of this shift was the journal *Tribuna* which was published from January 1969. This weekly newspaper was the first official and legal party publication representing the anti-reformist voice in Czechoslovak politics.[61] Under its chief editor, Švestka, *Tribuna* became a nation-wide mouthpiece of staunch anti-reformism. It contained not only political tracts and articles besmirching various aspects of reform communism, but also denunciatory texts which vilified reform-oriented politicians, intellectuals and local activists. Apart from *Tribuna*, the anti-reformists also created organisations that aimed to coordinate and sustain their operations. Bodies such as the Leninist Youth Union and the Left Front were founded in March and December 1969 respectively, but they remained marginal, short-lived and ultimately failed to transform the ultra-leftist and anti-reformist currents in the party into a coherent and influential political force with significant social support.[62] The last throw of the dice for the neo-Stalinists came in the first half of 1970. The main ringleaders were the staunchly pro-Soviet parliamentarians Jaroslav Trojan and Soňa Pennigerová, backed, it seems, by Jodas and several other 'super-normalisers' who demanded that Husák initiate a 'Stalinist settling of accounts' with the Prague Spring reformers. Described by Kieran Williams as a 'motley, feckless crew', their campaign fizzled out even before the deaths of Jodas in June and Trojan in a car accident in August 1970. Nevertheless, their insistent sniping was sufficient to irritate Husák, who privately complained to Brezhnev that he was 'fed up with pockets of opposition from Stalinists who had Moscow's protection'.[63]

In sum, after the Warsaw Pact intervention the neo-Stalinist cliques became the vanguard of radical anti-reformist rhetoric. Their ideological extremism and intense pro-Soviet sympathies ensured that they were unable to generate much enthusiasm from the vast majority of the population as well as from the ruling party elites. However, contrary to the pre-invasion period they behaved like activists whose ideas were in accordance with the new power relations determined by the Soviet military presence in Czechoslovakia. Although their dogmatic positions were increasingly unacceptable for the promoters of 'normalisation', Jodas and Brovják, with the connivance of a handful of high-ranking *apparatchiks* such as Kapek and Nový, acted as shock-troops pushing the boundaries of what was possible or even thinkable in Czechoslovak politics. As was shown in an excellent recent case study on the normalisation process at the prestigious Charles University Faculty of Arts in Prague, those party activists who perceived themselves as the so-called 'healthy core' (*zdravé jádro*), be they ultra-leftists or pure opportunists, were quite prepared to enact coercive and punitive policies at the micro-level.[64] Their visibility in enterprises and collectives enabled the smooth introduction of 'consolidation' measures, for example ideological 'screening' and ultimately party cleansing. In the specific case of Charles University, this small but vocal minority of militants contributed to the normalisation of a former reformist stronghold. However, when they finished this job, the most intransigent neo-Stalinists were gradually removed from important positions because their extremism endangered the stability of the 'normalised' institution which was grounded to a large extent on conformism and docility.

The fate of Jodas and his peers, the Left Front and other virulent neo-Stalinists was similar to that of the 'healthy core' at Charles University. They fulfilled their role and then quickly lost political significance. Their stance was too provocative for Husák's emerging 'consolidation' system, which was built on social stability, the 'quiet life' and political disengagement. There was no place for any kind of radical in this era of 'socialist *Biedermeier*'. Having completed their part in the convoluted development towards 'consolidation', the ultra-leftists were rewarded with official sinecures or social benefits.[65] Therefore, they did not succeed in their efforts to establish some form of neo-Stalinist regime. Well-known anti-reformists and arch-conservatives like Bil'ak and Kapek distanced themselves from the adherents of the 'great leap backwards' and acted rather as doctrinal watchdogs—party hard-liners who guarded political orthodoxy based on the absolute rejection of the Prague Spring and unconditional acceptance of the Warsaw Pact 'fraternal assistance'.

Conclusion

The neo-Stalinist groupings and cliques that we have examined in this chapter were, at first glance, bit players in the dramas that unfolded in Czechoslovakia in the years 1968–70. They were numerically marginal, organisationally isolated, often ridiculed and reviled. And it is easy to understand why. Angry old men like Jodas and Nový stood, uncomprehendingly, outside the complex processes of socio-cultural modernisation and political democratisation that encapsulated the Prague Spring. But this does not mean that they should be ignored by historians or that their broader influence should be overlooked. In order to rediscover the impact of these political outcasts, it is necessary to reconfigure our interpretation of the Prague Spring. In conventional readings, communists at all levels of the Czechoslovak party, save a tiny minority of conspicuous ultra-conservatives, willingly embraced the Dubčekite vision of 'socialism with a human face' and passionately rallied behind the new post-January leadership. This was indeed the case for many party members, notably younger cadres in the main cities. However, our evidence suggests that for many other local and regional officials and loyalists 1968 was a time of confusion, doubt, upheaval and disarray, typified by the rise of social phenomena that were either largely alien (for example, youth sub-cultures and new 'Western-like' life styles) or completely hostile (K-231, KAN and the revitalisation of the Social Democrats). When the renowned 'dissident' chronicler of normalisation, Milan Šimečka, famously characterised it as the 'restoration of order', for these disoriented communists it was a truly positive development, signalling a return to 'socialist stability' as they knew it.[66] Thus, we can postulate that the Prague Spring did not represent merely a sharp reformist 'break' or innovation in party history, but was marked just as much by conservative continuities across the 1968 divide.

This 'continuity thesis' in turn implies a fresh analysis of the nature of 'normalisation'. Our hypothesis is that in the course of 1969 and thereafter, Husák's 'consolidation' found relatively fertile soil in the KSČ not only because of the 'fear factor' generated by the party screenings and the accompanying opportunism, pragmatism and careerism of many communists, but also because of the critical stances towards risky and untested reformist schemes that were embedded in the party rank-and-file and *apparat* well before the August occupation. The constant interplay and tension between, on the one hand, the proponents of technocratic modernisation and, on the other, entrenched conservatism which had punctuated the 1960s continued to exist in varying degrees after 1969. That is, residual impulses of reformism were tentatively adopted, or better adapted, by Husák and the 'realists', while at the same time resilient conservative mentalities and policies undoubtedly gained the upper hand after the invasion. Hence, the normalisation process displayed certain hybrid tendencies: purges of party and non-party 'oppositionists', but no return to the show trials and violent repressions of the Stalinist era; a more authoritarian polity, but with far-reaching ameliorative welfare and social measures; ritualistic ideologised campaigns, but stopping short of mass ideological mobilisation; a tacit recognition of the salience of 'law' and a functioning judiciary, but periodic crass state intervention in the legal system; and a commitment, at least in theory, to professional 'expertise', but combined with an onslaught against autonomous culture and academia. In these circumstances, the sectarian tenets and activist propensities of the neo-Stalinists were incompatible with the bureaucratic routinism and de-politicised rhetoric (the 'quiet life') of a 'normalisation' regime that sought a 'third way' between the Stalinism of the 1950s and the reform communism of the 1960s.

Acknowledgements We wish to thank Jitka Bílková, Pavel Kobera, Božena Vlčková, Jitka Vondrová and especially Jiří Hoppe for their kind assistance in locating archival sources for this chapter.

Notes

1. For the classic works on the Prague Spring, see note 9 in Kevin McDermott and Matthew Stibbe's chapter in this volume.

2. See V. Prečan, 'Seven Great Days. The People and Civil Society during the "Prague Spring" of 1968-1969', in F.M. Cataluccio and F. Gori (eds), *La Primavera di Praga* (Milan, 1990), pp. 165-75; J. Pecka et al. (eds), *Občanská společnost 1967-1970*, 2 vols (Prague and Brno, 1998); T. Vilímek, 'Občanská společnost a její význam v období Pražského jara', *Paměť a dějiny*, vol. 2, no. 2 (2008), pp. 6-17; O. Tůma and M. Devátá (eds), *Pražské jaro 1968: Občanská společnost—média—přenos politických a kulturních procesů* (Prague, 2011); and B. Vlčková, *Ohlas událostí roku 1968*, 2 parts (Prague, 2012).
3. On this thorny debate, see H. G. Skilling, 'Czechoslovak Political Culture: Pluralism in an International Context'; and D. W. Paul, 'Czechoslovakia's Political Culture Reconsidered', in A. Brown (ed.), *Political Culture and Communist Studies* (Basingstoke, 1984), pp. 115-33 and 134-48 respectively.
4. P. Urbášek, 'Jak "pancéřové divize" bránily socialismus', *Listy*, no. 4 (2006), pp. 17-24, available at http://www.listy.cz/archiv.php?cislo=064&clanek=040604 (last accessed 24 October 2016). The 'Jodasovci' were those pre-war sectarian communists from Prague's working-class Libeň district associated with Josef Jodas. A similar group formed around Emanuel Famíra.
5. For insights into the Hradec Králové neo-Stalinists, see O. Felcman, '"Ultras" v Hradci: Aktivity prosovětských sil na Královéhradecku na podzim 1968', *Soudobé dějiny*, vol. 15, no. 3-4 (2008), pp. 639-69. It is rumoured that Rudolf Černý was an unofficial, but active, collaborator of the Czechoslovak security police, the StB.
6. Archiv bezpečnostních složek (Archive of the Security Services—ABS) Brno-Kanice, O1-1, inv. jedn. 7, Krajská správa (KS) SNB Ostrava, 'Materiály k činnosti protisocialistických sil v severomoravském kraji v letech 1968-1971', pp. 9-10.
7. The only evidence of cross-border contact we have found is a clandestine meeting between Ostrava and Katowice (Poland) 'ultras' in early May 1968. For details, see K. Jiřík, 'Co se projednávalo na tajné schůzce katovických a ostravských komunistů v Cieszyně 3.-4.5.1968?', *Těšínsko*, vol. 41, no. 4 (1998), pp. 10-13.
8. See, for example, J. Moravec, *Antipoučení* (Prague, 1990), pp. 55-7.
9. Some Czech workers interpreted Dubček's promotion as a form of takeover by the Slovaks and a few even thought that the Slovaks 'wanted an independent state'. One non-party worker quipped 'we will now be called the Slovak Republic'. See ABS, Brno-Kanice, f. L1 1, inv. jedn. 58, KS SNB Ústí nad Labem, 'Denní informace—ohlas na opatření ÚV KSČ z ledna 1968', pp. 1-7, 22.
10. For speculations on this murky campaign, see J. Vondrová, *Reforma? Revoluce? Pražské jaro 1968 a Praha* (Prague, 2013), pp. 32-3.

11. A type-written copy of the letter, together with a four-page resolution, is deposited in the Národní archiv České republiky (National Archive of the Czech Republic—NA), Archive of the Central Committee of the KSČ (AÚV KSČ), f. 02/7, sv. 4 Odbor informací, nezpracovaná část, a.j. Informace únor-červenec 1968. 'Informace', no. 12, 28 February 1968, pp. 1–25, quotations at 1–5, 7, 8, 12, 19, 20, 24. All five signatories were bearers of various party and state honours, Jodas having been awarded the 'Order of the Republic'.
12. Hubert Ripka (1895–1958) was a leader of the Czech National Socialist Party (a parliamentary party not to be confused with its German namesake) and a fierce opponent of the communists before the February 1948 takeover. Thereafter, he went into foreign exile for the second time, having already been a member of Edvard Beneš's London-based government during World War II. The epithet 'social fascist' was a particularly incendiary Stalinist term of abuse for European Social Democrats originally popularised in the Comintern in the late 1920s and early 1930s.
13. For details, see K. Dawisha, 'The 1968 Invasion of Czechoslovakia: Causes, Consequences, and Lessons for the Future', in K. Dawisha and P. Hanson (eds), *Soviet-East European Dilemmas: Coercion, Competition, and Consent* (London, 1981), pp. 21–2. See also Zbigniew Wojnowski's chapter in this volume.
14. NA, f. 02/7, sv. 4, 'Informace', no. 21, 22 March 1968, pp. 1–5, quotations at pp. 3 and 5.
15. See, among many examples, NA, f. 02/7, sv. 4, 'Informace', no. 13, 7 March 1968, p. 9; 'Informace', no. 17, 11 March 1968, p. 1; Archiv Ústavu pro soudobé dějiny (Archive of the Institute of Contemporary History—AÚSD), fond Komise vlády ČSFR pro analýzu událostí let 1967–1970, SII/105, k. 121, 'Výzkum názorů komunistů hlavního města Prahy k demokratizačnímu procesu ve straně a společnosti', July 1968, pp. 14–18. Also J. Vondrová et al. (eds), *Komunistická strana Československa: Pokus o reformu (říjen 1967—květen 1968)* (Prague and Brno, 1999), pp. 138–9, 364–76, especially p. 372. On the 'information vacuum', see Vondrová, *Reforma?*, p. 30.
16. Vondrová et al. (eds), *Komunistická strana Československa*, p. 417.
17. On the impact of the 'technocrats', see J. Hoppe et al., *'O nový československý model socialismu'. Čtyři interdisciplinární vědecké týmy při ČSAV a UK v 60. letech* (Prague, 2015).
18. J. Vondrová (ed.), *Mezinárodní souvislosti československé krize 1967–1970. Dokumenty ÚV KSSS 1966–1969*, vol. 4, no. 4 (Prague and Brno, 2011), p. 105.
19. Archiv Českého rozhlasu (Czech Radio Archive—AČR), 'Dopisy od posluchačů, 1965–68', 4 May 1968. For more anti-Semitic vitriol, see communications from 15 May, 19 and 22 June.

20. For the letter and Goldstücker's remarkably restrained response, see R. A. Remington (ed.), *Winter in Prague: Documents on Czechoslovak Communism in Crisis* (Cambridge, MA, 1969), pp. 189–94. An anti-Goldstücker leaflet, though not explicitly anti-Semitic, was circulated in Plzeň in late May. See ABS (Prague), Hlavní správa Státní bezpečnost, 'Denní svodky' (DS), no. 113, 28 May 1968, pp. 4–5.
21. Skilling, *Czechoslovakia's Interrupted Revolution*, p. 273, fn. 45. The issue of anti-Semitism in Czechoslovakia, both before and after the invasion, was widely reported in the foreign media. See E. Litvinoff, 'The Use of Antisemitism in the Czechoslovak Affair—A Dossier', in K. Coates (ed.), *Czechoslovakia and Socialism* (Nottingham, 1969), pp. 109–49. For the even worse situation in Poland, see Tony Kemp-Welch's chapter in this volume.
22. NA, f. 02/7, sv. 4, 'Informace', no. 18, 12 March 1968, p. 3; 'Informace', no. 21, 22 March 1968, pp. 30–1, 34.
23. NA, f. 02/7, sv. 4, 'Informace', no. 13, 7 March 1968, pp. 1, 9, 10; 'Informace', no. 17, 11 March 1968, pp. 12, 17, 19; 'Informace', no. 20, 21 March 1968, p. 5.
24. AÚSD, f. Komise, DI/109, k. 4, 'Hodnocení mimořadných okresních a krajských konferencí strany', 18 July 1968, pp. 5–7.
25. For a similar argument, see J. Vondrová, 'Rozkol v KSČ během Pražského jara', in J. Dejmek and M. Loužek (eds), *Srpen 1968: Čtyřicet let poté* (Prague, 2008), pp. 139–58.
26. ABS, DS, no. 92, 29 April 1968, p. 6. See also DS, no. 26, 2 February 1968, p. 2; no. 73, 3 April 1968, p. 5; no. 88, 23 April 1968, p. 5; no. 97, 6 May 1968, pp. 2–3.
27. ABS, DS, no. 153, 17 July 1968, p. 4.
28. Cited in M. Kramer, 'Ukraine and the Soviet–Czechoslovak Crisis of 1968 (Part 1): New Evidence from the Diary of Petro Shelest', *Cold War International History Project Bulletin*, no. 10 (1998), p. 238.
29. ABS (Prague), B/102, kr. 3, 'Seznam osob, které v době 1.1.1968 do současné doby spáchaly z politických důvodů sebevraždu', pp. 1–7.
30. Vondrová et al. (eds), *Komunistická strana Československa*, p. 430.
31. NA, f. 0/27, sv. 4, 'Informace', no. 23, 26 March 1968, p. 23; ABS, DS, no. 73, 3 April 1968, p. 5. See also the references to 'spiritual terror' infecting sections of the media, including *Rudé právo*, in NA, f. 0/27, sv. 4, 'Informace', no. 35, 4 May 1968, p. 6.
32. NA, f. 02/1, sv. 85, a.j. 84/88, 'Informace o dopisovém ohlasu na články v Rudém právu Jak manipulují s A. Dubčekem....', (part 2), 15 September 1988, pp. 24, 29–30.
33. For lurid examples from 1956, see K. McDermott and V. Sommer, *The 'Club of Politically Engaged Conformists'? The Communist Party*

of *Czechoslovakia, Popular Opinion and the Crisis of Communism, 1956*, Cold War International History Project, Working Paper No. 66 (Washington, DC, 2013), pp. 34–6.
34. Z. Mlynář, *Night Frost in Prague: The End of Humane Socialism* (London, 1980), p. 41.
35. NA, f. 02/7, sv. 5, 'Informace', no. 52, 10 August 1968, p. 8.
36. For details on these groups, see J. Hoppe, *Opozice '68. Sociální demokracie, KAN a K 231 v období Pražského jara* (Prague, 2009).
37. Vondrová (ed.), *Mezinárodní souvislosti*, no. 4, pp. 95–6.
38. Vondrová et al. (eds), *Komunistická strana Československa*, p. 148.
39. AÚSD, f. Komise, DI/108, kr. 4, 'Dopis člena ÚV KSČ s. V. Nového předsednictvu ÚV KSČ', p. 5. The insidious term 'second centre' was increasingly being used by Soviet and Czechoslovak hard-liners to refer to those radical progressives and intellectuals in the apparatus who were, *inter alia*, allegedly undermining the leading role of the party.
40. Vondrová et al. (eds), *Komunistická strana Československa*, p. 378.
41. NA, f. 02/7, sv. 4, 'Informace', no. 34, 2 May 1968, pp. 8–9; f. 02/7, sv. 5, 'Informace', no. 52, 10 August 1968, p. 29.
42. AÚSD, f. Komise, DII/108, kr. 17, 'Informační zpráva o politické situaci v jednotkách Lidových milicí....', 10 June 1968, p. 22.
43. ABS (Brno-Kanice), O2–1, inv. jedn. 1, KS SNB Ostrava, 'Bezpečnostní situace, 25.7.–20.8.1968', p. 172.
44. NA, f. 02/7, sv. 5, 'Operativní informace', no. 6, 7 September 1968, p. 20.
45. NA, f. 02/7, sv. 4, 'Informace', no. 38, 27 May 1968, p. 27.
46. Vondrová (ed.), *Mezinárodní souvislosti*, no. 4, pp. 99–100. On the use of the slogan in the Soviet Union, see S. Fitzpatrick, *Tear Off the Masks! Identity and Imposture in Twentieth-Century Russia* (Princeton, NJ, 2005).
47. Vondrová (ed.), *Mezinárodní souvislosti*, no. 4, pp. 116–29, quotations at 125, 127, 128.
48. J. Vondrová and J. Navrátil (eds), *Mezinárodní souvislosti československé krize 1967–1970: Červenec—srpen 1968*, vol. 4, no. 2 (Prague and Brno, 1996), p. 49.
49. Jodas's interview, published on 8 June, is reprinted in J. Hoppe (ed.), *Pražské jaro v médiích: Výběr z dobové publicistiky* (Prague and Brno, 2004), pp. 199–202.
50. M. Kun, *Prague Spring: Prague Fall: Blanks Spots of 1968* (Budapest, 1999), pp. 17–18; S. V. Kudriashev (ed.), *Leonid Brezhnev: Rabochie i dnevnikovye zapisi*, vol. 2 (Moscow, 2016), pp. 233–7, 242, 245–55, 257–78, 281–3, 287–8, 290–1, 295–6. We wish to thank John Morison for alerting us to this source.
51. NA, f. 02/7, sv. 5, 'Operativní informace', no. 2, 30 August 1968, pp. 24–5.

52. NA, f. 02/7, sv. 5, 'Operativní informace', no. 3, 2 September 1968, pp. 2–3, 17–23; and 'Operativní informace', no. 5, 5 September 1968, pp. 1–2, 20.
53. NA, f. 02/7, sv. 5, 'Operativní informace', no. 6, 7 September 1968, pp. 1–2.
54. Our account of the Brovják group is based on K. Jiřík, 'Frakční činnost předválečných členů KSČ v Ostravě v letech 1968–1969', in *O sovětské imperiální politice v Československu v letech 1945–1968. Sborník příspěvků* (Olomouc, 1995), pp. 25–41.
55. A second *aktiv* was held in November 1968 with the well-known anti-reformist Vilém Nový as the main orator.
56. For Bil'ak's version of his exchanges with Brovják, see V. Bil'ak, *Paměti Vasila Bil'aka. Unikátní svědectví ze zákulisí KSČ*, vol. 2 (Prague, 1991), p. 184.
57. There are several reports on this important meeting. Our account is based on AÚSD, f. Komise, A/229, k. 99, 'Zpráva ze schůze komunistů... Praha 8'; AÚSD, f. Komise, A/204, k. 99, 'Souhrnná zpráva ze schůze starých komunistů... v Praze 8'; and AÚSD, f. Komise, A/476, kr. 109, 'Schůze starých komunistů... referát Kapka'.
58. AÚSD, f. Komise, A/229, k. 99, 'Zpráva', p. 3.
59. For reports on the January meeting, see AÚSD, f. Komise, A/230, k. 99, 'Zpráva o schůzi ... 22.1.1969'; and AÚSD, f. Komise, CI/137, k. 41, 'Zpráva o schůzi v libeňské Čechii, 22.1.1969'.
60. AÚSD, f. Komise, DI/164, k. 6, 'Usnesení 106. schůze PÚV KSČ z 8.11.1968', pp. 10/1, 44/2.
61. The history of *Tribuna* is summarised in J. Železný, 'Vznik týdeníku Tribuna jako první legální tiskové platformy antireformních sil v roce 1969', *Sborník Národního muzea v Praze, Řada C—Literární historie*, vol. 57 (2012), pp. 53–7. In October 1969, *Tribuna* issued a celebratory article commemorating the first anniversary of the Čechie meeting. See V. Trvala, 'My z libeňské Čechie', *Tribuna*, 8 October 1969, pp. 3–4.
62. Urbášek, 'Jak "pancéřové divize"'. For an overview of the allegedly dense network of Left Front regional organisations, see 'Levá fronta v krajích', *Levá fronta*, September 1970, p. 15.
63. For details, see K. Williams, *The Prague Spring and Its Aftermath: Czechoslovak Politics, 1968–1970* (Cambridge, 1997), pp. 244–8, quotations at pp. 244, 245 and 247.
64. J. Jareš et al., *Náměstí Krasnoarmějců 2: učitelé a studenti Filozofické fakulty UK v období normalizace* (Prague, 2012), pp. 82–100.
65. Jiřík, 'Frakční činnost', p. 37.
66. M. Šimečka, *The Restoration of Order: The Normalization of Czechoslovakia, 1969–1976* (London, 1984).

The Impact of the Prague Spring on the USSR

Zbigniew Wojnowski

The Prague Spring marked the end of de-Stalinisation in the USSR.[1] Over the previous 15 years, the Soviet leadership had searched for ways to rekindle popular faith in the communist system after the traumas of Stalinism. Following Nikita Khrushchev's 'Secret Speech' at the Twentieth Congress of the Communist Party of the Soviet Union in February 1956, rank-and-file party members were encouraged to take a more active role in debating and implementing policy. Most prisoners were released from the Gulag in the first few years after Stalin's death as the new leadership relied more on persuasion and material incentives, and less on terror and coercion, to mould people into Soviet citizens. Censorship was relaxed, though fundamental aspects of the political, social and economic system were still beyond criticism in the USSR's public culture.[2] These ambitious attempts to foster new forms of 'participatory citizenship' were curtailed with Khrushchev's ouster from the Kremlin in October 1964.[3] But until the Warsaw Pact invasion of Czechoslovakia, Leonid Brezhnev's team still saw gradual economic

---

Z. Wojnowski (✉)
University of Roehampton, London, UK
e-mail: zbig.wojnowski@roehampton.ac.uk

© The Author(s) 2018
K. McDermott and M. Stibbe (eds.), *Eastern Europe in 1968*,
https://doi.org/10.1007/978-3-319-77069-7_4

reform and limited intellectual and cultural openings as a means of winning popular legitimacy.[4]

Soviet relations with Czechoslovakia and other East European satellite states reflected the broader dynamics of de-Stalinisation. Czechoslovakia remained politically, militarily and economically dependent on the USSR. At the same time, the late 1950s saw the emergence of special organisations devoted to promoting new types of transnational contacts between the Soviet Union and Czechoslovakia. Their goal was to demonstrate the international success of Soviet-style socialism. Soviet travel to Eastern Europe was a particularly important means of fostering faith in the communist project among the population of the USSR: trips to the satellite states were meant to include ordinary blue-collar workers, eclipsing 'any significant expression of ethnic or national difference…in favor of a shared socialist/working class identity'.[5] Soviet and Czechoslovak citizens engaged with the transnational friendship project for a variety of reasons, ranging from personal memories of World War II 'to professional interests to attempts to further transnational friendships made in other contexts to a desire for goods and culture unavailable at home'.[6]

The 1950s and the 1960s also witnessed the rise of new transnational contacts that were beyond the Kremlin's control.[7] Especially (though not exclusively) in the USSR's western borderlands, Soviet citizens learned about the outside world from western radio stations broadcasting into the country, as well as East European newspapers, radio and television. East European broadcasts and publications featured items that Soviet censors considered 'antisocialist'.[8] At the same time, the Soviet leadership was reluctant to stop the flow of news from the USSR's satellite states, lest socialist friendship be exposed as a mere propaganda façade. By the late 1960s, Soviet leaders looked upon a fast globalising world with apprehension. When Alexander Dubček launched his reforms in Czechoslovakia, people in the USSR were surprisingly well-informed about the momentous events across their western border.

As Soviet citizens commented on the Czechoslovak crisis widely, Thaw-era notions of what it meant to be Soviet and what it meant to be socialist crumbled. From the Politburo's perspective, the Czechoslovak events were part of a broader international crisis facing communism that encompassed student protests in Poland, escalating tensions with China and a break with Nicolae Ceauşescu's socialist Romania.[9] In this context, Czechoslovakia represented the most sustained and ambitious attempt to reform a regime that very closely resembled the Soviet model.

Dubček's experiment was thus a testing ground for Soviet policies and ideas. Commenting on the Prague Spring reforms and the Warsaw Pact invasion of Czechoslovakia, leaders and citizens of the USSR reflected not only on their country's foreign policy, but also on the extent to which it was possible to increase political participation, open borders and relax censorship without undermining party control over society and inducing instability. The Soviet-led invasion of Czechoslovakia was a clear sign that the Brezhnev leadership would no longer pursue or tolerate attempts at democratisation within the bloc's communist parties or in society more broadly. Ambitious attempts to increase citizens' participation in debating and implementing policy thus ended with a bang in August 1968.

This clear anti-reformist direction created deep rifts in Soviet society. Some citizens turned to illegal means to defend the de-Stalinisation agenda. At the same time, faced with a major crisis of the socialist system that challenged Soviet ideas of progress, leaders of the USSR were able to rally many citizens around the idea that Soviet interests had to be protected against the supposed chaos emanating from Eastern Europe, as well as a potential 'fifth column' at home. In various public forums, citizens underlined their loyalty to the Soviet homeland and its titular ethnic groups. While it is impossible to judge levels of genuine belief, these public articulations of Soviet patriotism shaped social and political dynamics in the USSR during the late 1960s. The 'search for socialism' that had animated state–society relations over the previous fifteen years was over in 1968. Instead, ethnically and geographically defined Soviet patriotism, often framed in xenophobic terms, became the main tool of social and political mobilisation in the USSR.

My analysis encompasses developments in Moscow, where the top Soviet leadership as well as members of the intelligentsia followed the Czechoslovak crisis in detail. But the chapter focuses in particular on Soviet Ukraine. Ukraine lay in the west of the USSR and it shared a border with Czechoslovakia.[10] Its inhabitants were therefore very well-informed about the Prague Spring. In the borderland region of Transcarpathia, memories of Czechoslovak rule in the interwar period made the crisis seem very close to home.[11] Moreover, the example of Czechoslovakia's rising autonomy from Moscow followed by a military crackdown on Dubček's reforms carried particular significance in the USSR's non-Russian periphery, which itself had a complicated relationship with the Soviet centre in Moscow.

Official Reactions

The Prague Spring sparked a crisis of identity among the Soviet leadership. Throughout the first half of 1968, Brezhnev in particular was keen to salvage the idea that political and economic reform was possible in the Soviet bloc and, by extension, in the USSR itself. He was therefore reluctant to crack down on 'socialism with a human face' that promised to lend Soviet-style regimes new legitimacy. But other members of the Politburo were also painfully aware that Dubček's reforms challenged Soviet-made visions of what it meant to be socialist. The Warsaw Pact invasion of Czechoslovakia pushed Soviet leaders to search for new sources of legitimacy at home and abroad, as attempts to involve citizens in debating and implementing policy were now associated with chaos and violence.

In conversations with Soviet diplomats in Prague in early 1968, Dubček presented his reforms as a fight against 'violations of party discipline', excessive bureaucracy and attempts to concentrate all political power in the hands of just one individual. These ideas echoed Brezhnev's own slogans that had helped him to justify the overthrow of Khrushchev in 1964.[12] In January and February 1968, the Kremlin did not therefore express alarm at the unfolding events in Czechoslovakia. The tide turned in March when, concerned by the removal of former party leader Antonín Novotný from the office of president, major changes in Communist Party cadres and increasingly free mass media in Czechoslovakia, Moscow issued a stern warning to Prague. Even then, members of the Politburo insisted that some of the most confrontational phrasing prepared by Soviet Foreign Minister Andrei Gromyko and the head of the KGB Yurii Andropov be dropped from the letter they drafted.[13] An eyewitness recalled 'long and heated' arguments in the CPSU Politburo during deliberations on the Czechoslovak crisis.[14] Top Soviet leaders were clearly at a loss about how to interpret Dubček's policies. Prime Minister Alexei Kosygin, for example, was a very harsh critic of Czechoslovak reforms in March 1968, but seemed to take a more positive view of Dubček after a visit to Karlovy Vary in May. He continued to question the idea of a military intervention in Czechoslovakia at Politburo meetings: 'We will take our armies in, and then what?'. Even in early August, shortly before the invasion, Moscow harboured hopes that the bilateral Čierna nad Tisou agreements would help to avoid open confrontation with Czechoslovakia.[15]

Soviet leaders knew that their own legitimacy was at stake in Czechoslovakia. Albeit highly critical of the mooted idea to introduce a multi-party system in Czechoslovakia, Brezhnev still wanted inhabitants of the socialist camp to believe that communist parties and state institutions could bring more prosperity and opportunities for citizens to participate in power.[16] In May 1968, the head of the Supreme Soviet Nikolai Podgornyi was likewise alarmed that an overly heavy-handed approach in Czechoslovakia would convince 'enemies of socialism' that the system was broken.[17] Further down the Communist Party hierarchy, after Khrushchev's economic policies that had effectively devolved much decision making to the non-Russian republics were reversed in 1965,[18] the Prague Spring was seen as a promising sign that political power might once again be de-centralised along national lines. Soviet Ukrainian party activists often travelled to Czechoslovakia in 1968 to gather information and influence Slovak politics in particular; many drew inspiration from the example of Slovakia successfully lobbying for more autonomy from Prague.[19]

Yet many influential Soviet leaders were early advocates of crushing Dubček's reforms. The foreign ministry, along with the KGB and the GRU (the organisation in charge of Soviet reconnaissance operations), were the main channels through which Politburo members learned about events across the border. From November 1967, they painted a dark picture of Czechoslovak politics, raising alarm about the relaxation of censorship in Czechoslovakia which, in their view, weakened communist ideology. Equally important, they associated freedom of speech with the rise of anti-Soviet stereotypes, stressing that the Czechoslovak mass media presented Soviet people as 'downtrodden and backward'.[20] In contrast to the late 1950s and early 1960s, public debate was increasingly seen not as a means of fostering faith in socialism, but rather as a threat to the unity of the Soviet bloc. Moscow was much more preoccupied with the lack of censorship and emerging political pluralism in Czechoslovakia than about Ota Šik's explicitly market-oriented economic reforms.[21]

From the Kremlin's perspective, the political turmoil and new cultural openings of 1968 were a concern insofar as they threatened Czechoslovakia's place in the Warsaw Pact. The Defence Minister Andrei Grechko was especially worried about the spread of anti-Soviet propaganda among Czechoslovak soldiers.[22] As the man who represented the Soviet Politburo in Prague during the invasion in August, General

Kirill Mazurov, put it in an interview conducted over 20 years later: '[i]t was difficult for us to imagine that a bourgeois parliamentary republic could take shape along our borders, one flooded with West Germans and behind them, Americans. This was totally incompatible with the interests of the Warsaw Pact'.[23] Less commonly, Politburo members expressed concern about the infrequent Czechoslovak irredentist claims to Soviet territory. In June 1968, for example, the Politburo informed Prague about their outrage at the pamphlets they discovered in Czechoslovakia. Their authors claimed that the region of Transcarpathia, annexed by the USSR at the end of World War II, should be returned to Czechoslovakia.[24]

In the course of 1968, sceptical about the new participatory public culture across their western border, Soviet leaders grew ever keener to limit access to information and public debate in the USSR itself. The Ukrainian party boss Petro Shelest was especially vocal in condemning developments in Czechoslovakia, berating Brezhnev for indecisiveness during the crisis (later he even claimed that the Soviet First Secretary fainted when the decision to invade Czechoslovakia was taken).[25] Like other leaders of territories bordering on Czechoslovakia, including Władysław Gomułka in Poland and Walter Ulbricht in East Germany,[26] Shelest was alarmed by the potential spillover of the Czechoslovak crisis. He thus called for suppressing the flow of information from Czechoslovakia into the USSR's Ukrainian borderlands.[27] The Soviet hardliners gained more traction with Brezhnev by mid-1968, as developments in Czechoslovakia seemed to slip out of Dubček's control.[28] The limits of permissible expression shrank accordingly. Czechoslovak and Romanian publications were subjected to Soviet censorship in the summer of 1968, even though books and newspapers from East European socialist countries had previously been free from such controls.[29] Censorship control over Soviet publications also grew harsher as the Czechoslovak events unfolded.[30]

The Search for Legitimacy

The political and cultural shifts of 1968, however, did not just entail limiting citizens' access to information. Rather, the Prague Spring sparked a search for redefining the USSR's relationship with its allies in Soviet public culture. Soviet propaganda drew on a sense of great power pride and ethnic prejudices to justify the USSR's continuing interference in

Eastern Europe as it became clear that Soviet-style socialism had failed to create friendly relations between the USSR and Czechoslovakia. The prominence of geographically and ethnically defined identities in Soviet public culture had far-reaching implications for identity politics at home.

Even after the Warsaw Pact invasion of Czechoslovakia, officials in the USSR continued to present Soviet-style socialism as an ideology powerful enough to bridge national divisions and accommodate national differences. After a brief lull, the Soviet-Czechoslovak Friendship Society revived international travel between the two countries. In late 1968 and 1969, as Rachel Applebaum puts it, Soviet tourists visiting Czechoslovakia engaged in a quest for 'mutual understanding' with the Czechoslovak citizens they encountered.[31] In order to justify the military invasion, the press frequently drew on the stock phrases about proletarian solidarities during official agitation meetings on Czechoslovakia.[32] Still, painfully aware that citizens learned about the Czechoslovak crisis from foreign sources of information before the Soviet media,[33] opinion leaders in the USSR were worried that slogans about international socialist friendship rang hollow in 1968. Czechoslovak broadcasts made it very clear that Dubček had a different interpretation of what it meant to be 'socialist' than his Soviet counterparts.[34] Rifts in Soviet relations with the communist parties of France and Italy, as well as Romania, Albania and Yugoslavia, cast further doubt on the strength of friendly transnational ties grounded in a common ideological outlook.[35] Before the invasion, with Czechs and Slovaks complaining about the USSR's control over their natural resources, the KGB wrote of 'peace and friendship' as meaningless phrases that masked much more 'messy' international relations.[36]

For the Soviet regime, socialism thus turned from a legitimating discourse into a contested idea and even a symbol of foreign policy failures. For those who saw Dubček as a committed Leninist, the Soviet military intervention signalled deep rifts within the socialist movement. For those who believed that Czechoslovakia was overrun with counter-revolutionaries, it was clear that Soviet-style socialism failed to spread across borders. This may partly explain why the Politburo approached the rhetoric of 'revolution' and 'communism' with great caution. In editing the appeal that pro-Soviet Czechoslovak leaders sent to Brezhnev with a request for military assistance, Politburo members heeded the advice of the secretary in charge of ideology Mikhail Suslov and decided that it would be best not to refer to the alleged pro-Soviet Czechoslovak forces as 'revolutionary'. In another appeal written to citizens of Czechoslovakia on behalf of Warsaw Pact members concerned about the unfolding events in Prague, Soviet leaders addressed 'workers', 'peasants', 'the national intelligentsia', 'Czechs' and 'Slovaks', but decided to remove references to 'Communist party members' as the progressive pro-Soviet elements in Czechoslovakia.[37] In defining 'us' versus 'them', the Politburo was more at ease with appealing to social and ethnic rather than political or ideological allegiances.

As the socialist ties that bound the USSR and Czechoslovakia were visibly shaken, the Soviet mass media evoked a sense of great power pride to justify the USSR's continuing interference in Eastern Europe. In this way, the mounting crisis in Czechoslovakia marked a return to geographically and ethnically defined patriotism that had helped mobilise citizens behind Stalinist policies.[38] Amir Weiner shows that the memory of World War II was particularly crucial for legitimising the USSR's actions in Czechoslovakia.[39] Moreover, the Soviet press defined the socialist camp as a union of closely related Slavic nations, grounded in supposedly natural inborn affinities older than Soviet socialism.[40] In line with these broader trends, the central Soviet newspaper *Krasnaia zvezda* ('Red Star') described the concept of 'Central Europe' as a hostile assault on natural affinities. The concern was that historians who wrote about 'Central Europe' implied that Soviet bloc states (as well as western Ukraine) were part of the Habsburg and not the Russian historical sphere of influence.[41] Although the Soviet Union's satellites included countries with non-Slavic majority populations, Soviet propaganda cast Eastern Europe as a predominantly Slavic community, united against German and Jewish outsiders.

Simplistic xenophobic slogans played an important role in Soviet public culture during 1968. According to Polish diplomats in Moscow, the anti-Semitic speech that Gomułka delivered after the student protests in Warsaw in March found great resonance in the USSR itself.[42] Along with other statements published in the USSR in the aftermath of the student demonstrations, the speech fanned the fear of '[West] German imperialism', 'Zionism' and 'cosmopolitanism' as destructive forces that threatened the Slavs of Eastern Europe.[43] In the summer of 1968, the Soviet media continued to mobilise popular fears of German 'revanchism'. They publicised proclamations by the organisations of Sudeten Germans who pressed the West German government not to recognise post-war borders, and emphasised that nationalists in Austria and West

Germany would threaten the USSR itself if they gained control over Czechoslovakia.[44] The Soviet news agency TASS framed the Warsaw Pact invasion of Czechoslovakia as part of an age-old European struggle for peace that pre-dated the establishment of the USSR.[45]

Soviet propaganda raised anxieties about Czech and Slovak nationalism during 1968. Informing party activists about the unfolding developments in July 1968, for example, the Politburo wrote about the 'specificity' of Czechoslovakia and its communist party, underlining that the 'bourgeoisie' never emigrated after the establishment of socialism in the country in 1948. Class enemies had infiltrated the party and were now on course to restore capitalism in Czechoslovakia. The implication was clear: Czechs were inherently suspect, as even membership in the communist party was no sure sign of loyalty. In contrast, not only Soviet communists, but all 'Soviet people' were ready to defend revolutionary achievements.[46] The language of socialism thus masked rather crude distinctions made on the basis of ethnicity and citizenship. Anti-Czechoslovak narratives were further promulgated after the invasion. For instance, the short documentary 'The Counter-Revolution Shall Not Succeed' (*Kontrrevoliutsiia ne proidet*), screened before feature films in Soviet cinemas, depicted foreigners across the border as dangerous radicals.[47]

Xenophobic incidents were likewise on the rise in late 1968 and 1969. When a group of sixty-one Czechoslovak miners and engineers from Ostrava came to Lviv to visit the Soviet soldiers whom they had supposedly befriended back home during the autumn of 1968, the trip took a nasty turn. One guest came up to a Czech woman who was dancing with a Soviet army soldier, slapped her in the face and called her a 'Russian swine'.[48] Similarly, after the series of anti-Soviet demonstrations that followed the infamous USSR–Czechoslovakia ice hockey matches in March 1969, Soviet citizens attended special informational meetings. They learnt about crowds of angry protesters who destroyed the Aeroflot offices in Prague and, even worse, vandalised monuments commemorating Soviet soldiers who had 'liberated Czechoslovakia from fascism in 1945'. Although Dubček tried to dismiss these actions as isolated cases of hooliganism, Soviet agitators insisted that anti-Soviet nationalism was in fact widespread in Czechoslovakia, with right-wing forces infiltrating such 'socialist' institutions as the official trade unions. Propaganda further played on Soviet fears of encirclement, emphasising that anti-Soviet sentiment in Czechoslovakia was promoted by the USA, West Germany and China.[49]

The shifts in Soviet public culture that occurred in 1968 had far-reaching implications for identity politics at home. Evoking the supposedly eternal and natural ethnic bonds among Slavs, Soviet leaders were intolerant of any expression of complex, multi-national borderland identities. From their perspective, every political-administrative unit in the Soviet bloc and each resident of the socialist camp could be described in unambiguous national terms. The Soviet authorities looked upon national minorities with suspicion at a time when the nation turned into the primary locus of identity. They thus hoped to see the Slovaks curtail the activities of the Ukrainian minority in eastern Slovakia, concerned that their interpretation of what it meant to be Ukrainian undermined state-approved narratives of Ukrainianness promoted within the USSR itself. The KGB was particularly alarmed by the revival of the Greek Catholic Church in Czechoslovakia because this institution, banned in the USSR, was seen as a vehicle for articulating Ukrainian identities defined in opposition to the Soviet state.[50] From the Soviet perspective, Slovakia would be a much more reliable neighbour if it was simply Slovak rather than multi-national.

On the Soviet side of the border, non-titular ethnic groups without their own national republics came under suspicion. Most prominently, after the 1967 Six Day War the ethno-centric turn in public culture fuelled anti-Semitic rhetoric in the USSR.[51] During agitation meetings organised in 1968, participants asked many awkward questions concerning the role of Jews in East European disturbances.[52] For their part, likely in response to popular accusations of disloyalty, some Soviet citizens of Jewish origin found it expedient to emphasise publicly that they were loyal to the USSR.[53] When high-ranking Soviet officials such as Petr Demichev discussed both anti-Semitism and Zionism as problems plaguing the socialist camp, they revealed their own anti-Semitic prejudice. Demichev even claimed in a conversation with a Polish diplomat in Moscow that the rise of anti-Semitism was the fault of the Jews themselves: 'Zionist forces have become distinctly more active. The masses can feel it. In consequence, we can observe a backlash in the form of anti-Semitic moods'.[54] Furthermore, some Soviet citizens of Polish and Czech origin also found it necessary to openly highlight their alienation from their rebellious 'external homelands' as ethnicity turned into a marker of loyalty.[55]

With the importance of geographically and ethnically defined patriotism on the rise, the limits of permissible national expression shrank even among the non-Russian ethnic groups that had their own nationally designated republics in the USSR. This represented a major departure from Thaw-era policies. During the early 1960s, the party leadership in Ukraine was surprised by levels of resistance to Russification and attempts to curtail the rights of the republics. In order to avoid an open confrontation with dissidents and to increase their own autonomy from Moscow, some party officials sought legitimacy within their republic by presenting themselves as Ukrainian national leaders. These communists expected a measure of support from members of the Politburo in Moscow.[56] In 1968, portrayals of the Prague Spring acted as a warning against over-emphasising Ukrainian distinctiveness in the USSR. Federalism in Czechoslovakia was hardly discussed in the Soviet Ukrainian press in 1968 and 1969, and it did not figure at all in public anti-Czechoslovak polemics. Reports from agitation meetings show that residents of the Ukrainian SSR asked about the relationship between Czechs and Slovaks over and over again,[57] but it seems that party activists found the subject too sensitive to discuss publicly.[58] With the Slovaks striving towards greater autonomy in Czechoslovakia, the authorities wanted to prevent inhabitants of Ukraine from questioning the position of their own republic in the USSR. These developments fed into high politics in Soviet Ukraine. It is possible that Shelest's vocal condemnation of Dubček's reforms was an attempt to demonstrate to Moscow that his own limited endorsement of Ukrainian culture was different from Czechoslovak demands for more autonomy from Moscow.[59] Still, developments in Czechoslovakia helped to discredit Shelest's relatively liberal national policy. In contrast, his main rival in Kyiv, Volodymyr Shcherbyts'kyi, had no scruples about subordinating the republic's interests to those of the Soviet state. As such, he was seen as more reliable by the Kremlin and his position in the Ukrainian party was strengthened during 1968.[60]

A New Consensus

The Brezhnev regime successfully redirected popular frustrations away from its own policies, and towards foreign and domestic 'enemies'. Many citizens embraced the state's patriotic rhetoric, rallying behind the Soviet state as a representative of their interests defined in opposition to 'nationalists' and 'imperialists' abroad, as well as ethnic minorities at home. Expressions of Soviet patriotism did not necessarily reflect genuine belief, but they shaped the parameters of Soviet public discourse in 1968.

In various forums, as socialism turned into a contested notion during 1968, citizens underlined their loyalty to the Soviet vision of what it meant to be properly socialist. In May 1968, an engineer from Mukachevo, close to the Slovak-Ukrainian border, thus stated that his father had died in Czechoslovakia during World War II fighting for 'a life without the rich' for the Czechoslovak people. Now his achievements were being undermined, he despaired, because the Czechoslovak party was in no hurry to build socialism, and some of its members were even 'anti-communist'.[61] Two months later, a pensioner from the Sumy region in northern Ukraine claimed that Dubček's democracy would mirror Masaryk and Beneš's pre-war 'bourgeois republic', with the 'working class' condemned to 'hunger, unemployment, executions and imprisonment'. It was necessary to increase 'revolutionary alertness', he concluded.[62]

More often, however, public statements of support for the USSR's policies in Czechoslovakia were underpinned by loyalty not to the party or the cause of building communism, but rather to the Soviet state framed in geographical and ethnic terms. Especially in the borderlands, Sovietness was defined in opposition to the supposedly threatening Czechs and Slovaks. In this vein, after 21 August two students from Uzhhorod wrote to their parents in Lviv and Kamianets-Podilskyi relaying rumours that the Czechs wanted Transcarpathia back.[63] In preparation for what seemed to be impending war, some residents of Transcarpathia bought great quantities of soap, salt and matches, whilst others prepared to leave the region and escape eastwards.[64] Fear of war, combined with memories of victory over Nazi Germany, framed citizens' public declarations of loyalty to the Soviet Union. A villager from Transcarpathia described his outrage at the slanderous claims broadcast by the West German radio station *Deutsche Welle* which attacked 'our party and state'. He followed this statement by an account of his native village in Volhynia, which was 'burned to the ground' by the Nazis, and ended by writing that (given the opportunity) he would avenge the death of his father.[65] For many, Soviet policies had a distinctly personal dimension, as people who overtly supported the invasion of Czechoslovakia spoke about their friends and relatives in the army.[66] The public seemed receptive to increasingly xenophobic official narratives in August 1968. According to local officials, inhabitants of Chernivtsi applauded the 'heroic acts' of the Soviet Army and reacted very vocally to images of 'sabotage' aimed at 'our soldiers' when they watched the propaganda film 'The Counter-Revolution Shall Not Succeed'.[67]

Public statements of support for the Soviet invasion of Czechoslovakia were often painfully jingoistic and it is difficult to assess levels of genuine belief behind them. However, they should not be dismissed as mere conformity, for geographically and ethnically defined Soviet patriotism also framed criticism of Soviet foreign and domestic policies. At a time when Moscow still considered a range of options in Czechoslovakia, some citizens reportedly expressed a desire for more decisive military measures to be implemented. During an informal conversation with his colleagues that was later related to the KGB, for example, a teacher from Transcarpathia argued that it was necessary to install a new leadership in Prague that could then request Soviet military assistance.[68] It is, of course, hard to gauge how widespread such views were, and it is conceivable that Shelest devoted disproportionate attention to pro-interventionist sentiment in his reports in order to exert pressure on Moscow to suppress the Prague Spring. But similar statements were also recorded after the August invasion. Several participants in public meetings called for a still stricter policy in Eastern Europe, asking why the army did not invade Romania. The KGB classified such views as 'criticism'.[69] Citizens also articulated disappointment with the 'softness' of the Soviet occupation in Czechoslovakia.[70] At agitation meetings in Zaporizhzhia, for example, members of the audience asked about the USSR's failure to locate and destroy the underground radio stations in Czechoslovakia with all the advanced technology at its disposal.[71]

Citizens further expressed isolationist sentiments at odds with the USSR's continuing interference in East European politics. For example, the notion that the USSR should look after its own interests fuelled anti-war opinions in Soviet Ukraine. In correspondence with Moscow, Shelest reported the views of women collective farmers from a village in Transcarpathia who complained that their husbands were drafted into the army in the midst of spring field works, just because the Czechoslovak leaders were not able to cope with their own problems.[72] Keen to ensure that citizens perceive Soviet socialism as a successful system with global appeal, some opinion leaders were alarmed when participants in public meetings suggested that Soviet interests did not coincide with those of the USSR's socialist allies. In Poltava, for example, a non-party collective farmer stated that all of Eastern Europe 'feeds off us', echoing more widespread complaints about Soviet subsidies to the socialist satellite states,[73] but he supposedly 'understood his mistake' after the deputy head of a local council visited the collective farm to explain the intricacies of 'internationalist help'.[74] Soviet patriotism defined in opposition to the socialist states of Eastern Europe helped citizens express diverse and even contradictory opinions about the desirable direction of the USSR's foreign policy.

Public discussions of the Czechoslovak crisis further provided a forum for criticising the Soviet mass media. Soviet institutions and the debates about the Prague Spring which they organised allowed citizens to build social and political capital. Speakers at agitation meetings typically acted as leaders of public opinion at home, promising to ensure that members of their local communities would toe the official line.[75] These self-proclaimed leaders of popular opinion sometimes criticised the Soviet authorities for failing to provide enough information about the unfolding events. After the publication of the speech by the Polish communist leader, Gomułka, in which he blamed Jews for student unrest in Poland, some citizens demanded that a similarly clear statement should be produced with regards to Czechoslovakia.[76] During the highly controlled public meetings held to discuss the Prague Spring, citizens further picked up on inconsistencies in Soviet mass media coverage of Czechoslovakia.[77] Some self-identified Soviet patriots claimed that incomplete information about the situation in Czechoslovakia was conducive to the appearance of harmful information and rumours.[78] In July 1968, for example, the KGB reported that students, teachers and other employees of the Odesa civil engineering institute complained that the secrecy surrounding the Czechoslovak events fuelled the popularity of hostile foreign radio stations, proposing that newspapers should publish short information about the course of events on a day-to-day basis.[79] They were not dissidents opposed to Brezhnev's new course, and indeed they embraced the language of xenophobia that overcame the socialist camp in the late 1960s, but they still claimed the right to voice limited criticism of how Moscow handled information about the unfolding crisis.

From the Soviet leaders' point of view, censorship was not a sufficient means of keeping the population in check. Soviet patriotism defined in geographical and ethnic terms provided a powerful legitimating discourse for Brezhnev at the height of the Czechoslovak crisis, but it also pushed the Kremlin to reflect on the need to find new ways of providing information to loyal and engaged citizens.

Dissent

Brezhnev's fears that the crushing of Dubček's reforms would shake popular faith in the ability of Soviet institutions to evolve and better represent society's interests were not entirely unfounded. The Warsaw Pact invasion of Czechoslovakia was an important impetus for the growth of the Soviet dissident movement, whose members no longer found it possible to work within the confines of official culture to achieve their political goals. 'Dissent' refers to those opinions that Soviet leaders classified not merely as 'mistaken' or 'harmful', but outright 'illegal'. The KGB registered such dissenting voices among university students, members of the creative intelligentsia, soldiers and members of the Jewish minority, with most reports concentrating on citizens who did not belong to the communist party.[80] Dissidents were few and far between, but most expressed a surprisingly coherent set of views, arguing that the USSR's great-power nationalist politics represented a betrayal of socialist ideals. They sometimes echoed 'loyal' criticism of Soviet policy, condemning the invasion of Czechoslovakia and calling for more information to be provided to citizens. However, dissident views were underpinned by the belief that Dubček, and not Brezhnev, had the right idea about how to fix Soviet-style regimes. Soviet leaders and dissidents themselves knew full well that such views were now firmly outside the limits of the permissible.

Soviet intellectuals concerned about creeping 're-Stalinisation' of the socialist camp saw the Prague Spring as a rallying call for defending civic rights at home and abroad. Most famously, seven individuals gathered on Red Square in Moscow on 25 August 1968. They carried banners calling for the USSR to withdraw its armies from Prague, and underlining that they were fighting 'for your freedom and ours'. The protesters were brutally punished: two ended up in a labour camp, three were exiled from Moscow and one was sent to a mental hospital. Natalia Gorbanevskaia, who was still breast-feeding her small child at the time, was released. She played a leading role in establishing and running the *samizdat* publication *The Chronicle of Current Events (Khronika tekushchikh sobytyi)*.[81] Publicising statements by Soviet intellectuals and translations of Czechoslovak documents, *The Chronicle* turned into a source of news about the unfolding events at home and abroad and thus helped to shed dissent of its predominantly literary character in 1968.[82]

For Soviet dissidents, civic rights were tied intimately with freedom of speech. They drew on Khrushchev-era narratives of 'citizenship' (*grazhdanstvennost'*),[83] bemoaning the fact that citizens' ability to participate in politics was ever more severely curtailed. In an attempt to evaluate the Czechoslovak events, many *samizdat* materials emphasised that 'freedom of expression' was the only guarantee of democracy and economic progress in the Soviet bloc.[84] They likewise warned 'all citizens' that silence had already led to one disaster: the rise of Stalinism.[85] Dissidents thus emphasised that residents of the USSR had a social and political responsibility to criticise the party leadership, but they were far from questioning the legitimacy of the Soviet state as such. Rather, they imagined themselves as part of a distinctly 'Soviet' community of citizen-activists committed to a vision of society in which leaders were held accountable through open debate and protest. In this vein, an inhabitant of Dnipropetrovsk complained about the lack of information concerning demonstrations in Poland and changes in Czechoslovakia in the official press and on television. He sarcastically recalled how Soviet leaders kissed Novotný in front of cameras earlier, yet now could not find words to defend him (he suggested that perhaps they should have kissed him behind closed doors to make it more pleasant for everyone). His letter was highly confrontational, stating that the press was afraid to publish news from Eastern Europe lest Soviet students be inspired to protest against censorship, concentration camps or unfair trials.[86]

Dissent never translated into organised opposition to the Soviet state. But neither was post-Prague non-conformity confined to a mere handful of Moscow intellectuals who published in *samizdat*. Liudmila Alekseeva documented several instances where citizens collected signatures under pro-Dubček petitions or simply refused to vote on resolutions approving the Soviet invasion of Czechoslovakia at public meetings held across the USSR.[87] The Ukrainian historian Volodymyr Dmytruk has also shown that views explicitly critical of Soviet policies in 1968 were registered throughout Soviet Ukraine.[88] Sending anonymous letters and spreading illegal pamphlets, dozens of people embodied active resistance to the state's attempts at curtailing public debate.[89] Party and KGB reports suggested that many non-conformists in the provinces and in the non-Russian parts of the USSR saw themselves as part of the same culture of dissent as their Moscow counterparts, citing the example of a student from Lviv who claimed that her friends should follow the example of Moscow dissidents.[90]

Non-conformist critiques of Soviet policies in Czechoslovakia were often explicitly grounded in socialist ideas. As self-proclaimed 'communists',[91] many *samizdat* authors underlined their commitment to Dubček's reform socialism. They reprinted the Czechoslovak party's Action Programme from April 1968. The Soviet Union should learn how to build socialism from the Czechs—read the four leaflets discovered in Chernihiv on 24 August—as the struggle in Czechoslovakia was not a fight between communism and capitalism, but rather a battle between new and old ideas within socialism.[92] For those citizens who believed that Moscow betrayed the socialist cause in 1968, real socialism was still embodied by some members of Brezhnev's own team. An anonymous letter from Zhdanov (Mariupol) in the Donetsk region condemned the 'bandit' invasion of Czechoslovakia and Brezhnev's 'revisionist' system, ending in gripping slogans: 'Out with Brezhnev! Long live Kosygin!'[93] The authors did not explain why they held a positive opinion of the Soviet Prime Minister, but it is likely that they associated him with the abortive economic reforms of the mid-1960s which represented the last concerted attempt by the Kremlin to improve the functioning of Soviet institutions.[94]

Underground publications attacked the Warsaw Pact invasion of Czechoslovakia as an expression of 'imperialism', quite unbecoming of a socialist state committed to de-colonisation and internationalist friendship.[95] In this vein, in July 1968 a self-styled 'group of honest communists' penned an open letter expressing the hope that the USSR would not risk discrediting itself 'by invading a brotherly country'.[96] Such views were often underpinned by anti-capitalist sentiment and continuing faith that Soviet-style socialism offered an attractive alternative path to modernity. Official reports quoted dozens of individuals who claimed that the intervention would weaken the communist movement in the whole world.[97]

The national question acquired a new urgency for dissidents as the limits of permissible non-Russian expression in the USSR shrank. Throughout the latter half of the 1960s, 'ethnic minority *samizdat* championed "genuine socialism" and "the restoration of Lenin's norms"' as a guarantee of greater national autonomy for republics in the USSR.[98] In line with this, during the Prague Spring and its aftermath, some authors who published their views in the underground sought to defend 'Ukrainian rights', but also underlined their commitment to the Soviet Union and its official ideology. For example, an anonymous member of the Ukrainian writers' union distributed a letter among Soviet citizens, in which he or she commented at length on the situation in Czechoslovakia, as well as complaining that the Soviet authorities were prejudiced against Ukrainian culture. Although the author was critical of Soviet nationalities policy, he or she still appealed to an official Soviet institution, the writers' union, to rectify the problem.[99]

Anti-Soviet Nationalism

It was mostly in the USSR's western borderlands that some residents went further and rejected the Soviet state and socialism in its entirety, rather than calling for the reform of the system. On 27 August, the Lviv regional party secretary claimed that 'nationalist' and anti-Soviet elements had intensified their hostile activities after the Warsaw Pact invasion of Czechoslovakia.[100] At the height of the Prague Spring, the national solution was the most immediately obvious alternative to Soviet socialism for those citizens who rejected existing state structures. For instance, the KGB quoted a man from Stryi who claimed that the only way to solve the Czechoslovak problem was to grant 'freedom and independence' to all peoples in Eastern Europe, including Ukraine.[101] This type of dissidence was not new in 1968, but rather represented continuities from earlier Ukrainian nationalist resistance to the USSR which was now weaker than at any point since the establishment of Soviet rule in the region during World War II.[102] At least in the KGB's view, explicitly anti-Soviet attitudes were mostly confined to individuals who had already developed a hostile relationship with the authorities, with many having spent time in the Gulag for nationalist resistance to Soviet rule during and in the immediate aftermath of World War II.[103] This suggests perhaps that the Prague Spring emboldened citizens with anti-Soviet convictions, but did not in fact increase the reach or affect the claims of anti-Soviet Ukrainian nationalism.

Anti-Soviet Ukrainian nationalism carried a range of different connotations. Anecdotal evidence suggests that in some cases it framed explicit calls for inter-ethnic violence. For instance, a metal worker from Lviv boasted that he had identified a house belonging to a Russian man in order to occupy it during the coming war.[104] For others, anti-Russian nationalism helped frame economic complaints. Immediately after the invasion, an employee of a furniture factory in Chernivtsi stated that the 'Moskali' (a derogatory term for Russians) prevented the people of Czechoslovakia from 'living well',[105] and a local resident claimed that the Ukrainians would be richer had it not been for 50 years of 'Muscovite oppression'.[106] In some cases, nationalism was associated with support for private ownership. A woman employed at the bread factory in Uzhhorod stated that 'the Russians take everything away'. At the suggestion that it was still better to live under the Russians than the Germans, she retorted that the Germans would 'give people their land'.[107] Finally, anti-Soviet Ukrainian nationalism helped citizens articulate opposition to religious oppression in the USSR. In particular, the legalisation of the Greek Catholic Church in Czechoslovakia during 1968 emboldened some faithful in Ukraine to call for similar measures at home.[108]

Conclusion

The Prague Spring marked a shift in Soviet identity politics. The events of 1968 made it abundantly clear that socialist allegiances were not tantamount to loyalty to the Soviet state and its titular ethnic groups. In the search for popular legitimacy, leaders of the USSR downplayed the internationalist ideas of the previous decade, when Khrushchev sought to rekindle popular faith in socialism as an ideology that united class-conscious, ideologically committed people across borders. This is because the idea that socialist institutions would involve citizens in debating and implementing policy, or that socialism would help to construct a new type of international relations based on anti-imperialist commitments, was largely discredited by 1968.

Expression of 'socialist' identities was now largely confined to underground culture. The few, but surprisingly, vocal proponents of reform turned to illegal means such as unsanctioned demonstrations, underground publications and illegal pamphlets to defend the now largely abandoned de-Stalinisation agenda. They called for 'openness' and the 'spiritual renewal' of Soviet society, demanded a return to 'Leninist' nationalities policy and criticised Brezhnev's 'imperialist' foreign policy. Bar a few scattered calls for independence from the USSR in the western borderlands, dissenting voices did not normally echo ideas of anti-Soviet nationalism or a sense of cultural and historical distinctiveness that Amir Weiner focuses on in his study of territories incorporated into the USSR after 1939.[109] Rather, dissent was mostly grounded in a sense of Soviet patriotism that underpinned demands for political representation, access to information and freedom of speech. The geography of dissent in 1968 did not, therefore, conform to the stereotypical division into unstable borderlands and a compliant centre. This may partly explain why, some 20 years later, ideas about reforming socialism inspired by the Prague Spring entered the USSR's mainstream culture as Mikhail Gorbachev sought to radically overhaul the Soviet system.[110]

Yet it would be a mistake to assume that citizens lost faith in the ability of the Soviet state to represent their interests because they could no longer debate what socialism was or what communism should be; or to argue that residents of the USSR only remained acquiescent due to Brezhnev's material handouts.[111] After the Prague Spring buried the Soviet Thaw, many inhabitants of the USSR did not see the Soviet state as an 'ageing revolution' that had lost its impetus, but rather as an embodiment of their ethnically and geographically defined interests.[112] Although it is impossible to judge levels of genuine belief behind public statements of approval for Soviet foreign policy in 1968, ethnically and geographically defined Soviet patriotism was a powerful tool that helped citizens to manifest their patriotic credentials and thus improve their social standing and even voice limited criticism of official policy.

Far from signalling the beginning of 'stagnation', the Czechoslovak crisis pushed Soviet leaders to search for new ways of shaping state–society dynamics in the USSR. The Prague Spring highlighted the urgent need to develop Soviet television that would help isolate citizens from harmful foreign-produced information and ideas.[113] After the upheavals of 1968, Soviet and East European leaders did not close borders between the USSR and its satellite states. On the contrary, transnational cultural and social ties grew over the 1970s. As faith in the power of socialism to bind the USSR and its allies crumbled, Soviet media professionals developed new types of popular culture that lent Eastern Europe a great degree of cultural integrity, and East European organisations developed ties and infrastructure that allowed for the rise of international tourism on an unprecedented scale. But Eastern Europe was increasingly defined not as a 'socialist commonwealth' united by left-wing values and ideas, but rather as a confederation of closely related ethnic groups that looked to Moscow for protection against Western European and American aggression.[114]

Notes

1. Some of the ideas and evidence presented in this chapter have previously appeared in Z. Wojnowski, *The Near Abroad: Socialist Eastern Europe and Soviet Patriotism in Ukraine, 1956–1985* (Toronto, 2017).
2. For example, see J. Fürst, P. Jones and S. Morrissey, 'The Relaunch of the Soviet Project, 1945–1964', *Slavonic and East European Review*, vol. 86, no. 2 (2008), pp. 201–7.
3. On the shrinking limits of the permissible, see D. Kozlov, *The Readers of* Novyi Mir*: Coming to Terms with the Stalinist Past* (Cambridge, MA, 2013), pp. 239–62.
4. J. Suri, 'The Promise and Failure of "Developed Socialism": The Soviet "Thaw" and the Crucible of the Prague Spring, 1964–1972', *Contemporary European History*, vol. 15, no. 2 (2006), pp. 138, 148, 150–3.
5. A. Gorsuch, *All This is Your World: Soviet Tourism at Home and Abroad after Stalin* (Oxford, 2011), pp. 88, 106–10.
6. R. Applebaum, 'The Friendship Project: Socialist Internationalism in the Soviet Union and Czechoslovakia in the 1950s and the 1960s', *Slavic Review*, vol. 74, no. 3 (2015), p. 507.
7. See A. Gorsuch and D. Koenker, 'Introduction: The Socialist 1960s in Global Perspective', in A. Gorsuch and D. Koenker (eds), *The Socialist Sixties: Crossing Borders in the Second World* (Bloomington, IN, 2013), pp. 1–21.
8. A. Weiner, 'Déjà Vu All Over Again: Prague Spring, Romanian Summer, and Soviet Autumn on Russia's Western Frontier', *Contemporary European History*, vol. 15, no. 2 (2006), pp. 172–4.
9. On Romania, see "Ceauşescu's Finest Hour? Memorialising Romanian Responses to the Warsaw Pact Invasion of Czechoslovakia", by Calin Goina, in this volume; Weiner, 'Déjà Vu', pp. 164–71. On the repercussions of the Polish crisis, see Wojnowski, *The Near Abroad*, pp. 106, 112, 114, 121–3, 126–7.
10. O. Bazhan edited a fascinating collection of KGB reports on popular opinion about the Prague Spring in Soviet Ukraine. See O. Bazhan (ed.), '"Praz'ka Vesna" u dokumentakh Galuzevoho derzhavnoho arkhivu Sluzhby Bezpeky Ukrainy', *Z arkhiviv VUChK-GPU-NKVD-KGB*, no. 1–2 (2008), pp. 54–137.
11. On the importance of Transcarpathia during the Prague Spring, see Weiner, 'Déjà Vu', pp. 174–6.
12. O. Pavlenko, 'Sovetskie informatsionno-analiticheskie i operativnye materialy po chekhoslovatskomu krizisu 1968 goda', in N.G. Tomilina et al.

(eds), *Prazhskaia vesna i mezhdunarodnyi krizis 1968 goda: stat'i, issledovaniia, vospominaniia* (Moscow, 2010), p. 61.
13. M. Prozumenshchikov, '"Vy poimete, chto my ne imeli drugogo vykhoda". Problemy razrabotki i priniatiia reshenii vysshim sovetskim rukovodstvom v khode chekhoslovatskogo krizisa 1968 goda', in Tomilina, *Prazhskaia vesna: stat'i*, pp. 19-20.
14. 'Memoir of Andrei Aleksandrov-Agentov on Internal Soviet Deliberations about Czechoslovakia (excerpts)', in J. Navrátil et al. (eds), *The Prague Spring 1968: A National Security Archive Documents Reader* (Budapest, 1998), p. 102.
15. Prozumenshchikov, 'Vy poimete', pp. 20-1, 32-3.
16. Suri, 'The Promise', pp. 138, 148, 150-3; Pavlenko, 'Sovetskie informatsionno-analiticheskie i operativnye materialy', p. 50.
17. Prozumenshchikov, 'Vy poimete', pp. 21-2.
18. On the fight against 'localism', see A. Nove, *An Economic History of the USSR, 1917-1991* (London, 1992), p. 368.
19. G. Hodnett and P. Potichnyj, *The Ukraine and the Czechoslovak Crisis* (Canberra, 1970), pp. 116-17.
20. Pavlenko, 'Sovetskie informatsionno-analiticheskie i operativnye materialy', pp. 50, 59.
21. Prozumenshchikov, 'Vy peimete', p. 26.
22. Prozumenshchikov, 'Vy poimete', p. 20.
23. 'The Recollections of Kirill Mazurov', in Navrátil et al. (eds), *The Prague Spring*, p. 434.
24. 'Postanovlenie Politbiuro TsK KPSS v svyazi s rasprostraneniem v ChSSR "Obrashcheniia" tak nazyvaemogo "Komiteta Deistviia za demokraticheskuiu sotsialisticheskuiu Chekhoslovakiiu, granitsy i territoriia kotoroi byli ustanovleny 50 let nazad"', 18 June 1968, in N. G. Tomilina et al. (eds), *Prazhskaia vesna i mezhdunarodnyi krizis 1968 goda: dokumenty* (Moscow, 2010), p. 99.
25. P. Shelest, *Spravzhnii sud istorii shche poperedu. Spohady, shchodennyky, dokumenty, materialy*, edited by Iurii Shapoval (Kyiv, 2003), p. 331.
26. Pavlenko, 'Sovetskie informatsionno-analiticheskie i operativnye materialy', p. 72.
27. M. Kramer, 'The Czechoslovak Crisis and the Brezhnev Doctrine' in C. Fink et al. (eds), *1968: The World Transformed* (Cambridge, 1998), p. 144; Tsentral'nyi Derzhavnyi Arkhiv Hromads'kykh Ob"ednan' Ukrainy, Kyiv (TsDAHO), f. 1, op. 25, s. 28, ark. 98.
28. Suri, 'The Promise', pp. 146-7.

29. O. Lavinskaia, 'Tsenzura v SSSR i ogranicheniia informatsii o sobytiiakh v Chekhoslovakii', in Tomilina et al. (eds), *Prazhskaia vesna: stat'i*, p. 133.
30. V. Baran, *Ukraina: Novitnia istoriia* (Lviv, 2003), p. 283.
31. R. Applebaum, 'A Test of Friendship: Soviet-Czechoslovak Tourism and the Prague Spring', in Gorsuch and Koenker (eds), *The Socialist Sixties*, pp. 213–32.
32. For example, Digest of Soviet Ukrainian Press 12:10: H. Nikol'nikov, 'The Struggle of V.I. Lenin and the CPSU for Consolidating the Principles of Proletarian Internationalism', from *Radians'ka Ukraina*, 3 September 1968.
33. Derzhavnyi Arkhiv L'vivs'koi Oblasti, Lviv (DALO), f. P3, op. 10, s. 248, ark. 3–4, 87–89; TsDAHO, f. 1, op. 25, s. 14, ark. 26–30; TsDAHO, f. 1, op. 25, s. 32, ark. 15–20; Rossiiskii Gosudarstvennyi Arkhiv Noveishei Istorii, Moscow (RGANI), f. 1, op. 60, d. 28, ll. 65–6.
34. TsDAHO, f. 1, op. 25, s. 37, ark. 9–12.
35. Prozumenshchikov, 'Vy poimete', p. 31.
36. Pavlenko, 'Sovetskie informatsionno-analiticheskie i operativnye materialy', p. 52.
37. Prozumenshchikov, 'Vy poimete', p. 36.
38. T. Martin, *The Affirmative Action Empire: Nations and Nationalism in the Soviet Union, 1923–1939* (Ithaca, NY, 2001), p. 450.
39. Weiner, 'Déjà Vu', pp. 186–9.
40. Wojnowski, *The Near Abroad*, p. 148.
41. Current Digest of the Soviet Press (CDSP) 20:21, 12 June 1968: V. Kozyakov, 'What the American Policy of "Building Bridges" Aims At', *Krasnaia zvezda*, 24 May 1968.
42. Archiwum Akt Nowych, Warsaw (Archive of Modern Records—AAN), z. 1354, s. XIA, t. 84, ss. 269–70.
43. CDSP 20:14, 24 April 1968: 'Speech by Comrade W. Gomułka at Meeting with Warsaw Party Aktiv', *Pravda*, 22 March 1968; B. Kowalski, 'On Certain Theses of Israeli and West German Propaganda', *Literaturnaia gazeta*, 3 April 1968.
44. A. Filitov, 'SSSR, FRG i Chekhoslovatskii krizis 1968 goda', in Tomilina et al. (eds), *Prazhskaia vesna: stat'i*, p. 82.
45. 'Postanovleniie Politbiuro TsK KPSS "O zaiavlenii TASS"', 19 August 1968, in Velichanskaia (ed.), *Chekhoslovatskii krizis*, p. 201.
46. 'Postanovleniie Politbiuro TsK KPSS "Ob informatsii partiinogo aktiva o sobytiiakh v Chekhoslovakii"', 7 July 1968, in Velichanskaia (ed.), *Chekhoslovatskii krizis*, pp. 119–20.
47. Wojnowski, *The Near Abroad*, pp. 119–20.
48. TsDAHO, f. 1, op. 25, s. 255, ark. 2–5.

49. M. Prozumenshchikov, 'Skol'zkii led "Prazhskoi vesny"', ili o roli sporta v istorii sovetsko-chekhoslovatskikh otnoshenii', in Tomilina et al. (eds), *Prazhskaia vesna: stat'i*, p. 148; 'Postanovleniie Politbiuro TsK KPSS "Ob informatsii po Chekhoslovakii"', 23 March 1968, in Tomilina et al. (eds), *Prazhskaia vesna: dokumenty*, p. 27; 'Postanovleniie Politbiuro TsK KPSS "Ob informatsii dlia partiinogo aktiva o sobytiiakh v Chekhoslovakii"', 10 April 1969 in Velichanskaia (ed.), *Chekhoslovatskii krizis*, pp. 526–8.
50. Hodnett and Potichnyj, *The Ukraine*, pp. 117–19.
51. Weiner, 'Déjà Vu', p. 180.
52. TsDAHO, f. 1, op. 25, s. 14, ark. 131–3.
53. Derzhavnyi Arkhiv Odes'koi Oblasti, Odesa (DAOO), f. P11, op. 19, s. 702, ark. 4–11. As Yaacov Ro'i argues in his study of Soviet Jewish reactions to the 1967 Six Day War, statements like these were likely underpinned by Jewish fear of anti-Semitism. '[I]t is reasonable to assume that many Jews, especially older ones who remembered the propaganda campaigns of early 1949 and early 1953, genuinely feared the negative results of the Six Day War might have on them and made every effort to dissociate Soviet Jewry from the activity and policy of the Israeli government and to condemn them'. 'The Soviet Jewish Reaction to the Six Day War' in Y. Ro'i and B. Morozov (eds), *The Soviet Union and the June 1967 Six Day War* (Stanford, CA, 2008), p. 258.
54. AAN, z. 1354, s. XIA, t. 84, s. 308.
55. DAOO, f. P11, op. 20. s. 88, ark. 15–26; TsDAHO, f. 1, op. 25, s. 37, ark. 93.
56. B. Lewytzkyj, *Politics and Society in Soviet Ukraine, 1953–80* (Edmonton, 1987), pp. 100, 134.
57. TsDAHO, f. 1, op. 25, s. 14, ark. 131–3; TsDAHO, f. 1, op. 25, s. 35, ark. 6–7; TsDAHO, f. 1, op. 25, s. 39, ark. 10–14.
58. Hodnett and Potichnyj, *The Ukraine*, pp. 116–17.
59. Hodnett and Potichnyj, *The Ukraine*, p. 78; Lewytzkyj, *Politics and Society*, p. 119; Kramer, 'The Czechoslovak Crisis', p. 144.
60. Lewytzkyj, *Politics and Society*, p. 204.
61. TsDAHO, f. 1, op. 25, s. 28, ark. 102–12.
62. TsDAHO, f. 1, op. 25, s. 35, ark. 6–7.
63. TsDAHO, f. 1, op. 25, s. 28, ark. 102–12.
64. Bazhan, 'Praz'ka Vesna', pp. 70–1, 73, 105; TsDAHO, f. 1, op. 25, s. 28, ark. 102–12.
65. RGANI, f. 5, op. 60, d. 26, ll. 160–72.
66. DALO, f. 3, op. 10, s. 248, ark. 20–3.
67. TsDAHO, f. 1, op. 25, s. 33, ark. 111–15.
68. TsDAHO, f. 1, op. 25, s. 28, ark. 12–13.

69. TsDAHO, f. 1, op. 25, s. 39, ark. 10–14.
70. Derzhavnyi Arkhiv Kyivs'koi Oblasti, Kyiv, f. P5, op. 7, s. 822, ark. 42–3.
71. TsDAHO, f. 1, op. 25, s. 39, ark. 10–14.
72. TsDAHO, f. 1, op. 25, s. 28, ark. 102–12.
73. For more examples of complaints about Soviet exports, see Wojnowski, *Near Abroad*, pp. 15, 27, 44–5, 182, 191–3, 205.
74. TsDAHO, f. 1, op. 25, s. 39, ark. 142–4.
75. Wojnowski, *The Near Abroad*, pp. 116–19.
76. DAOO, f. P11, op. 19, s. 702, ark. 4–11.
77. TsDAHO, f. 1, op. 25, s. 14, ark. 131–3.
78. Bazhan, 'Praz'ka Vesna', p. 86.
79. DAOO, f. 11, op. 20, s. 88, ark. 15–26.
80. Wojnowski, *The Near Abroad*, pp. 125–8.
81. L. Alekseeva, *Istoriia inakomysliia v SSSR: Noveishii period* (Benson, VT, 1984), pp. 264–5.
82. *Khronika tekushchikh sobytii* (KhTS), 31 December 1968.
83. For a discussion of *grazhdanstvennost'*, see S. Costanzo, 'Amateur Theatres and Amateur Publics in the Russian Republic, 1958–71', *Slavonic and East European Review*, vol. 86, no. 2 (2008), p. 394.
84. KhTS, 30 June 1969.
85. *Sobranie dokumentov Samizdata* (SDS), Document AS69: Valentin Komarov, 'Otkrytoe pis'mo v sviazi s okkupatsiei Chekhoslovakii'.
86. RGANI, Moscow, f. 5, op. 60, d. 26, ll. 39–71.
87. Alekseeva, *Istoriia inakomysliia*, pp. 264–5.
88. V. Dmytruk, *Ukraina ne movchala: Reaktsiia ukrains'koho suspil'stva na podii 1968 roku v Chekhoslovachchyni* (Kyiv, 2004).
89. Bazhan, 'Praz'ka Vesna', pp. 111–16.
90. Wojnowski, *The Near Abroad*, p. 128.
91. KhTS, 28 February 1970.
92. TsDAHO, f. 1, op. 25, s. 31, ark. 141–3.
93. Bazhan, 'Praz'ka Vesna', p. 93.
94. For a discussion of the Kosygin reforms, see A. Shubin, *Ot zastoia k reformam: SSSR v 1917–85 gg* (Moscow, 2001), p. 119.
95. KhTS, 31 October 1969; KhTS, 31 August 1970.
96. SDS, Document AS108: P. Grigorenko, A. Kosterin, V. Pavlinchuk, S. Pisarev, I. Iakhimovich, 'Otkrytoe pis'mo "Kommunistam Chekhoslovakii, ko vsemu chekhoslovatskomu narodu"', 28 July 1968.
97. Bazhan, 'Praz'ka Vesna', pp. 84, 94–6.
98. D. Zisserman-Brodsky, *Constructing Ethnopolitics in the Soviet Union: Samizdat, Deprivation, and the Rise of Ethnic Nationalism* (New York, 2003), p. 197.

99. SDS, Document AS970, Chlen spilki pysmennykiv Ukrainy, 'Lyst do Olesia Honchara i sekretariv SPU pro kul'turni vidnosyny mizh Ukrainoiu i ChRSR', 1968.
100. DALO, f. P3, op. 10, s. 248, ark. 87–9.
101. Bazhan, 'Praz'ka Vesna', p. 90.
102. The most violent nationalist resistance to Soviet rule in western Ukraine occurred in the 1940s and early 1950s. See A. Statiev, *The Soviet Counterinsurgency in the Western Borderlands* (Cambridge, 2010). As Amir Weiner writes, in 1968 'there was no young and violent constituency similar to the returning nationalist guerrillas and underground activists who tried to seize the moment in 1956'. Weiner, 'Déjà Vu', p. 186.
103. They thus referred to one culprit as a 'famous nationalist'. Bazhan, 'Praz'ka Vesna', p. 97.
104. Bazhan, 'Praz'ka Vesna', pp. 71–2.
105. TsDAHO, f. 1, op. 25, s. 38, ark. 141–3.
106. Bazhan, 'Praz'ka Vesna', p. 90.
107. Bazhan, 'Praz'ka Vesna', pp. 97–8.
108. Dmytruk, *Ukraina*, p. 228.
109. Weiner, 'Déjà Vu', pp. 159–94.
110. On the relationship between the Prague Spring and Gorbachev's reforms, see M. Gorbachev and Z. Mlynář, *Conversations with Gorbachev: On Perestroika, the Prague Spring, and the Crossroads of Socialism* (New York, 2003).
111. For a critique of this paradigm of stagnation, see Wojnowski, *The Near Abroad*, pp. 23–5.
112. For a discussion of the 'ageing revolution', see Weiner, 'Déjà Vu', pp. 159–94.
113. TsDAHO, f. 1, op. 31, s. 3607, ark. 1–9.
114. Wojnowski, *The Near Abroad*, pp. 141–73.

Ideological Offensive: The East German Leadership, the Prague Spring and the Warsaw Pact Invasion of August 1968

Matthew Stibbe

On 1 October 1964 Ernst Engelberg, one of the GDR's most prominent academics, professor of history at the University of Leipzig, director of the Institute for History at the Academy of Sciences in East Berlin, and president of the (East) German Historians' Association, submitted a report on a trip he had made three weeks earlier to Vienna to attend a conference on the theme 'Austria-Hungary and the First International'. The conference was significant as it brought together nineteenth-century specialists working on both sides of the Iron Curtain. Engelberg, as an ultra-loyal member of East Germany's ruling Socialist Unity Party (SED), was always alert to any attempt by non-communist scholars to challenge the legitimacy of Marxist-Leninist interpretations of history. What especially concerned him on this occasion, however, was the appearance of Hans Mommsen, a rising star in left-liberal academic circles in the West German Federal Republic (FRG) and later a very

M. Stibbe (✉)
Sheffield Hallam University, Sheffield, UK
e-mail: m.stibbe@shu.ac.uk

© The Author(s) 2018
K. McDermott and M. Stibbe (eds.), *Eastern Europe in 1968*,
https://doi.org/10.1007/978-3-319-77069-7_5

eminent historian of Weimar and Nazi Germany. Mommsen had begun his career in the early 1960s with a series of publications on workers' movements in the nineteenth-century Habsburg Monarchy. He was also known to be a member of the West German Social Democratic Party (SPD) and to support its new policy of *Wandel durch Annäherung*—or achieving positive change in the FRG's relationship with Eastern Europe via a policy of rapprochement and dialogue. But most worryingly of all— according to Engelberg's report—Mommsen appeared to be on familiar *Du* terms with several card-carrying Czechoslovak communist historians who attended the conference and to have convinced them that their and his understanding not only of the Habsburg past but of the European present might be set on a slow path towards convergence:

> It seems to me that the ideological position and political tactics of a man like Hans Mommsen should be studied very carefully by us ... [He] has won a great deal of acclaim for his detailed study on 'Social Democracy and the Nationalities' Question in the Multi-National Habsburg state', not only among left-liberal and social democratic historians ..., but also among communist scholars in the Habsburg successor states, especially among the Czechoslovak comrades. For them Mommsen is the 'next best thing to a Marxist' [*eine 'Beinahe Marxist'*] [and] a sympathiser with the Czech and Slovak liberation movements. He is also very clever at displaying his 'understanding' for the supposedly progressive elements in all nineteenth- and twentieth-century movements towards European integration.[1]

Engelberg's suspicions of Mommsen were increased when the latter criticised his own paper for displaying 'conservative authoritarian' tendencies with regard to the Habsburg nationalities' question and/or for being unduly influenced by Karl Marx and Friedrich Engels' early writings on the place of 'historic' and 'non-historic' nations in the unfolding of their materialist conception of history.[2] For Engelberg, later famous as the GDR's chief biographer of Bismarck, the key political lesson of 1848– 49 was the failure to unite the German people from below on a republican, democratic and 'großdeutsch' basis, with German-speaking Austria and Bohemia included. While still critical, in the 1960s, of 'reactionary' elements in Bismarck's 'kleindeutsch' programme, he was already on a path that would lead him, by the 1980s, to present the Iron Chancellor's military victories over Denmark, Austria and France as being a 'historically progressive moment'—on the grounds that national unification was a pre-condition for the emergence of a disciplined, organised, self-conscious working class as an independent force in politics.[3] This was of course very much at odds with both Mommsen's and many of the less dogmatic Czechoslovak historians' interpretation of the relationship between the rising consciousness of 'labour' interests and the 'national awakening' in nineteenth-century Bohemia, which tended to highlight the emergence of a common democratic-humanist and socialist 'European' culture that transcended shifting geopolitical and linguistic frontiers. For them, Bismarck remained an arch-conservative Prussian militarist and enemy both of the cosmopolitan spirit behind the 1848 'springtime of peoples' and of the multifarious labour movements that were formed at the time of the First International from 1864 to 1872.[4]

At first glance, this clash between different strains of Marxism that occurred at a conference of nineteenth-century specialists in 'neutral' Austria in 1964—some three to four years before the key events discussed in this volume took place—might seem to be of arcane interest only. However, in this chapter I shall argue that Engelberg's conference report is of broader relevance because of how closely it anticipates some of the central themes in the SED's reaction to the Prague Spring and its hard-line defence of the Warsaw Pact invasion of Czechoslovakia on 20–21 August 1968. This can be seen on three different levels. First, Engelberg feared that leading Czechoslovak historians were becoming susceptible to 'revisionist' views of the past, particularly in regard to the historical relationship between class and nation in the development of socialist consciousness. The rehabilitation in 1963 of certain Slovak communists imprisoned in the 1950s for 'national-deviationist' tendencies, the most prominent of whom was the future party first secretary Gustáv Husák, and a gradual thaw in the attitude of Marxist historiography in Czechoslovakia towards the Czech and Slovak national movements of the past, were indeed early signs of what was to come in 1968.[5]

Second, Engelberg feared that Mommsen's advocacy of a 'value-free' approach to the human sciences, or what he called his 'sociologism' (*Soziologismus*), might have a superficial attraction to Czechoslovak scholars who were looking for ways of restricting the party's leading role in the development of scientific knowledge. There were indeed certain parallels with Czech reformer Ota Šik's attempts from the early 1960s to persuade the hard-line regime of Antonin Novotný to relax central controls over the Czechoslovak economy, with the party gradually re-positioning itself as a disinterested mediator between conflicting material demands rather than the enforcing instrument of the 'dictatorship of the proletariat'. For anti-reformers like Engelberg, there was nothing 'Marxist', and indeed something deeply suspect, in the new fad for 'dressing oneself up as ideologically open-minded'. Science, in his view, could never be 'value-free'; rather, its task was to stand on the side of the working class, the producers and creators of wealth, against the class of exploiters, the bourgeoisie.[6]

Finally, Engelberg was concerned that Mommsen, and 'standing behind him, the full weight of the West German history profession', might use academic contacts with Czechoslovak colleagues 'in order to isolate the GDR politically and morally from other states', and especially from neighbouring socialist countries in Eastern Europe.[7] Since the early 1960s 'fraternal' bonds between the SED and the Czechoslovak Communist Party (KSČ) were put under strain by awareness of the small but increasing numbers of West German students and academics visiting Czechoslovakia, and vice versa, and by fears that these contacts could lead to the promotion of 'counter-revolution' along the Czech–German and German–German frontiers. Even after the building of the Berlin Wall in 1961, Germany was still imagined by political leaders on both sides of the Iron Curtain as a single nation partitioned into two rival states.[8] This meant that in the eyes of East Germany's rulers, Czechoslovak academics who engaged in dialogue with West German colleagues, who published in Western journals, and who talked, implicitly or explicitly, about a falling away of ideological barriers, were not only in danger of undermining the unity of the Soviet bloc. They were also potentially calling into question the very *raison d'être* of one of its core, front-line members: the GDR. In his 1964 conference report Engelberg could already name some examples, among them Jiří Kořalka, author of a 1963 study of the social democratic movement and the Czech national question in nineteenth-century Bohemia (and incidentally a former student of Ota Šik), who had been invited to give several guest lectures at West German universities.[9] The fact that Engelberg could interpret such contacts as an existential threat to the East German state may seem odd—even paranoid and delusional—from today's perspective. However, viewed from the mind-set of the time, his stance bears witness to the peculiar 'intensity' with which Cold War antagonisms could be confronted and experienced in the divided post-1948 (and post-1961) German/Central European landscape.[10]

Using Engelberg's conference report as a starting point, this chapter will first explore the reactions of the SED leadership to the political challenges posed by the Prague Spring. It will also consider what the East German secret police or Stasi's careful monitoring of public opinion in the immediate aftermath of the Warsaw Pact invasion can tell us about the regime's evolving domestic priorities and security interests. A central argument will be that the GDR's distinctive ideological position in 1968 can only be understood in terms of the triangular relationship—real and imagined—between East and West Germany and Czechoslovakia. This three-way connection was also linked in a direct manner to the Nazi past, especially given the SED's concerns to avoid giving credence to any comparisons that might be made between Hitler's seizure of the Sudetenland and Bohemia/Moravia in 1938–39 and East Germany's participation in the Soviet-led military invasion of Czechoslovakia in 1968. When it comes to examining the Stasi's monitoring of public opinion, the chapter will focus on the administrative district—or *Bezirk*—Magdeburg, which contained not only the city of Magdeburg (population on 31 December 1967: 268,064)[11] and surrounding towns and villages, but part of the heavily guarded inner-German border, including the main east-west crossing point at Marienborn-Helmstedt. However, in respect to reactions from the SED leadership, the GDR-wide picture will be at the centre of analysis and attention.

THE PRAGUE SPRING AND THE SED LEADERSHIP

East Germans in the 1960s were long used to propaganda identifying the FRG—or the 'rulers in Bonn'—as being the chief and irreconcilable enemy of the GDR. So-called Western freedoms were dismissed by the East German media and party ideologues as being little more than freedom for militarists, monopoly capitalists, right-wing newspaper magnates and neo-Nazis to plot a revanchist war against the peace-loving states of the Soviet bloc. West Germany, it was argued, was not a model for East Germans to follow, particularly given its recent and wholehearted support for the American war in Vietnam and for extreme forms of anti-communism (dressed up as 'anti-extremism') at home.[12] The formation of a 'grand coalition' in Bonn in December 1966, with the SPD entering government at federal level for the first time in the FRG's history and SPD leader Willy Brandt serving as Foreign Minister and Vice Chancellor, was interpreted as the latest phase in the West's campaign to isolate the GDR internationally.[13] This was especially the case when the new West German administration began to explore ways of gradually expanding its commercial and political links in Eastern Europe, beginning with the establishment of formal diplomatic relations with Romania (in January 1967) and Yugoslavia (in January 1968), and the opening of a trade mission in Prague (in August 1967). The GDR responded by reiterating the ideological unity and military preparedness of the Soviet bloc, and by insisting on strict observance of the principles agreed to at a conference of European communist parties in Karlovy Vary in April 1967, namely that Western recognition of East Germany, together with abandonment of the FRG's claim to be the only legal representative of the German nation and formal acceptance of existing territorial borders in Eastern Europe, were vital preconditions for any deeper cooperation with European NATO countries on questions of peace and security.[14]

While opposition to the West was a familiar theme in SED propaganda, the East German population was less prepared in 1968 for ideological attacks on an important ally like Czechoslovakia. Unlike the German–German border, the GDR's frontier with the ČSSR was relatively open and tens of thousands of East Germans visited the country each year in the 1960s.[15] True, in internal reports from 1963 onwards, SED cultural officials had, like Engelberg, expressed doubts about the slow relaxation of censorship in Czechoslovakia, particularly in the sphere of film and literature.[16] However, public criticism of a fellow socialist country was still considered taboo and at odds with the principles of 'proletarian internationalism'. Even in 1968, the change of rulers at the top of the KSČ was initially greeted with customary—if rather quiet—approval in the chief SED newspaper, *Neues Deutschland*.[17] As a Slovak and longstanding party apparatchik, Alexander Dubček was regarded as a 'centrist' who was capable of restoring some kind of equilibrium between the Czech and Slovak halves of the ČSSR while taking cautious steps towards modernisation of the Czechoslovak economy. Moreover, SED first secretary Walter Ulbricht had little time for Dubček's predecessor, Novotný, considering him to be an 'incorrigible "dogmatist"'.[18] There was as yet no hint in East Berlin of any desire to interfere in the new course adopted by the KSČ's Central Committee at its 5 January plenum.

Within a matter of weeks, however, the SED leadership began to show deep unease at some of the changes being proposed by figures close to Dubček, in particular the move towards greater freedoms in the cultural and economic spheres. Top level internal party discussions and memoranda raised concerns that the KSČ was in danger of being taken over by counter-revolutionary elements who were planning to loosen Czechoslovakia's ties with the other Warsaw Pact countries and abandon the country's commitment to a common military defence of Eastern Europe's post-1945 borders. The spectre of a re-run of Hungary in 1956 loomed large in such reports, as did the possibility that the KSČ might open out to the West German regime, heralding the prospect of a unilateral Czechoslovak recognition of the government in Bonn.[19] Signs that the new rulers in Prague intended to experiment with a wide-reaching rehabilitation programme for communist and non-communist victims of the purges and political show trials of the early 1950s also rang particular alarm bells in East Berlin, not least as the GDR itself had only engaged in a very limited form of de-Stalinisation after 1953/56 and held any critical discussion of the Stalin era to be potentially damaging to its own legitimacy.[20]

Over the next few months the East German leadership repeatedly drew attention to the dangers of a rapprochement between West Germany and Czechoslovakia and the threat this posed to existing border arrangements (and therefore to peace and security) across the region. The FRG and its media were accused of deliberately exploiting the democratisation measures within the KSČ in order to launch a new form of 'psychological warfare'.[21] Or as Ulbricht put it at a summit of Warsaw Pact leaders (without Romania) in Dresden on 23 March 1968, the course taken by the reform communists in Prague was handing 'the enemy material for a campaign against [all] the socialist countries', not least the GDR.[22] Particularly worrying in this respect was evidence of a secret meeting in Prague on 17–19 April 1968 between Czechoslovak leaders and Egon Bahr, a senior figure in the SPD who was close to Brandt.[23] The meeting took place just one week after the KSČ published its 'Action Programme', which announced, among other things, that the ČSSR would henceforth 'pursue a more active European policy' and promote 'mutually advantageous relations with all states'.[24] This was of course completely at odds with the SED's understanding of the meaning of 'proletarian internationalism', whereby solidarity between socialist countries and a common commitment to upholding existing alignments in Europe were considered to be sacrosanct.

Given such hostile views of the Prague Spring, which were shared by Ulbricht's successor-in-waiting, Erich Honecker, by the East German ambassador in Prague, Peter Florin, and by the Minister of State

Security, Erich Mielke and his deputy, Bruno Beater, it is perhaps not surprising that the SED leadership was fully behind the Soviet-led invasion that took place four months later.[25] After 21 August, the official state media even sought to give the impression that troops from the East German army, the NVA (*Nationale Volksarmee*), had been directly deployed across the GDR's southern frontier into Czechoslovakia as part of 'Operation Danube'. In fact, after 1989 it turned out that this claim was false: intelligence and reconnaissance efforts aside, the NVA's involvement had effectively been restricted to securing the Czech-East German border and providing logistical assistance to the invading Soviet forces. Even so, the GDR had played a crucial part in background preparations for military action, and two armed divisions of the NVA had been ready to cross into Czechoslovakia alongside combat troops from the USSR, Poland, Hungary and Bulgaria, until ordered at a very late stage by Moscow to stay put in East Germany.[26] Even after this, there was virtually unanimous agreement within the leaderships of both the NVA and the SED that the Warsaw Pact invasion was necessary in order to 'safeguard peace' and preserve the socialist order across the region.[27] Shortly before his death in 2002, Werner Eberlein, a senior SED functionary who became first party secretary in Magdeburg in 1983 and a Politburo member in 1986, repeated the view that the KSČ had in effect abandoned communism in the spring and summer of 1968, with Šik's proposed economic reforms pointing almost certainly to the eventual restoration of capitalism on Czechoslovak soil.[28]

There is still some controversy about Ulbricht's exact motives in 1968, and in particular whether he was in favour of a full-scale military strike from the outset, or rather preferred a political solution up until the final decision to invade was announced to assembled Warsaw Pact leaders in the Kremlin on 18 August 1968. Much attention has focused on his meeting with Dubček at Karlovy Vary six days earlier, on 12 August 1968. Here he exhorted Dubček to take back control of the mass media in Czechoslovakia, but otherwise refrained from drawing overt attention to ideological disagreements between the SED and the KSČ.[29] At a bizarre joint press conference held on the following day he confessed to having been surprised when it was announced, on 26 June, that the ČSSR had formally abolished censorship of the press. 'When we learned [about this] … we were astonished, because we have never known anything like this. We have never had press censorship [in the GDR], and, as you can see, we have got along quite well without [it]'.[30]

One interpretation of Ulbricht's behaviour is that he feared that too much liberalisation in Czechoslovakia, particularly if it provoked Soviet military intervention, would take the shine off his own economic reforms in the GDR, which he intended to present as a 'model' for other Warsaw Pact states to follow.[31] Ulbricht believed that his 'New Economic System of Planning and Leadership', launched in 1963 and renamed the 'Economic System of Socialism' in 1967, would make a 'decisive contribution' both to the modernisation of socialism and to the renewal of Marxist-Leninist ideology.[32] Science and technology, partly imported from the West, were harnessed with the aim of generating improvements in productivity, while some aspects of the administrative-command system were relaxed without letting go of key instruments of party control. The problem in Czechoslovakia, from this point of view, was that the reformers there were presenting a more radical vision of how to shape a modern industrial society under socialism, a vision that deviated substantially and dangerously from established Leninist norms. At the earlier-mentioned meeting of Warsaw Pact leaders in Dresden in March 1968, Ulbricht had already given an answer as to why he thought this had happened in the ČSSR in particular: 'Because for 10 years no ideological battle has been fought there, no systematic ideological fight, not for 10 years! This is a fact'.[33]

However, a more straightforward explanation for Ulbricht's stance at Karlovy Vary is his fear that the step-by-step removal of barriers to freedom of expression in Czechoslovakia not only represented a betrayal of Leninism, but would also damage the international reputation of the GDR and its claim to be a separate—and more progressive—German state. It would legitimise internal opposition, including from figures like the East German chemist Robert Havemann who had been expelled from the SED in 1964 after publicly criticising aspects of party dogmatism. Combined with a renewed push to rehabilitate the victims of Stalinist terror, it would lead to a permanent airing of grievances and a constant reiteration of the mistakes of the past. Even before 1968, artists and writers in the ČSSR were given too much freedom to criticise or to engage in 'decadent' forms of subjectivity and introspection, distracting them from their true task of 'engineering' the souls of the future.[34] On the other hand, Ulbricht remained convinced that a strong, centrist and ideologically steadfast Czechoslovak regime, open to socialist forms of economic modernisation but committed to combating all surviving remnants of 'bourgeois' ideology in society, culture and relations of production, was essential for the realisation of his strategy to achieve Western recognition of the GDR. The only way of countering Dubček's reformist brand of socialism and ending the threat of counter-revolution on the GDR's southern border was to apply further pressure on the KSČ leadership—short of military intervention if possible, but by force of arms if necessary.

On the Eve of the Invasion

When the leaders of the 'Warsaw Pact five' met for crisis talks in the Polish capital on 14–15 July 1968, and again in Bratislava on 3 August, this time with Czechoslovak officials present, military action was clearly on the cards. Indeed, it was explicitly demanded by Bulgarian party leader Todor Zhivkov in Warsaw on 15 July, although for the time being this option was postponed. Instead, Leonid Brezhnev followed Ulbricht's recommendation that the Czechoslovak Central Committee be sent an open letter offering 'fraternal' advice on the internal measures required to counter the present 'counter-revolutionary' threat.[35] When the so-called 'Warsaw Letter' did not produce the desired response, the armed forces and internal security organs of all five countries were placed on a state of high alert.[36]

In East Berlin, fears of an existential threat to state security should communism be dismantled in the ČSSR merged with more immediate concerns about the exposure of young people to the ideas of the Prague Spring. The 'guarded liberalization' introduced in the GDR after 1963 in respect to youth policy had already been put into reverse in October 1965, when hundreds of young 'beat music' fans clashed with police in Leipzig following a decision by the district authorities to withdraw performance licences from local bands.[37] The new campaign against Western 'beat music' was reinforced by a crackdown on cultural dissent and 'American-inspired immorality and decadence' announced by Honecker at the eleventh plenum of the SED's Central Committee in December 1965.[38] From 1966 Department 2 of the Stasi's Main Department XX (*Hauptabteilung* XX), which dealt with political underground movements, was handed new responsibilities for guarding over youth and educational establishments.[39] Nonetheless, in 1968 'subversive' political ideas were still able to make their way across the border, either via informal contacts in holiday spots and summer camps in the GDR or through East German returnees from trips to the ČSSR bringing back illicit pro-Dubček or West German publications with them.[40] One of the most feared documents was the 'Two Thousand Words Manifesto', penned by the Czech writer Ludvík Vaculík and published on 27 June 1968, which called for a summer of protest action in favour of freedom of speech and against those communist officials who were resisting change: 'It took several months before many of us believed it was safe to speak up; many of us still do not think it is safe. But speak up we did, exposing ourselves to the extent that we have no choice but to complete our plan to humanize the regime'.[41] Equally alarming was an article written by East German dissident Robert Havemann that appeared in the West German newspaper *Die Zeit* on 31 May 1968 and made clear his sympathies for the Dubček line:

> A crucial part of democracy is democratic control of the government from below. This means the right to express opposition, whether in public, in the press, radio and television, or in parliament … I believe that the resolution of the German question in the interests of socialism and democracy will be unimaginably quickened and eased if the path which the CSSR is currently taking is also pursued by us [in the GDR].[42]

Calls for greater freedoms to air specific grievances against the existing system were already being heard in East German universities, as Stasi reports from 1967 and 1968 indicate.[43] On several campuses after March 1968, students and professors were denounced by police informers or members of the official youth organisation, the FDJ (*Freie Deutsche Jugend*), for voicing open support for Dubček or at least for arguing that the Czechoslovaks should be allowed to pursue their own path to socialism free from outside interference.[44] A hard-line anti-Dubček speech made by SED ideology chief Kurt Hager at a philosophy congress on 25 March 1968 led a handful of opposition youth activists in Leipzig to circulate flysheets calling for democratic change under the slogan: 'Doktrinäre in den Ruhestand! Rehabilitierung für Prof. Havemann!' ('Send the dogmatists into retirement! Rehabilitation for Prof. Havemann!').[45] The influence of the Prague Spring, and/or the Western media, was also blamed for the almost 6% of the electorate who had voted no or abstained in the referendum on the new East German constitution in April, and in particular for the 'hostile-negative' behaviour of some of the students at Berlin's Humboldt University, who had peppered pro-'yes' posters with the catchphrase 'ČSSR—our role model'.[46] Yet solidarity between young people on both sides of the border could also express itself in less directly political ways, for instance in a common liking for Western bands and accompanying clothes and lifestyles.[47] For the Stasi this too was a matter of tangible concern. In late July 1968, for instance, rumours that a Rolling Stones concert was due to take place in Prague at an unspecified date prompted the deputy Minister of State Security, Beater, to send instructions to all administrative districts (*Bezirke*) asking them to put measures in place to stop young people from travelling to the Czechoslovak capital, especially those whose 'outward appearance suggests a proclivity to rowdy behaviour, who have previous criminal convictions, or who look like they would not represent the GDR in a worthy fashion'.[48]

The link drawn between policing 'beat music' fans at home and efforts to limit or monitor unofficial contacts between East German and Czechoslovak youths is a clear illustration of the Stasi's own implacable opposition to 'liberalisation' of any kind. Nonetheless, it was also the result of a genuine fear that developments in Prague could take a violent turn, as they had done in Poland and then Hungary in 1956, with the GDR and the socialist order across Eastern Europe subsequently put at risk. This can be seen most vividly in a report written by a group of undercover Stasi officers from Department VIII of the Magdeburg district administration who visited Karlovy Vary and Prague on a fact-finding mission on 17–19 August 1968, on the very eve of the invasion. It is worth citing here at length because of the insights it gives into the mentality of those who were responsible for organising the crackdown on internal dissent after 21 August.

The report painted a picture of a socialist regime in a state of rapid dissolution and vulnerable to penetration by Western media and intelligence outlets. This was already evident as the officers crossed the frontier into the ČSSR from Schmilka in Saxony (*Bezirk* Dresden). Czechoslovak border guards and customs officials were reportedly lax in their control of travel documents. Worse still were the scenes in the border zone between West Germany and the ČSSR near Cheb, which was supposed to be a restricted area (a *Sperrgebiet*). Here the Stasi officers observed 'several meetings between GDR and West German citizens ... Both groups came in private cars which they parked up in more remote roads or country lanes'. Meanwhile, units of the Czechoslovak army encountered *en route* to Karlovy Vary and Prague 'left an unmilitary and disorderly impression, accentuated by their [slovenly] haircuts and dress code'.[49] A strike by NATO forces would meet with very little patriotic-military opposition from the Czech side of the border, it was implied.

In Prague itself, the officers came across crowds of up to two hundred 'unkempt youths' at Wenceslas Square. Next to them was a VW bus belonging to the West German TV station 'Sender Freies Berlin' (SFB), equipped with cameras and staffed by reporters who engaged in conversations with passers-by of all ages. In other parts of the city spontaneous 'meetings' of anywhere between fifty and seventy youths at a time were taking place. Their behaviour was of a highly sexualised nature: 'They ... kissed each other on the street and embraced each other in a very intimate way, without any regard to who was observing them'. Their appearance was 'scruffy' and 'dirty' and their minds had apparently been poisoned by Western ideas:

> The show cases in front of cinemas advertised mostly western films, with sex and crime being the dominant themes. Among others, the British film 'Help', with the Beatles, 'Old Shatterhand' from West Germany, 'Quyenne' from America but also the [East German] DEFA film 'Heroin' were being shown ... Western newspapers, apart from communist ones, were not openly on sale, but many passers-by could be seen holding them and they are somehow getting [into the country] ... Many shops were offering postcards of western actors. Postcards depicting members of the Czechoslovak government, especially [Ludvík] Svoboda, and figures from Czech history, were also on sale.[50]

Two men, a West German and a Czech, approached the officers after noticing their East German number plates, and spoke to them 'in a ... quite insolent and brazen manner'. The conversation turned threatening when the Czech man told them that the division of Germany was all the fault of the 'Spitzbart', the nickname commonly given to Ulbricht because of his goatee beard. West Germans were to be found everywhere in central Prague, as were Czech 'Gammlertypen', young layabouts without any obvious work to do. Furthermore, while 'the majority of the population did not seem to be at all impressed by these negative apparitions', they did not appear to be doing anything to oppose them either, but rather went about their daily lives in a 'very carefree ... and aimless' way.[51]

Finally, the officers were keen to emphasise the difference in living standards between the ČSSR and the GDR. The economic reforms in Czechoslovakia were unbalanced, leading to a 'stark contrast between those cities that have become a magnet for tourists, and smaller towns, mainly in the border regions, which appear bleak and deserted'. The beneficiaries were few and far between, apart from Westerners looking for a cheap holiday. Even they could not afford the more expensive hotels in Prague and Karlovy Vary, meaning that many rooms were left vacant.[52] The welfare of ordinary Czechoslovak citizens and the duty of the state to inculcate in them a positive enthusiasm for socialist work and discipline, international proletarian solidarity and military defence against the 'imperialist' powers had been ignored, was the implication, while Ulbricht's reforms in the GDR had produced a more prosperous, modernised, future-oriented economy—which was nonetheless placed in jeopardy by dint of having such an unstable neighbour on its southern border. The situation was deeply alarming, but interestingly the authors of the report did not suggest any immediate remedies, and clearly did not know what was about to happen next.

The Aftermath of the Invasion

In the hours immediately following the invasion of 20–21 August, the SED Central Committee issued a joint communiqué with the East German Council of State and Council of Ministers defending the Warsaw Pact's operation as a necessary act to prevent 'the overthrow of socialism and the installation of a pro-Western, pro-imperialist, state capitalist regime in Czechoslovakia'.[53] At the same time, the Stasi began to broaden the scope of what was known as 'Operation Genesung' ('Operation Recovery'), the codename for a set of measures designed to safeguard the GDR internally from pro-reform ideas brought into the country by Czechoslovak visitors and/or promoted by East German sympathisers. As Mielke explained in a letter to the heads of all operational departments on 27 August 1968, the aim was to document '[h]ostile actions by citizens of the CSSR and other patterns of behaviour which indicate an oppositional attitude towards the GDR, the socialist camp and all progressive forces'. Particular attention was to be paid to 'incidents on the state border [between the] GDR and [the] CSSR, on GDR territory … [and] in the CSSR, as well as in West Germany, West Berlin and other non-socialist countries'.[54]

In *Bezirk* Magdeburg the Stasi collected regular reports on popular opinion in the first few weeks after the invasion.[55] One area of concern was the road and rail crossing into West Germany at Marienborn-Helmstedt. Employees of the East German railway, the Reichsbahn, for instance, were allegedly greeted on arrival at Helmstedt on 21 August with open hostility from their West German counterparts. This took various forms, from references to Hitler's 1938 annexation of the Sudetenland to tongue-in-cheek accusations that NVA soldiers had only taken part in the invasion because they wanted to try out the beer in Plzeň.[56] One East German train driver was greeted with the taunt: 'What are you doing still turning up here? You are one of the 100 per cent-ers [i.e. totally loyal supporters of the GDR, M.S.] so why aren't you joining the others going to the CSSR?'.[57] Trusted East German lorry drivers returning from trips to the West 'unanimously reported that they were abused and threatened' while driving through the FRG.[58] One day after the invasion a student from West Berlin was stopped at the German–German border because he was displaying a pro-Dubček poster in his car window. After a thorough search he was found to be in possession of 'inflammatory literature' from the West German Socialist Student Society (SDS) criticising the 'measures taken by the Warsaw Pact countries'.[59]

Among East Germans living in *Bezirk* Magdeburg, the most common complaint after 21 August was the inadequacy of reporting in the official GDR media, forcing people to rely on Western news outlets.[60] Women factory workers in particular were identified as being anxious for husbands and sons serving in the NVA, especially as they had no idea of their whereabouts.[61] Instances of panic buying (*Angsteinkäufe*) in shops were reported across the district.[62] The NVA's apparent involvement in the invasion was criticised for the damage that it might do to the GDR's reputation as an anti-militarist, peace-loving state. Indeed, this was a more common sentiment than expressions of direct support for Dubček's reform-style communism. Already by 22 August voices were heard in some parts of *Bezirk* Magdeburg that the invasion was a 'reflection of the weakness, rather than the strength of the socialist camp'.[63] Knowledge of the critical stance taken by the ruling communist parties in Romania, Albania and Yugoslavia, and also by some communist parties in Western Europe, particularly the French and Italian, gave rise to renewed uncertainty.[64] Even more confusion was caused in late August by the decision on Moscow's part to allow most of the kidnapped leaders of the reform wing of the KSČ, including Dubček, Josef Smrkovský and Oldřich Černík, to remain in office after the conclusion of lengthy discussions in the Kremlin. Magdeburgers wondered what this meant, especially as the same reformers had been denounced as 'counter-revolutionaries' in the official GDR media in the immediate aftermath of the invasion.[65]

The exact number of East Germans arrested and interrogated for political offences after 20 August—including for acts such as distributing illegal flysheets, painting pro-Dubček or anti-Soviet slogans on walls, verbally abusing members of the *Volkspolizei* (People's Police), making drunken insults against Ulbricht or, more rarely, carrying out minor acts of sabotage against the NVA or Red Army forces stationed in the GDR—is difficult to establish with any certainty. In the Stasi files for the Magdeburg district, information exists on twenty-nine individuals held between 24 August and 15 September.[66] Across the whole GDR, some 1290 people had been placed under formal investigation for 'anti-state activities' by the end of November 1968, with 506 cases handled by the Stasi's criminal case review department (Main Department IX) and 784 by the *Volkspolizei*, the transport police or military prosecutors.[67] Both the Magdeburg and the GDR-wide Stasi sources indicate that at least two-thirds of those who were picked up by state security organs were under 25 years of age, with a preponderance of young men born between 1945 and 1950. Interestingly, students and intellectuals made up only a small proportion of the total, indeed less than 10% in both sets of figures. There was also no evidence of any organised networks of protestors, only isolated acts carried out by individuals or small groups whose expressions of frustration with the socialist system were more or less spontaneous, and often alcohol-induced.[68] In respect to the 506 cases investigated by Main Department IX of the Stasi, the largest group was made up of skilled workers (37.3%), followed by unskilled workers (19.9%) and apprentices (14.5%).[69] If young working-class men were most prominent among those arrested for overt acts of opposition, however, unease at the invasion could be found among both sexes and all age groups, including those who were old enough to have direct personal memories of 1939, 1953 and 1956.[70]

As part of 'Operation Genesung', attention shifted from early September 1968 towards a more targeted campaign aimed at identifying and isolating those East German citizens who 'openly or covertly glorify the counter-revolutionary goings-on in the CSSR'.[71] Some court cases were pursued by state prosecutors, and jail terms handed out, although again it is difficult to say how many individuals were affected. In late October 1968 *Neues Deutschland* provided details on two cases brought against a group of seven young people in East Berlin whose parents belonged to the political and academic elite or were prominent dissidents. Among them were 18-year-old Frank Havemann and 16-year-old Florian Havemann, sons of Robert Havemann; 23-year-old Thomas Brasch, son of the deputy Minister for Culture Horst Brasch; Sandra Weigel, the 20-year-old grand-daughter of the actress (and widow of Bertolt Brecht) Helene Weigel; and Erika Berthold, the 18-year-old daughter of Lothar Berthold, director of the SED's Institute for Marxism-Leninism.[72] While this group eventually had their sentences suspended, less well-known figures had to serve their jail terms in full, usually on top of extended periods spent in pre-trial detention. In practice, though, the overall prison population did not rise significantly in 1968–69 and there was no return to the 'open' political terror practiced in the late 1940s and 1950s.[73] Part of the reason for this may have been fears that high visibility trials would be exploited by the West German press.[74]

As an alternative to judicial methods, various forms of 'hidden' psychological pressure were placed on known critics of the Warsaw Pact invasion from the academic, trade union, media and cultural worlds that were designed to isolate them from colleagues, damage their professional reputations and dissuade them from engaging in 'subversive' activities.[75] Among serving members of the NVA who were caught up in the protests or who in some way criticised the invasion, twenty were given jail sentences between 1968 and 1970, while many more were demoted or subjected to internal disciplinary procedures, with lasting effects on their careers.[76] There was also a purge of suspected oppositional elements from the SED's own ranks, albeit nothing like on the scale witnessed at various points in the late 1940s and 1950s (especially in 1948–49, 1951, 1953 and 1956–58). By the end of 1968, according to a report produced by the Central Party Control Commission, a total of 3358 members and candidate members had been investigated for displaying 'hostile-negative' attitudes towards the Warsaw Pact's military intervention in Czechoslovakia. Of these, 522 received some kind of formal sanction: 223 were expelled from the party (including twenty serving members of the NVA), fifty-five had their membership cancelled, 109 received a 'severe reprimand' and 135 a 'lesser reprimand'. Informal warnings were given to a further 297. In 1961 total membership of the SED stood at 1.61 million, in 1967 at 1.77 million and in 1971 at 1.91 million, so that the vast majority of ordinary party activists were unaffected.[77]

One lasting concern was over the 'political-ideological situation' among students, with the SED Politburo commissioning a special report from the Central Committee on this theme, which it received and endorsed on 28 January 1969. The report concluded that the student body as a whole had behaved loyally in the wake of developments in 1968. Indeed, to some extent students still represented, as they had in the 1950s and early 1960s, the most politically reliable segment of young people. Nonetheless, certain 'backlogs' were also noted 'in the work of the party and the FDJ'. A minority of students had fallen prey to 'bourgeois-philosophical ideas, for instance those advanced by Kafka, Marcuse, Sartre, Böll [and] Enzensberger', while others were showing an unhealthy interest in 'radical left [*linksoppositionellen*] theories, especially those adopted by students in West Germany and other capitalist countries'. The result was 'that the events in the CSSR and the remedial action taken [by the Warsaw Pact] are not always judged from the viewpoint of their class character, and in particular from the perspective of the intensifying international struggle between socialism and capitalism'.[78]

At first sight this interest in students may seem strange, as the Stasi's own analyses of arrest statistics, which it also presented to the higher bodies of the party, made clear that the majority of youths detained for political offences in the wake of the invasion were not students, but young workers and apprentices.[79] Nonetheless, the focus on students makes sense in relation to the SED's understanding of the long-term 'causes' of the Prague Spring (and of events in Warsaw in March 1968), and the manner in which similar threats to the socialist order might be countered in the future. The expansion of higher education and skilled technical jobs in the 1960s gave rise to concerns about the emergence of a new class of technocrats who wished to separate science and the production of new knowledge from Cold War politics and the class struggle—for instance by arguing that East Germany should have stayed out of the Warsaw Pact's measures for pragmatic reasons even when they recognised that military action against the Prague Spring had been justified in a formal political and geo-strategic sense.[80] These technocrats were considered to be a bigger threat than the small number of students who criticised the Soviet intervention on radical leftist or pacifist grounds, for example by comparing it with US aggression in Vietnam; and the even tinier minority who looked for ways of 'improving' socialism and re-energising anti-fascist 'praxis' within the metaphysical realm of Marxist (or Hegelian) theories about 'alienation'.[81] This is because, as the Central Committee report put it, in their 'false' belief in the inter-dependence of different scientific models and their calls for a more open 'information policy', the new class of 'apolitical' technocrats were displaying ignorance of the 'power question', or rather the 'global design pursued by imperialism in its struggle against the socialist system across the world'.[82]

Even so, numbers expelled from universities or jailed in the aftermath of August 1968 were relatively small. In total 127 disciplinary proceedings were launched, with particular concerns focused on the fourth year of the mathematics course at Halle, the chemistry students at the Technical College in Merseburg-Leuna, the information technology course at the Technical University in Dresden, and the history department at the Humboldt University in Berlin.[83] Twenty-nine students were investigated for attempting to flee to the West, and nineteen were reported to have successfully escaped. A further forty-five were arrested for other offences in connection with the events of August 1968.[84] The main solution was to be found in the isolation of perceived trouble-makers and a rejuvenation of ideological work among the main body of students. This also helped to pave the way for the more conservative political climate under Honecker, particularly in the late 1970s and 1980s, whereby ideological separation (*Abgrenzung*) from the West was combined with a greater emphasis on improved methods of cadre selection, the expansion of military training in schools and institutes of higher education, and the creation of a GDR-specific form of state patriotism.[85]

Conclusion

In his 2008 study *Der Traum von der Revolte*, Stefan Wolle points to the paradox that in East Germany in 1968 'little or nothing happened' on a grand scale and the fact that this year still appears as a significant turning point in the biographies of many individuals, especially members of what he calls the GDR's 'middle generation', namely those born in or around the years 1945–50. The 'dream of revolt', he contends, or rather the dream of a democratised socialism, continued to be borne by many of this generation—in fact, *his* generation—'right through to the autumn of 1989'.[86] It also played a bigger role than is often recognised in the dissident movements that began to emerge in the late 1970s and 1980s to create what Mike Dennis refers to as an 'alternative political culture … articulated outside official channels' and focused on new causes such as peace, environmental protection and human, women's and gay rights.[87]

Whether August 1968 was a more important staging post in the fall of the GDR than other points, such as August 1961 (building of the Berlin Wall) or November 1976 (the dissident songwriter Wolf Biermann's summary deprivation of GDR citizenship) would seem doubtful, however.[88] The evidence presented in this chapter would suggest that while the invasion of August 1968 deeply unsettled many East Germans, it did not lead to organised protests or to a sense that sustained opposition 'from below' might bring eventual changes to the system. It is true that the regime instigated a series of harsh measures against individuals and small groups who voiced their rejection of the official explanation for the crushing of the Prague Spring. When Czech student Jan Palach set himself on fire on 16 January 1969 in protest against the erosion of Dubček's reform agenda, the Stasi's Main Department XX ordered an immediate launching of 'heightened political-operative measures' in all East German universities and institutes of higher learning, with particular attention to be paid to individuals who had already come to attention during the previous year's 'Operation Genesung'.[89] A new department, Department XX/7, was also created later that year to guard over intellectuals and the cultural sector.[90] Nonetheless, while the regime remained committed to discrediting dissenters and isolating them professionally and socially, the relatively small number of people who were criminalised for political acts by being placed in front of courts would also suggest a reluctance to create martyrs. Indeed, more artists and intellectuals were arrested, placed on publication blacklists, deported to the FRG, harassed by the Stasi or expelled from the East German Writers' Association for protesting on behalf of Biermann in 1976 than for criticising the Soviet-led invasion in 1968.[91]

What 1968 signalled, above all else, was the commitment of the higher echelons of the SED to a hard-line version of Marxism-Leninism, one that precluded any engagement with the cosmopolitan, European-integrative agenda set out in the KSČ's April 1968 'Action Programme'. The closer economic relations forged with West Germany after the signing of the Basic Treaty between the FRG and the GDR in 1972 did nothing to change this, other than confirming the paradigm shift in official policy on the 'German question'—from Ulbricht's notion of 'one nation in two states' to Honecker's emphasis on the creation of a distinct 'socialist German nation' with its own past and future trajectories. The historian Ernst Engelberg took this thinking to its logical conclusion in his Bismarck biography in 1985. Bismarck's unification of Germany belonged to the progressive phenomena that paved the way for the creation of the GDR and the concentration of power in the hands of the working class, he argued.[92] Czechoslovakia, on the other hand, did not seem to have any 'progressive' moments in its historical past, at least until the 'power question' was settled in favour of communism in 1948. Before 1989, alternative left-wing narratives of recent Central European history were scarcely possible in East Germany, even if the cause of democratic socialism remained close to the hearts of at least some members of the '1945–50 generation' who had been inspired by the example of the Prague Spring in 1968.

NOTES

1. E. Engelberg, 'Bericht über meine Reise nach Wien zu dem internationalen Symposium "Österreich-Ungarn und die 1. Internationale" vom 6.9 bis 13.9.1964', 1 October 1964, p. 4, in Stiftung Archiv der Parteien und Massenorganisationen der ehemaligen DDR im Bundesarchiv (SAPMO-BArch), DY 30/IV A2/9.04/334. Engelberg had also clearly read Mommsen's work, *Die Sozialdemokratie und die Nationalitätenfrage im habsburgischen Vielvölkerstaat* (Vienna, 1963).
2. In particular this is a reference to Engels' famous articles in the *Neue Rheinische Zeitung* in 1848–49 in which he insisted that only the 'historic nations' of Central Europe, the Germans, Magyars, Italians and Poles, were destined to play a vital role in the revolutionary movement from feudalism to capitalism to socialism. See C.C. Herod, *The Nation in the History of Marxian Thought: The Concept of Nations with History and Nations without History* (The Hague, 1976).
3. E. Engelberg, *Bismarck: Urpreuße und Reichsgründer* (East Berlin, 1985), here pp. 761–2.
4. See, for instance, Mommsen's essay 'Nationalitätenfrage und Arbeiterbewegung in Mittel- und Osteuropa' (1971), reproduced in Mommsen, *Arbeiterbewegung und nationale Frage: Ausgewählte Aufsätze* (Göttingen, 1979), pp. 81–101, in which he also cites the works of several Czechoslovak colleagues, including František Jordán, Jiří Kořalka and Zdeněk Šolle. All of the latter were strong supporters of Dubček's reforms in 1968, and at least two of them, Kořalka and Šolle, faced long-term bans on publishing in the wake of the post-1969 'normalisation' process in Czechoslovakia. See also J. Connelly, *Captive University:*

The Sovietization of East German, Czech, and Polish Higher Education, 1945–1956 (Chapel Hill, NC and London, 2000), p. 190.
5. See M. Górny, *The Nation Should Come First: Marxism and Historiography in East Central Europe* (Frankfurt-am-Main, 2013), esp. pp. 42–5.
6. Engelberg, 'Bericht über meine Reise', p. 4.
7. Ibid., p. 5.
8. C. Kleßmann (ed.), *Zwei Staaten, eine Nation: Deutsche Geschichte, 1955–1970* (Göttingen, 1988); T. Lindenberger, 'Divided, but not Disconnected: Germany as a Border Region of the Cold War', in T. Hochscherf, C. Laucht and A. Plowman (eds), *Divided, but not Disconnected: German Experiences of the Cold War* (Oxford and New York, 2010), pp. 11–33.
9. Engelberg, 'Bericht über meine Reise', p. 5. See also J. Kořalka, *Severočeští socialisté v čele dělnického hnutí českých a rakouských zemí* (Liberec, 1963).
10. Lindenberger, 'Divided, but not Disconnected', p. 12.
11. *Statistisches Jahrbuch der Deutschen Demokratischen Republik*, edited by the Staatliche Zentralverwaltung für Statistik, Vol. 13 (East Berlin, 1968), p. 12.
12. See S. Wolle, *Der Traum von der Revolte: Die DDR 1968* (Berlin, 2008), esp. pp. 24–34.
13. See, for instance, H. Kröger, *'Neue' Ostpolitik in Bonn?* (East Berlin, 1967); H. Barth, *Bonner Ostpolitik gegen Frieden und Sicherheit: Zur Ostpolitik des westdeutschen Imperialismus von Adenauer und Erhard bis zu Strauß/Kiesinger* (East Berlin, 1969).
14. On the 1967 Karlovy Vary conference, see J.G. Kerr, *The Road to Helsinki: An Analysis of European International Relations Leading to the Conference on Security and Cooperation in Europe* (Bloomington, IN, 2015), pp. 13–15. The Romanian and Yugoslav communist parties were conspicuously absent from the proceedings, but some West European communist parties attended. Other principles established at the conference included the demand that the FRG not be given its own or jointly controlled nuclear weapons, and that the 1938 Munich agreement be declared unlawful from the outset, in opposition to the West German claim that it had simply been superseded by events.
15. In 1967–68, 2.6 million East Germans travelled to the ČSSR, and 1.1 million Czechoslovaks made trips to the GDR. See T.S. Brown, 'East Germany', in M. Klimke and J. Scharloth (eds), *1968 in Europe: A History of Protest and Activism, 1956–1977* (Basingstoke, 2008), pp. 189–97 (here p. 194).
16. See, for instance, the concerns expressed by Günter Witt, deputy Minister of Culture and leader of the GDR delegation to the XIV International Film Festival in Karlovy Vary, in a report to the SED Politburo, 13

August 1964. Copy in SAPMO-BArch, DY 30/IV A 2/9.01/27. Also G. Erbe, *Die verfemte Moderne: Die Auseinandersetzung mit dem 'Modernismus' in Kulturpolitik, Literaturwissenschaft und Literatur der DDR* (Opladen, 1993).
17. See A. Mitter and S. Wolle, *Untergang auf Raten: Unbekannte Kapitel der DDR-Geschichte* (Munich, 1993), p. 421.
18. M. Frank, *Walter Ulbricht: Eine deutsche Biografie* (Berlin, 2001), p. 412; P. Grieder, *The East German Leadership, 1946–73: Conflict and Crisis* (Manchester, 1999), p. 174.
19. See the extensive discussion in L. Prieß, V. Kural and M. Wilke, *Die SED und der 'Prager Frühling' 1968: Politik gegen einen 'Sozialismus mit menschlichem Antlitz'* (Berlin, 1996), esp. pp. 37–71.
20. On this issue see M. Stibbe, 'The Limits of Rehabilitation: The 1930s Stalinist Terror and its Legacy in post-1953 East Germany', in K. McDermott and M. Stibbe (eds), *De-Stalinising Eastern Europe: The Rehabilitation of Stalin's Victims after 1953* (Basingstoke, 2015), pp. 87–108.
21. Prieß et al., *Die SED*, p. 52.
22. Stenographic Account of the Dresden Meeting, 23 March 1968, reproduced in J. Navrátil et al. (eds), *The Prague Spring 1968: A National Security Archive Documents Reader* (Budapest, 1998), pp. 64–72 (here p. 69).
23. Report on Secret Discussions between the International Department of the KSČ's Central Committee and Egon Bahr of the West German Social Democratic Party, 17–19 April 1968, reproduced in ibid., pp. 108–11.
24. The KSČ's 'Action Programme', April 1968, reproduced in ibid., pp. 92–5 (here p. 95).
25. On Honecker and Florin see Prieß et al., *Die SED*, pp. 58–60, and on Beater, see I.-S. Kowalczuk, *Stasi konkret: Überwachung und Repression in der DDR* (Munich, 2013), pp. 146–7.
26. This, in particular, is the conclusion reached by Rüdiger Wenzke, the leading historian of the NVA. See, for instance, his essay 'The Role and Activities of the SED, the East German State and its Military during the "Prague Spring" of 1968', in M.M. Stolarik (ed.), *The Prague Spring and the Warsaw Pact Invasion of Czechoslovakia, 1968: Forty Years Later* (Mundelein, IL., 2010), pp. 137–64 (here pp. 151–8). Also his book, *Die NVA und der Prager Frühling 1968: Die Rolle Ulbrichts und der DDR –Streitkräfte bei der Niederschlagung der tschechoslowakischen Reformbewegung* (Berlin, 1995).
27. Wenzke, 'The Role and Activities', p. 153.
28. W. Eberlein, *Geboren am 9. November: Erinnerungen* (Berlin, 2000), p. 351.

29. Grieder, *The East German Leadership*, pp. 175–6.
30. Frank, *Walter Ulbricht*, p. 414; Wolle, *Der Traum von der Revolte*, p. 145.
31. M. E. Sarotte, *Dealing with the Devil: East Germany, Détente, and Ostpolitik, 1969–1973* (Chapel Hill, NC and London, 2001), pp. 17–21.
32. Prieß et al., *Die SED*, p. 53.
33. See note 22 above.
34. The phrase comes from Stalin—see F. Westerman, *Engineers of the Soul: The Grandiose Propaganda of Stalin's Russia* (London, 2010), p. 34. On Ulbricht's negative use of concepts like 'decadence' in relation to cultural policy, see also Erbe, *Die verfemte Moderne*, pp. 81–2.
35. K. Williams, *The Prague Spring and its Aftermath: Czechoslovak Politics, 1968–1970* (Cambridge, 1997), p. 119.
36. Wenzke, *Die NVA*, pp. 95–8; Prieß et al., *Die SED*, p. 195.
37. N. Frei, *1968: Jugendrevolte und globaler Protest* (Munich, 2008), pp. 203–4.
38. See also A. McDougall, *Youth Politics in East Germany: The Free German Youth Movement, 1946–1968* (Oxford, 2004), p. 200; M. Fenemore, *Sex, Thugs and Rock 'n'Roll: Teenage Rebels in Cold-War East Germany* (Oxford and New York, 2007), p. 32; M.-D. Ohse, '"Keinen Dubček, keinen Ulbricht": 1968 und die Jugend in der DDR', in A. Ebbinghaus (ed.), *Die letzte Chance? 1968 in Osteuropa: Analysen und Berichte über ein Schlüsseljahr* (Hamburg, 2008), pp. 170–8 (here esp. pp. 172–3).
39. S. Schädlich, *Briefe ohne Unterschrift: Wie eine BBC-Sendung die DDR herausforderte* (Munich, 2017), p. 117.
40. According to information sent by Politburo member Albert Norden to Ulbricht on 26 July 1968, the number of East German visitors to the ČSSR had reached 244,000 in June 1968 and 154,000 in the first half of July. In addition 214,000 Czechoslovaks had entered the GDR in June and 90,000 in the first half of July. See Wolle, *Der Traum von der Revolte*, p. 150.
41. The 'Two Thousand Words Manifesto', 27 June 1968, reproduced in Navrátil et al. (eds), *The Prague Spring*, pp. 177–81 (here p. 179).
42. R. Havemann, 'Sozialismus und Demokratie: Ein freisinniges Wort zu der Umwälzung in der Tschechoslawakei', *Die Zeit*, 31 May 1968, reproduced in Havemann, *Warum ich Stalinist war und Antistalinist wurde: Texte eines Unbequemen*, edited by D. Hoffmann and H. Laitko (Berlin, 1990), pp. 206–10 (here p. 209).
43. On the situation in East German universities, see Mitter and Wolle, *Untergang auf Raten*, pp. 400–9.
44. See also Wolle, *Der Traum von der Revolte*, pp. 127–30.
45. Ohse, '"Keinen Dubček, keinen Ulbricht"', p. 175.
46. On a turn-out of 98.05%, 94.49% voted 'yes', meaning that 5.62% of those entitled to vote either abstained or voted 'no'. In Berlin, the 'yes'

vote was only 90.96%. See Prieß et al., *Die SED*, p. 140; Kowalczuk, *Stasi konkret*, pp. 145–6; McDougall, *Youth Politics*, pp. 206 and 213.
47. As Dorothee Wierling argues, the self-consciously de-politicised nature of non-conformist youth culture in the GDR, which was a direct reaction to state domination of the political sphere, can be contrasted with the highly politicised nature of youth and student protests in West Germany and West Berlin in 1968—see D. Wierling, 'Opposition und Generation in Nachkriegsdeutschland: Achtundsechziger in der DDR und in der Bundesrepublik', in C. Kleßmann, H. Misselwitz and G. Wichert (eds), *Deutsche Vergangenheiten—eine gemeinsame Herausforderung: Der schwierige Umgang mit der doppelten Nachkriegsgeschichte* (Berlin, 1999), pp. 238–52 (here esp. pp. 243–6).
48. MfS Berlin/Stellvertreter des Ministers, Telegram, 24 July 1968. Copy in Der Bundesbeauftragte für die Unterlagen des Staatssicherheitsdienstes der ehemaligen Deutschen Demokratischen Republik (BStU), MfS, Bezirksverwaltung Magdeburg, AS 7/73, Bd. 7, Bl. 41.
49. Informationsbericht über eine Reise in die CSSR vom 17.08 bis 19.08.1968, 21 August 1968, in BStU, MfS, Bezirksverwaltung Magdeburg, AS 7/73, Bd. 3, Bl. 4–6 (here Bl. 4). Department VIII dealt with 'Enquiries and Observation'—see M. Dennis, *The Stasi: Myth and Reality* (London, 2003), p. 53.
50. Informationsbericht über eine Reise in die CSSR, Bl. 5.
51. Ibid., Bl. 6.
52. Ibid., Bl. 4–5.
53. Erklärung des ZK der SED, des Staatsrats und des Ministerrats der DDR zur Intervention in der ČSSR, *Neues Deutschland*, 21 August 1968, reproduced in Kleßmann (ed.), *Zwei Staaten, eine Nation*, pp. 586–7.
54. Schreiben Mielkes an die Leiter der Operative[n] Haupt-/selbst. Abteilungen im Hause, 27 August 1968, reproduced in M. Tantzscher (ed.), *Maßnahme 'Donau' und Einsatz 'Genesung': Die Niederschlagung des Prager Frühlings 1968/9 im Spiegel der MfS-Akten*, 2nd edn (Berlin, 1998), p. 103.
55. The reports can be found in BStU, MfS, Bezirksverwaltung Magdeburg, AS 7/73, Bd. 3 and Bd. 5.
56. Ibid., Bd. 3, Bl. 8 (Information, 21 August 1968).
57. Ibid., Bd. 3, Bl. 10 (Information, 22 August 1968).
58. Ibid., Bd. 5, Bl. 32 (Mood Report, 25 August 1968).
59. Ibid., Bd. 5, Bl. 72 (Mood Report, 6 September 1968).
60. Ibid., Bd. 5, Bl. 2, 8 and 53 (Mood Reports, 21 and 31 August 1968).
61. Ibid., Bd. 5, Bl. 5 and 41 (Mood Reports, 21 and 28 August 1968).
62. Ibid., Bd. 5, Bl. 7 and 20 (Mood Reports, 21 and 22 August 1968).
63. Ibid., Bd. 5, Bl. 13 (Mood Report, 22 August 1968).

64. Ibid., Bd. 5, Bl. 34, 59 and 66 (Mood Reports, 28 and 30 August, 5 September 1968).
65. Ibid., Bd. 5, Bl. 38 and 41 (Mood Reports, 27 and 28 August 1968). See also note 53 above.
66. See 'Inhaftierungen', n.d., in BStU, MfS, Bezirksverwaltung Magdeburg, AS 7/73, Bd. 7, Bl. 3–11.
67. Wolle, *Der Traum von der Revolte*, p. 160. The Stasi's HA IX (Main Department IX) was reponsible for 'criminal investigation and interrogation'—see Dennis, *The Stasi*, p. 54.
68. Wierling, 'Opposition und Generation', pp. 247–8; Brown, 'East Germany', pp. 191–2.
69. Einschätzung der HA IX zu den in Ermittlungsverfahren des MfS festgestellten Angriffen gegen die Hilfsmaßnahmen der fünf sozialistischen Bruderstaaten, 27 November 1968, reproduced in Tantzscher (ed.), *Maßnahme 'Donau'*, pp. 122–9 (here pp. 126–7).
70. Kowalczuk, *Stasi konkret*, p. 149; Brown, 'East Germany', p. 192.
71. Schreiben Mielkes an die Leiter der Bezirksverwaltungen ... etc., 2 September 1968, reproduced in Tantzscher (ed.), *Maßnahme 'Donau'*, pp. 117–19 (here p. 117).
72. On the members of this group, and in particular the gender roles within it, see U. Kätzel, 'Geschlechterrolle und das 1968er Aufbegehren in der DDR', in Ebbinghaus (ed.), *Die letzte Chance?*, pp. 183–94.
73. F. Werkentin, *Politische Strafjustiz in der Ära Ulbricht: Vom bekennenden Terror zur verdeckten Repression*, 2nd edn (Berlin, 1997), pp. 269–72.
74. Mitter and Wolle, *Untergang auf Raten*, pp. 453–5.
75. Werkentin, *Politische Strafjustiz*, pp. 275–7.
76. Wenzker, 'The Role and Activities', p. 163.
77. A. Malycha and P.J. Winters, *Die SED: Geschichte einer deutschen Partei* (Munich, 2009), pp. 189 and 415; Werkentin, *Politische Strafjustiz*, p. 274.
78. Information zur politisch-ideologischen Situation unter den Studenten, 28 January 1969, in BStU, MfS, Archiv der Zentralstelle, SED-KL, 828, Bl. 40–56 (here Bl. 41).
79. Wolle, *Der Traum von der Revolte*, p. 161; Werkentin, *Politische Strafjustiz*, pp. 267–8; Wenzker, 'The Role and Activities', p. 161; Wierling, 'Opposition und Generation', p. 247; Ohse, '"Keinen Dubček, keinen Ulbricht"', pp. 176–7; Frei, *1968*, p. 206.
80. See also Stimmung der Bevölkerung zur Lage in der CSSR, 18 September 1968, in BStU, MfS, Bezirksverwaltung Magdeburg, AS 7/73, Bd. 5, Bl. 76–8 (here Bl. 78).
81. See, for instance, the memoirs of Rita Kuczynski (b. 1944), a philosophy student at the Humboldt University in 1968, who notes that the idea of 'improving' socialism and overcoming the problem of 'alienation' at

universal/global level via immersion in Hegelian and early Marxist texts had a quite different meaning in East as opposed to West Germany. Indeed, while it could lead to calls for more internal democracy in the party and universities, and elicit some sympathy for the reforms of the Prague Spring, it was also quite compatible with the notion that GDR-style anti-fascism was *already* the most humane and progressive of all political systems, and with willing endorsement of the leading role of the SED in state and society. See R. Kuczynski, *Mauerblume: Ein Leben auf der Grenze* (Munich, 1999), esp. pp. 81–110.
82. Information zur politisch-ideologischen Situation unter den Studenten (as note 78), Bl. 44–5.
83. Ibid., Bl. 47.
84. Ibid., Bl. 56. Cf. Mitter and Wolle, *Untergang auf Raten*, pp. 475–6.
85. See C. Jordan, *Kaderschmiede Humboldt-Universität zu Berlin: Aufbegehren, Säuberungen und Militarisierung 1945–1989* (Berlin, 2001), esp. pp. 165–7 and 178–85; and A. Saunders, *Honecker's Children: Youth and Patriotism in East(ern) Germany, 1979–2002* (Manchester, 2007), esp. pp. 31–45.
86. Wolle, *Der Traum von der Revolte*, pp. 13–14.
87. Dennis, *The Stasi*, p. 157.
88. See also the sceptical views expressed by Wierling, 'Opposition und Generation', pp. 250–2; and Brown, 'East Germany', p. 194.
89. See Stellvertreter Operativ an alle Kreisdienststellen, Abteilung XX, 21 January 1969, in BStU, MfS, Bezirksverwaltung Magdeburg, AS 7/73, Bd. 7, Bl. 84–5.
90. Dennis, *The Stasi*, p. 32.
91. H. Weber, *Geschichte der DDR*, 2nd edn (Munich, 2000), pp. 304–7; S. Schädlich, *Immer wieder Dezember: Der Westen, die Stasi, der Onkel und ich* (Munich, 2009), pp. 29 and passim.; Kuczynski, *Mauerblume*, pp. 159–62.
92. Engelberg, *Bismarck*. See also Alan L. Nothnagle, *Building the East German Myth: Historical Mythology and Youth Propaganda in the German Democratic Republic, 1945-1989* (Ann Arbor, MI, 1999), pp. 186-8.

'To Hell with Sovereignty!': Poland and the Prague Spring

Tony Kemp-Welch

Political and social responses in Poland to the Prague Spring of 1968 can only be understood in relation to the developments of the preceding twelve years. On 25 February 1956, Nikita Khrushchev had famously denounced Stalin and his authoritarian rule at the concluding session of the Twentieth Congress of the Soviet Communist Party. Foreign delegates were excluded from the meeting, but, following the dissemination of the 'secret speech' to communist parties abroad, an English translation soon appeared.[1] Uniquely in the Soviet bloc, the ruling Polish United Workers' Party (PZPR) had the text translated and thousands of copies soon circulated, prompting a fervent nation-wide debate.[2] The year 1956 was the heyday of Polish revisionists who sought a post-Stalinist communism that did not depend on repression and coercion. Following a false start in June 1956 with the brutal suppression of the workers' 'Poznań uprising', the process culminated in the peaceful 'Polish October' when the hitherto disgraced reformist-communist, Władysław Gomułka, was reinstated as First Party Secretary with reluctant Soviet backing. Gomułka had been dismissed under Stalinism in

---

T. Kemp-Welch (✉)
School of History, University of East Anglia, Norwich, UK
e-mail: A.Kemp-welch@uea.ac.uk

© The Author(s) 2018
K. McDermott and M. Stibbe (eds.), *Eastern Europe in 1968*,
https://doi.org/10.1007/978-3-319-77069-7_6

1948 and immediately after his return to power made major shifts from Stalinist orthodoxy, allowing private agriculture, ending persecution of the Catholic Church and briefly lifting restrictive censorship.[3] His impulse for change soon petered out, however, following the Soviet repression of the Hungarian Revolution in November 1956 and from the late 1950s Polish politics reverted to stagnation. As a result, many Poles looked abroad for signs of change, including discussions of a 'regulated market economy' in the Soviet Union and Hungary in the early 1960s, and above all the dramatic events of the Prague Spring. But Gomułka was implacably opposed to the Czechoslovak reforms.

This chapter considers both domestic and external factors that caused his reaction. At home, he faced anti-government protests, notably the student-led 'March Events' of 1968, and a notorious anti-Semitic campaign within Poland's party leadership. Abroad, Gomułka repeatedly stressed that West German 'revanchism' might seek to undermine Poland's post-1945 frontiers. We will conclude with Poland's participation in the Warsaw Pact invasion of Czechoslovakia and the reactions of the Polish population to the Prague Spring innovations and to the invasion itself.

The 'March Events', Anti-Semitism and the Dresden Meeting

On 5 January 1968, Alexander Dubček replaced Antonín Novotný, the Czechoslovak party leader since the death of Stalin in March 1953, and thereafter moved cautiously towards reform. From the outset, he reassured his Soviet and East European allies that his aim was simply to make communism correspond more closely to the economic and political conditions of the country. For this to be achieved, a measure of democratisation was necessary, as was the rehabilitation of victims of the Stalinist terror from the late 1940s and early 1950s. Dubček deliberately avoided terms controversial in Soviet vocabulary such as 'revisionism': he spoke merely of 'socialist renewal' and revival. Even so, he found Brezhnev and his aging colleagues obdurate: 'In contrast to early post-revolutionary attitudes, late Stalinism was marked by a self-deceptive arrogance in relation to other countries'.[4]

Dubček's first meeting with Gomułka on 7 February 1968 at Ostrava, an industrial city in Moravia close to the border with Poland, was equally disappointing. The Polish leader, who was then sixty-three, struck him as embittered: 'I knew he had failed to meet the hopes of his early supporters.

At the same time, I did not realise how adamantly he opposed reform; I only discovered this later'.[5] Gomułka's six-hour harangue stressed geopolitics. 'The international communist movement finds itself in a difficult situation. We may say the decisive role in this movement is that of the Soviet Union and the other countries of the Warsaw Pact. Even so, these countries are beginning to sound a bit creaky (*trzeszczeć*). This atmosphere spreads across the whole movement'. He stated that Poles who advocated 'full sovereignty' were neglecting the role of the Soviet Union whose military power was the vital protector of Poland's national interest and the sole guarantor of its post-1945 western borders with Germany. He concluded on a domestic note: 'We want your party to be strong. If you're in a good situation, that helps us. If your situation worsens, our rogue elements will rear their heads'. Indeed, they already had: 'We now have trouble with writers and students over the theatrical production of *Dziady* (Forefathers Eve)'.[6]

Adam Mickiewicz's classic drama had been playing in Warsaw since October 1967, the fiftieth anniversary of the Bolshevik Revolution. Why its subject-matter, Poland's struggle for freedom under late eighteenth- and nineteenth-century Tsarist rule, had been thought suitable by the theatrical censorship was not clear and audience reactions to the anti-Russian passages grew. Duly alarmed, the authorities banned the play from 30 January 1968, which, paradoxically, happened to coincide with a favourable notice in *Pravda*, the Soviet party's daily newspaper. The last performance attracted an immense audience, including three hundred without tickets. When the curtain fell there was a ten-minute ovation and the foremost dissident Karol Modzelewski, who together with Jacek Kuroń had formed a group of dissident student activists known as the 'commandos' (*komandosi*), cried out from the gallery: 'Independence without censorship'.[7] Some three hundred spectators left the theatre and congregated at the Mickiewicz statue nearby, festooning it with flowers and the national flag. This first public street manifestation for more than a decade shocked the communist leadership.

University students kept up the pressure. They drew up a petition: 'We, Warsaw youth, protest against the decision to ban performances of Adam Mickiewicz's *Dziady* at the Great Theatre in Warsaw. We protest against a policy cutting us off from the progressive traditions of the Polish nation'.[8] It had strong support, particularly in the Departments of Philosophy, History and Political Economy and in halls of residence. The petition with 3145 signatures was presented to the Polish parliament (*Sejm*) on 16 February.[9] The protest became international when two student leaders, Adam Michnik and Henryk Szlajfer, were interviewed by the French newspaper *Le Monde* and their account was broadcast back to Poland by Radio Free Europe. In response, the authorities expelled them from Warsaw University.

When a special session of the Polish Writers' Union met in closed session on 29 February, the four hundred present heard a defence of the ban on *Dziady* from the Minister of Culture. He argued that audiences had exploited a tendentious production, but unpersuaded writers responded by attacking the party's cultural policy. Stefan Kisielewski declared that state censorship was a 'scandalous dictatorship of ignoramuses over Polish cultural life'. Veteran writer Antoni Słonimski concluded that little was left of the achievements of the 'Polish October' of 1956. 'First writers censor themselves, then they are censored by editors and publishers'. While he acknowledged that Polish leaders had carried out the initial stages of de-Stalinisation, restoring the rule of law, these were now distant memories. Nonetheless, there were encouraging signs abroad. 'Democratic and genuine humanism is reaching us from our colleagues in Czechoslovakia. We watch with hope the activities of our Czechoslovak neighbours'.[10]

On 8 March, two thousand Warsaw University students assembled 'to defend academic freedom' and university autonomy. Speakers noted that although freedom of expression was guaranteed by Poland's Constitution, the authorities had banned *Dziady*. They deplored the expulsion of Michnik and Szlajfer and welcomed the anti-censorship stance adopted by the Writers' Union. A secret party document on 'excesses at Warsaw University' reported that, alongside anti-government slogans, came the chant 'Poland awaits her own Dubček'.[11] While dispersing peacefully, the students were attacked by plain-clothed officers, secret police and 'workers'' militia emerging from buses marked 'excursion' parked outside the university gates. Some seventy students were arrested and many more injured by police brutality. So began the famous 'March Events'. The official media portrayed student activists as an alien and perverse elite who had nothing in common with normal and honourable Poles. Despite this, the protests in Warsaw against a political dictatorship imposed by Moscow, a stagnant economy and the abolition of citizens' freedom were rapidly endorsed across the country.

In mid-March, the secret police in Kraków reported student attempts to disrupt 'public order' by posters and pamphlets. Among these were: 'Long live the student-worker alliance'; 'Don't let police truncheons rule

Poland'; 'Don't let cut-throats drink the blood of students'; 'The whole of Poland awaits her Dubček'.[12] Technical University students marched through the streets of Częstochowa to the residence of the Rector proclaiming: 'We are with Warsaw'; 'Long Live Czechoslovakia'; 'Long Live Dubček'.[13] Other student demonstrations took place in Gdańsk, Gwilice, Katowice, Lublin, Łódź, Poznań, Szczecin and Wrocław. Protests by students in Białystok, Bydgoszcz, Olsztyn and Toruń were accompanied by non-academic disturbances elsewhere. In all, demonstrations took place in about one hundred localities and anti-government leaflets and slogans were distributed in 140 cities and towns throughout the country.[14]

Rampant turmoil in society reflected, and was matched by, disunity in the party. By early spring 1968, Polish communism was complicated by the so-called 'Partisan' faction within the PZPR. These hardliners, coalescing around General Mieczysław Moczar, the Minister of the Interior, expounded a perennial, multi-functional and populist agenda: 'anti-Zionism'. Its immediate origins extended back to the Six Day War of June 1967, when Israel captured land from Jordan, Egypt and Syria, thereby doubling in size. At the time, many Poles were sympathetic, drawing parallels between Israel's fight for survival and Poland's past struggles for independence. Though state media was rather neutral at first, this soon changed into official denunciations of 'Israeli aggression' and expressions of solidarity with the Arab nations. Gomułka attacked Israel and claimed that Polish support for the country only came from 'Zionist circles of Jews who are Polish citizens'.[15] There were at most 30,000 Jews in Poland's 32 million population, mainly elderly people, whose offspring were widely integrated into secular culture. Nonetheless, the Polish Ministry of Interior, the Security Services and the army's Chief Political Authority—all infiltrated by Soviet officials—began to screen and identify 'hidden Zionists' in various institutions. As Dariusz Stola, the leading historian of this movement, notes, the 'Partisans' revived a medieval notion of Jews as 'chimera'. Instead of appealing to the Polish public on grounds of communist ideology, such as historical determinism or class loyalty, they spearheaded a campaign against phantasmagorical monsters.[16]

As a result of this anti-Semitic onslaught, it is estimated that approximately 15,000 Polish Jews were forced into emigration in the course of 1968.[17] When news of the purge spread, the Polish ambassador in Prague received dozens of protest letters. Most notably, the Czechoslovak Writers' Union condemned 'anti-Semitic propaganda unleashed in the Polish press, radio and TV' and defended professors sacked from

Warsaw University.[18] These included the philosopher Leszek Kołakowski, sociologists Zygmunt Bauman and Maria Hirszowicz and political economist Włodzimierz Brus, all of whom emigrated to posts at British universities. Addressing the Institute of International Politics in Prague on 14 June, the distinguished American-Polish academic Zbigniew Brzezinski referred to recent pogroms in Poland as 'social fascism rather than communism'. He argued that parts of the Polish political elite had responded to legitimate social aspirations with anti-Semitism, a reaction he described as anti-intellectual, primitive and chauvinistic.[19]

Gomułka made his first public comments on the 'March Events' after eleven days of silence. He addressed several thousand party activists in the Congress Hall in Warsaw, which was bedecked with banners such as 'Down with the Agents of Imperialism and Reactionary Zionism' and 'We Demand the Complete Unmasking and Punishment of Political Activists'. While condemning dissident writers, he placed student protests in the context of reaction or revisionism rather than Zionist instigation. He denied that 'Zionism' was a danger to Poland, though recognised that there were individual cases of dual identity within the Jewish community, some of whom were more attached to Israel than Poland: such people should 'sooner or later leave our country'. Instead of demanding mass migration, he focused his critique on 'imperialist reactionaries and enemies of socialism' allegedly at work in Czechoslovakia.[20] Gomułka also repeated his warnings to Soviet leaders. 'Reactionary centres operated and inspired by foreign intelligence services' in Czechoslovakia were seeking to extend their activities more widely. His complaints were given extra moment by Czechoslovak students who held huge demonstrations in May to condemn political repression and anti-Semitism in Poland.[21] Brezhnev passed these complaints on to Dubček, calling on him to stop 'interfering in [Poland's] internal affairs'.[22]

At this time, the 'Partisans' extended their targets to include senior members of the Polish party, notably Edward Ochab, who had been a progressive Prime Minister during the 1956 uprising. Under 'Partisan' pressure, he was forced to resign from the Politburo on 8 April. Asked in retirement about the March protests, he insisted they had expressed the discontent of a much wider public. 'These students, after all, weren't fascists, counter-revolutionaries or any kind of bourgeoisie: that's why the situation demanded a serious consideration of our mistakes and serious talks'.[23] His resignation letter had stated: 'As a Pole and a communist it is with the greatest outrage that I protest against the anti-Semitic campaign which is being organised in Poland by various dark forces'. Before resigning he had explained this to Gomułka, who to some extent realised he himself might become a target. But Gomułka replied that events in Poland must be considered in a wider context: 'serious counter-revolutionary preparations were under way in Czechoslovakia, similar to the ones in Hungary in 1956'.

Soviet leaders concurred. Yuri Andropov, former ambassador to Hungary in 1956 and now head of the KGB, told the Soviet Politburo that recent events in Czechoslovakia 'are very reminiscent of what happened in Hungary'.[24] Brezhnev immediately telephoned Dubček to express concern about the 'emergence of patently anti-socialist forces'. In none too subtle language, he told the Czechoslovak leader that unless he moved rapidly to suppress 'anti-socialist elements ... the Hungarian events of 1956 might soon be repeated'.[25] In light of the emerging disquiet about developments in Czechoslovakia, the Eastern bloc leaders decided to convene a top-level multilateral meeting of communist party officials from the USSR, Poland, the GDR, Hungary, Bulgaria and Czechoslovakia in Dresden on 23 March. Here, for the first time, the Czechoslovaks were in private roundly condemned by their erstwhile allies for unleashing the spectre of reform.

Gomułka rhetorically asked the delegates 'Why shouldn't we draw conclusions from Poland's experience in 1956? Why not draw conclusions from what took place in Hungary? They all began in the same way, comrades. In our country and in Hungary it all began with the writers. It started with the Petőfi Circle, and with us the same. Intellectuals have been acting like this since 1956 ... And in your country it also started with the intellectuals'. Pursuing the analogy, he stated:

> I don't want to remind you, comrades, of the student events in our country, because I already talked about this at length to the Warsaw party *aktyw*. Czechoslovak comrades, I think this fits your situation 90%. The more you look at it, the more it looks the same. It all starts with the arts. Under the flag of defending culture and defending freedom, under this mask, the enemy, the counter-revolution, foreign intelligence works. They want to stir people up and achieve their goals this way.[26]

It is hardly surprising that Dubček considered that his harshest critic was Gomułka, with Walter Ulbricht, the East German leader, only slightly less arrogant. Although Brezhnev 'put on the face of a worried parent', he was equally stinging in his comments.[27]

In public, however, the summit's communiqué made no direct reference to the contentious events in Czechoslovakia, outside of expressing its confidence that 'the working class and all the working people of the C.S.R. [sic—Czechoslovakia] … will ensure the further development of socialist construction in the country'. Instead, the authors preferred to focus on 'questions of European security'. West German *Ostpolitik* was described as an attempt to subvert 'the interests of the German Democratic Republic and the other socialist states'.[28] The strategic importance of Czechoslovakia was seen as crucial. It was the only Warsaw Pact country to have a border both with NATO and the USSR. Indeed, according to an intelligence report from the Bavarian Ministry of the Interior, Czechoslovak border guards had dismantled a series of barbed wire and electric fences on the frontier with West Germany.[29] To Prague, the purpose of the Dresden joint statement was immediately apparent. On 28 March, 134 Czechoslovak writers told their leadership: 'The Dresden communiqué has made clear to us that you must resist pressures based on doubts about our internal measures … You should not forget that your primary responsibility is to the people of this country'.[30] On the same day, the Polish Consul-General in Ostrava reported a demonstration 'in support of Polish students and professors', crying 'Long Live Democracy' and 'We wish you a Dubček'. The crowd of several hundred included local students and even school-children.[31]

THE ACTION PROGRAMME AND RISING TENSIONS

The Czechoslovak Communist Party unveiled its 'Action Programme' on 5 April. Rejecting the Stalinist thesis of antagonistic classes, which 'no longer existed', the programme proposed 'a frank exchange of views and democratisation of the whole social and economic system'.[32] A special plenum held in Moscow on 9 April discussed the strategic implications. It concluded that Soviet security, and that of the entire bloc, was now threatened by 'imperialist subversion'. Karen Dawisha explains this widening agenda in terms of Soviet high politics: 'If Czechoslovakia became the "weak link" in the Warsaw Pact, East Europeans and, more importantly, the Soviet defense establishment could legitimately enter the political debate over the reform movement'.[33] On 16 April, Gomułka told the Soviet Ambassador to Warsaw, Averki Aristov: 'The process whereby socialist Czechoslovakia will be transformed into a bourgeois republic has already begun'. The liquidation of democratic centralism was granting leeway for bourgeois expression, as was the formation of non-communist trade unions. Such 'counterrevolutionary plans' being concocted in Prague were 'having an increasingly negative effect on Poland' and he called on the Soviets 'to intervene immediately'.[34]

When the Warsaw Pact chief, Marshal Yakubovsky, visited Poland three days later, Gomułka claimed 'counter-revolutionary forces are trying to change the status of Czechoslovakia in the direction of bourgeois democracy'. He cited the new constitution and electoral regulations, the demand for an extraordinary party congress, the 'destabilising' political ambitions of other parties under the slogan of 'legal opposition', and moves among communists to reactivate a Social Democratic Party. All this had implications abroad: 'Our interests are without doubt linked to the situation in Czechoslovakia. Disorganisation of their army practically opens the frontier with the German Federal Republic'. Even minor disturbances in the German Democratic Republic could have untold consequences. It was 'essential to preserve the Warsaw Pact through the Russian army in Czechoslovakia'.[35]

A series of Polish diplomatic protests about the unsettling effects of the Prague Spring culminated in a formal *démarche* on 6 May. This complained of 'malicious and inimical commentary' on Poland in the—now uncensored—Czechoslovak press.[36] At the same time, the Polish Politburo ordered the Foreign Ministry and Press Bureau of the Central Committee to prepare a paper for party activists on the 'situation in Czechoslovakia'.[37] The working plan for this document was to focus on 'revisionist right-wing views' which had allegedly taken hold of the Czechoslovak Communist Party.[38] Gomułka elaborated on these themes at a secret summit of Warsaw Pact leaders in Moscow on 8 May. When the Hungarian leader János Kádár dismissed the Czechoslovak 'Action Programme' as 'a big zero ... nothing', he was interrupted by Gomułka:

> What does all this mean? It means equality for all existing ideologies; it means the legalization of bourgeois ideology. And that is not just to be found in some programme. It exists in practice today in Czechoslovakia. That same Action Programme says that this year guarantees of free assembly and opportunities to create voluntary social organizations conforming to the interests and needs of different strata of the population will be inscribed into the constitution.[39]

Two weeks later, on 22 May, Gomułka expressed further concerns to the Soviet Ambassador. The Romanian and Yugoslav leaders, Nicolae Ceauşescu and Josip Broz Tito, had invited Dubček to visit their countries. Dubček himself had tentatively suggested that Poland and Czechoslovakia, together with Romania and Yugoslavia, might present a reformist counter-weight to the Soviet Union. Gomułka had been horrified by this suggestion. 'In Cde. Gomułka's opinion these three countries are united by their attraction to the West. Their common wish is to leave the socialist camp and to set up something in the nature of an unofficial alliance that might be formed among them'.[40] There is an echo here of the Ostrava meeting in February when, according to Dubček's later reminiscences, he had obliquely mentioned to a sceptical Gomułka that Poland, Czechoslovakia, Hungary and Romania might jointly constitute an informal 'Warsaw Four'.[41]

The strategic importance of Czechoslovakia had been increasing for some time. One aspect of détente in Europe was a fundamental reappraisal of West German attitudes to the East European states: *Ostpolitik*.[42] But Moscow was determined to prevent a re-opening of the 'German question'. Following the establishment of diplomatic relations between West Germany and Romania in early 1967, Soviet leaders had summoned European communist parties to a conference at Karlovy Vary in Czechoslovakia and told them that none could follow suit. Moscow was now focussing on the 'northern tier' of the Warsaw Pact—Poland, East Germany and Czechoslovakia—which had become the most significant members of the Eastern bloc.[43] The new analysis was spelt out to the Czechoslovak leadership at a bilateral summit in Moscow on 4 May 1968.

On 23 May, Soviet leaders formed a high-level 'Commission on the Czechoslovak Question' whose members included the chief ideologue Mikhail Suslov—who was later a key figure in the Polish crisis of 1980–81—and Ukrainian party leader Petro Shelest, who feared contamination from Czechoslovakia in his domain. As Mark Kramer notes, rather than delegating and getting bogged down by lower-level bureaucratic manoeuvring, 'the CPSU Politburo, led by Brezhnev, exercised tight control over Soviet policy'. The Commission kept a daily watch over Czechoslovak developments and reported to Brezhnev directly. Preparations to invade Czechoslovakia had begun on 5 April, under the code-name 'Operation Danube'. One month later, the Soviet Defence Council decided to send a high-level mission to Prague and to use large-scale military manoeuvres as a prelude to any future invasion.[44] Consequently, Warsaw Pact staff exercises began on Czechoslovak territory on 20 June.

While significant contingents of Soviet-led troops manoeuvred in Czechoslovakia, Dubček's leadership abolished prior censorship, leaving responsibility to editors for what they published. It was in this unprecedented situation that Ludvík Vaculík's incendiary 'Two Thousand Words' manifesto was published on 27 June in the Writers' Union weekly, *Literární listy*. This extraordinary article declared support for democratic reforms, but also advocated resistance to Soviet pressures. 'There has been great alarm recently over the possibility that foreign forces will intervene in our development. Whatever superior forces may face us, all we can do is stick to our positions, behave decently, and initiate nothing ourselves. We can show our government that we will stand by it, *with weapons if need be*, if it will do what we give it a mandate to do'.[45] Philip Windsor regards this as a turning-point in the Czechoslovak crisis:

> To call on the government to move faster, to declare a willingness to resort to arms, at a time when Warsaw Pact forces were entrenching themselves in the country, was bound to polarize the extremes which the government had sought to avoid and had almost succeeded in avoiding at every turn hitherto: a polarisation between the internal demands of the Czechoslovak peoples and the external demands of Czechoslovakia's allies.[46]

The response from Moscow was immediate and unambiguous. On 28 June, Foreign Minister Andrei Gromyko issued a strong condemnation of imperialism in general and *Ostpolitik* in particular. Though not mentioning Czechoslovakia by name, he delivered a stark warning to the Soviet Union's allies: 'To defend the gains and cohesion of states belonging to our socialist commonwealth is our sacred duty, to which our country will be loyal despite all trials ... Those who hope to break even one link in the socialist commonwealth are planning in vain'.[47]

Though Warsaw Pact military manoeuvres were scheduled to end on 2 July, Soviet troops remained in Czechoslovakia in considerable numbers. The threat of force was thus palpable. However, Moscow went to great lengths to reassure the USA and its allies that such an intervention was solely an 'internal affair' of the Soviet bloc. The Kremlin also implied that the USSR would not act unilaterally, as in 1956, but with the participation of other members of the Warsaw Pact. Gomułka was most willing to take part. According to notes of his speech to the Polish Politburo on 5 July, Gomułka 'told Brezhnev that military intervention is necessary, but he replied that the matter is still open'. The Soviet leader said there was still a 'paper' phase: letters, conferences and so on. Yet Gomułka saw time as of the essence. The Czechoslovak party was planning an extraordinary congress for September at which democratic centralism would be eliminated. Under the guise of social democracy, the country would become a bourgeois republic. It was therefore urgent to 'organise an opposition' of loyal Czechoslovak hard-liners (Vasil Bil'ak, Alois Indra and others) in order to prevent the country from 'leaving our camp'. Before the situation became even more complicated it was necessary to say to Moscow: 'We will move in with our army, because our security is involved too. To hell with sovereignty!'[48]

Following Gomułka's outburst at the Politburo session, a PZPR Central Committee Plenum was convened on 8–9 July. Although discussions concentrated principally on the 'March Events', the theses adopted for the next party congress condemned 'revisionism' as 'the main ally of imperialism' and denounced West Germany. While conceding that it was the sovereign right of each party to determine its own policies, they also declared that this did not mean that 'each party and each socialist country can establish its own policy in international matters, disregarding the voluntarily-accepted alliance concepts, as well as the opinions and policies of other parties and socialist states'.[49]

Poland and the Invasion

By July 1968, it was thus clear that tensions between Prague and its Warsaw Pact allies were reaching boiling point. In an attempt to put even more pressure on the Dubček leadership, the Soviet leaders decided to hold multilateral talks to which the Czechoslovaks were invited. Dubček realised he could not reject Brezhnev's summons out of hand. Instead, he suggested the meeting be attended 'by *all* European socialist countries, which would include Romania and Yugoslavia'.[50] Since Romania would not attend and Yugoslavia was non-aligned, this was evidently a delaying tactic. While Prague prevaricated, the other five Pact members met in Warsaw on 14–15 July. In a private discussion beforehand, Gomułka told Brezhnev not to be 'deceived' or 'hoodwinked' by Dubček. A military response to the Prague Spring was now unavoidable: anything less would be an 'empty gesture'.[51]

Ulbricht was equally vehement: 'The Czech plan for counter-revolution is clear. We cannot have any further doubt about this. The counter-revolutionaries want to prepare the [September] congress to eliminate Marxism-Leninism. The "Two Thousand Words" [manifesto] is unambiguously counter-revolutionary. Then they will hold multi-party elections and try to annihilate the [communist] party, and then want to change the constitution'. Responding to Hungarian hesitations, he declared: 'I don't know, comrade Kádár, why you can't see this? Don't you see that the next blow from imperialism will fall on Hungary? Can't you see that imperialist circles are now focused on the Hungarian intelligentsia'. In a further dig, this time directed at Gomułka, Ulbricht referred to the recent lecture by Brzezinski in Prague and promised to send him a transcript.[52] Gomułka had frequently castigated Brzezinski—whose works he had probably never read—as an 'imperialist running-dog' and one of Poland's worst enemies.[53]

While abjuring any 'intention to interfere in matters that are purely the internal affair of your party and state', the 'Warsaw Letter', released on 15 July, asserted that 'we cannot agree that hostile forces should push your country off the socialist path and threaten to detach Czechoslovakia from the socialist community. This is no longer your affair alone'.[54] The Letter set out two essential elements of the future 'Brezhnev Doctrine': (1) the subordination of national interests to those of the international communist movement as defined in Moscow (not Bucharest or Beijing); and (2) 'not only the *right*, but also the *duty* of socialist states to come to the defence of socialism, wherever it might be threatened'.[55] It was a *carte blanche* for interventionism, but at the same time the Soviet Politburo formulated one last-ditch negotiating strategy for bilateral talks.[56] These took place on 29 July to 1 August at Čierna nad Tisou on the Slovak-Ukrainian border. By all accounts, the atmosphere between the two sides was miserable and no unambiguous decisions were taken, although the Soviets believed Dubček had promised to undertake specific measures to bring events in Czechoslovakia under control. It was also agreed that a further multilateral meeting should be convened in Bratislava on 3 August.

Before setting out for the Slovak capital, Gomułka told the Czechoslovak Ambassador to Warsaw, Antonin Gregor, that no political 'solution' could be successful without a change of leadership in Prague. In his view, the 'democratization process' had 'already caused ... difficulties among various sections of the [Polish] public, especially the clergy'.[57] As Zdeněk Mlynář, a close associate of Dubček, later observed about the Bratislava meeting: 'Walter Ulbricht and Wladyslaw Gomulka [sic!] were hostile, vain, and senile old men. It was quite clear that they had no interest in understanding the developmental problems of their own countries, let alone of their neighbours. Both of them fairly radiated a self-satisfied intoxication with their own power'. Harmony had not been helped either by Shelest's 'shameless statements' at the Čierna summit that Czechoslovakia was trying to wrest the Carpatho-Ukraine from the Soviet Union or by his overt anti-Semitism directed against the Czech delegate, František Kriegel.[58]

The main task at Bratislava was to formulate a joint communiqué. The statement, adopted on 3 August, asserted: 'The task of supporting, consolidating and defending [the] gains [of socialism], achieved through the heroic efforts and self-sacrificing labour of each nation, is the common international *duty* of all the socialist countries'. It affirmed: 'Such was the unanimous opinion of all participants at the meeting'.[59] Following this apparent unanimity, relations appeared to relax and the Soviet ruling troika and their East European counterparts left for their summer holidays. However, on 17 August the Soviet Politburo voted unanimously to 'provide assistance and support to the Communist Party and people of Czechoslovakia through the use of armed forces'.[60] On the following day at a meeting in Moscow, Brezhnev informed his Polish, East German, Hungarian and Bulgarian counterparts of the Kremlin's decision.

The invading forces were primarily Soviet (170,000 troops) and Polish (40,000), with much smaller numbers of East Germans, Hungarians and Bulgarians (a further 20,000–25,000).[61] The intervention took place on the night of 20–21 August, ostensibly 'by invitation' of certain Czechoslovak politicians. The Soviet news agency, TASS, was authorised to state that 'the party and government leaders of the Czechoslovak Socialist Republic have asked the Soviet Union and other allied states to render the fraternal Czechoslovak people assistance, including assistance with armed forces'. The request was to eliminate the 'threat emanating from the counter-revolutionary forces which have entered into collusion with foreign forces hostile to socialism'.[62] According to Mlynář, Dubček, after being transported to Moscow, was told by Brezhnev that he was no longer reliable. Though the Soviet leader had long defended 'our Sasha', that stage was now over. Instead, he launched into an extensive account of Soviet sacrifices in World War II. The outcome was Soviet security, guaranteed by the post-war division of Europe and specifically the fact that Czechoslovakia was linked to the USSR 'forever'. Hence, the western borders of Czechoslovakia were the common borders of the 'socialist camp'. Brezhnev opined: 'Today it might seem impossible for you to accept it all ... But look at Gomulka [sic!]. In 1956, he too was against Soviet military assistance [to Hungary], just as you are. But if I were to tell him today that I was about to withdraw the Soviet army from Poland, Gomulka would jump into a special plane and fly here to plead with me not to do it'. Mlynář noted that Brezhnev did not use technical terms like 'sovereignty' or 'national independence' or any official clichés about 'mutual interests of the socialist countries'. There was only one concern: Soviet soldiers had fought their way to the Elbe in 1945 and 'that is where our real Western borders are today'.[63]

While post-invasion 'negotiations' between the Soviet and Czechoslovak leaders were underway in Moscow, five-power talks were also held in the Soviet capital from 24 to 26 August. Here, Brezhnev reported to his Warsaw Pact allies that he had insisted Dubček and the Czechoslovak Prime Minister, Oldřich Černík, must act in the spirit of the Čierna and Bratislava accords. 'The Czechoslovak comrades must understand that if they fail to do this there will be bloodshed in Czechoslovakia. In such a situation the allied troops cannot retreat even a single step'. Soviet Premier Aleksei Kosygin said: 'We are now in a position of strength. At Čierna we had an agreement, but no strength to back it up'. Gomułka was adamant: 'Do we want to capitulate or not? If Dubček and Černík go back to Prague, the counter-revolution will go further'. The Czechoslovak Party is 'reforming as a social democratic party which will then move on to counter-revolution'. The balance of forces in Europe was also shifting: 'Czechoslovakia is effectively outside the Warsaw Pact and so is the Czechoslovak army. We have only the territory of Czechoslovakia, but no majority among the population, party or military. What's really happening there is a counter-revolution, led by the intelligentsia. A majority of the population remains passive. Communists fear to show their heads. The situation is worse than Hungary in 1956'[64]

Meanwhile, back home the Polish party held emergency meetings on 21 August to inform the rank-and-file about the five-power military intervention. A Central Committee letter to all members criticised the Czechoslovak media for attempting to present the Bratislava Declaration as a 'victory' and as 'rescuing sovereignty'. Their press and publications 'undermined the Warsaw Pact and the principles of internationalism, unity and solidarity of the socialist countries'.[65] The Soviet Politburo sent explanatory missives. The first said the invasion was necessary since 'it had been established that the counter-revolutionary forces had a large quantity of munitions at its disposal'.[66] The second letter informed Western communist parties that the decision to base Soviet troops on Czechoslovak soil was necessary in order 'to guarantee the security of the socialist camp in the light of strengthening revanchist and neo-Nazi forces in West Germany'.[67]

Gomułka stressed similar themes in his address to the Central Committee on 29 August. Here, he spelled out the need for unity in the Warsaw Pact. Though it had been ruptured long ago with the expulsion of Yugoslavia from the Cominform in 1948 (before the Pact was formed) and the increasingly independent stance pursued by Romania under Ceauşescu, the further loss of Czechoslovakia could not be contemplated. The Czechoslovaks had talked about 'neutrality', but 'could East Germany become neutral? It would be rapidly swallowed up by the German Federal Republic'. Then Poland would face an entirely new situation in Europe: 'the rebirth of Germany with pre-war boundaries, the German Democratic Republic gobbled up by the Federal Republic, creating a mighty German state'.[68] A 'Letter to all Party Organisations', issued on 3 September, rehearsed these apocalyptic visions.[69]

POLISH REACTIONS TO THE INVASION

The Soviet-led occupation of Czechoslovakia aroused strong reactions among a relatively wide strata of the Polish population, even soldiers participating in the events. For example, many Polish troops stationed in northern Moravia expressed surprise at the absence of American 'imperialists' and West German 'revanchists' against whom they had been told they were deployed.[70] The East European military units were soon withdrawn and they were not included in the bilateral Soviet-Czechoslovak 'Treaty on the Temporary Presence of Soviet Forces in Czechoslovakia' signed on 16 October 1968. There were also fierce responses from Czechoslovaks living on Polish soil. Reports from Kraków describe the 'great indignation' of the Slovak population in Nowy Sącz, Nowy Targ and Zakopane. They threw stones, attacked public and tourist buses and addressed 'various abusive epithets ("swine", etc.)' to local Poles. There was a flurry of 'inimical' pamphlets, posters and graffiti: 'Long live Dubček and his party! We don't want a repeat of September 1939 and the Hungarian events of twelve years ago. We condemn the military intervention in Czechoslovakia' (Rabka); 'Gomułka has raised his hand against Czechoslovakia. For Your Freedom and Ours. The Soviets have occupied Czechoslovakia. You are not alone!' (Brzeg); 'Brezhnev is an aggressor, a criminal. We demand the withdrawal of armies from Czechoslovakia' (Opole).[71] A group of fifty students met the party secretary in Koszalin and sharply criticised the Warsaw Pact invasion, stating that this breached the sovereignty of Czechoslovakia.[72]

Other Polish reactions were similarly negative. Pamphlets discovered by the security services pilloried the invasion: 'Communists are the imperialists against Czechoslovakia. We demand the release of Dubček. Communist imperialists: go home!' (Poznań); 'USSR—aggressor. Long live Czechoslovakia. Long live Dubček. Brezhnev—Hitler!' (Konin); 'The road to socialism does not lead through Moscow' (Gostyn); 'Disgrace! Down with aggression. Occupiers go home. Hitler-Brezhnev-Gomułka-Ulbricht-Kádár-Zhivkov' (Zakopane, on the way to Morskie Oko).[73] There were also workers' protests: 'Strike! Long Live a Free Czechoslovakia. Long Live Polish workers and students. Down with strangling freedom' (Wrocław).[74] But one should not over-estimate the scale and nature of the public response. Undoubtedly, many citizens were stunned by the invasion and Poland's participation in it, but few were prepared to voice their anger in public. Nor were intellectual reactions particularly extensive, with some honourable exceptions. Jerzy Andrzejewski published a critical 'Open Letter' in *Le Monde* on 27 September, and Bronisław Geremek, Krystyna Kersten and several other leading members of the Institute of History, Polish Academy of Sciences, returned their party cards.

After the Warsaw Pact invasion, Poland's hopes for political change from within the communist regime were abandoned. Attention switched from inner-party revisionism to society-wide initiatives, notably workers' movements. Thus, paradoxically, the Soviet occupation of Czechoslovakia carried out in order to restore the status quo in central Europe ultimately undermined it. Instead of increased stability there was greater uncertainty. Polish leadership elections in November 1968 saw Gomułka entering into an alliance with one of his previous adversaries, Edward Gierek, to contain the pressure of Moczar and his acolytes. While apparently successful, Gomułka's tenure of office was still fragile. The new Presidium no longer included figures who had long favoured détente in Europe, such as Adam Rapacki whose plan for a nuclear-free zone in central Europe dated back to 1957. Ideas of economic reform and social pluralism disappeared from the official political agenda. In December, Kuroń and Modzelewski were sentenced to three and a half years in prison and the following February Michnik received three years. Other activists were handed somewhat shorter sentences.[75] The Polish news agency PAP announced that some 5264 Polish citizens 'of Jewish origin' had been given passports to Israel. Many others, possibly twice this number,[76] took one-way exit visas to Vienna and then settled in Amsterdam, Paris or New York.

Despite these harsh measures, pressures 'from below' began to change the political context. By autumn 1970, many Polish families spent half their budget on food. A decade's stagnation of real wages left them in no position to pay more. Nonetheless, the Politburo announced a 40% increase on basic foodstuffs, notionally offset by cheaper prices for expensive durables, such as television sets and kitchen appliances, beyond the reach of ordinary households. The start date for the price hikes was ten days before Christmas. It led immediately to major strikes on the Baltic coast, which were crushed by force. Gomułka received no support from Moscow and promptly resigned. 'December 1970' was a brutal forerunner of the more peaceful 'Polish August' a decade later. Then, the independent trade union movement 'Solidarity' was legalised under the Gdańsk Agreement of 31 August 1980 and, after ten years of struggle against the communist monopoly of power, formed the world's first post-communist government in summer 1989.[77]

Notes

1. *The Anti-Stalin Campaign and International Communism: A Selection of Documents* (New York, 1956), pp. 1–89.
2. T. Kemp-Welch, 'Khrushchev's "Secret Speech" and Polish Politics: The Spring of 1956', *Europe-Asia Studies*, vol. 48, no. 2 (1996), pp. 181–206.
3. P. Machcewicz, *Polski Rok 1956* (Warsaw, 1993), enlarged edition published in English under the title *Rebellious Satellite: Poland 1956* (Stanford, CA, 2009).
4. A. Dubček, *Hope Dies Last: The Autobiography of Alexander Dubček* (New York, 1993), p. 134.
5. Dubček, *Hope Dies Last*, p. 135.
6. Archiwum Akt Nowych (Archive of Modern Records—AAN), Warsaw, Polish United Workers' Party (PZPR), 237/XIA/33, pp. 278–80.

7. Interview with Modzelewski in A. Friszke, *Anatomia Buntu. Kuroń, Modzelewski i komandosi* (Kraków, 2010), p. 514.
8. AAN 237/XVI/586 (6 February 1968).
9. T. Torańska, *Jestesmy. Rozstania '68* (Warsaw, 2008), p. 397.
10. AAN, 237/XVIII/319, 'Walne zebranie Oddzialu Warszawski Związek Literackich Polskich (29. 2. 1968)'.
11. AAN, 237/VII *Informacja* nr. 9/A/4346, 'Odgłosy na temat ekscesow na Uniwerystecie Warszawskim (10. 3. 1968)'.
12. J. Kwiek (compiler), *Marzec 1968 w Krakowie w dokumentach* (Kraków, 2005), p. 110.
13. K. Rokicki and S. Stepien (eds), *Oblicza Marca 1968* (Warsaw, 2004), pp. 104–5.
14. Torańska, *Jestesmy*, p. 398; J. Eisler, 'March 1968 in Poland', in C. Fink et al. (eds), *1968: The World Transformed* (Cambridge, 1998), pp. 246–7.
15. D. Stola, *Kampania antysyjonistyczna w Polsce, 1967–1968* (Warsaw, 2000), chapter two.
16. D. Stola, 'Fighting Against the Shadows: The Anti-Zionist Campaign of 1968', in R. Blobaum (ed.), *Anti-Semitism and Its Opponents in Modern Poland* (Ithaca, NY, 2005), pp. 284–300.
17. S. Garsztecki, 'Poland', in M. Klimke and J. Scharloth (eds), *1968 in Europe: A History of Protest and Activism, 1956–1977* (Basingstoke, 2008), pp. 179–88 (here p. 184).
18. M. Górny, 'Wydarzenia marcowe w opinii czechosłowackiej', in *Marzec 1968. Trzydziesci lat pozniej, tom 1: Referaty* (Warsaw, 1998), pp. 210–11.
19. Górny, 'Wydarzenia marcowe', p. 217.
20. Gomułka's speech in *Trybuna ludu* (Warsaw) 19 March 1968, translated in *Pravda* on 22 March.
21. J. Eisler, *Polski rok 1968* (Warsaw, 2006), pp. 732–3.
22. M. Kramer, 'The Kremlin, the Prague Spring and the Brezhnev Doctrine', in V. Tismaneanu (ed.), *Promises of 1968: Crisis, Illusion, and Utopia* (Budapest, 2011), pp. 285–370 (here pp. 329–30).
23. All quotations in this paragraph are from T. Torańska, *Oni. Stalin's Polish Puppets* (London, 1987), p. 82.
24. M. Kramer, 'The Czechoslovak Crisis and the Brezhnev Doctrine', in Fink et al. (eds), *1968*, pp. 111–72 (here pp. 123–4).
25. Kramer, 'The Kremlin, the Prague Spring', p. 304.
26. AAN, KC (Central Committee) PZPR, tom 1, paczka 298, n.p.
27. Dubček, *Hope Dies Last*, p 141.
28. Cited in R.A. Remington (ed.), *Winter in Prague: Documents on Czechoslovak Communism in Crisis* (Cambridge, MA, 1969), p. 56.
29. K. Dawisha, *The Kremlin and the Prague Spring* (Berkeley, CA, 1984), p. 53.
30. 'Open Letter', *Literární listy* (Prague), 28 March 1968.

31. Górny, 'Wydarzenia marcowe', pp. 210–11.
32. Remington (ed.), *Winter in Prague*, pp. 88–137.
33. For details on the plenum, see Dawisha, *The Kremlin and the Prague Spring*, pp. 56–61, quotation on p. 60.
34. 'Cable to Moscow from Soviet Ambassador to Warsaw Averki Aristov ...', 16 April 1968, in J. Navrátil et al. (eds), *The Prague Spring 1968: A National Security Archive Documents Reader* (Budapest, 1998), pp. 103–4.
35. L. Pajorek, *Polska a 'praska wiosna'. Udział Wojska Polskiego w interwencji zbrojnej w Czechosłowacji w 1968 roku* (Warsaw, 1998), p. 96.
36. AAN, 237/X1A, pp. 327–30.
37. AAN, 237/X1A, pp. 331–4.
38. AAN, 237/X1A, p. 342.
39. 'Minutes of the Secret Meeting of the "Five" in Moscow, May 8, 1968', in Navrátil et al. (eds), *The Prague Spring*, pp. 138–9.
40. 'Cable from the Soviet Ambassador in Warsaw ...', 22 May 1968, in Navrátil et al. (eds), *The Prague Spring*, p. 147.
41. 'Alexander Dubček's Recollections of the Crisis ...', part 2, 10 August 1990, in Navrátil et al. (eds), *The Prague Spring*, p. 306.
42. J. Fiszer and J. Holzer (eds), *Recepcja Ostpolitik w RFN i w krajach bloku kommunistycznego: Polska, ZSRR, NRD, Czechosłowacja, Węgry* (Warsaw, 2004).
43. P. Windsor and A. Roberts, *Czechoslovakia 1968: Reform, Repression and Resistance* (London, 1969), p. 8.
44. Kramer, 'The Kremlin, the Prague Spring', pp. 310–12, 318–19.
45. L. Vaculík, 'Two Thousand Words that Belong to Workers, Farmers, Officials, Scientists, Artists, and Everybody', in Navrátil et al. (eds), *The Prague Spring*, pp. 177–81 (italics added).
46. Windsor and Roberts, *Czechoslovakia 1968*, p. 50.
47. A Gromyko, 'On the International Position and Foreign Policy of the Soviet Union', *Pravda*, 28 June 1968.
48. 'Notatka posiedzenia Biura Politycznego 5 lipca 1968 r.', in L. Kamiński (ed.), *Wokół praskiej wiosny. Polska i Czechosłowacja w 1968 roku* (Warsaw, 2004), pp. 190–2.
49. *Trybuna ludu*, 13 July 1968.
50. Dubček, *Hope Dies Last*, p. 162.
51. Kramer, 'The Kremlin, the Prague Spring', pp. 335–6.
52. AAN, KC PZPR, tom 24, paczka 193, n.p.
53. E. Weit, *Eyewitness: The Autobiography of Gomulka's Interpreter* (London, 1973), pp. 203–4.
54. 'The Warsaw Letter, July 14–15, 1968', in Navratil et al. (eds), *The Prague Spring*, pp. 234–8.

55. Dawisha, *The Kremlin and the Prague Spring*, p. 212 (italics in original).
56. Kramer, 'The Kremlin, the Prague Spring', p. 338.
57. 'Polish Views of the Situation in Czechoslovakia ...', 2 August 1968, in Navratil et al. (eds), *The Prague Spring*, p. 319.
58. Z. Mlynář, *Night Frost in Prague: The End of Humane Socialism* (London, 1980), pp. 152, 155.
59. 'Statement by the Communist and Workers' Parties of Socialist Countries', *Pravda*, 4 August 1968 (italics added).
60. Kramer, 'The Kremlin, the Prague Spring', p. 347.
61. H.G. Skilling, *Czechoslovakia's Interrupted Revolution* (Princeton, NJ, 1976), p. 714. In fact, the East German contribution was limited to a tiny number of intelligence and reconnaissance units. For further details, see "Ideological Offensive: The East German Leadership, the Prague Spring and the Warsaw Pact Invasion of August 1968" by Matthew Stibbe in this volume.
62. Cited in E.H. Judge and J.W. Langdon (eds), *The Cold War Through Documents: A Global History*, 3rd edn (Lanham, MD, 2018), pp. 216–17.
63. Mlynář, *Night Frost in Prague*, pp. 237–42.
64. AAN, KC PZPR, tom 54, 'Protokol ze spotkania partyjno-rządowych delegacji Bułgarii, NRD, Polski, Węgier i ZSSR (Moskwa, 24–6 sierpnia 1968 r.)', p. 119.
65. AAN, 237/VII/5790, KC PZPR, tom 1, 'Do wszystkich organizacji partyjnych' (21 August 1968), pp. 269–72.
66. Russian State Archive of Contemporary History (RGANI), Moscow, f. 1, op. 72, d. 201, ll. 31–40 (2 September 1968).
67. RGANI, f. 3, op. 72, d. 214, ll. 55–78 (28 October 1968).
68. AAN, 237/X1/367, tom 73, Speech to Central Committee, 29 August 1968.
69. AAN, 237/X1/213, 3 September 1968.
70. L. Kowalski, *Kryptonim 'Dunaj': Udział wojsk polskich w interwencji zbrojnej w Czechosłowacji w 1968 roku* (Warsaw, 1992), pp. 180–91.
71. AAN, 237/VII/5790, 'Zachowanie obywatelstwo czecznosti na terenie Polski' (21 August 1968).
72. AAN, 237/VII/5790, tom 1, p. 328.
73. AAN, 237/VII/5790, tom 2, Report of 26 August 1968, pp. 364–5.
74. W. Suleja, *Dolnośląski Marzec '68. Anatomia protest* (Warsaw, 2006), pp. 338–9.
75. The fullest account, including their court speeches, is in Friszke, *Anatomia Buntu*, pp. 737–883.
76. Torańska, *Jestesmy*, p. 401.
77. See A. Kemp-Welch, *The Birth of Solidarity*, 2nd enlarged edition (London, 1991).

Hungary 1968: Reform and the Challenge of the Prague Spring

Csaba Békés

By the late 1960s, Hungary was the most de-Stalinised country in the Soviet bloc and had gained a solid reputation in the international arena. Radical economic measures were introduced in Budapest at precisely the same time as the changes began in Czechoslovakia in January 1968. The challenge of the Prague Spring compelled the Hungarian leaders to conduct secret mediations between Prague and Moscow from the outset with the aim of avoiding the military 'option' to the Czechoslovak crisis. Regrettably, these efforts proved to no avail. In this chapter I will chart the reaction of the Hungarian communist leaders to the Czechoslovaks' innovatory reforms, recount Budapest's complex attempts at conciliation, assess Hungary's military contribution to the Soviet-led invasion, and, finally, discuss the responses of Magyar intellectuals and society to the crushing of the Prague Spring in August 1968. In order to do this, some historical contextualisation is required.

C. Békés (✉)
Hungarian Academy of Sciences, Institute of Political Science,
Budapest, Hungary
e-mail: Bekes.Csaba@tk.mta.hu

Internal Developments, 1956–68

Following the brutal suppression of the Hungarian Revolution by Soviet armed forces in early November 1956, a new pro-Moscow government was installed under János Kádár. Its fundamental task was the long-term reconsolidation of the communist dictatorship. The primary means of creating political stability and pacifying society was Kádár's novel 'quality of life policy' that aimed to rapidly improve living standards for the great majority willing to distance themselves from the revolution, while severely punishing those who were found 'guilty' or resisted.[1] However, building 'consumer socialism' depended on a well-functioning economy and it soon became apparent that the development of the Hungarian economy, which was massively reliant on external sources and foreign trade, could only be achieved if the leadership was able to exploit both Eastern and Western relations. In regard to the Soviet Union, this meant above all providing Hungary with stable supplies of raw materials and energy resources at 'friendly' prices (that is, well below world market rates) and as for the West, it entailed Hungary's partial re-admittance into the world economic system by adopting the advanced technologies necessary for modernisation.

The maintenance of Kádár's political power was predicated on a strategy of continual two-front struggle. Immediately after 1956, the main goal was to eliminate 'revisionist' opponents in the leadership, but by the beginning of the 1960s a renewed programme of de-Stalinisation had been initiated. In the first place, this signified a resumption of the rehabilitation of the purge victims of the late 1940s and early 1950s, following a break in this process immediately after 1956, but it also resulted in the removal of 'leftists' from their positions of authority. Thus, Kádár had successfully turned Hungary into a 'Khrushchevian model state' by the middle of the 1960s,[2] something the Soviet leader himself was never able to achieve in his own country. Just a few short years after the 1956 revolution, Hungary, of all the Soviet bloc states, was regarded as having made the most significant progress towards de-Stalinisation: political stability was nigh-on total, the agricultural sector was almost fully collectivised and living standards were continuously rising. It is remarkable that even a top secret White House memorandum from April 1964 claimed that 'Hungary has perhaps gone farther than any other satellite in de-Stalinising the communist system and the movement in that direction continues'.[3]

Another important Kádárist strategy to improve social cohesion was greater freedom of movement. This essentially inexpensive measure, in place from 1964, permitted Magyars to travel to Western states every three years, while unlimited visa-free travel to Soviet bloc countries (except the USSR) was also made possible.[4] As a consequence, tourism expanded enormously: in a country of ten million inhabitants in 1968, 929,000 Hungarians travelled abroad (compared to only 200,000 in 1959) and 4.3 million visitors entered Hungary (a mere 400,000 in 1959). In the cultural field, a relatively liberal policy was emerging by the end of the 1960s. On the basis of the 'Three T' doctrine (*tilt, tűr, támogat*: ban, tolerate, support) of differentiation introduced in 1957, 'socialist' art became one of several recognised trends. Hence, many Hungarian as well as Western non-socialist, though not 'anti-socialist', novels were published, and Western movies, including cartoons (Huckleberry Hound) and television series, were also more and more frequently broadcast. Western pop music was gradually assimilated and in 1966 a series of annual televised pop festivals was launched. In August 1968, the winner of the festival, watched by a large majority of the population, was the band *Illés* with their song *Amikor én még kissrác voltam* ('When I Was Still a Boy'). The group effectively created Hungarian rock music in the mid-1960s and the song was a rather sceptical piece, openly condemning the dark conditions of the 1950s and also criticising the hypocrisy of contemporary society.

The most spectacular changes, however, occurred in 1968. The New Economic Mechanism (NEM), introduced on 1 January 1968, represented the first profound structural reform in a communist state since Lenin's New Economic Policy in 1921 and became the most radical economic measure ever undertaken in the Soviet bloc.[5] Prepared between 1964 and 1968 by hundreds of experts and scholars, which in itself was a novel approach to state planning in a communist country, NEM combined a planned economy and collective ownership with elements of a market economy, reduced the role of central planning, improved the input of companies in production and partially liberalised prices and wages. Officially, it was called an economic reform, but from the off it was understood that it would be coupled with political and cultural amendments, including major changes in fields such as education, science and academic research.[6] Projects for constitutional and electoral reform and reinforcing 'socialist legality' were likewise well under way after 1967.

Foreign Policy

By the mid-1960s, Hungary had gone through a process of 'double emancipation'. First, Hungary's diplomatic isolation from the West after the crushing of the 1956 revolution was overcome in December 1962 when the Hungarian issue was finally removed from the agenda of the UN General Assembly following a secret deal between Washington and Budapest. As a result, the black sheep of the family was once again regarded as simply one of the states of the Soviet bloc. Second, by this time the emancipation of all bloc states (except the GDR) was completed in three directions: in their relationship with the USSR, the West and the Third World. Consequently, their international status was upgraded from 'Soviet satellite' to a member of a mighty politico-military alliance: the Warsaw Pact.

In the foreign policy sphere, the year 1963 was a true caesura for Hungary. The two-day visit of UN Secretary General U Thant in July was a symbolic event, officially terminating Hungary's diplomatic isolation and creating favourable circumstances for normalising Budapest's relationship with the Western world. A series of spectacular successes was inaugurated by U Thant's visit starting with the upgrading of diplomatic ties with many Western countries: ministers, government delegations and representatives of various social organisations paid regular visits on a mutual basis, and Western journalists, public figures, scholars and artists often visited Hungary.[7] In September 1964, Hungary became the first Soviet bloc state to sign an agreement with the Vatican, which, though leaving a number of questions unresolved, played an important role in ameliorating conditions for the Hungarian Catholic Church.[8] On the basis of the positive American assessment mentioned above, relations with the USA also began to improve in 1964, but after the escalation of the Vietnam War in February 1965 this rapprochement deteriorated as the Hungarian government, together with other members of the Warsaw Pact, sharply condemned the aerial bombardment of North Vietnam.

More generally, Hungarian foreign policy in the decades after the 1956 revolution is still often presented as determined solely by the manifest dependency on the USSR. However, my extensive archival research conducted since 1990 suggests that it can only be properly explained and understood in the framework of a novel theoretical concept: 'tripartite determinism'. While (1) affiliation to the Soviet empire ostensibly implied enforced restrictions, (2) the dependence on the West in terms of advanced technology, trade contacts and subsequent loans produced a similarly strong bond. At the same time, (3) Hungarian foreign policy had to perform a delicate balancing act to pursue specific national objectives in terms of a pan-East Central European lobby-contest.[9] Although this tripartite determinism of Hungarian foreign policy had always existed in some form and magnitude, the import of the three factors became essentially equally weighted from the mid-1960s. This theory can also be interpreted in a wider context and with certain restrictions applies to the entire Soviet bloc. The above three determinants were valid for Hungarian, Polish, Romanian, East German[10] and to a lesser extent Czechoslovak and Bulgarian foreign policy, especially from the early to mid-1960s. Meanwhile, Hungarian diplomacy, at Moscow's initiative, was engaged in a serious, albeit ultimately unsuccessful, mediation effort aimed at finding a negotiated settlement to the Vietnam War. These developments also enhanced Hungary's prestige in the Eastern bloc. Hence, by the mid-1960s the country had become a kind of 'model state' for the West in the context of de-Stalinisation and relative internal 'liberalism'. In sum, by the end of the 1960s, together with the Soviet Union, Poland and Romania, Hungarian diplomacy assumed an important role in international politics and this position was strengthened further when, in January 1968, Hungary became a non-permanent member of the UN Security Council for two years.

The Challenge of the Prague Spring and Kádár's Mediation

The introduction of NEM in Hungary in January 1968 was rightly seen as a radical attempt at reforming the communist economic system, and so, not surprisingly, it was viewed with much suspicion not only in Moscow but in the other allied states. Therefore, from early in 1968 the main goal of the Hungarian leadership was to offer clandestine support for the 'renewal process' in Prague in the hope of forming a reform coalition with Czechoslovakia that could act as a pressure group for the revitalisation of the communist system throughout the bloc. Consequently, the other crucial political aim was to avoid a 1956-type military solution. This policy required subtle diplomacy and a triangular system of mediation among Kádár, Dubček and Brezhnev. Kádár attempted to persuade the Czechoslovak leaders to be moderate, to slow down the pace of reform, to acknowledge realities and respect the level of tolerance of

Moscow. On the other hand, he tried to convince the Kremlin and other Soviet bloc leaders, at least up to the middle of July and even beyond, to show more understanding and patience towards Czechoslovakia because the cause of socialism was not yet critically endangered there. Kádár's mediation was fulfilled in the course of a number of bilateral and multilateral meetings. Between January and August 1968, Kádár met Dubček nine times altogether, five times bilaterally (on three occasions in secret) and on four occasions at multilateral gatherings.[11] During the same period, Kádár met Brezhnev seven times, but their most important channel of communication was by telephone: they talked almost every week and sometimes more often.

At the first multilateral meeting of the Warsaw Pact leaders, excluding Romania, on the Czechoslovak crisis in Dresden in March 1968, Kádár wanted to demonstrate his support for the Prague reformers, but at the same time he pointed out the perils inherent in their present situation. He insisted that Czechoslovakia had not yet—contrary to the assertions of Brezhnev and the Polish party leader Władysław Gomułka—reached the stage of counter-revolution. Kádár recognised, however, that in a number of ways conditions in Prague resembled those that had preceded the Hungarian 'counter-revolution' of 1956.[12] At the next summit, held without the Czechoslovaks in Moscow on 8 May, the representatives of the Soviet bloc states, except Kádár, saw the position as obviously counter-revolutionary. From now on, the idea gained ground that consolidation through political means was to be achieved by pro-Moscow 'healthy forces' seizing power internally. Kádár acknowledged in his statement that there was widespread anarchy in Czechoslovakia and that it was being exploited by anti-socialist forces. Nonetheless, he continued in his attempts to convince his comrades that the incumbent Czechoslovak leadership only needed sufficient support in order to get things under control. Thus, the situation was indeed perilous but counter-revolution had not yet gained the upper hand in the country.[13]

The official visit of a Czechoslovak party and government delegation to Hungary that had originally been planned for March finally took place on 13 and 14 June.[14] Brezhnev telephoned Kádár on the eve of the meeting and urged him to help Dubček understand 'the dangers that are threatening the Czechoslovak party, socialism and himself'.[15] During the sojourn, Kádár in public assured his guests of his backing for their efforts to consolidate the situation. In private, however, he sounded a note of warning. The Hungarian experiences of 1956 showed that it was necessary to curb democratisation and to draw an unmistakable line against deviations and hostile tendencies; otherwise the party was bound to lose control.[16] Towards the end of June, Kádár travelled to Moscow at the head of a party delegation. Here, Brezhnev painted a sombre picture: Dubček was gradually drifting to the right, which was growing in strength, Czechoslovakia was getting ever closer to going down the road of Yugoslavia and its further trajectory might even take it into the bourgeois camp. The Hungarian leadership differed at that time from the Soviet line on a number of issues, therefore it seemed important to maintain the goodwill of the Kremlin to tolerate the reforms in Hungary. Kádár presumably felt that the time had come to make it clear that, while the Hungarian Socialist Workers' Party (HSWP) favoured a political solution to the Czechoslovak crisis, it would support military intervention as a measure of last resort, if a political settlement could not be achieved and the continued existence of the socialist order was in jeopardy.[17]

At the meeting of the 'Five' (USSR, Poland, GDR, Hungary and Bulgaria) on 14–15 July in Warsaw, Kádár gave a detailed report on his secret meeting with Dubček and Prime Minister Oldřich Černík in Komárom held at their request the previous day,[18] and underlined the threat inherent in Czechoslovakia, which had, however, not yet reached the stage of counter-revolution. Kádár's conciliatory speech was immediately subject to an unprecedented attack by the GDR leader Walter Ulbricht and his Bulgarian counterpart Todor Zhivkov. The former not only resolutely and openly condemned Kádár's point of view, but added that it might well be the case that Hungary's internal problems would be next in line for a 'solution' at a future meeting of the Warsaw Pact. In these circumstances, Kádár thought it expedient to repeat in front of his critics the 'declaration of loyalty' that he had issued two weeks before in Moscow. In an unexpected second speech, he announced that the Hungarian leadership agreed with the evaluation of the Soviets and was 'prepared to take part in all joint actions'.[19]

Towards the Invasion

After the Warsaw meeting of the 'Five', Kádár concentrated on persuading Brezhnev to make one last-ditch effort at a Soviet–Czechoslovak *tête-à-tête*. It was intended that the Soviets would make it clear to Dubček and his comrades that, in case they continued to do nothing to stop developments that bore all the hallmarks of total disintegration, there would have to be outside intervention to save socialism. Kádár had the impression that he had succeeded in frightening Dubček and Černík in Komárom; at the end of the discussions, when they realised the danger they were in, both men had burst out crying.[20] He hoped that a final warning by the Soviets would prove effective and trigger at long last the administrative measures required for a consolidation of the Czechoslovak communist system. The Soviet–Czechoslovak meeting on their common border at Čierna nad Tisou at the end of July was mainly the result of Kádár's tireless efforts at mediation, but its results were meagre. At the ensuing summit of the 'Six' in Bratislava at the beginning of August, Kádár confronted Dubček quite openly with the alternatives the Czechoslovak party faced. Either they themselves used force to stop certain counter-revolutionary tendencies or force would be applied against them from outside. He illustrated this with his own example and underlined that in 1956 it had been necessary to use deeply unpopular measures to save Hungarian communism in a context that was much more difficult; yet he had done what had to be done.[21]

At Brezhnev's invitation, Kádár travelled to Yalta on 15 August. During the negotiations everyone knew that a decision in favour of a military solution was in the offing. Kádár now concentrated on potential developments after the intervention. The situation being as it was, he consented to the military option,[22] yet he emphasised that in the long term only a political settlement could ensure success. The struggle to correct the mistakes made in Czechoslovakia before January 1968 had to be continued and Prague must not relinquish its two-front battle. At this stage, Kádár was pursuing a dual goal: first, he was trying to make sure that post-invasion Czechoslovakia would be allowed to re-establish the communist order with minimum political interference from Moscow and, second, he was attempting to broaden the domestic manoeuvring space for all states in the Soviet bloc. At Yalta, Brezhnev entrusted a last mediation mission to Kádár, intimating that the Hungarian party was the only one, in addition to the Soviet, that Dubček might be prepared to heed. The meeting took place in Komárno on 17 August.[23] Dubček, who in Komárom on 13 July had acknowleged the mistake of not attending the Warsaw conclave, now changed his position and declared that his leadership's decision had been correct. He told Kádár that he was at present dealing solely with the forthcoming extraordinary party congress set for early September. Kádár warned Dubček that if the Czechoslovaks disregarded basic problems, such as the leading role of the party and the fight against right-wing forces and held parliamentary elections after the congress without a firm political platform, this would lead to unpredictable consequences, clearly referring to the possibility of a 'bourgeois restoration'. As a communist, Dubček must have been well aware that such a capitulation would not be tolerated by the Kremlin. By the end of the meeting Kádár was sure that the situation in Czechoslovakia was hopeless and he had no illusions about the decision to be taken by the 'Five' the following day in Moscow.

Hungary and the Military Invasion of Czechoslovakia

The June 1953 uprising in East Berlin, the workers' revolt in June 1956 in Poznań and the 'Polish October' crisis of the same year did not raise the highly sensitive issue of whether other countries of the Soviet bloc should participate in restoring order and the consolidation process. This dilemma was posed in a different way after the suppression of the Hungarian Revolution in November 1956. Although both the Romanian and Czechoslovak leaders offered armed assistance to the Soviets in cracking down on Budapest,[24] no joint military invasion occurred. However, punitive political intervention—still basically unknown to the public and historians alike—by five Warsaw Pact states did take place between 1 and 4 January 1957. This collective bloc 'tribunal' was organised by the leaders of the Bulgarian, Czechoslovak, Hungarian, Romanian and Soviet parties.[25] The Kremlin's main motivation behind the meeting was to discuss the imminent programme statement of the infant Kádár government, which included the possibility, eventually rejected, of maintaining a special kind of multi-party system.[26] The other important matter discussed at the tribunal was the fate of Imre Nagy, the reform communist leader of the revolution. It is evident that a key joint decision was arrived at, which opened the way for court proceedings and eventually the conviction and execution of Nagy and his associates in 1958. In other words, they were no longer treated as political prisoners but rather as common criminals.[27]

In several ways, then, the 1956 Hungarian Revolution acted as a crucial catalyst for strengthening the multi-lateralisation of the Soviet bloc. This process of emancipation received a new dynamic during the 1960s and by the end of the decade the Warsaw Pact had developed into a political-military organisation that granted its members significant room for manoeuvre.[28] The challenge of the Prague Spring coincided with the Soviet bloc's campaign for convening a pan-European security conference aimed at stabilising the 1945 status quo. This was coupled with unstinting efforts to promote the image of a cooperative and peace-loving USSR and Eastern bloc in general. Therefore, it was vital for Moscow to avoid a military 'solution' to the Czechoslovak crisis for as long as possible, and, in case there was no other alternative, responsibility had to be shared with the other Soviet bloc countries. This is why it was essential for the Kremlin to persuade its partners to participate in the invasion: at this pivotal juncture in East–West relations a joint action had symbolic importance. While Moscow obviously had to reckon with Romania's absence, Bulgaria, which had to send troops via Soviet territory, was allowed to send only two regiments.[29] The East German and Polish leaderships, ardent opponents of the Prague Spring, provided two and three divisions respectively,[30] while the reluctant ally Hungary sent just one. At least this was how it was communicated to, and perceived by, the outside world. Today we know that at the very last minute Brezhnev banned the East German army from crossing the border, because he had been convinced by conservative hard-liners in Prague about the psychological dangers of German soldiers marching once again on Czechoslovak soil.[31] This created one of the most absurd situations in the history of foreign invasions: the population of the invaded country was outraged at the non-existent 'presence' of its neighbour's army, while the invader proudly lied to its own people and the rest of the world for decades that GDR ground troops had crossed the East German border into Czechoslovakia on 20–21 August, although this never happened.

In Hungary's case the initial 'request' on 10 July 1968 by Marshal Grechko, the Soviet Defence Minister, to Lajos Czinege, his Hungarian counterpart, for three divisions was coupled with an explicit falsehood: he claimed that Kádár had already given his consent to this decision. An exchange of letters and a telephone conversation between Kádár and Brezhnev soon clarified that Grechko's assertion lacked any basis. Until this time, Magyar military leaders had hoped that Hungary might avoid participating in an invasion; now the task was to bargain for the smallest possible contribution. At first this endeavour seemed successful, as in the official invitation forwarded to the Hungarian leadership on 22 July the Soviets asked for the involvement of 'at least one division, or if this is not possible, a smaller unit'. The Hungarian reply on the same day confirmed the country's participation 'with one division in reduced number'. Moscow was also permitted to send a Soviet division to Czechoslovakia through Hungary. In reality, though, the Soviets outmanoeuvred the Hungarians: by constantly changing the conditions during the invasion, in late August the latter eventually were forced to 'voluntarily' double their contribution and send army units equalling approximately two full divisions with some 20,000 troops, 155 tanks, 200 canons and 99 fighter planes.[32] With benevolent Soviet acquiescence, however, what survived in public memory was that the reluctant ally took part in the invasion with only the smallest possible units.

The Hungarian troops participating in 'Manoeuvre Zala' were subordinated to the commander of the Southern Soviet Army Group as early as 28 July and operated under Soviet command until their return from Czechoslovakia in late October. After being in readiness for three weeks, the soldiers moved to southern Slovakia at 00:00 hours on 21 August, where they occupied a territory of 11,500 km^2 and established eleven garrisons. Although they met no opposition by the Czechoslovak army, as it was ordered not to resist, Hungarian troops were prepared to fight the 'enemy' and quell any armed popular resistance. Some of the local military leaders bluntly declared that they would have fought against the aggressors had there not been the order of President Svoboda to the contrary. In spite of the original Soviet plans to introduce military administration in the occupied areas, this never happened. While the local authorities everywhere condemned and protested against the intervention, in most cases they were prepared to cooperate with the occupying forces in 'restoring order'.[33]

The population, however, received the Hungarian troops with open hostility. This surprised the military as the majority of the population belonged to the large Magyar ethnic minority living in southern and eastern Slovakia. All of 'Upper Hungary' (present-day Slovakia) had been detached from Hungary in the Trianon peace treaty of 1920, although the southern part of the region was inhabited overwhelmingly by Hungarians. In November 1938, the Magyar-populated part of Slovakia was reattached to Hungary in the First Vienna Award, which was based on the ethnic principle. After World War II, however, the decision made by Hitler and Mussolini was declared null and void by the Allies and the region became part of the restored Czechoslovak state. Interestingly, the size of the occupied area by the Hungarian army in 1968 was almost identical with the region reattached to Hungary in the First Vienna Award (12,000 km^2), just thirty years before. To the great surprise of the military leaders, the local Hungarian populace, which a generation earlier had celebrated the marching Hungarian army as liberators, now supported the Dubček leadership unanimously and bitterly protested against the invasion together with the Slovaks, labelling the action an aggression and the Hungarian troops invaders. There were many ferocious demonstrations and in two towns, Nitra and Nové Zámky, the crowd had to be dissolved after firing warning shots. In the latter case, a tragic outcome was avoided only by the judicious decision of the local commander to withdraw troops from the town to a nearby forest.[34]

Violent clashes were, however, rare. In Hungarian-controlled territory altogether a mere four soldiers died (traffic incidents, suicide, careless weapons handling) and there were two local victims who died in accidents. From the beginning of September, military leaders urged the withdrawal of the troops arguing that their further presence would do more harm than good. While the Soviets originally favoured a long-term joint occupation, and then planned for allied soldiers to stay throughout the winter, eventually by the end of October all non-Soviet forces had been pulled out. The return of Hungarian personnel was a low key publicity event: it was reported that the army had fulfilled its 'internationalist duty' to defend the socialist system in Czechoslovakia, but the political leadership itself was not particularly proud of this contribution. The public, of course, knew nothing about the many signs of dissent and protest in the army. According to a secret report prepared by the Interior Ministry in January 1969, there were 252 cases of 'incitement' in connection with the invasion. More than half of these were issues connected to listening to Radio Free Europe and commenting on and spreading the news of the 'enemy radio'. Nevertheless, very few cases were taken to military court. The only person to be jailed was a soldier sentenced to sixteen months in prison for criticising the Soviet Union. Another private suggested that perhaps an 'atom bomb should be dropped on the garrison in the town of Eger' so that he should not have to join up.[35] He received a ten-month suspended prison sentence.

Post-invasion Prospects

After the invasion on 20–21 August, an unexpected opportunity arose for Kádár to positively influence the course of events. On the first day of the crisis management talks of the 'Five', which took place parallel to the joint Soviet-Czechoslovak 'negotiations' on 24–26 August in Moscow, he was a fervent advocate of the need to find a compromise with the legitimate Czechoslovak leadership. Ulbricht and Zhivkov, however, insisted on sticking to the original dictatorial solution: the formation of a 'revolutionary government of workers and peasants' following the Hungarian model of 1956.[36] Given that there were a number of powerful Soviet supporters of a radical outcome, Kádár, with his plea for Dubček and his comrades, came down clearly on the side of the 'realist' alternative favoured by Brezhnev and Kosygin. He thereby contributed to a political compromise that involved the incumbent Czechoslovak leaders and culminated in the signing of the Moscow Protocol.

During the period of 'normalisation' in Czechoslovakia that began in earnest in 1969, the Hungarian party continued to play a moderating role between Moscow and Prague. It hoped that the sobering experience of the violent end of the Prague Spring would eventually result in the emergence of a modestly reform-oriented political agenda in Czechoslovakia, akin to the Hungarian model. According to this logic, many achievements of the Prague Spring would be preserved, just as the Kádárist regime had incorporated several goals of the failed revolution of 1956, albeit not the introduction of a multi-party system. Then the two reformist states in the Soviet bloc would form a virtual alliance that would help them avoid isolation and they could together fight successfully for the renewal of the communist system on pragmatic grounds. Indeed, from a historical perspective it is clear that the Prague Spring would have led to the restoration of parliamentary democracy without foreign intervention as eventually occurred in 1990. In reality, the Soviet leadership demonstrated extreme patience and self-restraint during the eight months of the crisis, as a military 'option' already in March following the abolition of censorship in Czechoslovakia would not have been irrational from their imperial perspective. From that time on, there was little hope that the Czechoslovak leadership would be able to push the genie of democracy back in the bottle. Yet, learning the lesson of their fatal mistake of intervening in Budapest too early during their first military incursion on 24 October 1956, the Soviets tried to find a political resolution according to the Kremlin's norms, executed by local communists and thus averting the need for Soviet armed aggression. Therefore, during the Czechoslovak crisis Brezhnev and his comrades for some eight months attempted to apply the 'Mikoyan doctrine',[37] that is, they relied on local actors and did their best to avoid using Soviet or joint allied military forces to 'restore order'. Initially, this meant persuading the Dubček leadership to acknowledge the limits of Moscow's tolerance, and then in the second stage, hoping to have the restoration implemented by pro-Soviet 'healthy forces' in the Czechoslovak party itself via an internal takeover. In the end, however, they had no other option than to use what would soon become known as the 'Brezhnev Doctrine' to stop the dangerous process of political transition by a military invasion.

The general public both at home and abroad rightly raised the question, which is timely even today: what would have happened if Hungary had not joined the armed coalition? From a moral viewpoint, this political step had incalculable consequences. Although everybody knew, including the people of Czechoslovakia, that the decision was not made voluntarily by a legitimate Hungarian government, the fall into sin was evident. Hungary's participation in the occupation of Czechoslovakia was a serious historical crime, which cannot be remedied by a subsequent apology. Moreover, one member of the Soviet bloc, Romania, did not take part in the invasion, albeit it was not invited to. What is more, Ceauşescu openly condemned the action and this had no perceivable negative consequences for Romania. Indeed, the Hungarian leadership, despite Soviet pressure, could also have declined to participate. Today we know that despite the original plans—as mentioned earlier—the East German army also did not join in the intervention, although this was a last-minute decision taken in Moscow rather than East Berlin. Since Romania's absence was an obvious fact, a negative decision on participation would automatically have placed Kádár in the same camp as Ceauşescu. This would not have been an attractive alternative, not only because Kádár was on bad terms with the Romanian leader, but also because the main principles of Hungarian foreign policy were totally contrary to that of Bucharest. In their 'separatist' policy, the Romanians were continually seeking maximum publicity in order to 'sell' their 'deviation' to the West as much as possible. For Kádár, however, the most important criteria were predictability and trustworthy partnership in international relations both with the East and the West.

This trustworthy status, which Kádár had been conscientiously constructing since 1956, would have been severely jeopardised if Hungary had opted out of the invasion. Kádár was not afraid that the USSR would once again occupy Hungary since this could hardly have taken place as retaliation. Rather, he was fearful that losing the confidence of the Soviet leadership would have a strong negative impact on the political and economic development of his country. The first victim would have been the economic reform being introduced at the time, which a few years later still earned the disapproval of Moscow and as a result had to be significantly limited. Nevertheless, many of its key elements were retained and it was never terminated, as mistakenly stated in numerous works. The removal of Kádár would also have been a logical option just as Dubček was replaced under Soviet pressure in April 1969, followed— for much less deviance—by Ulbricht in May 1971 and the Polish party leader Stanisław Kania a decade later in October 1981.

All in all, we can say that Kádár might have wished to stay out of the invasion but his mental constitution as a communist leader was unsuitable for taking such a radical step against the Kremlin. In many ways, his position was the opposite of Ulbricht's, whose acute desire to participate by including East German troops in the invasion ground force—again in order to reassure Moscow of the GDR's loyalty and lessen Soviet distrust of its more modest 1960s-style economic reforms—was in the end, for very good reasons, not granted. Had Hungary's leaders opted to stay out of the Warsaw Pact intervention, they would not have been able to achieve the relative independence they managed to secure in the 1970s and 1980s precisely on the basis of their reliability. In other words, Hungary, the 'happiest barrack in the Soviet camp', would have been less happy (although very few Hungarians know it, the Poles also think they had this self-same honourable title). Most likely Hungary would have ended up with a 'neither fish, nor fowl' kind of political line that would have been similar to the period of normalisation in Czechoslovakia under Gustáv Husák. In sum, in a moral sense Hungary paid a high price for the invasion, damaging its international reputation as a model 'de-Stalinised' communist state, but in a material sense it was probably better off.

Social Reactions to the Prague Spring

On 12 September 1968, the HSWP Politburo discussed an extensive policy paper evaluating the national and international effects of the crisis in Czechoslovakia.[38] The most remarkable and blunt statement was that although Hungarian society tolerated the invasion and Budapest's participation in it as an unavoidable step, it did not agree with it. According to the document, the basis of this consent was the party's largely successful efforts to improve political and economic conditions in the country since 1956. Indeed, while the invasion, and especially Hungarian involvement in it, came as a great surprise and shock for society, generally it was silently accepted, not because confidence in the regime was so excessive—as the document somewhat optimistically suggested—but because by 1968 most people felt they had something to lose.

The only public protest, which became known internationally, was made by five Hungarian philosophers and sociologists. From 14 to 24 August 1968, some seventy prominent Marxist and left-wing scholars gathered at a conference on Marxism in Yugoslavia. The symposium, devoted to the theme 'Marx and Revolution', was organised by the famous Zagreb avant-garde periodical *Praxis* in the town of Korčula, located on a tiny island off the Dalmatian coast. It was part of the regular 'Korčula Summer School', which was attended every summer by non-conformist Marxist and left-wing philosophers from Western as well as East European countries.[39] As news of the intervention in Czechoslovakia spread, the conference was interrupted and a joint declaration was drafted and published harshly condemning the invasion. The protest was expressed in the form of an appeal 'to all Communist, Socialist and progressive forces all over the world to condemn this aggressive act'. The appeal compared the situation of Czechoslovakia with that of Vietnam, and Soviet belligerence with 'that committed by Hitler's Germany'.[40] György Márkus, Vilmos Sós, Zádor Tordai, Ágnes Heller and Mária Márkus—aware of the potential consequences—signed the petition. Moreover, the Hungarian participants also delivered a separate declaration to the French news agency AFP, publicly attacking the intervention. The announcement stated that the Hungarian scholars, as Marxists and socialists, were completely conscious of their responsibility for the evolution of the socialist movement, and they went on:

> We consider that the intervention of certain countries of the Warsaw Pact constitutes a serious danger to the process of the renaissance of socialism and to the renaissance of Marxist theory which has been taking place in recent times. Regardless of the consequences, our duty is to try everything possible in order to further the development of authentic socialism and genuine social democracy.[41]

In Hungary, too, there were several isolated negative reactions to the invasion, but these did not get much publicity at the time. The world-renowned Marxist philosopher György Lukács and former Prime Minister András Hegedűs (1955–56), now head of the research group for sociology at the Hungarian Academy of Sciences (HAS), wrote letters to the HSWP Central Committe condemning the intervention. Lukács, who had been readmitted to the party only a year before,[42] announced that he would withdraw from all political and social activities in protest.[43] In similar fashion, the party meeting of the HAS research group for sociology unanimously passed a resolution rejecting the HSWP's decision to participate in the invasion. In the communist establishment the only visible protest was the resignation of András Tömpe, a veteran of the Spanish Civil War, from his post as Hungarian Ambassador to East Germany. Another initiative could have produced the first organised political protest in Hungary since 1956: a few young authors launched a campaign to sign a declaration condemning the Soviet bloc's military intervention. However, the movement soon failed because neither Lukács nor Gyula Illyés, the most influential representative of the so-called 'rural writers', supported the idea.[44]

The HSWP Politburo discussed these protests at its session on 3 September 1968. At the end of the debate, Kádár declared that the party would apply a differentiated approach to these actions, ranging from 'comradely friendly talks' with the culprits to extreme measures.[45] In the event, retaliation for these deviant acts was relatively mild as the Hungarian leadership itself took part in the invasion only half-heartedly. Hegedűs was replaced as head of the research group for sociology, Tömpe was made director of the Corvina Publishing House, while three of the Korčula 'five'—Márkus, Sós and Tordai—were expelled from the party, the other two not being party members.[46]

CONCLUSION

The failure of the Prague Spring taught both Hungarian leaders and society serious lessons. For Kádár and his colleagues, it compelled them to realise that radical political reforms in a Soviet bloc state, even if originally promoted and controlled by the party, could eventually lead to unpredictable and tragic consequences. The shocking warnings of the Soviets, outmatching even Stalin and Khrushchev combined, to the captive Czechoslovak leaders during the Kremlin 'negotiations' in late August must have been truly enlightening about how the Brezhnevite Politburo understood the real nature of the relationship between Moscow and its allies: 'They stated that they have a strategic interest in this region and they will never give it up... [therefore] the Soviet leadership is determined to crush any kind of Czechoslovak resistance, even if it means repopulating the country'.[47] The immediate reaction in Budapest was extreme caution in the planned extension of NEM beyond the economic sphere and in the long run it reinforced Kádár's conviction that his policy of 'constuctive loyalty' was the only feasible strategy towards Moscow. Thus, even his enormous mediation efforts during the Prague Spring, which could have been utilised to raise his popularity, had to be kept secret, so that the story could only be told in the 1990s after the collapse of the communist regime. While the majority of society silently accepted the harsh realities albeit with an unconfessed feeling of shame, the Prague Spring did eventually trigger the emergence of organised political opposition in Hungary. Although no public protests were made in 1968—with the exception of the Korčula declaration—a decade later in 1979 250 intellectuals signed a solidarity statement in support of the Czechoslovak human rights initiative, Charter 77.

Notes

1. The thesis that Kádár's 'carrot and stick' policy started immediately after the revolution and not in the early 1960s, as previously thought, was introduced by M. Kalmár, *Ennvaló és hozomány. A kora kádárizmus ideológiája* (Budapest, 1998).
2. Hungary was first described as a 'Khrushchevian model state' by the historian F. Fehér, 'A hruscsovista mintaállam', in *A stabilitás vége. Magyar Füzetek*, 8th edn (Paris, 1981), p. 27. It should be noted that an initial phase of de-Stalinisation had already been undertaken by the reform communist Imre Nagy from 1953 to 1955.
3. Memorandum from the Special Assistant for National Security (Bundy) to President Johnson, 14 April 1964, *Foreign Relations of the United States, 1964–1968. Eastern Europe*, vol. 17 (Washington, DC, 1996), p. 301.
4. P. Bencsik and Gy. Nagy, *A magyar úti okmányok története 1945–1989* (Budapest, 2003).
5. On the economic reform in 1968, see I.T. Berend, *The Hungarian Economic Reforms, 1953–1988* (Cambridge, 1990).
6. On the cultural field, see M. Kalmár, 'Az optimalizálás kísérlete. Reformmodell a kultúrában. 1965–1973', in J.M. Rainer (ed.), *"Hatvanas évek Magyarországon"* (Budapest, 2004), pp. 161–98. For an in-depth study of the Soviet system in Hungary, see M. Kalmár, *Történelmi galaxisok vonzásában. Magyarország és a szovjetrendszer, 1945–1990* (Budapest, 2014).
7. S. Bálint (ed.), *A szocializmus útján: A népi demokratikus átalakulás és a szocializmus építésének kronológiája, 1944. szeptember-1980. április.* (Budapest, 1982), pp. 603–30.

8. On Hungarian–Vatican relations, see Z. Ólmosi (ed.), *Mindszenty és a hatalom. Tizenöt év az USA-követségen* (Budapest, 1991); Gy. Gyarmati, 'A Mindszenty-ügy "diplomáciai" rendezésének kudarca', *Történelmi szemle*, vol. 42, no. 1–2 (2000), pp. 1–2, 69–90.
9. For the first use of this concept, see Cs. Békés, 'Hungarian Foreign Policy in the Soviet Alliance System, 1968–1989', *Foreign Policy Review*, vol. 2, no. 1 (2004), pp. 87–127, also available online at: http://www.rev.hu/portal/page/portal/rev/tanulmanyok/kadarrendszer/foreign_policy
10. For the GDR, the Western relationship meant above all their unique and highly controversial relationship with the Federal Republic of Germany.
11. For a detailed account of Kádár's mediating role, see Cs. Békés, 'Hungary and the Prague Spring', in G. Bischof et al. (eds), *The Prague Spring and the Warsaw Pact Invasion of Czechoslovakia in 1968* (Lanham, MD, 2011), pp. 371–95; also T. Huszár, *1968. Prága, Budapest, Moszkva. Kádár János és a csehszlovákiai intervenció* (Budapest, 1998).
12. For the full text of Kádár's speech, see Stiftung Archive der Parteien und Massenorganisationen im Bundesarchiv, Zentrales Parteiarchive, Berlin, (SAPMO BArch. ZPA), IV 2/201/778. Minutes of the Dresden Meeting, 23 March 1968. The speech is printed with omissions in S. Karner et al. (eds), *Prager Frühling. Das internationale Kriesenjahr 1968*, vol. 2: *Dokumente* (Cologne, Weimar and Vienna, 2008), pp. 451–9.
13. J. Navrátil et al. (eds), *The Prague Spring 1968: A National Security Archive Documents Reader* (Budapest, 1998), p. 138.
14. The Czechoslovak delegation consisted of Dubček, Oldřich Černík, Vasil Bil'ak and Jiří Hájek.
15. Hungarian National Archives (MNL-OL), M-KS-288, f. 47/743. ő. e. Memorandum of a telephone conversation between Kádár and Brezhnev, 12 June 1968.
16. Huszár, *1968*, p. 117.
17. Huszár, *1968*, p. 135.
18. Huszár, *1968*, p. 135; MNL-OL, M-KS-288, f. 4/93. ő. e., Minutes of the meeting of the HSWP CC, 7 August 1968.
19. Navrátil et al. (eds), *The Prague Spring 1968*, pp. 215–21, 229.
20. Huszár, *1968*, p. 216; MNL-OL, M-KS-288, f. 5/462. ő. e., Minutes of the meeting of the HSWP Politburo, 15 July 1968.
21. Huszár, *1968*, p. 228.
22. For the role of the Hungarian army in the invasion of Czechoslovakia, see I. Pataky, *A vonakodó szövetséges. A Magyar Népköztársaság és a Magyar Néphadsereg közreműködése Csehszlovákia 1968 évi megszállásában* (Budapest, 1996).
23. MNL-OL, M-KS-288, f. 5/467. ő. e., Minutes of the meeting of the HSWP Politburo, 20 August 1968.

24. Cs. Békés, *Az 1956-os magyar forradalom a világpolitikában* (Budapest, 2006), 2nd enlarged edition, p. 94.
25. Cs. Békés et al. (eds), *The 1956 Hungarian Revolution. A History in Documents* (Budapest, 2002), p. 487.
26. Cs. Békés and M. Kalmár, 'A szovjet-kelet-európai viszony átalakulása a korai Hruscsov korszakban', *Acta Scientiarium Socialium. Historia, Oeconomica, Paedagogia, Philosophia, Sociologia*, no. 46. (2016), pp. 17–33.
27. On the Imre Nagy case, see Gy. Litván, 'A Nagy Imre-per politika háttere', in *Világosság*, no. 10 (1992), pp. 743–57; J.M. Rainer, *Nagy Imre 1953–1958. Politikai életrajz*, vol. 2 (Budapest, 1999).
28. On the Warsaw Pact, see V. Mastny and M. Byrne (eds), *A Cardboard Castle? An Inside History of the Warsaw Pact, 1955–1991* (Budapest, 2005); Cs. Békés, 'Cold War, Détente and the Soviet Bloc: The Evolution of Intra-Bloc Foreign Policy Coordination, 1953–1975', in M. Kramer and V. Smetana (eds), *Imposing, Maintaining and Tearing Open the Iron Curtain: The Cold War and East-Central Europe, 1945–1989* (Lanham, MD, 2014), pp. 247–78. On the concept of 'emancipation' in the Warsaw Pact, see Cs. Békés, 'The Warsaw Pact and the Helsinki Process, 1965–1970', in W. Loth and G.H. Soutou (eds), *The Making of Détente: Eastern and Western Europe in the Cold War, 1965–75* (London, 2008), pp. 201–20.
29. On Bulgaria, see "1968: A Bulgarian Perspective", by Jordan Baev, in this volume; and I. Skálová, 'Bulgarian Participation in Suppressing the "Prague Spring" in August of 1968', in M.M. Stolarik (ed.), *The Prague Spring and the Warsaw Pact Invasion of Czechoslovakia, 1968* (Mundelein, IL, 2010), pp. 171–92.
30. On Poland, see "'To Hell with Sovereignty!': Poland and the Prague Spring", by Tony Kemp-Welch, in this volume; and Ł. Kamiński, 'The "Prague Spring", Poland and the Warsaw Pact Invasion', in Stolarik (ed.), *The Prague Spring*, pp. 95–127.
31. On the GDR, see "Ideological Offensive: The East German Leadership, the Prague Spring and the Warsaw Pact Invasion of August 1968", by Matthew Stibbe, in this volume; and R. Wenzke, 'The Role and Activities of the SED, the East German State and its Military during the "Prague Spring" of 1968', in Stolarik (ed.), *The Prague Spring*, pp. 137–64. It should be noted that Ivan Pataky, a Hungarian military historian, published information about the GDR's non-intervention as early as 1996. See Pataky, *A vonakodó szövetséges*, p. 150.
32. Pataky, *A vonakodó szövetséges*, pp. 45, 59.
33. Pataky, *A vonakodó szövetséges*, pp. 126–35.
34. Pataky, *A vonakodó szövetséges*, pp. 102–5.

35. 'Prágai tavasz: mégsem "testvéri segítségnyújtás"?', *Múlt-kor: Történelmi magazin*, 11 January 2013. Available at: https://mult-kor.hu/20130111_ pragai_tavasz_megsem_testveri_segitsegnyujtas (last accessed on 29 November 2017).
36. For details on the negotiations of the 'Five' on 24–26 August 1968, see Navrátil et al. (eds), *The Prague Spring 1968*, pp. 474–6; MNL-OL, M-KS-288, f. 4/95. ő. e., Minutes of the Meeting on 27 August 1968; Huszár, *1968*, pp. 272–4.
37. For the concept of the 'Mikoyan doctrine', see Cs. Békés, *Cold War, Détente and the 1956 Hungarian Revolution*, Working paper No. 7, International Center for Advanced Studies, New York University (2002).
38. MNL-OL, M-KS-288, f. 5/471. ő. e., Minutes of the HSWP Politburo, 13 September 1968.
39. Z. Antic, 'Leading Marxist Philosophers Protest Against the Invasion of Czechoslovakia, 1968', Open Society Archives Document. http://osaarchivum.org/files/holdings/300/8/3/text/78-1-20.shtml (last accessed on 29 November 2017). The 'Korčula Summer School' was particularly well attended in 1968. Besides approximately seventy philosophers and scholars, there were about 300 students from Yugoslav, West German, Austrian, French, Italian and British universities.
40. Antic, 'Leading Marxist Philosophers'.
41. Antic, 'Leading Marxist Philosophers'. On Hungarian dissident reactions to the invasion of Czechoslovakia, see also J.M. Rainer, 'PrágaKorcula-Budapest, 1968. augusztus 21', *Élet és Irodalom*, vol. 52, no. 32 (2008), n. p.
42. Lukács had been a party member before 1956, but he was not re-admitted to the reorganised HSWP until 1967.
43. Rainer, 'Prága-Korcula-Budapest'.
44. Rainer, 'Prága-Korcula-Budapest'.
45. MNL-OL, M-KS-288, f. 5/470. ő. e., Minutes of the HSWP Politburo, 3 September 1968.
46. Rainer, 'Prága-Korcula-Budapest'.
47. MNL-OL, M-KS-288, f. 47/744. ő. e., Report by Imre Kovács, Hungarian Ambassador in Prague, for János Kádár, 31 August 1968.

1968: A Bulgarian Perspective

Jordan Baev

The history of the Prague Spring and Warsaw Pact invasion of Czechoslovakia in 1968 has been thoroughly rewritten since the end of the Cold War. Yet certain key 'blank spots' in the historiography of these events still exist, among them the role played by a small Balkan communist state—Bulgaria. As important new Bulgarian political, diplomatic, military and security records have become accessible in recent years, there is now a chance to throw more light on the issue. This chapter discusses several lesser known themes: the input of the Bulgarian leadership in the Warsaw Pact decision-making process in favour of military intervention in Czechoslovakia; the participation of Bulgarian units in the invasion and their behaviour as an occupying force in an allied country; the reports and interpretations of official Bulgarian representatives in Prague and Bratislava concerning the reactions of various strata of Czechoslovak society; the influence of the Prague Spring and invasion on the Bulgarian public; and the consequences of these events for Bulgarian foreign and domestic policy and for developments in the Balkans as a whole.

Four different versions have been offered regarding the role played by the Bulgarian communist leader, Todor Zhivkov. The oldest variant

J. Baev (✉)
Rakovski National Defense College, Sofia, Bulgaria

puts forward the thesis that Zhivkov was the first East European leader to press Leonid Brezhnev to take the 'extreme step' of sending foreign troops into Czechoslovakia. This interpretation emerged from statements made by Foreign Minister Petar Mladenov at a Bulgarian Communist Party (BCP) Central Committee (CC) plenary session in July 1973.[1] In the early post-Cold War years, another hypothesis was raised which asserted, on the basis of official public statements and comments, that up to July 1968 the Bulgarian government had a relatively moderate approach to the Czechoslovak problem.[2] A third version, introduced by Zhivkov himself in his interviews with Western journalists and reconfirmed time and again during the disputes he had with his opponents in 1993, was his claim that he sympathised with the Prague Spring, but was obliged to adapt his position to suit the Kremlin's dictates.[3] In the early 1990s, the Bulgarian historian Vesela Chichovska posited yet another view—Zhivkov was Brezhnev's closest confidante and as such was used as an 'intermediary' during the initial attempts to exert influence over the Czechoslovak party leader Alexander Dubček.[4]

Following the declassification of relevant archival records in the 1990s and beyond, more realistic interpretations of Bulgarian involvement in the military intervention appeared, although these were largely restricted to national historiography with limited impact on the international academic community.[5] In addition, new evidence came to light in the memoirs of leading participants in the events.[6] Crucially, scholars also had the opportunity to reveal and analyse a number of hitherto secret documents from Zhivkov's personal files together with material from the Bulgarian diplomatic, military and security archives. All this has contributed to a more consistent and nuanced representation of the 'Bulgarian perspective' on the turbulent year 1968.

Bulgaria and the Decision-Making Process on Intervention

The first East European leader to draw Moscow's attention to the situation in Czechoslovakia—as early as January 1968—was Władysław Gomułka. Together with his East German counterpart, Walter Ulbricht, Gomułka was one of the severest critics of the Prague Spring and from the beginning of March both declared themselves firmly against the 'anti-socialist counter-revolution' in Czechoslovakia. As for the role of 'mediator', it was actually assigned, as Csaba Békés notes in his chapter, to the most moderate of the East European leaders—the Hungarian party boss, János Kádár. Zhivkov's attitude was rather double-faced. Initially, at least until the beginning of July 1968, his official and public position was really quite cautious. A second completely different stance, however, was confidentially exposed at Warsaw Pact summits as well as at secret BCP Politburo and Secretariat meetings. In his personal talks with Brezhnev, he not only expressed his solidarity with the Soviet stance, but also demonstrated a certain initiative.

In February 1968, on the occasion of the twentieth anniversary of the 1948 communist takeover in Czechoslovakia and less than two months after Dubček's appointment as leader of the Czechoslovak Communist Party (KSČ), Warsaw Pact dignitaries met in Prague. In the speeches delivered by the attending heads-of-state there was no hint whatsoever of any discord. Zhivkov declared 'full unanimity' with the 'expert and wise' leadership of the KSČ, stating: 'There have never been and there continue to be no matters of difference between us'.[7] A gathering of the Warsaw Pact Political Consultative Committee (PCC) took place ten days later, on 6–7 March 1968, in Sofia. The official communiqué on the 'open exchange of views' did not even mention Czechoslovakia. Nor did developments there appear in the text of the declaration made at the joint BCP CC and Council of Ministers plenary about the PCC summit. However, in a confidential report at the end of March 1968, Zhivkov himself explained:

> During the Warsaw Pact PCC session, we decided to share with the Soviet comrades our anxiety over events in Czechoslovakia. I had a special meeting with Comrades Brezhnev and Kosygin at which I expressed our concern with the situation, pointing out that we must do all we can, including taking even the ultimate risk, as we cannot permit counter-revolution to get into full swing in Czechoslovakia and as a consequence lose that country. What is Czechoslovakia's significance? Czechoslovakia is in the middle of the socialist bloc; it is a state of relatively great importance within the socialist system, both politically and economically. We categorically declared to Comrades Brezhnev and Kosygin that we had to be prepared to put our armies into action.[8]

Zhivkov's statement is indirectly confirmed by documents in the archives of the former Communist Party of the Soviet Union (CPSU) in Moscow. At a CPSU CC Plenum on 21 March 1968 dedicated to Czechoslovakia, Brezhnev remarked: 'In Sofia and afterwards, Comrades

Zhivkov, Gomułka and Kádár requested us to undertake steps to regulate the situation in Czechoslovakia'. Therefore, it was decided to convene a meeting of Soviet, East German, Polish and Hungarian representatives with the Czechoslovak leadership in Dresden. At Zhivkov's explicit insistence, a Bulgarian delegation was invited to take part in the proceedings.[9] Expressions such as the following are typical of those delivered to the BCP Politburo regarding the Dresden discussions: 'The attention of the Czechoslovak comrades has been drawn to the necessity of looking more closely at their people, at those whose heads need to be examined ... so that the incipient counter-revolution will be cut short'. Should the Czechoslovak leadership fail to implement the necessary measures to 'smash counter-revolutionary acts' the other Warsaw Pact countries would not be able 'to remain indifferent since they have bonds of unity with Czechoslovakia as well as common interests and they cannot permit a counter-revolution in the heart of Europe'.[10] At a special BCP CC Plenum on 29 March, Stanko Todorov, the Central Committee Secretary, delivered a detailed fifty-five page report on the Dresden meeting stating that all the East European leaders had displayed serious concerns about the 'disturbing situation' in Czechoslovakia. They were alarmed, in particular, by public demands for a return to the principles of 'Masarykian democracy' and for 'positive neutrality' in Czechoslovak foreign policy.[11]

The BCP Politburo thus gave perfectly clear guidelines on how the Bulgarian embassy in Prague and the domestic mass media were to portray events in Czechoslovakia. While early reports by Raiko Nikolov, Political Counsellor at the embassy, attempted to analyse the 'interesting processes' taking place in Czechoslovakia, the memoranda of Ambassador Stoyan Nedelchev after March 1968 ominously warned of a 'creeping counter-revolution', a position in full harmony with Sofia's views.[12] The hardening stance of the Bulgarian party leadership was also influenced by the intensification of 'confidential channels' of information received by State Security and Ministry of Defence sources. On 30 March 1968, the Chairman of the Committee for State Security, General Angel Solakov, despatched top secret intelligence reports to Zhivkov, which claimed that a 'leading anti-socialist centre' had been created in Prague against the 'pro-Moscow conservatives'. This hypothetical 'centre' was headed by František Kriegel with the participation of Ota Šik, Jiří Pelikán, Eduard Goldstücker and other leading reformists. The document warned that the intentions of the 'centre' were to isolate Dubček and announce Czechoslovakia's 'neutrality' outside the Warsaw

Pact Treaty Organisation. According to Bulgarian State Security informers, Kriegel had established confidential contacts with West German SPD leaders Willy Brandt and Helmut Schmidt, while Goldstücker allegedly maintained connections with Simon Wiesenthal's 'Zionist' headquarters in Vienna. In another intelligence memorandum to Zhivkov, Gen. Solakov sent additional data about Kriegel and Goldstücker.[13] On 12 April 1968, General Dobri Dzhurov, Minister of National Defence, informed the BCP Politburo about the deliberations of a Bulgarian military delegation in Prague with their Czechoslovak counterparts. The main conclusion was that 'a clandestine centre' had been established in Prague, which attempted 'to use Dubček and [President] Svoboda for its own reactionary' purposes.[14] In mid-May, high-ranking Bulgarian State Security representatives visited Czechoslovakia and their summary report, containing critical estimates of the 'demoralisation' of the Czechoslovak intelligence services and 'contradictory' activity of the Minister of the Interior, Josef Pavel, was sent personally to Zhivkov.[15]

In the second half of April 1968, a Bulgarian state and party delegation, headed by Zhivkov, paid an official visit to Czechoslovakia. The aim was to sign a new bilateral treaty of cooperation and mutual assistance between the two countries. Zhivkov's talks with Dubček on 23 April in Prague and with the arch-conservative Slovak party leader Vasil Bil'ak on 24 April in Bratislava focused on the situation in the country and 'the deep crisis which Czechoslovak society is now suffering'. Later, in private discussions with a closed circle of elite party activists, Zhivkov emphasised:

> From the very moment we stepped on Czechoslovak territory ... we felt that there is another ruling body in Czechoslovakia, operating in parallel with the Central Committee, created within the Central Committee and the Presidium ... This is a revisionist centre and it is clearing the way for counter-revolution, which is rampant in Czechoslovakia.[16]

Particularly interesting are the Bulgarian delegation's clandestine gatherings with representatives of the Czechoslovak 'sound hard-line'. At one such meeting, Central Committee Secretary Drahomír Kolder allegedly said: 'Tell the Soviet comrades that the situation here is so difficult that our own resources are insufficient to control it'. Another Czechoslovak communist functionary pointed out to his Bulgarian guests: 'The Central Committee officials and system of authority are paralysed'.

According to Zhivkov's testimony, his confidential talks with Bil'ak were organised like an underground criminal action:

> Bil'ak agreed with all my assessments and conclusions. Our delegation went to a night club. He took me from the club in a 'Volga' car, and going out through a different exit we went to his office in the Central Committee building and commenced our talks there. Bil'ak thinks our way, but Dubček sees things differently ... He is an absolutely inept person. He has neither the political, nor the personal courage which a leader should have to steer the sound forces against counter-revolution and revisionism.

At its meeting on 6 May 1968, the Soviet Politburo debated for the first time the idea of an armed intervention in Czechoslovakia. It should be noted that the political decision to launch a Warsaw Pact operation against Czechoslovakia was preceded by a proposal drawn up by the Soviet military command. The initial formulation was made by the General Staff of the Soviet armed forces on 8 April 1968.[17] Two days after the CPSU Politburo discussion of the matter, the leaders of Poland, Hungary, the GDR and Bulgaria were summoned to Moscow. Zhivkov later reported:

> We informed the Soviet comrades and comrades Gomułka, Kádár and Ulbricht of our impressions from our visit to Czechoslovakia ... Our assessments were confirmed at the Moscow meeting. New additional facts were presented that made it clear that the KSČ is actually incapacitated and that the revisionists are clearing the way for counter-revolution. We agreed that we should do everything to help the healthy forces in their struggle against counter-revolution ... we will use military force, and will never let the counter-revolution go ahead.[18]

Concrete planning for the eventual military operation started at the Warsaw Pact Joint Armed Forces' Unified Command sometime in the second half of June 1968. As is well known, Warsaw Pact military exercises under the code-name 'Šumava' took place in Czechoslovakia from 20 June to 11 July 1968. During that time, as a participant later recalled, 'a number of points relating to the introduction of allied troops on the territory of Czechoslovakia were worked out'.[19]

Meanwhile, on 30 June the Bulgarian Ambassador to Prague informed the BCP CC, in somewhat exaggerated terms, that the internal political crisis in Czechoslovakia had turned into an irreversible process which would end in 'unfavourable consequences' unless the 'healthy forces' inside the KSČ acted immediately. At the same time, the famous 'Two Thousand Words' manifesto was urgently sent to Sofia. On 5 July, the BCP Politburo dispatched a very severe letter to the KSČ Presidium describing the Manifesto as a counter-revolutionary appeal and a 'provocation' not only against the KSČ, but also against the Soviet Union and its East European allies.

In response to the growing turmoil in Czechoslovakia, it was decided to convene a special meeting of the leaders of the USSR, Bulgaria, East Germany, Poland and Hungary to be held in Warsaw on 14–15 July. Controversially, the KSČ Presidium declined to take part. In the so-called 'Warsaw Letter', adopted by the five parties at the gathering and addressed to the Czechoslovak Central Committee, the 'Brezhnev Doctrine' regarding the 'limited sovereignty' of members of the socialist commonwealth was outlined for the first time. Following the Bulgarian delegation's return from the Polish capital on 16 July, the BCP Politburo discussed the situation,[20] and at an extraordinary plenum on 26 July CC Secretary Stanko Todorov delivered a detailed report on the results of the Warsaw summit. Its content completely undermines the claims made later in the West that Bulgaria opposed Soviet intervention in Czechoslovakia[21]:

> Comrade Todor Zhivkov began his speech by emphasising that the Bulgarian delegation agreed with the assessment of the current situation in Czechoslovakia made by Com. Gomułka and Com. Ulbricht. 'Our delegation, however, does not accept the evaluation and the conclusion regarding the position in Czechoslovakia made by Comrade Kádár'. The task we now all face is what to do in these circumstances. Each one of us ... bears historical responsibility for the fate of socialism in Czechoslovakia ... it is not only a domestic problem of Czechoslovakia. This problem concerns each one of us, the whole socialist entity, and our joint defence. Without our strong support, the healthy forces inside the country will find it difficult to organise themselves ... The sound domestic forces must feel our unwavering support, the help of our parties, the aid of our countries, the assistance of our armed forces and the help of the Warsaw Pact as a whole.

Moreover, the planned operation in Czechoslovakia was also considered a 'preventive strike' against Western policy in Eastern Europe:

Above all, Czechoslovakia will be saved as a socialist country, a member of our socialist family [and] the counter-revolutionaries and imperialists will be taught yet another lesson. They will see that each of their attempts to restore capitalism in any socialist country is doomed to fail—that opportunism in the international communist and labour movements will be dealt a blow.[22]

In compliance with the plenum's resolutions, the Bulgarian press launched a 'campaign of clarification' of the situation in Czechoslovakia in the spirit of the 'Warsaw Letter'. This provoked an official protest from the Czechoslovak Foreign Minister, Jiří Hájek, at a meeting with the Bulgarian Ambassador Nedelchev on 27 July 1968.[23]

Rising diplomatic tensions were not the only noteworthy events of those hot summer days. From 28 July to 6 August, the Ninth World Youth and Student Festival was held in Sofia with the participation of more than 20,000 representatives from 138 countries.[24] Accordingly, from spring onwards the Bulgarian secret services were mobilised to take counter-measures against expected 'imperialist', 'revisionist' and 'pro-Maoist' ideological propaganda.[25] Among the more absurd political decisions was a recommendation from the CC Secretariat to the Organisational Bureau of the festival 'to undertake actions to prevent any eventual visit and concerts by the Beatles'.[26]

The official Czechoslovak delegation to the Ninth Youth and Student Festival numbered 508 representatives. They were accompanied by an additional 380 young tourists from Czechoslovakia and about eighty journalists (Czechoslovak TV alone sent sixteen reporters). The activities and contacts of the Czechoslovak delegates and guests were carefully monitored by Bulgarian secret agents and recounted in several confidential memoranda. For example, on 30 July 1968 Col.-Gen. Solakov informed Zhivkov that Bulgarian police and border guards had confiscated from the visitors numerous boxes of 'propaganda materials', among them translations of the 'Two Thousand Words' manifesto. The 'provocative behaviour' of some Czechoslovak representatives and journalists 'had obviously been planned in advance'. At the official opening ceremony in the streets of Sofia, several delegates shouted 'provocative' slogans against the Bulgarian civil militia and demanded 'more democracy' with appeals like 'Sofia, wake up!' About forty Czechoslovak delegates organised an 'unauthorised' discussion in front of their residence with other foreign guests and local citizens, aiming to 'tell the truth about the situation in Czechoslovakia'. In response, Solakov proposed that the Bulgarian

Foreign Ministry should deliver a verbal reprimand to the Czechoslovak Ambassador, while the secretary of the Organisational Bureau of the festival, Petar Mladenov, officially protested to the leaders of the Czechoslovak delegation 'about the behaviour of some of their members'.[27]

PARTICIPATION OF BULGARIAN TROOPS IN THE WARSAW PACT INVASION

At 1 a.m. on 21 August, the armed forces of the five Warsaw Pact countries taking part in 'Operation Danube' entered Czechoslovak territory. Bulgarian involvement consisted of military formations from two regiments of the Third Army, totaling 2164 troops.[28] The modest size of this contingent, compared with that of other Warsaw Pact forces, shows that the Bulgarian role in the operation was essentially symbolic.[29] It was the only Warsaw Pact state which had no land border with either Czechoslovakia or the Soviet Union. Furthermore, it was quite unthinkable that Bulgarian soldiers might cross the territories of Yugoslavia and Romania either on land or by air. It was also clear that Bulgarian participation in the military operation was required not for any practical reason, but because of the persistent request of the Bulgarian leaders to contribute to the joint action.

As early as mid-July, the Bulgarian forces chosen to take part in the Warsaw Pact operation were installed in field camps undergoing intensive military and psychological preparation. They trained in strict isolation from the civilian population in order to preserve the utmost secrecy. In fulfilment of a hand-written battle order of 23 July 1968 for 'participation in a military exercise' on Soviet territory, units of the 12th Elhovo regiment under the command of Col. Alexander Genchev were transported on the evening of 24 July from the Bulgarian Black Sea naval base of Atia to the USSR. Three days later formations of the 22nd Harmanli regiment led by Col. Ivan Chavdarov were flown from the Bulgarian airforce base at Uzundzhovo to the Soviet Union. According to the battle order, at the moment of their transportation the two Bulgarian regiments came under the control of the Supreme Commander of the Warsaw Pact Joint Armed Forces. A special Bulgarian operative liaison group was created at the JAF Unified Command, headed by First Deputy Chief of General Staff Lt.-Gen. Hristo Dobrev.[30] In execution of the Unified Command plan, by the end of July the Bulgarian units were located on the territory of the Lvov and pre-Carpathian military districts in Soviet Ukraine.

On 30 July 1968, the Chairman of the State Security Committee, General Solakov, approved the draft plan for a secret security operation 'Blow' to complement preparations for the military 'Operation Danube'. The security plan included both additional intelligence and counter-intelligence actions to be undertaken at the start of 'Danube'. The Foreign Intelligence Service (PGU-KDS) was instructed to strengthen its 'rezidentura' (intelligence stations) in Austria and West Germany. Bulgarian counter-intelligence services were to organise stricter surveillance over Bulgarian citizens in Eastern Europe, establish 'operational control' over the diplomatic personnel of the Czechoslovak, Yugoslav and Romanian embassies in Sofia, and prevent Czechoslovak citizens who stayed in Bulgaria at the beginning of the military operation from 'leaving the country'.[31]

In his subsequent detailed account to the BCP Politburo, Minister of Defence Dzhurov reported that as early as 1 August 1968 the Bulgarian Military Command was given instructions to fulfil the following tasks:

> The 12th APC Infantry Regiment acting within the structures of the 128th [Soviet] APC Infantry Division was to move to ZHNIATINO [western Ukraine], KOŠICE and BANSKÁ BYSTRICA [eastern and central Slovakia]. By the 20th hour after crossing the border it was to gain command of the ZVOLEN and BANSKÁ BYSTRICA regions. It had to gain control of important administrative-political and military sites: ZVOLEN airport, the post and telegraph office, the regional broadcasting station, the political parties' clubs, the militia department and the barracks and warehouses.
>
> Two flights were to transfer the 22nd APC Infantry Regiment from KOLOMIA airport (USSR) to RUZYNĚ and VODOCHODY aerodromes. The regiment had to organise perimeter defence of the aerodromes, not allowing capitalist states or Czechoslovak civilian and military aircraft to land or take off. In case of necessity, the regiment had to be ready to send forces into Prague in order to assist the 7th [Soviet] Airborne Division.[32]

In his memoirs, General Atanas Semerdzhiev stated that in the late afternoon of 18 August 1968 he and Dzhurov were urgently summoned by Zhivkov, who had just returned from Moscow. He informed them briefly: 'We agreed it should start the day after tomorrow. The government will pass a resolution tomorrow. Romania is not participating. You will be given details by the Unified Command'. Semerdzhiev also recollected that:

> Our military units were put under the operational command of a specially created Staff headed by Col.-Gen. Ivan Pavlovskii, Commander-in-Chief of Soviet land forces. Consequently, we - our national military command - were discharged from any responsibility in respect of the planning, organisation and management of the forthcoming operations. Our only obligation, and we had to fulfil it immediately, was to 'put into words' the verbal instruction we had just received from Todor Zhivkov in the form of a written order.[33]

In the rush to carry out the instructions, the strictly confidential orders—made out only in single hand-written copies—were sent to the commanders of the 12th Elhovo and 22nd Harmanli regiments on 19 August, while the official resolution of the Bulgarian government bearing the signature of Zhivkov was issued the next day. Both directives were of similar content and read:

> The attacks of the Czechoslovak counter-revolutionary elements against the people's power are becoming ever sharper. The Communist Party and the socialist system in the country appear to be in serious danger. The reactionaries are making particular efforts to divide Czechoslovakia from the Warsaw Pact and to set it against the other socialist states. In order to terminate the counter-revolution, I ORDER the Regiment to proceed to the execution of the battle tasks entrusted by the Commander-in-Chief of the Warsaw Pact Joint Armed Forces for the defeat of the enemy elements within the terms and areas according to the Action Plan. All directives of the Commander-in-Chief of the Warsaw Treaty Joint Armed Forces for the implementation of these tasks have to be executed strictly and unquestioningly.
> Gen. Dzhurov.[34]

The deployment of Bulgarian troops on Czechoslovak territory and the reactions of the local population were laboriously described in a report by the Minister of Defence prepared for the Bulgarian leadership on 30 September 1968.[35] Several isolated acts of resistance were documented during the 12th regiment's advance on Zvolen and Banská Bystrica in central Slovakia: the construction of barricades, stone attacks and even rifle fire, which caused minor injuries to twenty-one soldiers and eight officers from the regiment. In addition, the Bulgarian military had to react to other 'provocations' by Slovak 'hooligan' and 'prostitute' underground organisations, and 'under the instructions of the Soviet comrades' to close temporarily the publication of the local newspapers *Smer* ['Direction'] and *Vpred* ['Forward'], which had appealed for armed struggle against the Allied Forces.[36]

Units of the 22nd Harmanli regiment were transported by air to Prague in order to guard Czechoslovakia's primary airport, Ruzyně. The field diaries of the Bulgarian military formations reported a number of incidents during their two-month stay on Czechoslovak territory. In his reports to Sofia, Col. Dimitar Naidenov, representative of the Chief Political Directorate of the Bulgarian national army, mentioned some of the armed incidents:

> On 22 August at 01.55 a.m. positions of two of our formations were fired on. Around 02.40 a.m. two shots were fired over the company of Captain Gochkov, and around 02.44 a.m. there was shooting at the battle rows of Captain Valkov's company originating from nearby buildings. On 24 August at 01.07 a.m. an intensive round of automatic gunfire was directed at Officer Dimitrov's formation. At the end of August, the Bulgarian military newspaper, 'A Sentry at Ruzyně', published an article in which it was stated: 'On the night of 26 to 27 August shots were fired at the position of Warrant-Officer Vassilev from adjacent houses'.[37]

Similar information was given in General Dzhurov's report of 30 September 1968:

> On 30 August in the vicinity of the 22nd APC Infantry Regiment an underground warehouse with explosives (23 wooden boxes - 75-g explosives, 5 wooden boxes - 400-g explosives, 7 wooden boxes - plastic explosive and 12 wooden boxes - fuses, out of which 8 wooden boxes were ready for use) and 136 pcs mines for detonating explosives to destroy railway tracks were found. On 31 August in the same region another warehouse with 2 submachine guns and 2 pcs P-105 radio-transmission equipment was discovered.[38]

Bulgarian units did not participate directly in any military operations and the entire time they were stationed on Czechoslovak territory (21 August–23 October) they were under strict Soviet command. They suffered only one fatality. On the evening of 9 September 1968, Junior-Sergeant Nikolai

Nikolov was shot with three bullets from a 7.65 mm pistol. According to the subsequent investigation made by the Czechoslovak authorities, three Czechs murdered him in order to steal his submachine gun.[39] The official Bulgarian verdict, however, concluded that he was 'kidnapped'. While in a drunken state he had stopped two of the Czechs on the road from Prague to Kladno and asked them to take him to Karlovy Vary. Extrapolating from this, one contemporary version claims that he was probably trying to reach the border with West Germany.[40]

Reactions in Bulgaria

During the Prague Spring and following the Warsaw Pact intervention on 21 August 1968, there were isolated acts of protest among Bulgarian intellectuals. Three History Department students at the University of Sofia were arrested and sentenced to varying prison terms and several of their professors were expelled from the BCP.[41] State Security services carefully monitored all reactions, especially among representatives of the Bulgarian academic and artistic communities.[42] In accordance with the security operation 'Blow', at the time of the invasion strict 'operational control' was likewise organised over the Czechoslovak youth vacationing at the Bulgarian Black Sea resorts. Typical is a report by the State Security Chief in Burgas district, dated 26 August 1968, on the situation at the International Youth Vacation Camp in Primorsko and the 'Sunny Beach' resort:

> The Camp chiefs, following our instruction, warned an Italian journalist and a West German as well as the rest of the West European tourists not to meddle in these matters and recommended them to enjoy their holidays instead ... There are those progressive-thinking young people from England, Austria and West Germany who say that the measures taken were correct, if not even a bit delayed ... Czech citizens working here as musicians, waiters or experts at the Neftozavod [petrol processing plant] protested against the presence of Soviet troops in Czechoslovakia. They said the Czech people approved of the order they had established and other countries had no right to interfere.

The same State Security dossier also reported on negative reactions and comments of Bulgarian citizens:

> There are people, representatives of the intelligentsia, who directly accuse our leaders of interfering in Czech affairs - for their obedience to Moscow. With a certain amount of anger, hostile elements express their regret that the restoration [of capitalism] in Czechoslovakia was prevented. Dr Delcho Delchev, a member of the BCP working in Sofia, said: 'I cannot believe there is a counter-revolution in Czechoslovakia. These are nothing but fabrications meant to justify the intervention of Soviet troops and the Bulgarian part in these dangerous events. But look who's governing us. Todor Zhivkov is an obedient boy. Western communist parties will not approve the armed intervention. I reckon there will be a lot of important consequences'. The architect Yancho Chonkov is reported to have said: 'Force is force. The Soviets will impose a new order in Czechoslovakia, never mind the whole world saying they sympathise with the Czechs. One should be realistic about the events. Nothing will change' ... After urgent investigations, the persons concerned will be warned in respect to their above-mentioned statements.[43]

As 'preventive counter-measures' to the influence of the Prague Spring in Bulgaria, political control and censorship were visibly strengthened in the second half of 1968 and into 1969. Several plays, poems, satirical publications and movies were banned, among them works by well-known authors like Radoi Ralin and Georgi Markov. A few academic monographs by social scientists, like the young philosopher Asen Ignatov, were harshly criticised for their lack of 'class and party perspective' and for falling under the 'influence of decadent Western ideas'. Emerging popular rock musicians, and many university students in general, were persecuted for their 'improper "hippy" appearance, fashion and behaviour' occasioned by Western counter-culture models. The BCP leadership also incited the publication of various denunciatory media editorials lambasting ideological 'deviations', both from rightist 'opportunistic' and leftist 'dogmatic' and 'pro-Maoist' positions.

The Bulgarian Embassy in Prague and General Consulate in Bratislava documented numerous protests from different strata of Czechoslovak society against the armed intervention. Various reports from Czechoslovakia after 21 August bemoaned the 'great mistake' made by the Warsaw Pact countries, whose actions had 'hurt the national dignity of the Czechs and Slovaks'. Prior to the invasion, General Kodaj, Commandant of the East Czechoslovak Military District, had supported hard-line positions, often stating that more decisive actions were required against the 'anti-socialist forces'. Yet early in November 1968,

Kodaj admitted to Stefan Velikov, the Bulgarian Consul General in Bratislava: 'The shock was too great'. He explained how he felt offended on the night of 20–21 August: 'He was nearly arrested; his headquarters were surrounded and machine gunners rushed into his office'. The Czechoslovak military commander underlined several times during his confidential talks that there had been no need to send Warsaw Pact regiments. The Commander of the Bratislava Garrison backed this opinion, saying that 'our countries have lost a lot with the invasion'.[44]

Repercussions in the Balkans

Soon after the invasion of Czechoslovakia, various experts and commentators speculated about Warsaw Pact 'plans' for armed intervention against Romania and Yugoslavia. Western media reported on this throughout the second half of 1968 and into early 1969.[45] Although US diplomatic and intelligence channels confirmed that 'there is no reliable evidence' for such a military operation, Lyndon B. Johnson's administration discussed the necessity of strengthening contacts with Tito's regime in Belgrade.[46] Bulgarian archival sources categorically reject the hypothesis that any plans for intervention against Romania or Yugoslavia were ever discussed in the Warsaw Pact structures, as well as any re-deployment of Soviet troops in Bulgaria.[47] On the contrary, in a top secret cable to the chief of Soviet military intelligence, Col.-Gen. Petr Ivashutin, dated 28 August 1968, his Bulgarian counterpart, Lt.-Gen. Vasil Zikulov, reported on the stationing of Yugoslav tank and artillery units in the cities of Zaječar, Niš and Pirot close to the border with Bulgaria. General Zikulov also stated that there was no evidence of the mobilisation of troops in Italy, Greece and Turkey (the NATO Southern Flank) in response to the Warsaw Pact action in Czechoslovakia.[48]

The occupation significantly aggravated relations between Romania and its Warsaw Pact allies. Early in the morning of 21 August 1968 an extraordinary meeting of the Romanian Communist Party leadership was urgently convoked. The main decisions were to mobilise the so-called 'Patriotic Guard' in the spirit of an 'all-people's territorial national defence' and to announce at a special parliamentary session a declaration on the 'Basic Principles of Romanian Foreign Policy'.[49] On 23 August, party boss Nicolae Ceaușescu requested through the ambassadors of the USSR, Hungary and Bulgaria in Bucharest urgent consultations with the governments of these neighbouring countries, while on 24 August he departed for Belgrade for talks with Tito. The media commentaries after their deliberations specified that the two Balkan leaders had discussed 'their ability to repulse with joint forces an eventual aggression by the Soviet Union, Bulgaria and Hungary'.[50] The voice of the Romanian mass media became more balanced and moderate only after the confidential talks between Ceauşescu and the Soviet ambassador Aleksandr Basov on the afternoon of 25 August.[51]

To understand Soviet policy towards Romanian 'dissidence' inside the Warsaw Pact, it is necessary to stress two significant differences between the situation in Czechoslovakia and Romania. In the first place, Ceauşescu's domestic policies conformed to communist orthodoxy. Unlike Dubček's 'socialism with a human face', they were repressive, authoritarian and devoid of any ideological challenge to the established political model. Second, Romania was the only Warsaw Pact member state, together with Poland, that bordered entirely with other socialist countries and therefore from the military-strategic point of view Romania was not regarded as being so crucial as Czechoslovakia in the common defence against NATO. What is more, Ceauşescu never demonstrated any inclination to leave the Eastern bloc, whereas in Moscow and beyond it was feared that the Czechoslovaks were wavering on this pivotal issue.

Nevertheless, the disagreements between Bucharest and her East European allies in August 1968 effectively terminated the participation of Romanian armed forces in joint Warsaw Pact military operations for a considerable period. At the end of October 1968, an annual meeting of the heads of Warsaw Pact military intelligence services (initially planned for the beginning of September) took place in Bucharest. The Romanian hosts attended the first plenary session, but declined to discuss the questions of mutual cooperation in the field of strategic, operational and radio-electronic intelligence directions. Moreover, the chief of Romanian military intelligence service, Colonel Dumitru, refused to sign the concluding protocol of the meeting.[52] In March 1969, the fleets of the USSR, Bulgaria and Romania carried out naval exercises in the Black Sea basin for the last time in four years; they were renewed only in April 1973.[53] Between 1970 and 1972, Romania sent only General Staff observers, but not troops, to Warsaw Pact drills, and it was not until 1975 that multilateral military exercises were once again held on Romanian territory.[54]

Another consequence of the military intervention in Czechoslovakia was the increased activity of Mao's China in the Balkans. On the evening of 21 August, the Chinese diplomatic representative in Bucharest was asked directly by a senior Romanian official about the possibility of Chinese support in case of Soviet aggression against Romania. Two days later, after consultations with Mao, the Chinese Prime Minister Zhou Enlai encouraged the Romanian ambassador in Beijing, Aurel Duma, to resist Soviet 'social imperialism' and even declared: 'If it is necessary, we will deliver arms to Romania!'[55] Discussions between Mao Zedong, Zhou and the Albanian Minister of Defence, General Beqir Balluku, in Beijing on 1 October 1968 were also revealing. The Albanian guest informed his hosts about a surprising redeployment of large numbers of Soviet troops (ten airborne divisions with approximately 40,000 servicemen) in Bulgaria immediately after the Czechoslovak invasion. According to the talks in the Chinese capital, the Kremlin was 'undoubtedly' preparing a forthcoming military invasion of Yugoslavia and Romania. As noted above, all recently declassified archival evidence categorically demonstrates that such 'confidential information' was totally groundless, but it was considered quite reliable in Beijing and Tirana. During the talks, Chairman Mao remarked that in these circumstances even Tito's government could be considered 'our indirect ally' because of its problems with Moscow. Zhou Enlai expanded on Mao's thoughts by proposing the establishment of a 'Balkan union', consisting of Albania, Romania, Yugoslavia and China spearheaded against 'Soviet hegemony'.[56] However, the Albanian leader, Enver Hoxha, declined the prospect of an 'anti-Soviet bloc' if it meant the participation of his personal foe, Tito. Nevertheless, shorthand reports of private conversations between Zhivkov and Brezhnev in the 1970s clearly display the Soviet leader's constant and growing concern about the possibility of a 'pro-Chinese' and 'anti-Soviet bloc' in the Balkans.[57]

CONSEQUENCES

The Bulgarian communist authorities were explicit and unanimous in their statements concerning the necessity of their actions, which had allegedly saved the Czechoslovak people from a 'counter-revolution' and had prevented an inevitable Western intervention. They firmly maintained this position when challenged by representatives of Western European communist parties who had opposed the military operations in

Czechoslovakia. During the extremely long and controversial discussions with the head of the International Department of the Italian Communist Party, Carlo Galluzzi, on 16 September 1968, the BCP leaders constantly reiterated that: 'We do not consider our interference a mistake. We believe that by our timely intervention, we put an end to the dangerous process of counter-revolution which could only have ended with a victory of the counter-revolution ... That would have signified a dreadful blow for the defence of the socialist camp in Europe'.[58] Even five years later, Zhivkov maintained the same view in his talks with the Italian 'Euro-communist' leader Enrico Berlinguer.[59]

The invasion of Czechoslovakia with the participation of Bulgarian troops helped to shape several features of Bulgarian foreign and internal policy in subsequent years. On the one hand, Soviet-Bulgarian relations and the personal ties between Brezhnev and Zhivkov were consolidated. Soon afterwards this was demonstrated by means of considerable Soviet economic aid to Bulgaria. For instance, during Zhivkov's visit to Moscow in September 1968 a delivery of large quantities of Soviet natural gas, petrol and electric energy was agreed. That marked the beginning of a new stage of bilateral relations through which in the course of the next decade the Bulgarian communist government enjoyed significant economic benefits. At the same time, there was an upsurge in the systematic re-armament of the Bulgarian armed forces with modern Soviet weaponry, a step also motivated by the on-going crisis in the Middle East and the turmoil in Cyprus in 1973–74.

On the other hand, the events in Czechoslovakia directly influenced the hardening of the internal political line of the communist regime in Bulgaria. More severe 'preventive' measures were undertaken mainly against eminent representatives of the intelligentsia, though these repressive acts did not foment any 'dissident' activity similar to that in Central European countries. The suppression of the Prague Spring and adoption of the 'Brezhnev Doctrine' generated pessimistic attitudes in Bulgarian society, feelings that Bulgaria had no political alternatives, that its political destiny had been predetermined much earlier and imposed by means of the infamous 'percentage agreement' between Churchill and Stalin in October 1944 and the Yalta agreements of February 1945. The Bulgarian position also resulted in a deterioration of the country's relations with two other Balkan communist states—Tito's Yugoslavia and Ceauşescu's Romania. Finally, Bulgaria's participation in the military occupation of Czechoslovakia was used as a suitable argument by the Turkish and Greek governments to request significantly more military aid from NATO, as well as the consolidation of its Southern flank, requests that were in the event rejected at the NATO Council session held in November 1968.

From a wider perspective, there is no doubt that the invasion of Czechoslovakia prompted an organisational strengthening of both NATO and the Warsaw Pact, affected within several months of the intervention. Furthermore, the aggravation of the political and military confrontation in Central and Eastern Europe and the categorical condemnation of the Soviet actions by West European governments and public opinion interrupted and delayed for many months the initial talks on the convocation of a joint conference for security and cooperation in Europe. In the end, however, taking into consideration all the pros and cons, it must be concluded that the military intervention in Czechoslovakia blocked all attempts and strivings in the Soviet bloc countries for even the most moderate economic and political reforms for at least four or five years, and in some cases substantially longer.

Notes

1. Central State Archive (TsDA), Sofia, f. 1-B, op. 58, a.e. 85, p. 128.
2. M. Kramer, 'The Prague Spring and the Soviet Invasion of Czechoslovakia: New Interpretations (part 2)', *Cold War International History Project Bulletin*, no. 3 (1993), pp. 2–13 (here pp. 4–6).
3. T. Zhivkov, *Sreshtu nyakoi lazhi* (Sofia, 1993). Zhivkov's exact words in an interview with an American journalist in November 1991 were: 'From today's point of view, I've no doubt that it was an occupation and that nothing can justify it. But at that time, we were allies and had to participate. I could do nothing by myself. I was not exactly ordered to participate, but I could not refuse. The fate of our country was at stake. The Soviet Union could have cut us off economically, and we would not have survived for more than a month'. *New York Times*, 28 November 1991. However, this version was not mentioned in Zhivkov's recollections of more than 700 pages, *Memoari* (Sofia, 1997).
4. V. Chichovska, 'Bulgaro-chehoslovashkite otnoshenia prez 40-te—60-te godini', *Minalo*, no. 2 (1994), p. 75.
5. J. Baev, *Voennopoliticheskite konflikti sled Vtorata svetovna vojna i Bulgaria* (Sofia, 1995), pp. 192–210; J. Baev, 'Bulgaria and the Political Crises in Czechoslovakia (1968) and Poland (1980/81)', *Cold War International History Project Bulletin*, no. 11 (1998), pp. 96–101; J. Baev, *Sistemata za*

evropeiska sigurnost i Balkanite v godinite na Studenata vojna (Sofia, 2010), pp. 189–202; I. Baeva, *Bulgaria i Iztochna Evropa* (Sofia, 2001), pp. 124–43; I. Baeva, *Iztochna Evropa prez XX vek* (Sofia, 2010), pp. 190–208, 306–44, 449–61; V. Migev, *Prazhkata prolet-68 i Balgaria* (Sofia, 2005).

6. For instance, see the memoirs of the former Chief of the Bulgarian General Staff, Col.-Gen. Atanas Semerdzhiev, *Prezhivyanoto ne podlezhi na obzhalvane* (Sofia 1999), pp. 244–8.
7. *Foreign Policy of the People's Republic of Bulgaria. Documents*, vol. II (Sofia, 1971), p. 422.
8. TsDA, f. 1-B, op. 58, a.e. 4, pp. 96–9.
9. R. Pikhoia, 'Chekhoslovakiia 1968: Vzgliad iz Moskvy. Po dokumentam TsK KPSS', *Novaia i noveishaia istoriia*, no. 6 (1994), p. 11.
10. TsDA, f. 1-B, op. 35, a.e. 127, pp. 6–13.
11. TsDA, f. 1-B, op. 58, a.e. 4, pp. 2–57.
12. Diplomatic Archive of the Ministry of Foreign Affairs (DA), Sofia, op. 24-P, a.e. 2988, pp. 8–14, 50–9.
13. Central Archive of the Bulgarian State Security and Military Intelligence Services (COMDOS), Record Group 'M', f. 1, op. 10, a.e. 694, pp. 50–9, 184–6. The Bulgarian Counter-intelligence Service had its agent (aka 'Gorast') in Kriegel's entourage. His dispatches were also delivered to the head of the KGB group in Czechoslovakia, General Mikhail Kotov. It should be noted that all four named Czech reformers were of Jewish descent.
14. State Military History Archive (DVIA), Veliko Tarnovo, f. 24, op. 10a, a.e. 21, pp. 8–12.
15. COMDOS, Record Group 'M', f. 1, op. 10, a.e. 695, pp. 83–4 and 204–8.
16. This quotation and the subsequent ones by Kolder and Zhivkov are from TsDA, f. 378-B, op. 1, a.e. 206, pp. 1–4.
17. A. Okorkov, *Sekretnye voiny Sovetskogo soiuza. Pervaia polnaia entsiklopediia* (Moscow, 2008), pp. 648–61.
18. TsDA, f. 378-B, op. 1, a.e. 206, pp. 5–7.
19. S. Zolotov, 'Shli na pomoshch druziam', *Voennoistoricheskii zhurnal*, no. 4 (1994), pp. 14–17.
20. TsDA, f. 1-B, op. 35, a.e. 255, pp. 1–2.
21. *Radio Free Europe Background Reports*, Open Society Archives, Budapest, f. 300, sub-fond 20, folder 1, box 89.
22. TsDA, f. 1-B, op. 58, a.e. 12, pp. 44–8.
23. DA, op. 24-P, a.e. 3020, pp. 202–3. Hájek also delivered a letter from Czechoslovak Prime Minister Oldřich Černík to Zhivkov outlining the additional measures taken to protect the Czechoslovak state border with West Germany.

24. Previous festivals were held in Prague (1947), Budapest (1949), East Berlin (1951), Bucharest (1953), Warsaw (1955), Moscow (1957), Vienna (1959) and Helsinki (1962).
25. For the massively detailed security service's reports, see COMDOS, Record Group 'M', f. 24, op. 1–343. Soviet and East European secret services sent more than ninety officers to Sofia during the festival.
26. TsDA, f. 1-B, op. 36, a.e. 131, p. 16; COMDOS, Record Group 'M', f. VI-L, a.e. 282, vol. 1, p. 75. This mirrors similar concerns in the GDR to prevent East German youths from travelling to Prague to attend what was in fact a non-existent Rolling Stones concert in late July 1968. For details, see "Ideological Offensive: The East German Leadership, the Prague Spring and the Warsaw Pact Invasion of August 1968", by Matthew Stibbe, in this volume.
27. COMDOS, Record Group 'M', f. 1, op. 10, a.e. 697, pp. 132–8. According to a KGB memorandum, several members of the Czechoslovak youth delegation intended to organise a meeting in front of the Soviet embassy in Sofia with the slogan: 'Stop Soviet interference in the internal affairs of Czechoslovakia'.
28. The Third Bulgarian Army, deployed in south-east Bulgaria near the Greek and Turkish borders, was assigned to be an integrated part of the Warsaw Pact Joint Armed Forces.
29. One Hungarian, two East German and three Polish divisions, comprising more than 50,000 of the total 165,000 Warsaw Pact troops (26 divisions), were involved in the military operation. The full strength of the Warsaw Pact forces, both in the forward echelon and in reserve, numbered half a million servicemen. At the last moment, the East German divisions were ordered not to enter Czechoslovakia for 'psychological' reasons.
30. DVIA, f. 24, op. 10a, a.e. 22, pp. 172–6.
31. COMDOS, Record Group 'M', f. 1, op. 10, a.e. 445, pp. 240–8.
32. TsDA, f. 1-B, op. 49, a.e. 158, pp. 1–2.
33. Semerdzhiev, *Prezhivyanoto ne podlezhi na obzhalvane*, p. 244.
34. DVIA, f. 24, op. 10a, a.e. 22, pp. 37–8.
35. The Bulgarian Minister of National Defence regularly informed the BCP Politburo about the situation in Czechoslovakia and the participation of Bulgarian troops in the Warsaw Pact operation (Dzhurov reports, 13 and 30 September and 7 and 20 October 1968). See DVIA, f. 24, op 10a, a.e. 22, pp. 235–42, 276–80, 313–19.
36. TsDA, f. 1-B, op. 49, a.e. 158, pp. 2–5.
37. For field diaries, battle reports and summary information on the participation of Bulgarian troops in the invasion of Czechoslovakia, see DVIA,

f. 3, op. 6, a.e. 74, 94; f. 24, op. 10a, a.e. 21, 22; f. 343, op. 12, a.e. 4; f. 740, op. 11, a.e. 28.
38. TsDA, f. 1-B, op. 49, a.e. 158, p. 7.
39. The results of the investigation were included in a secret KGB Daily Bulletin sent from Moscow to Sofia on 30 September 1968. See COMDOS, Record Group 'M', f. 1, op. 10, a.e. 534, pp. 149–50.
40. See A. Nikolov, *Goreshtoto lyato na 68-a. Prazhkata prolet, bratskata pomosht i NR Balgaria* (Sofia, 2013), pp. 338–44.
41. *Homo Bohemicus*, no. 3 (1994), pp. 51–64. One of the students, Valentin Radev, languished in jail for eighteen months. He died from a heart attack at the age of forty-eight in 1995.
42. COMDOS, Record Group 'M', f. 1, op. 10, a.e. 699, pp. 129–37.
43. COMDOS, Record Group 'M', f. 1, op. 10, a.e. 696, pp. 90–100; a.e. 1435, pp. 9–11; f. 2, op. 2, a.e. 263, p. 69; op. 3, a.e. 322, pp. 129–37.
44. DA, op. 24-P, a.e. 2987, pp. 58–64.
45. The first analytical report of a hypothetical threat of Soviet military intervention in Romania was sent to the US President on 24 August 1968. See L. B. Johnson Library, Austin, Texas, National Security Council, Country File: Romania, box 204, 'Intervention in Romania'.
46. US Department of State, Intelligence Note, no. 827, 22 October 1968, National Archive Records Administration (NARA), College Park, MD, RG 59, Central Foreign Policy Files, 1967–1969, box 1917.
47. Bulgaria was the only Warsaw Pact country that had no Soviet troops on its territory from December 1947 until the end of the Cold War. The Red Army had previously withdrawn from Czechoslovakia in December 1945 (but returned in August 1968) and Soviet forces left Romania as late as September 1958.
48. COMDOS, Record Group 'VR', f. MF 000469, a.e. I-810, pp. 60–60a.
49. Central National Historical Archive (ANIC), Bucharest, CC PCR, Cancelarie, dosar 133/1968, pp. 2–4.
50. DA, Documentation Records, V/I/4—BTA-MINF, *Spetsialen Buletin*, no. 241, 27 August 1968.
51. However, in September 1968 the Romanian special counter-intelligence unit (code-named UM 0920/A), which had been established a year earlier with the task of counteracting potentially hostile KGB actions against Ceaușescu and his regime, was, in strict secrecy, significantly enlarged by around one hundred security officers and personnel.
52. COMDOS, Record Group 'VR', f. 23, op. 01288, a.e. 1057, pp. 4–5, 38–9, 68, 103–6; a.e. 1058, pp. 17, 124–32; f. MF 00825, a.e. 989, pp. 6–8.
53. DVIA, f. 1027, op. 13, a.e. 13, pp. 159–60.

54. DVIA, f. 48, op. 19, a.e. 21, pp. 137–64; f. 1027, op. 19, a.e. 21, pp. 1–12 and a.e. 22, pp. 45–98.
55. R. Budura (ed.), *Politica independenta a Romaniei si relatile Romano-Chineze, 1954–1975, Dokumente* (Bucharest, 2008), pp. 59–60.
56. X. Liu and V. Mastny (eds), *China and Eastern Europe 1960s–1980s* (Zurich, 2004), pp. 92, 98.
57. For more details, see J. Baev, 'Bulgaria and the Coordination of the East European Policy Toward China After the Sino–Soviet Discord (1960–1989)', in *New Sources, New Findings: The Relationship between China, the Soviet Union and Eastern Europe* (Beijing, 2014), pp. 351–2.
58. TsDA, f. 1-B, op. 60, a.e. 11, pp. 1–39.
59. TsDA, f. 1-B, op. 60, a.e. 74, pp. 1–68.

Ceauşescu's Finest Hour? Memorialising Romanian Responses to the Warsaw Pact Invasion of Czechoslovakia

Calin Goina

On 21 August 1968, Nicolae Ceauşescu, the 50-year-old leader of the Romanian Communist Party (RCP), addressed a huge crowd from the balcony of the Central Committee building in Bucharest[1]:

> Dear comrades, citizens of the Romanian land! The invasion of Czechoslovakia by the five socialist countries constitutes a grave mistake, a serious threat to peace in Europe and to the future of socialism on earth! (Acclamation) In the contemporary world, when people are fighting for their national independence and for equal rights, it is inconceivable that socialist states infringe on the freedom and independence of another state! (Acclamation) There is no justification, no reason, even for a single moment, for the idea of military intervention in the affairs of a brotherly socialist state! (Applause).[2]

C. Goina (✉)
Department of Sociology and Social Work, Babes-Bolyai University, Cluj-Napoca, Romania
e-mail: goinac@ucla.edu

It was an extraordinary spectacle, beginning with the way the leader addressed his audience. Perhaps consciously echoing Stalin's discourse following Hitler's invasion of the Soviet Union in June 1941, he used 'comrades', but also 'citizens', who lived not in the 'Socialist Republic of Romania', but in the 'Romanian land', evoking the medieval, more nationalist, connotation of the term. The speech was meant to be, and remained, a landmark in Romania's communist history with ramifications way beyond the country's borders.

My chapter aims to explore popular Romanian responses to Ceauşescu's discourse and to his public stand against the Soviet invasion of Czechoslovakia. I use the biographical method as my main instrument, focusing on a series of life-story interviews of party and non-party members on the August 1968 events. I do not look at the political elite. Instead, I document the reactions and memories of those who were far removed from the political centre living in a rural settlement located in western Romania, inhabited by Romanians, Romanian-Germans (*Schwaben*) and Roma.

Most experts on Romanian communism see August 1968 as the moment that the indigenous population backed the stance of their ostensibly reformist ruler, who had first come to power in 1965.[3] For example, Dragos Petrescu claims that 'Ceauşescu's display of national pride and complete independence created a special state of mind among the Romanian population and brought him broad popular support, which eventually gave legitimacy to single-Party rule in Romania'.[4] Highlighting this same peak of legitimacy, the editors of a volume of archival materials on 1968 chose as the title of their book *21 August 1968: Ceauşescu's Apotheosis*.[5] However, on the basis of my exploration of a variety of reactions to the invasion of Czechoslovakia, I conclude that notions of 'broad popular support' and 'Ceauşescu's finest hour' need to be qualified. While previous scholars seem to attribute singular significance to the August speech, referring to its wide and enthusiastic reception, I found that many Romanian citizens lacked concrete memories of the events and a few were less than sympathetic to Ceauşescu's position.

I begin with a brief historical overview of Romania's position in the Soviet bloc and its reluctance, alongside Albania, to condone what would soon be called the 'Brezhnev Doctrine'.[6] I then move on to a review of the main reactions among Romanian intellectuals to the August events before concluding with an in-depth account of my biographical explorations of the memories of 1968 in a small town—at that time no more than a village-commune—in western Romania.

THE HISTORICAL CONTEXT

How can we explain Romania's exceptionalism in 1968? Following William E. Crowther's argument, I reject unidimensional explications.[7] First, it is important to stress that militarily the Romanian regime, taking advantage of embryonic Sino–Soviet tensions, found itself in the fortunate position of soliciting and obtaining the complete withdrawal of Red Army troops from its territory in 1958. Second, the economy was an essential factor: the Romanian Communist Party (RCP) stubbornly implemented its economic programme of industrialisation and rebuffed Moscow's principle of specialisation within the socialist states which would have reduced Romania essentially to an agricultural producer. The result was that 'beginning in 1961 Kremlin leaders and the Romanians moved toward open confrontation'.[8] Last but not least, Nikita Khrushchev's 'secret speech' in February 1956 and the subsequent de-Stalinisation process pushed Gheorghe Gheorghiu-Dej, the then leader of the RCP, into an ideologically tense position, for as an old 'Stalinist' he ran the risk of being replaced by a Khrushchevite 'reformer' chosen by the Kremlin. This context favoured Dej's independent proclivities. In a trajectory similar to that of Mao, Albanian leader Enver Hoxha and the head of the French Communist Party, Maurice Thorez,[9] Dej distrusted Khrushchev's reforms and fearing the Kremlin's heavy hand he gravitated towards an increasingly autonomous nationalist stance, economically, culturally and ideologically. This campaign culminated in April 1964 when an RCP Central Committee plenum issued a 'Declaration' proclaiming that: 'There exists no "parent" party and "offspring" party, no "superior" and "subordinated" parties, but only the large family of communist and workers' parties having equal rights'.[10] This new independent political line was inherited and accentuated by Dej's successor, Ceaușescu, who after 1965 played the nationalist card with even greater enthusiasm.[11] It was precisely this principle of autonomy, originally adopted and promoted by Dej in the early-to-mid 1960s, that formed the basis of the RCP's position during the Czechoslovak crisis.

Throughout 1968, given Ceaușescu's independent stance, Romania was regarded by the Kremlin as an unreliable ally at best.[12] Hence, beginning with the Dresden meeting in late March, the Soviet leaders declined to invite RCP representatives to any of the multilateral gatherings of the socialist states that addressed the situation in Czechoslovakia. By the end of April, Ceaușescu was able to bolster his domestic power base by removing a potential rival, Alexandru Drăghici, from the

Politburo using the rehabilitation of Lucrețiu Pătrășcanu as a tool.[13] This was another signal of the nationalist turn he was embracing, alongside his anti-colonial discourse that all communist parties were equal. In May, Bucharest's struggle with Moscow was acknowledged by the French President, Charles de Gaulle, with an unprecedented state visit to communist Romania.

In a gesture of solidarity with the Czechoslovak leaders, Ceaușescu arrived in Prague on 15 August, only a week after Josip Broz Tito's visit, to sign a 'Czechoslovak-Romanian Treaty of Friendship, Collaboration and Mutual Assistance' valid for the next twenty years. Back in Romania, he declared in a public speech that 'we have been profoundly impressed' by developments in Czechoslovakia. Furthermore, 'we have returned with an even stronger conviction that the destinies of socialism and the Czechoslovak people are in safe hands, in the hands of the communist party and its leadership'.[14] But just a few days later, at 6.30 a.m. on 21 August, an emergency meeting of the RCP Executive Committee was convened. The participants were informed that 'at 3.00 a.m. a clerk from the Soviet Embassy brought an unsigned note that he left at the Chancellery of our Central Committee ... [announcing] that there are counter-revolutionary elements [in Czechoslovakia] and that, given the situation, at the request of the majority of the [Czechoslovak] Presidium the Soviet Union has intervened in that country'.[15] The Executive Committee decided to call a Central Committee plenum and a meeting of the Romanian government for later that day to decide the position the party should adopt towards the invasion.

The population was informed that morning via Radio Romania, so citizens who had access to a radio set could hear the following:

> Prague-ČTK news agency reports: yesterday, 20 August 1968 at around 11 p.m. troops belonging to the Soviet Union, the Polish People's Republic, the German Democratic Republic, the People's Republic of Hungary and the People's Republic of Bulgaria crossed the border of the Czechoslovak Socialist Republic. This happened without the knowledge of the President of the Republic, the President of the National Assembly, the Prime Minister and the First Secretary of the Czechoslovak Communist Party ... The Presidium of the Central Committee of the Czechoslovak Communist Party considers this act *an infringement not only of all the principles that govern the relationships between socialist states, but also a major infringement of international law.*[16]

Later that day, Romanians listened to their leader's speech in front of an estimated crowd of 100,000. Ceaușescu did not mince his words, making everyone aware that Romania might be invaded next:

> It has been said that in Czechoslovakia there is a danger of counter-revolution; there will be some, who, tomorrow perhaps, will say that here too, at this very meeting, we are manifesting counter-revolutionary tendencies. We answer all these people: the Romanian people will not allow anyone to step on the territory of our country.[17]

Indeed, the Romanian leadership feared that Soviet, Hungarian and Bulgarian military divisions might invade the country. Bucharest was not alone in its anxiety about potential Warsaw Pact aggression: Tito's Yugoslavia took certain defensive measures and even Austria sought 'discrete US and NATO guarantees to protect [its] vulnerable neutrality'.[18] An analysis of the reaction of the US State Department to the crisis shows that an invasion of Romania was treated with utmost gravity by Washington.[19] Consequently, Romania moved armed units to its borders, signalling that—unlike Czechoslovakia—an invasion would not go without a military response. In addition, a new doctrine was advanced by Ceaușescu, that of 'the war of the entire people'. He instituted so-called 'Patriotic Guards', civil defence units composed of armed civilians organised in companies and platoons under the leadership of the RCP. In these strained moments, many Romanians seemed eager to enlist in these formations, where they would be permitted to fight against the expected Soviet aggression.

His later actions seem to suggest that Ceaușescu did fear a potential Soviet invasion and that his speech and public stance were not manufactured purely for 'domestic purposes'. On 24 August, he held a secret meeting with Tito in the small Yugoslav town of Vršac, near the Romanian border. He asked Tito whether the Romanian army, in the event of defeat, could retreat to Yugoslavia. According to the notes of the conclave, Tito answered that he would welcome party leaders, but not armed troops, on Yugoslav territory.[20] Ceaușescu returned to Bucharest and, after a stalemate of a couple of days, recalled the army to their barracks and from then on explicit anti-Soviet discourse in the Romanian press was toned down. It should be noted that the idea of a second invasion, targeting Romania after Czechoslovakia, is not grounded in any available archival material or actual data on troop movements. I have been unable to locate any sources that could substantiate Ceauşescu's claim that a military invasion of Romania was being prepared. On the contrary, Jordan Baev in his contribution to this volume concludes that no military action was being considered against Romania. Furthermore, at the time the US military attaché in Hungary 'visited the border areas and could not detect any massive troop build-ups vis-à-vis Romania or Yugoslavia' while 'the CIA presented an "inconclusive" general picture'.[21] It is probable that Ceauşescu overplayed the threat, both domestically and in his messages to Washington. However, more detailed research is needed to discover whether he did so as part of a policy to ingratiate himself with the Americans or out of fear, as his encounter with Tito seems to imply.

Intellectual Reactions to Ceauşescu's Stance

The best-known response among Romanian intellectuals to the August 1968 events was that of the writer Paul Goma. Goma had been a political prisoner for two years (1957–59) because of his sympathetic attitude to the Hungarian Revolution of 1956: in solidarity with the Magyars, he had renounced his membership of the Communist Youth organisation. After his imprisonment, Goma was assigned forced domicile in a remote village where he remained until 1964. Despite this, on 22 August 1968 he asked to be readmitted into the Romanian Communist Party. And he was joined by several other intellectuals and writers, subsequently nicknamed '22 August members of the RCP', such as Mariana Costescu, A.D. Munteanu, Paul Schuster, Adrian Păunescu and Alexandru Ivasiuc. He later placed his gesture within a 'national framework':

> Ceauşescu's speech provoked by the invasion of Czechoslovakia was not an anti-Soviet one. The discourse from the balcony was patriotic: it called on all Romanians to defend the country—against the Russians, of course, but not against the Soviets. Therefore, in August 1968 several writers [the majority of whom were born in Bessarabia, today's Republic of Moldova] signed requests to be admitted [into the ranks of the party] as weapons were only being handed out to party members.[22]

This reaction illustrates the semantic essence of Ceauşescu's version of socialism: nationalist, 'patriotic' and mixed with strong anti-Russian sentiment.

The second type of response of Romanian intellectuals to the events of August 1968 was typified by Ion Ianoşi, a professor of aesthetics who also occupied an 'expert' position in the administrative apparatus of the RCP Central Committee. Ianoşi was the offspring of a rich Jewish family of Hungarian descent from Transylvania. Both he and his father were involved in communist activities before and during World War II, when the tiny communist party was illegal in Romania. After the war, young Ion was sent to study in Leningrad and became part of a new generation created by the party with stellar credentials: illegal communist activities combined with education in the USSR. Ianoşi was not in Romania on 21 August—as an intellectual favoured by the regime he had been permitted to travel to Vienna to attend the Sixteenth International Congress of Philosophy. But in retrospect he believed that 'Ceauşescu felt insulted by the fact that his support for the Czechoslovak regime, only days before the invasion, had been neglected [by the Soviets]. Besides that, he feared the danger that threatened him too. He did not have much in common with Dubček's reformism, but he did manage to enrage the Soviets'. Ianosi continued: '[Ceauşescu's] main worries were the national minorities and the intellectuals, that's why [in the immediate aftermath of the August 1968 invasion] he made speeches in settlements where a significant part of the population was constituted by Hungarians and at the General Assembly of Romanian Writers'.[23] Although Ianoşi's memoirs may well have been shaped by hindsight, it is not without significance that a seasoned communist and member of two minorities (Jewish and Magyar) should choose not to mention the potential Soviet invasion of Romania, but rather his feelings of unease at the nationalist and neo-Stalinist traits promoted by the new Romanian leader.

The third type of reaction to August 1968 is typified by Adrian Marino, the son of a well-to-do intellectual family who began as a very promising literary critic and assistant professor of literature. After the war, he got involved in anti-communist agitation and was arrested in 1949 for distributing National Peasant Party (PNŢ) literature aimed at young Romanians. He was imprisoned for seven years, followed by a further six years of forced domicile in a remote village in southern Romania. Only in 1963 was he allowed to move to Cluj, a Transylvanian university town. From 1964, he was permitted to write, initially under a pseudonym. Marino's lengthy memoirs are illustrative of another reaction to Ceauşescu's speech and the Soviet threat.[24] It is a reaction that is telling by its absence. Marino treats the August 1968 events, the famous speech and the fear of Soviet invasion as *non-events*, which do not deserve to be remembered and which had no impact on him, his life and his worldview. As we will see in the following section, this response is more common among Romanians than one would expect.

August 1968 Remembered in a Transylvanian Village

While it is certain that recollections recorded in 2017 are shaped by current contexts and by the life trajectory of the informant, the data provided by life-story accounts do provide valid material that adds to our understanding of the salience (or lack thereof) of the 1968 moment for 'ordinary' Romanians. In my attempt to explore the resonance of the invasion of Czechoslovakia in Romanian collective memory, I chose a rural settlement on the western Romanian plain, not far from the border with Hungary. It was a village in 1968 (a commune, according to the administrative categories of the day) and it is currently classified as a small town. In 1964, it had a total population of 14,077, of whom 7049 were Romanians, 6499 were ethnic Germans (*Schwaben*) and 346 were Hungarians.[25] The significant Roma community does not show up in the statistics as the official documents lacked this category. My estimate would be that the 1000–1500 Roma who lived in the village at the time were 'hidden' under the category 'Romanians'. Hence, an important reason for choosing this village was its ethnic diversity. More than that, the village had been a collectivisation success story, establishing a 'model *kolkhoz*' (collective farm) and often featuring in regime propaganda, and my oral history interviews confirm that the inhabitants tended to have a positive overall perspective on the evolution of their village under communism. Given these coordinates, I expected to find many people who would remember the August 1968 events. Last but not least, I have good knowledge of the place since I grew up there. I have also published two studies about it: one on the process of collectivisation and the other on local social history, following three successive generations of the same family from the late 1920s until 2010.[26] My previous work in the area allowed me to search for connections between the recollections of the events and the life trajectories and family background of my respondents.

The first step was to analyse the statistics I had gathered for my previous research regarding the extent to which villagers had access to the mass media in 1968. Of a total number of 3860 households with 14,833 inhabitants, 2400 (62%) had access to electricity. According to the data of the commune, 1876 families were recorded as paying the 'tax' for owning a radio (roughly 49%), but only 469 paid the tax for a TV set (12%). A subset of households (818, or 21% of the total) were exposed to a specific form of media: a loudspeaker installed usually in the kitchen, linked by cable to a small 'studio' located in the village, a 'studio' that broadcast national news, music and a small amount of local news. While TV coverage was incipient, and virtually negligible for our purposes, almost every second household in the village owned a radio and was exposed to national news coverage.

My qualitative study of the village consisted of ten days of research in June 2017. I conducted a series of twenty in-depth interviews (seven women and thirteen men) aged between sixty-seven and eighty-eight years old. There was one younger subject, sixty-one years old in 2017, who volunteered information on the events. I included all the ethnicities present in the village and all educational levels, actively seeking people who had fared well under 'real existing socialism' and those who had a lot to lose from it. I had previously known all the villagers I talked to, with the accidental exception of an ethnic German who had emigrated to Germany in the early 1990s and happened to visit the village during my research. I started the ethnographic interviews by mentioning 'August 1968' with the expectation that the interviewee would link the period with something significant to him or her, not necessarily the political events. If there was no recollection, I reminded them of the invasion, waiting for their eventual memories. In those cases when subjects had no remembrance of the events or of the discourse, I tended to explore their social trajectory around that year and what other political or historical events they recalled.

A story I often encountered echoes a confirmed myth that deserves separate research: a neighbour, a retired construction worker and rather well known as a fantasist, asserts that he witnessed Soviet tanks attempting to cross the Romanian border, only to be stopped by mines. In his account, the Russian tank driver is a beautiful blonde woman. He also 'remembers' the snow—in August! The tanks grinding to a halt at the frontier make up one of the most repeated tales I know about 1968. It was reiterated many times as I grew up, and was embellished in another interview with a college educated agronomist, born in 1938:

> It's nothing I know for sure, only hearsay … [but] some Russian armoured vehicles attempted to cross the Romanian border. Now, I don't know the truth, but people were talking … As it were, we had a weapon at the time,

a laser, and it was said that we used this weapon to repel the Russian tanks. That weapon was terrible! Now, who knows? We don't know what happened in reality.[27]

This theme of a mighty secret weapon—the only thing that could defeat the huge Soviet army—is a recurrent popular motif, the dissemination of which strengthens the argument that many Romanians were convinced of the invasion threat and made use of anything available to commemorate the (retrospective) 'sci-fi' victory of David over Goliath.

Before examining my main findings, a few words are necessary on methodology and theory. The crux of my research resides, of course, in the way social memory is conceptualised. It would be as misleading to claim that the memory of the 1968 events says nothing about what the interviewee lived and thought in 1968 as it would be to assert that it says everything about it. My perspective is informed by H. Gordon Bower's idea that 'an emotion serves as a memory unit that can enter into associations with coincident events. Activation of this emotion unit aids retrieval of events associated with it'.[28] I assume that current memories of August 1968 are influenced by my interviewees' emotional response to the news at the time. My initial exploration can be subsumed in three levels of emotional intensity of the memory of 1968. In my categorisation, one group of people had personal and emotional recollections of the events: the invasion of Czechoslovakia was perceived as a meaningful moment in their life-course, and therefore remembered with a certain amount of detail and implication. A second group of people proved to have certain memories of August 1968, but recount them as an external event without any personal involvement with the news and, as a rule, these subjects do not remember much about it. Last but not least is the third category of respondents—those who do not recall the event at all.

I will begin with a presentation of the positions I clustered under the first 'level of intensity'—those subjects who retrospectively claim that they resented at a personal and emotional level the events of August 1968. The first memory belongs to my late father, who passed away in 2004 and who used to tell me, in positive terms, about Ceaușescu's stance in 1968. A college-trained agronomist and member of the Communist Party, he participated in the first days of August 1968 in the Ninth International Youth and Student Festival in Sofia. He recalled that the Romanian delegation, as it entered the stadium, departed from the prescribed order of proceedings and formed with their bodies the letters CEAUȘESCU- DUBČEK, certainly not a spontaneous move, but something that had been planned by the Bucharest leadership. He stressed that they were given a very frosty reception by the delegations of the other socialist states and that he felt solidarity with Ceaușescu's stand on the Prague Spring.[29] The same solidarity is confessed by other villagers.

Petre (I have changed all my subjects' names) was twenty-four at the time, a conscripted soldier following his college graduation as an engineer specialising in agricultural machinery. On 21 August 1968, he was sent to the Romanian-USSR border to resist the anticipated Soviet attack on the country:

> So, during my military service ... we had to go through this [invasion of Czechoslovakia]. We didn't know why it happened, we thought it was a military exercise, an 'alarm'. It was 2 a.m. We received weapons, PPS automatic pistols ... they had a sort of rotor, stupid Russian weapons. They tended to jam ... One of our commanders, a colonel, asked us to go to the weapons depot ... At the depot, he explained to us [what was going on]. That man was crying and I could not understand, as I was a young lad, how it was possible to see a colonel crying. But he was and I remember him saying: 'I've got two daughters at home'. He had been through the war [WWII] and he knew what war means ... So we received ammo, real, not the stuff used for practice ... and we got on board trucks. As we served in a tank unit ... they told us that we were going to the border [with the USSR], to defend our country against the Russians. So, I shall not forget, all this happened most probably on the night of 23 August, I'm not sure of my memory. On 23 August [actually, 21 August], I heard Ceaușescu's speech. Calin, I'm telling you: it wasn't me alone. Every single one of us out there, had someone asked him: 'Are you willing to go [fight]? No one would have said no.' [leaves a significant break]

Petre's account fits with the general narrative of the events in Romanian historiography: he claims that he and his colleagues were more than willing to fight for the patriotic stance set out by Ceaușescu.

In terms of life trajectory, Petre was the second son of a poverty-stricken family of landless peasants:

> [My father] was a poor man. He was a servant his entire life, and after he returned from the war he received three and a half hectares of land [in the 1945 agrarian reform]. He was *very* hard-working, he didn't want to give away that land ... My father, for instance, was against the *kolkhoz* until he joined ... But when I tried to be admitted to college, they wouldn't allow me unless he joined the *kolkhoz*. That's when I saw my father crying.

However, both Petre and his younger brother managed to get to college, one ending up an engineer and the other a medical doctor. By 1968, according to Petre's reading, things had changed in the village:

> So, you asked me about the atmosphere in the village: I would have liked to see one person, just one who after five, seven or ten years in the *kolkhoz*, especially in our village, would have returned to work the land individually. I don't think there was one. And mind you, we had Germans, who were not kindly disposed toward the regime [and still they backed the *kolkhoz*].
>
> CG: Did your father side with Ceaușescu in 1968, or …?
> My father was on Ceaușescu's side.[30]

After graduating and completing his military service, Petre continued to work as an engineer in the village, eventually becoming the director of the local state-owned agricultural machinery company. Later, he was mayor for a single term. He eventually retired and now lives with his wife, also retired.

My second subject, Aurelia, born in 1948, is an ethnic Romanian with eight years of schooling. In July 1968, she had just given birth to her first son and lived as the wife of a railway worker in a neighbouring village in a rather isolated house belonging to the Romanian Railway Company. She remembers the events:

> Yes … we lived those moments in great fear. For there were tanks passing through the village. There were tanks moving towards the Hungarian border. Lord, I was shaking with fear, next to my baby. My mother was there too [to help]. Later that day Ceaușescu spoke, I saw him on TV, as we had recently bought a TV set. We bought it in installments. And I know that Ceaușescu said that he will not allow … Romania to be occupied. High emotions … for I saw, as I see you, the tanks passing by … the house was trembling as the tanks passed … Well, let me tell you, Romanians were fretful. I remember the wife of the head of the railway station, she was watching TV, her husband too, and everybody, a couple of neighbours came over: 'Oi-oi, may the war not come upon us, may the war not come upon us!'

She adds that the neighbours were wives of low-level railway employees who used to hang out around the wife of the railway station master and do chores for her. Aurelia was keeping far from the lady, as her goose sometimes entered the station master's yard, and that was causing trouble.

Women were scared, everybody was desperate and afraid of war!
CG: Were people supporting Ceaușescu, or did they rather wish he'd kept silent and steered us away from war?
No, people hoped he'd take care of us.
CG: So people supported him?[31]

Aurelia came from a medium-sized household of peasants. After graduating from the eighth grade, she married and the way she tells her life story is very much linked to her husband's career trajectory: as a wife of a mid-level employee at the railway company she had to follow him outside their native village. But Aurelia strove, and succeeded, to return. Although initially she did not work, she eventually joined the local *kolkhoz*, probably to help cover the expenses incurred by building a new house. She retired, lost her husband a couple of years ago and now lives with her younger son in the house she built in the early 1970s.

Of the twenty people interviewed for this project, five recalled with intensity and personal involvement the August 1968 days. I chose to present only two of them, for the other three (two men and one woman) belong roughly to the same category: like Petre, all are upwardly-mobile college-educated professionals (professors and agronomists) who were born between 1940 and 1946 and who describe in roughly the same terms their indignation about the invasion and their solidarity with Ceaușescu's stance.

In the second cluster of memories I rank those who did not evince any personal reaction to the events. They do remember the facts, yet they do not seem to be sympathetic to Ceaușescu's position and seem rather remote from the entire affair. Valtin is an ethnic German from the village, who was eighteen in 1968. In terms of his life trajectory, he came from a family of workers. He graduated from the eighth grade and then went to a vocational school. He entered a conversation I was having with an older relative of his whom I was asking about 1968. The woman did not recall anything, but at this point he intervened:

I remember...
CG: Oh, you do? How did you hear of it?
My father owned a radio ,,, TV sets were not common then, only later on, in the mid-1970s. I was already eighteen. I was playing football for the village team, the big one [meaning, he was not playing in the junior

league]. And they, the Russians, occupied the Czechs, and remained there I don't know how many years ... the troops were there until 1990, or was it 1989?

CG: I wonder, were locals afraid in 1968?
Yeah ... [he quotes] 'Oh, the Russians will come again!' ... You know, I came close to being born in Russia ... My mother and father met in Russia, they were there for five years in a labour camp after the war. She was pregnant when she returned [from the USSR] in November, and I was born in January. Two months difference, and I would have been a Russian [he laughs].

CG: Were your parents afraid, given their experiences?
They were afraid, they were ... they said: 'the Russians might return and then perhaps they'll take us off again to Ukraine' [their former labour camp].

In 1945, all Romanian ethnic Germans aged between eighteen and forty-five, male and female civilians, were forced by Soviet troops, with the blessing of the Allied Commission, to relocate to labour camps in the USSR for two to seven years to help 'rebuild' Soviet industry destroyed by the war. But Valtin did not engage with these traumatic events: as a youngster deep into his football passion, he registered something else newsworthy, something that had a resonance with his immediate family and their recent past; namely, his parents' fear that a Soviet occupation of Romania in 1968 might send them back to a Ukrainian labour camp.

CG: How did you see your future?
I didn't think of emigrating to Germany. No, nothing like that. There were a few guys who left for Germany [in the late 1960s], but it was only after 1980 that many more started to get out. In 1984, my sister left [for Germany] with her in-laws. Damn it all, I wasn't interested! I didn't think of it. I had a good job here. I was working with my wife and buddies in the coffin-making shop ... that was a part of the [state-sponsored] craftsmen cooperative.[32]

His life story emphasises the good times he had with his friends in the village in 1968. The fervent desire to escape Ceaușescu's Romania reached them only in the mid-1980s. Valtin tried to pay some Roma who promised to help him (and his wife and son) and three other family friends to cross illegally into Yugoslavia, but after having their documents checked by the police they were turned back in Timișoara, the last major town before the border. He assigns this additional check-up to a snitch in the village who might have warned the authorities. He finally left Romania legally in 1990 and has lived in Germany ever since.

Nicolae, an ethnic Romanian, was born in 1940. He is a high school graduate who worked in the post office. His family moved to the village when he was a child, coming from a distant mountain settlement where his grandparents and extended family continued to live. Nicolae was twenty-seven in 1968 and during the summer he took a trip back to his village of origin in the Apuseni mountains. He was there on 21 August:

> In the morning, I heard some acquaintances chattering and I asked them: what's the matter? So they told me that the Russians had invaded Czechoslovakia ... this was in 1968. And those men were saying: 'That's what's going to happen to us too!' They said this also because they'd heard Ceaușescu saying that he didn't agree [with the invasion], that the communist system does not condone, but condemns, such an act. He [Ceaușescu] was against it! And the people were scared, that Romania will be next in line ... You know how rumours spread, that's how it is!

Nicolae continued:

> So, in those days there were some people from our village up there in the mountains. They had been sent by the *kolkhoz* to sell watermelons at the market. I don't know who decided to send S [and] M as watermelon sellers. I don't know if you knew them, but both are Hungarians. And one of the locals ... took them on: 'what's with you, you want to take Transylvania back?!' So the two Magyars ran away ... to get protection from someone they knew ... You know what those Romanians from that region up in the mountains are like. They said: 'You [Hungarians] boasted that you'll cover the house of Avram Iancu [Romanian nationalist leader of the 1848 revolution] with Romanian hides?!' But the two escaped [without being molested], and I'm not sure whether they ever sent Hungarians to sell in that region again! [He laughs]
>
> CG: And that happened then, in those August days?
> Yes, yes...[33]

Again, Nicolae chose to share his story without mentioning himself or his attitude to the events. It is implicit that he was worried, but his narrative is neutral, never touching on his feelings or the way the news had an impact on him personally. However, what he chose to share is a very different story from what we usually hear. At this point his account resonates with the image evoked in Ianoși's memoirs: that Ceaușescu's patriotic stance triggered a nationalist response in the perception of some Romanians, who symbolically attacked the only 'enemy' they had at hand: two ethnic Hungarian peasants selling watermelons.

Nicolae's life trajectory is also one of upward mobility. His parents were on the receiving end of the agrarian reform of 1945. They relocated from their poor mountain origins to the village I cover in this study, where they received land. Nicolae grew up there, graduated from high school and in 1968 was working as a middle-level clerk in the Romanian Postal Office. He married a local mathematics teacher, has one son and retired a decade ago.

In this second cluster of memories I have categorised five out of my twenty subjects. Besides the two cases quoted here, I interviewed three men, one who was thirteen at the time, the other twenty-six and the third eighteen. All of them remember hearing the news, but nothing else. The first was very young and recalls the adults in the village gathering around the town hall to hear the broadcasts, which left an impression on him as a teenager. The second was an industrial worker and the third graduated from high school and failed to get admitted to college at the time (although he succeeded later). Both remember hearing the news, without any other details and without any personal reactions or involvement.

Finally, I will outline the third cluster of memoirists of 1968, the most important in my reading. In this cohort I gathered interviews with villagers who have no recollection at all of the events of August 1968. My mention of the invasion of Czechoslovakia, of the news covering the crisis and of Ceaușescu's discourse did not evoke anything in the minds of these people. I will review the main traits of each subject before offering a few conclusions on my ethnographical case study:

Maria: Romanian, female, born in 1946, college educated teacher, a local from the same generation (and life-long friend) as Petre, member of the Communist Party. Daughter of peasants, she had graduated from college, the first to do so in her family, by 1968.

Lica: Romanian, male, born in 1947 in a poor mountain area, relocated to the village for the tractor-drivers' vocational

	school. By 1968 he had a well-paid job as a tractor-driver, he recalls, and he was the first skilled worker in his peasant family.
Liliana:	Romanian, female, born in 1950. She worked in the laundry of the local hospital. In 1968 she was not yet married, living with her peasant family, all *kolkhoz* workers.
Resi:	Half-German, half-Hungarian, female, born in 1930. A high school graduate, she was the offspring of a rich land-owning family. She suffered from regime persecution and was not allowed to enrol in college in the late 1940s. By 1968 she managed to graduate from a vocational school for dental technicians and worked in this capacity until she retired.
Kati:	German, female, born in 1941 in the village. She acquired seventh grade education. By 1968 she was married to another ethnic German from the village and she worked at the local *kolkhoz* from where she has retired.
Gheorghe:	Roma, male, born in 1939, elementary education. He worked all his life as an industrial worker, initially unskilled, but by 1968 a skilled worker. One of the most respected members of his generation among the village Roma, especially for his intellectual abilities.
Mara:	Roma, female, born in 1947, elementary education. A housewife, occasionally working in the local *kolkhoz*.
Johan:	German, male, born in 1930, elementary education. Worked in the local *kolkhoz*. By 1968 he was a member of the *kolkhoz*'s construction workers' crew. He was proud of being a skilled and valued labourer.
Toni:	German, male, born in 1941, seventh grade education. Initially he opposed collectivisation, but by 1968 he worked in the local *kolkhoz* and appreciated the high income he managed to get there, thanks to his industriousness.
Stefi:	German, male, born in 1938, vocational training. In 1968, he was a driver for a factory in the neighbouring town, commuting from the village.

It is impossible to assume that these people did not hear anything about the invasion of Czechoslovakia. In one of the few peasant diaries that are available—a peasant with elementary education living in a remote village in Bistrita county—there is a short entry on 21 August 1968 mentioning 'the sad news' of the invasion. Interestingly enough, mixed with entries on the health of his cow he found August 1968 worthy of note, but not so the moon landing in the following year. Also, I cannot claim that the ten people who don't remember August 1968 are not being honest about it: all of them were gracious enough to grant me lengthy interviews and share with me the details of their lives and that of their families. The fact that memories are fluidly constructed and re-constructed is stressed time and again in social memory literature.[34] Once a thing or event was presented to the attention of the subject, it can and will be forgotten unless it is revisited or recalled. Also, in the vein of Bower, I contend that 'people recall an event better if they somehow reinstate during recall the original emotion they experienced during learning'.[35] It is highly probable that the people who forgot about August 1968 did not pay much attention to the news, and most certainly it did not resonate emotionally with them.

It is true that several interviews confirm that Romanians welcomed their leader's attitude towards the invasion of Czechoslovakia, as emphasised by the majority of scholars who have treated this subject. One respondent even relates a minor anti-Hungarian incident triggered—seemingly—by the nationalistic frame advanced and legitimated by Ceaușescu's discourse. However, the main finding of my limited research underlines that fifteen out of twenty interviewees report no personal or emotional engagement with the events: half of my subjects do not remember them at all, and five have but a cursory memory of 'something' in the news. Had the events of August 1968 been such a landmark in Ceaușescu's legitimacy, and that of Romania's communist regime, it is hardly believable that they could have been so neglected.

Conclusion

Certainly, a case study cannot hope to draw any definitive conclusions, but I hope it will allow me to advance a couple of hypotheses. It is striking that the subjects of the first cluster, those who recall the August events in detail, are, with one exception, highly educated ethnic Romanians. At the same time, those who remember the most are those who had been personally and emotionally involved with the events and who were not opposed to the regime: it is interviewees in this category who tended to resonate more with Ceaușescu's stance. On the other side, among those who don't remember much, if anything, of the events, I found people with elementary or mid-level education, but also two people with tertiary education. In this camp, ethnic minorities are dominant: only three out of ten are ethnic Romanians. In the intermediate category there are four ethnic Romanians and one German.

My project is both limited and made possible by the closing window of time: those who were eighteen in 1968 are now sixty-eight years old. My previous survey of this generation,[36] and the data focused on their life-course situation in 1968, highlight a perception of upward educational mobility, economic well-being and a much-appreciated break-up of the traditional pre-war rural way of life. In my reading, it is this experience of the modernising impact of the regime's policies as well as the relative economic prosperity experienced by my respondents that should be added to the explanation of the level of the regime's legitimacy in the late 1960s.[37] The anti-Russian rhetoric of 1968, as well as the appropriation of the 'nation' in the new political imaginary offered by Ceaușescu, are but parts of the explanation.

I conclude this case study of Romanian reactions to the invasion of Czechoslovakia with a question mark. My findings make me doubt the 'broad' impact and 'legitimacy' among Romanian citizens that Ceaușescu is said to have gained from his anti-Russian stance in 1968. The 21 August speech is not as present in the social memory as one would expect reading the historians and political scientists who have addressed the subject. Yet the time-frame of the events coincides with a point in the life-trajectories of a generation for whom the regime seemed to have provided a level of upward educational mobility and relative economic well-being, which should be regarded as additional factors in the 1968 equation. While more research is needed, I suggest that the claim that the 1968 events brought Romania's communist regime 'broad popular support, which eventually gave legitimacy to the single-Party rule' could, and most probably should, be qualified.

Notes

1. Ceaușescu lacked a solid education and, according to literary Romanian, mispronounced several words, especially neologisms.
2. P. Tutuleasa, 'Editie Speciala', in *Newsreel* (Bucharest, 1968).
3. C.L. Petrescu, 'Performing Disapproval Toward the Soviets: Nicolae Ceaușescu's Speech on 21 August 1968 in the Romanian Media', in M. Klimke et al. (eds), *Between Prague Spring and French May: Opposition*

and Revolt in Europe, 1960–1980 (New York, 2013), pp. 199–210; V. Tismaneanu, *Stalinism for All Seasons: A Political History of Romanian Communism* (Berkeley, CA, 2003); Pavel Campeanu, *Ceauşescu: The Countdown* (Boulder and New York, 2003); M. Retegan, *1968: Din Primavara Pana in Toamna* (Bucharest, 1998).
4. D. Petrescu, 'Continuity, Legitimacy and Identity: Understanding the Romanian August of 1968', *Cuadernos de Istoria Contemporanea*, no. 31 (2009), p. 88.
5. L. Betea et al. (eds), *21 August 1968: Apoteoza Lui Ceauşescu* (Iaşi, 2009).
6. M. Kramer, 'The Czechoslovak Crisis and the Brezhnev Doctrine', in C. Fink et al. (eds), *1968: The World Transformed* (Cambridge, 1998), pp. 111–72.
7. W.E. Crowther, *The Political Economy of Romanian Socialism* (New York, 1988).
8. Crowther, *The Political Economy*, p. 61.
9. M. Bracke, *Which Socialism? Whose Détente?: West European Communism and the Czechoslovak Crisis, 1968* (Budapest, 2007).
10. Petrescu, 'Continuity, Legitimacy and Identity', p. 74.
11. K. Verdery, *National Ideology under Socialism: Identity and Cultural Politics in Ceauşescu's Romania* (Berkeley, CA, 1991).
12. M. Prozumenshchikov, 'Politburo Decision-Making on the Czechoslovak Crisis in 1968', in G. Bischof et al. (eds), *The Prague Spring and the Warsaw Pact Invasion of Czechoslovakia in 1968* (Lanham, MD, 2010), pp. 103–43.
13. C. Goina, 'Rehabilitation in Romania: The Case of Lucreţiu Pătrăşcanu', in K. McDermott and M. Stibbe (eds), *De-Stalinising Eastern Europe: The Rehabilitation of Stalin's Victims after 1953* (London, 2015), pp. 132–49.
14. Petrescu, 'Continuity, Legitimacy and Identity', p. 79.
15. Betea et al., *21 August 1968*, p. 131.
16. Betea et al., *21 August 1968*, pp. 118–19 (italics added).
17. N. Ceauşescu, 'Cuvintul Tovarasului Nicolae Ceauşescu', *Scinteia*, 22 August 1968.
18. See G. Bischof, '"No Action": The Johnson Administration and the Warsaw Pact Invasion of Czechoslovakia in August 1968', in Bischof et al. (eds), *The Prague Spring*, pp. 215–36 (here p. 223).
19. The Johnson administration feared a spillover of the Czechoslovak crisis into Romania and twice hauled in the Soviet ambassador to the State Department to warn him that 'an invasion of Romania would have devastating consequences for US-Soviet relations and world politics'. Bischof, '"No Action"', p. 222.
20. Betea et al. (eds), *21 August 1968*, pp. 157–72.
21. Bischof, '"No Action"', pp. 221–2.

22. P. Goma, *Scrisuri 1972–1998* (Bucharest, 1999), pp. 355–6.
23. I. Ianoși, *Internationala Mea: Cronica Unei Vieti* (Iași, 2012), pp. 469–70.
24. A. Marino, *Viața Unui Om Singur* (Iași, 2010).
25. Anonymous, *Caietul Statistic Al Comunei Santana* (Arad, 1989).
26. C. Goina, '"Never Put Off Till Tomorrow What You Can Do Today!": A Case Study of a Model Kolkhoz: A "New Life" Santana (Arad Region)', in C. Iordachi and D. Dobrincu (eds), *Transforming Peasants, Property and Power: The Collectivization of Agriculture in Romania, 1949–1962* (Budapest, 2009); C. Goina, 'Social Mobility and Social Stratification in a Transylvanian Village: Historical Changes and Generational Experiences', PhD thesis (UCLA, 2012).
27. Interview with Ioan on 9 June 2017. Born in 1938, male, ethnic Romanian, college-trained agronomist, now retired.
28. H.G. Bower, 'Mood and Memory', *American Psychologist*, vol. 2, no. 36 (1981), p. 129.
29. I am extremely grateful to Aura Mocan, who was a member of the Romanian delegation to Sofia in 1968 and who kindly shared with me her memories of the event. I did not trust entirely what I recalled from old conversations with my father—I trust only the details that were confirmed by the independent account of Mrs. Mocan. Interviewed on 10 June 2017.
30. Interview with Petre on 11 June 2017. Born in 1944, male, ethnic Romanian, mechanical engineer, ex-mayor, now retired.
31. Interview with Aurelia on 14 June 2017. Born in 1948, female, ethnic Romanian, housewife, then *kolkhoz* worker, now retired.
32. Interview with Valtin on 14 June 2017. Born in 1950, male, ethnic German, coffin-maker, has lived in Germany since 1990.
33. Interview with Nicolae on 18 June 2017. Born in 1940, male, ethnic Romanian, postal office worker, now retired.
34. See, for example, L. Passerini (ed.), *Memory and Totalitarianism* (Oxford and New York, 1992); A. Corning and H. Schuman, *Generations and Collective Memory* (Chicago, 2015); J. Fentress and C. Wickham, *Social Memory: New Perspectives on the Past* (Oxford, 1992); M. Halbwachs and L.A. Coser, *On Collective Memory* (Chicago, 1992).
35. Bower, 'Mood and Memory', p. 147.
36. Goina, 'Social Mobility and Social Stratification in a Transylvanian Village'.
37. See, for instance, A. Stoica, 'Communism as a Project for Modernization: The Romanian Case', *Polish Sociological Review*, no. 120 (1997), pp. 313–31.

The 'June Events': The 1968 Student Protests in Yugoslavia

Kenneth Morrison

The student demonstrations in the Socialist Federal Republic of Yugoslavia (*Socijalistička federativna republika Jugoslavija*—SFRJ) were part of the broader wave of such events that took place in Western, Central and Eastern Europe throughout the early summer of 1968. While many of the dynamics that were present in protests elsewhere were evident in the Yugoslav context, and Yugoslav students were generally well-informed about the disturbances taking place in Poland, Czechoslovakia, France, West Germany and other countries, the main focus of the Yugoslav students' dissent was internal rather than external issues. The 'June Events', most pronounced in Belgrade but thereafter manifest in other cities, were the largest demonstrations to take place in the country since the end of World War II. They were built on the foundations of the anti-Vietnam War student activism of the mid-1960s, but while these protests had been organised by the state (and not initiated independently), the upheavals of June 1968 were different. The grievances and demands of the students were specific and framed in the context of Yugoslav social, economic and political developments of

K. Morrison (✉)
De Montfort University, Leicester, UK
e-mail: kmorrison@dmu.ac.uk

© The Author(s) 2018
K. McDermott and M. Stibbe (eds.), *Eastern Europe in 1968*,
https://doi.org/10.1007/978-3-319-77069-7_10

the 1960s. Moreover, they were not, on the whole, challenging the fundamentals of the Yugoslav political system or its underlying values; they were not seeking to overthrow the regime, but to provide a sharp critique of their own material conditions and what they regarded as the flaws *within* that system and a betrayal of the revolutionary ideas that underpinned it. The students called for more, not less, socialism. Their protest amounted to a denunciation of the growth of economic disparity, the rise of the bureaucratic class and a call for a return to the original principles of the socialist revolution. It elicited a response from the state that was relatively moderate. Understanding that the use of force to break the demonstrations might prove counter-productive, there was no brutal suppression of the demonstrations but, rather, an intervention by Josip Broz Tito, the President of Yugoslavia, that essentially acknowledged the legitimacy of the students' complaints. However, the state's response would, in the long term, decapitate those forces that had generated the intellectual energy that fostered the student movement.

This chapter analyses the roots of the student demonstrations in Yugoslavia and provides an overview of the political context in which the demonstrations took place. The ideological parameters of the student movement, the events that led to the June demonstrations and how the Yugoslav authorities sought to prevent a relatively limited small protest (and critique of the system) from becoming a platform for the expression of wider social, economic and political grievances will all be discussed. A key argument will be that although the Prague Spring had some influence on the 'June Events', internal developments and the example of radical Marxist, anti-authoritarian student movements in the West were more important.

THE CONTEXT OF THE 1968 EVENTS

Yugoslavia's position was unique in the wider context of the 1968 demonstrations. It was, of course, a socialist state, but it was not part of the Soviet orbit. Yugoslavia had been a firm ally of the USSR in the immediate post-World War II years, but it had ceased to be under the direct influence of the Soviet Union in 1948. The split between Yugoslavia and the USSR was fuelled by growing policy differences between Tito and Josef Stalin, who opposed Yugoslavia's tendency to forge an independent foreign policy. This led to the 1948 'Cominform Crisis', which culminated in the Tito–Stalin split and the expulsion of Yugoslavia from the Cominform.[1] The rift had significant domestic implications in the form of a purge of Stalinists, known as *ibeovci*, from the Yugoslav party-state, which constituted a major component of a renewed campaign of terror in the late 1940s and early 1950s.[2] In addition, the Yugoslav authorities re-conceptualised their model of communism, central to which was the notion of 'workers' self-management', an economic system that sought to give employees direct control over important state industries as a counter-balance against possible bureaucratisation of the party-state.

The events of June 1968 did not take place in a vacuum, but were integral to the wider wave of student demonstrations throughout Europe, a challenge to the leadership from within the ruling Yugoslav League of Communists (*Savez komunista Jugoslavije*—SKJ) from liberalisers who sought political and economic reforms, and from intellectuals in Croatia who were becoming increasingly vocal regarding Croatian cultural rights. Beyond Yugoslavia, the Prague Spring and the reforms initiated by Alexander Dubček, in particular, were followed intently by Yugoslav students, some of whom were also part of a growing student engagement with anti-war activism that had emerged since the mid-1960s. Organised anti-war unrest had begun in Yugoslavia in February 1965 following the beginning of the US military's 'Operation Rolling Thunder' in Vietnam and in the context of an increasingly febrile student politics. Protests against the Vietnam War were staged throughout Yugoslavia (in Belgrade, Zagreb, Novi Sad, Sarajevo and Skopje) in November and December 1966, with further mass anti-war demonstrations taking place in Belgrade in April 1968. But, as Radina Vučetić notes, these actions were largely coordinated by 'state-controlled student and party organizations' and not by students acting autonomously.[3] The focus of this outcry was also entirely on events outside Yugoslavia; they were not a critique of the country's policy vis-à-vis the war in Vietnam.

In terms of foreign policy, Yugoslavia, a founding member of the 'Non-Aligned Movement', maintained relatively close, though not too close, relations with both the USA and the Soviet Union, which gave the country a more weighty influence than it may otherwise have had in global affairs. Yugoslavia tacitly supported the non-aligned North Vietnamese in their war with the US, but adopted a cautious stance. On the one hand, the Yugoslav authorities and state media were deeply critical of the US role in the war, but on the other they were allied with the USA, from whom they received significant levels of aid. Thus, there were occasions when the Yugoslav government had to act to preserve this delicate balance. Protestors were afforded the right to express their dissent, but within limited parameters. Following an official anti-war meeting at the University of Belgrade in December 1966, for example, a group of students that included Vladimir Mijanović and Alija Hodžić,[4] both of whom would become key figures in future demonstrations, initiated a march to the US Cultural Centre and Embassy in Belgrade. The police intervened and clashes between them and students ensued.[5] Nevertheless, as Milan Petrović argues, the SKJ became, to a certain extent, something of a 'midwife' to the student movement, because it organised protests against the Vietnam War (thereby further politicising the student body).[6]

Even so, the 1968 student actions were much more than a straightforward extension of the anti-war movement that had developed throughout the mid-1960s. The so-called 'June Events' were not orchestrated by party or state-controlled student institutions and their main focus was on internal Yugoslav political, social and economic dynamics, not international factors. They took place during a general process of political liberalisation, marked primarily by the fall of Aleksander Ranković, hitherto the head of Yugoslav state security (*Uprava državne bezbednosti*—UDBA) in 1966. His removal represented a real blow to the conservative wing of the SKJ, who had endeavoured to ensure that reformist tendencies in the party (namely increased cultural, political and economic pluralism) were stymied. Conversely, liberals in the SKJ saw Ranković's demise as an opportunity to advance what they believed was a necessary drive toward market-oriented reforms and a democratisation of the party. But the economic reforms, launched in 1965, the objective of which was to tackle economic stagnation, led to high levels of unemployment, especially among the young.[7]

There existed a burgeoning perception among the youth that Yugoslavia's economic growth, though demonstrative of the success of the country's socialist 'self-management', had created as a by-product a 'new class', or 'red bourgeoisie', who had benefited more than others from the economic reforms. The protests of June 1968 were primarily driven, therefore, by what many students saw as a betrayal of the revolution and a deviation from the revolutionary path by some elements in the SKJ.[8] At its annual conference in 1966, the Yugoslav League of Students (*Savez studenata Jugoslavije*—SSJ) had taken, according to Boris Kanzleiter, 'an increasingly critical position regarding social problems and authoritarian political structures'. In addition to expressing dissatisfaction over growing wealth disparities, they demanded improved material conditions at the university and a greater level of student involvement in the reform and democratisation of university administration. This, he adds, 'was seen [to be] in line with the official reform discourse, but it also provided an opening for small groups of young activists, who called for more radical action to end shortcomings'.[9]

The student movement was influenced by the *Praxis* group of Marxist philosophy lecturers and professors, largely based at Belgrade and Zagreb universities, some of the leading figures of which were, or had been, members of the SKJ (among them Gavrilo 'Gajo' Petrović, Mihailo Marković and Milan Kangrga). Having first organised annual seminars on the Croat island of Korčula (the 'Korčula Summer School'), which began in 1963 and drew Marxist scholars of significant repute from Europe and beyond, they established *Praxis: A Philosophical Journal* in 1964. The *Praxis* group's core idea was that philosophy should be a 'merciless critique of everything that exists', and their questioning, however subtle, of the Yugoslav system of self-management inevitably brought them into conflict with the ruling SKJ.[10]

Many students, though, were concerned not with matters philosophical, but matters practical. Inter-generational tensions existed, regardless of the fact that the SKJ leadership was relatively youthful in comparison to governments in, say, 1960s Western Europe. Most senior positions were held by former wartime Partisans, who were perhaps only in their late forties or early fifties (and many in the middle ranks of the bureaucracy were even younger).[11] This meant that while the generational divide was smaller and less acute, there was also something of a 'logjam' created by the reluctance of a political class, who were still some years from retirement, to make way for youthful upward social mobility.[12] There was also indignation about the system of patronage in the SKJ, which allowed family members of influential people to hold jobs for which they were both ill-suited and unqualified. Thus, as Nick Miller concludes, the student protests may have been 'triggered by a relatively trivial incident', but they were 'fuelled by real resentments'.[13]

The 'June Events'

Despite disorder in other European cities, such as Paris, Milan, Frankfurt and West Berlin, there was little evidence of similar protest taking place in Yugoslavia in 1967. But though there had been signs that youthful expressions of dissent were becoming increasingly acute in the months preceding the 'June Events', such expressions were contained within the limited parameters of student politics.[14] During the spring and early summer of 1968—throughout the early months of the Prague Spring—there were, according to Dennison Rusinow, 'several anticipatory tremors of revolt', though these amounted to little and were not indicative of what was to follow.[15] Nevertheless, Yugoslav students were acutely aware of the revolutionary air elsewhere in Europe, an atmosphere that was given significant coverage in the Yugoslav media. According to the film-maker, Želimir Žilnik, then a student at the University of Belgrade and later one of the doyens in the *Crni talas* (Black Wave) of Yugoslav cinema:

> As Belgrade students we all listened to and watched the developments in Berlin, Bonn and Paris closely, and we engaged in street protests and petitions in support of the French National Student Union and the extra-parliamentary opposition in the Federal Republic of Germany. We were just waiting for a spark to ignite the fire. The spark came in the night of June 2 and 3.[16]

When the demonstrations began, however, their gravity came as something of a surprise even to those heavily involved in student politics.[17] The so-called 'June Events' began in Belgrade on the evening of 2 June 1968, when police were called to deal with disturbances at a building near the halls of residence in New Belgrade, known as *Studenski grad* (Student City).[18] The unrest was caused by a sizeable number of students being denied entry, on the basis that it was already at full capacity, to a concert called *Karavan prijateljstva* (Caravan of Friendship), which was being held in the hall of the adjacent Workers' University.[19] The venue had been changed at the last minute—it had been scheduled to take place at a nearby outdoor auditorium but had been moved to a smaller room because of predictions of heavy rain—meaning that demand for attendance far outstripped the capacity of the building.[20] Many of those in attendance were members of the Voluntary Youth Working brigades involved in 'New Belgrade 68'—the construction of New Belgrade (these infrastructural projects were known as *Omladinske radne akcije*—youth work actions).[21] Rising tension between these workers' brigades and the students who were attempting to enter the hall led to scuffles between the two groups, sufficient for the police to be summoned. Soon, however, rioting ensued between the students and police, leading the latter to use disproportionate force to clear protestors from the area surrounding the auditorium.

Thereafter, outraged students gathered in Student City to discuss their response to these incidents. In the early hours of 3 June thousands of students assembled and began marching towards the centre of Belgrade, some four miles away.[22] As they proceeded they were confronted at a railway underpass close to a complex of government offices in New Belgrade with several hundred police, who had orders to ensure that the demonstrators did not reach the centre.[23] Clashes ensued between the police and students, who had brought along an 'immobilised fire truck' captured in the earlier fracas, and the protestors were forced back towards their halls of residence. At 8.00 a.m. on 3 June, students reassembled in large numbers at Student City. They formed an *akcioni odbor* (action committee) and formulated a response to what they regarded as police brutality. The students discussed what Ralph Pervan calls 'serious and persistent problems (such as living conditions and employment)' and began to 'articulate criticism of certain basic aspects of the contemporary Yugoslav system'.[24] Conversely, the authorities and state media sought to explain the violence as a legitimate response to the unruliness perpetrated by a small 'band of hooligans' in the wider student body.[25]

After the conclusion of these meetings, the students again marched in procession to the railway underpass where they had been forced to retreat by the police in the early hours. There they were met once more by a police cordon and by a number of well-known SKJ leaders, among them Miloš Minić, the Serbian parliamentary speaker, Branko Pešić, the mayor of Belgrade and Petar Stambolić, the President of the Central Committee of the Serbian League of Communists (SKJ), who sought to negotiate with the students and bring an end to the tumult, but did little to assuage their concerns.[26]

The respected Montenegrin communist, Veljko Vlahović, a member of the federal party presidium, also entered the fray. In his youth he had studied in Prague, Paris and Moscow, had later fought in the Spanish Civil War and had been one of the wartime editors of the pro-communist Serb newspaper *Borba* ('Struggle'). Popular with young people, he sought to listen to the students' demands and discuss ways to seek a resolution.[27] In May 1968, he had said that the global student protests should be 'evaluated positively' and that the presence of slogans calling for 'self-management' during demonstrations in France and elsewhere was indicative of Yugoslavia being on the correct path.[28] Now he sat for three hours discussing the students' grievances and what could be done to address them. Though largely jovial and engaged with the protestors, he was anxious that there could be more trouble if they were to reach the city centre. Hence, he endeavoured to persuade the students not to proceed further and instead to return to Student City, an appeal that was not heeded by a determined coterie who expressed their wish to push on to the centre.[29] Then, at 12.00 noon, as party functionaries were close to an agreement with the demonstrators, the police intervened and clashes broke out, with those sent by the Yugoslav authorities to mediate between students and police in the midst of the melee. Minić received a blow to the head as he attempted to stop the police from beating students, and eventually he joined them in their retreat back to Student City.[30] The scene after the disturbances was, according to Dennison Rusinow, one of chaos. When it was all over, he noted, 'the field in front of the underpass was littered with bloodstained shoes and socks, shirts and blouses, and torn banners'.[31]

As a response to this, the students did not give up on their quest to reach the city centre, though they opted to move in smaller groups or by public transport towards university buildings scattered throughout Belgrade—most of them located in and around *Studenski trg* (Student Square). By then their leaders were already preparing the next phase of the protest, which involved occupying university premises and declaring a strike, a process which crystallised throughout 4 June.[32] The demonstrations thus began to evolve from a physical confrontation between students and the police to a dialogue between the former and the SKJ, in which the students displayed some restraint and seemed to understand the limits of the possible in the Yugoslav context (they did not, for example, criticise the existence of the regime, instead demanding reform).[33]

The following day, 5 June, students again gathered at Student Square. The potential for further clashes was apparent, but after a peaceful march the students returned to the university buildings across the street to continue their occupation of what they re-named the *Crvena Univerzitet Karl Marks* (Red University of Karl Marx). Banners bearing slogans such as 'Down with the Red Bourgeoisie', 'Down with Corruption' and 'Workers Work—Bureaucrats Enjoy' were hung from the windows of lecture halls and offices, as the students gathered in atriums and courtyards, in particular at the Faculty of Philosophy building, to attend the *zborovi* (meetings) that consisted of speeches, music recitals and performances. The most dramatic spectacle was given by the Slovenian actor, Stevo Žigon, who played Maximilien de Robespierre in a staging of scenes from Georg Büchner's play, *Danton's Death*.[34] The symbolism was clear. By ordering Danton's demise, for personal reasons rather than for the good of the republic, Robespierre had deviated from the ideals of the revolution and shifted towards tyranny. Žigon implied, therefore, that the 'red bourgeoisie' of the SKJ had also, in their dealings with the students, betrayed the principles of the revolution.

Other university buildings, such as 'Captain Miša's House' (the university rectory) were also occupied by students. Indeed, the rectory building became the centre of activity and the place where students listened to speeches by their comrades, professors and party officials.[35] Here, according to Rusinow, 'A variable crowd of two hundred or more students and faculty, plus others admitted by vigilant young "order-keepers" at the gate, stood or sat under the trees, talking, reading the latest bulletins issued by the faculty's action committee and by the university committee of the student federation, or listening to speeches being made from the platform'.[36] The students also sang a number of songs that expressed their acknowledgement of the achievements of their elders while venting frustration at their own exclusion from the shaping of the socialist revolution that had been started by previous generations:

> We know of the bravery of our father from the books
> And it is their dream that warms us
> Today and from now on our concern is
> Left, Left, Left!
>
> Now, before our eyes, like it was with [our elders]
> The star of the commune shines
> Youth is our privilege
> Left, Left, Left![37]

By early on 5 June, the demonstrations had spread to all university faculties across the city. The students called for more socialism, not less. They chanted slogans such as '*Više škole, manje kole*' ('More schools, less cars'), condemned economic reforms that had led to higher rates of unemployment and, more specifically, called for the sacking of the Belgrade police chief, Nikola Bugarčić.[38] The action committees also began to draft a series of demands that would take the form of a petition.[39] These included the immediate release of those students imprisoned after the violence at the New Belgrade underpass on 3 June, identification and prosecution of those police officers responsible for the beatings, and the disciplining of newspapers for distorting or misreporting these incidents. Their wider demands included action on growing social inequality, unemployment, freedom of public opinion and expression. Their main targets were the police chiefs and newspaper editors, and, in a more general sense, the 'New Class' of party and state bureaucrats.[40]

The students argued that state print media, on the whole, had misrepresented them—the daily newspaper *Borba* was singled out as especially hostile to the students, though they also condemned the daily *Politika*, as well as the *Tanjug* news agency and state television. A special edition of the student weekly newspaper, *Student*, was printed which told of events from their perspective. Though it did not normally publish for a three month period during the summer, the gravity of the situation dictated that a one-off edition had to be rushed to press. Kemal Kurspahić, who would later become the editor-in-chief of *Oslobodjenje* ('Liberation') in Sarajevo, was the newspaper's 'university news' correspondent and editor-on-duty in early June. He hurried to get the paper out so that it could be read by the growing numbers of students joining the protests and by their sympathisers. He soon ran into problems, however. In his own words:

> I picked up all the edited stories and, following the usual routine, went to the *Glas* printing company in Vlajkovićeva Street in the centre of the city. But the procedure was different this time. With an apologetic gesture, the manager on duty took the manuscripts to his office instead of distributing them to the typists. After an hour or so delay, he emerged from his room and, after another couple of hours, a special issue of *Student*—with only four pages of battleground reports was ready ... I took some copies and headed toward the exit. But the huge door was locked, and the guard at the entrance apologised. 'Sorry, police orders'. Soon, two trucks with riot police, again in full gear, pulled in front of the building and, holding their sticks, ordered us to leave immediately. The paper was banned with the frightening accusation of 'attempting to undermine the constitutional order'.[41]

The primary concern for the Yugoslav authorities was the potential escalation of the student revolt into wider society. Already taken aback by the rapid spread of the protests from Belgrade to other cities, as well as statements of support from students and high school pupils in Skopje, Novi Sad and Titograd (Podgorica), they were determined to restrict the demonstrations to the confines of the university.[42] Thus, the faculty buildings in which there were protests were sealed off and surrounded by police, and students who attempted to enter factories to talk to employees were forbidden from doing so (a number of enterprises were staffed with 'workers' guards' to prevent infiltration from students).[43] Workers, too, were showing occasional signs of being unsatisfied with their lot; there had been work stoppages in previous months, and there was a fear in the SKJ of cross-contamination between students and workers, as had happened in Hungary in 1956.[44] On the whole, however, the protest was contained; many citizens of Belgrade walked or drove past the university to read the slogans and observe the demonstration, but there were few evident manifestations of public interest beyond mere curiosity.[45]

The Spread of Discontent

While Belgrade was the epicentre of the turmoil, the fervour of the 'June Events' was seized upon by students in faculties and departments at several other university cities. Smaller scale, and shorter, protests took place in the capitals of other Yugoslav republics, such as Sarajevo in Bosnia-Herzegovina, Zagreb in Croatia and Ljubljana in Slovenia. In Zagreb, though there were heated meetings held in lecture halls and university buildings, there was 'no spill-over onto the streets'.[46] Nevertheless, local student politics in the Croatian capital had been far from humdrum before the June protests. In the spring of 1968, the leadership of the official student organisation at the University of Zagreb had been purged following an intervention by the Croatian League of Communists (*Savez komunista Hrvatske*—SKH). As Rusinow explains, 'As far as one could gather from the limited coverage in the press, the issues included a serious flirtation by the ousted [student] president and her followers with imported ideas about "student power" and the ideology of the "New Left"'.[47]

As the demonstrations in Belgrade intensified, the University Committee of the SKH issued a hastily-written statement expressing partial support for and solidarity with the Belgrade students, essentially stating that while they endorsed the aims of their peers in the capital, solutions should be pursued within the parameters of the Yugoslav self-management system and without recourse to disorder. More radical 'action committees' at the University of Zagreb drafted their own document, insisting upon demonstrations in support of change. Debates over the mechanisms that should be used, and the framework in which they should operate to achieve these aims, became a source of some friction among Croat students.[48]

In Sarajevo, students from a number of faculties at the university began to gather, though the main focus of the demonstrations there was the Faculty of Philosophy building. Among them was Radovan Karadžić, later the political leader of the Bosnian Serbs during the Yugoslav civil war of 1992–95 (and subsequently a convicted war criminal). One of the few protestors from the university's Medical Faculty (the vast majority were drawn from the Faculty of Philosophy), Karadžić gave energetic speeches and was clearly identifiable as a leading figure in the Sarajevo student movement. He was just one of several 1968ers in Yugoslavia (and elsewhere) whose criticism of the communist system later morphed into ethno-nationalism.[49] The June protests in Sarajevo were short-lived, however. After one day, police intervention put a quick end to the student revolt. Thus, while the spread of protests to Zagreb and Sarajevo represented a worrying development for the Yugoslav authorities, these demonstrations had essentially ended by 6 June.

'The Students Are Right!'—Tito Speaks

The official response from the SKJ in June 1968 had been to show some engagement with those student demands that did not overtly impugn the party and the system, while dismissing the more explicitly political demands that were directly censorious of the party. The revolutionary zeal of the students could be tolerated and understood, but a challenge to the legitimacy of the SKJ and the political system was dismissed as the 'work of extremists and of enemies of socialism'.[50]

As the upheavals continued in Belgrade, Tito broke his silence. Hitherto, he had not commented on the students' petition or intervened during the growing crisis, but on 9 June he chaired a joint session of the Presidency and the Executive Committee of the SKJ, before leaving to make a statement and an appeal to the students via television.[51] Watched by an estimated 10,000 students at Student City alone, he attempted to detach himself both from the repressive measures that the police had taken against students on 2 and 3 June and from the emerging new bureaucratic class. He cast himself as a socialist who retained the revolutionary spirit, said he was 'with the students' and essentially acknowledged the mistakes of the state and party leadership. He did not chide or berate the students but, instead, claimed to recognise that their misgivings were both legitimate and honourable; that their grievances about wealth inequalities, 'anti-socialist tendencies' and even their own financial circumstances and fears for future career prospects were valid.[52] In short, Tito agreed with the student demonstrators and committed himself to address and solve their problems, and invited all working people and students to join him in doing so. His words were well received by the students, who viewed the speech as *their* victory.[53] According to reports in the daily *Borba*, they greeted Tito's declaration with the wildest enthusiasm and loud expressions of approval.[54]

By essentially appeasing the students, Tito took the heat out of the situation. Following his speech, the strike and the occupations of university buildings ended and students celebrated 'their' triumph.[55] The 'June Events' were brought to a halt and normality, of a sort, returned. So ended a week-long stand-off that was characterised, in the main, by moderation on the part of both the students and the SKJ, with both exhibiting more of a commitment to mutual accommodation than in many Western countries that witnessed similar occurrences.[56] Tito rejected the notion that developments elsewhere had impacted on Yugoslavia or that events in Belgrade and other cities were related to the wider New Left demonstrations. He further argued that the students' anxieties could be resolved domestically, calming any public fears over outside intervention, such as the subsequent Warsaw Pact invasion of Czechoslovakia in August 1968, which he post factum publicly opposed.

The commitment to mutual accommodation did not last, however. In the wake of the protests, some of the reforms promised by Tito were implemented. These centred primarily on one of the students' demands—namely, that the SKJ do more to prevent corruption and self-enrichment inside the party. Tito commited to tackling this problem and, by so doing, hoped that most of the core issues and demands would be satisfied, and that others would soon dissipate.[57] Yet as Madigan Fichter notes, 'Beyond relatively cosmetic changes, the much deeper set of debates about social inequality and participatory government at the universities and beyond was not addressed in any serious way'.[58] Instead, the Yugoslav authorities dealt with those they regarded as more radical in the student movement incrementally and away from public glare. Indeed, the suppression of activists continued long after the protests had subsided. Some stood accused of supplanting and proliferating 'foreign ideas' or involvement with external foes ranging from the Central Intelligence Agency (CIA) to Maoism. At the same time, 'long-standing domestic enemies' (such as those supporting the ideas of the dissident Milovan Djilas or the hard-liner Ranković) were treated similarly.[59] In July 1968, the SKJ took measures against the student organisation at the Faculty of Philosophy in Belgrade, banning it from the party. In the wake of the protests, many of the *Praxis* academics faced formidable challenges in terms of their continued career progression, while the leaders of the student unrest were frequently harrassed. In later years, the *Praxis* professors came under mounting pressure and their journal subject to censorship (it was eventually dissolved in 1975). A longer-term process of suppression of leading *Praxis* figures culminated in the dismissal from the University of Belgrade of a group of radical Marxist academics known as the 'Belgrade Eight'.[60]

Officials in Sarajevo and Zagreb took an equally punitive approach, with several students either fined or banned from the SKH or the Bosnian League of Communists (*Savez komunista Bosne i Hercegovine—* SKBiH).[61] Gavrilo 'Gajo' Petrović, one of the leading figures in the *Praxis* group based in Zagreb, was among a number expelled from the SKJ. There is less evidence of the harsh measures taken against the Belgrade-based protestors, though many Croatian and Bosnian students were put under pressure or persuaded that it was not in their interests to cause trouble again. In August 1968, for example, Kurspahić, one of the editors of the *Student* newspaper, returned home to spend the summer with his family in Sanski Most (Bosnia-Herzegovina). While there he was visited by an agent from the Yugoslav state security, UDBA, who was keen to press him on the details of his work with the newspaper, and to gently remind him that he was being watched. Kurspahić did not return to *Student* thereafter, becoming instead the Belgrade sports correspondent for the Bosnian daily newspaper *Oslobodjenje*.[62]

Exactly two months after his televised address to students, Tito began a two-day visit to Czechoslovakia during which he was greeted enthusiastically by crowds in Prague. The Prague Spring may have influenced the Yugoslav students' own protests, but now Tito was being celebrated there as the first communist leader to resist Soviet domination. Tito had cautiously supported Dubček's reforms, but he also warned the Czechoslovak communists not to over-extend themselves.[63] Less than two weeks after Tito's visit, the Warsaw Pact 'Five', led by the Soviet Union, moved to crush the Prague Spring. In Yugoslavia, a new round of student-led protests in Kosovo in November 1968, entailing a different set of grievances, shifted attention away from the 'June Events'. The Kosovo demonstrations, which began at the Faculty of Humanities in the University of Pristina and spread to other localities in Kosovo and western Macedonia, represented not merely a critique of the SKJ but a highly sensitive call for greater autonomy for the Albanians of Yugoslavia.[64] As such, these protests initiated a quicker and far more robust response from the Yugoslav authorities than that witnessed in Belgrade, Zagreb and Sarajevo in June.

Conclusion

The 'June Events' were part of a wider wave of student demonstrations that took place throughout Europe in the summer of 1968. The means—street demonstrations, campus occupations, appeals to anti-authoritarianism—were indeed very similar. Nonetheless, the Yugoslav protests were different in that their character was determined less by global issues, whether connected with transnational opposition to hardline communism or to US imperialism, and more by a unique set of internal developments. The students' core argument was that communal interests had been replaced by those of a narrow sectoral elite in the SKJ. Their dissent was also underpinned by a call to restore socialism to its revolutionary origins. It was not, therefore, an attack on the fundamental values and ideologies of the SKJ, but a critique of aspects of the system— and within limited parameters. Nevertheless, the protests represented a challenge to a party and state that had appeared in generally good shape before the outbreak of the student unrest. The social impact of the economic reforms of 1965 had proved more potent than the leadership of the SKJ had anticipated, and they had not expected the scale and severity of the disorder that began on 2 June. The resultant student strike and occupation of university buildings had to be carefully contained to ensure that dissatisfaction could not be channelled too widely beyond the relatively narrow parameters of academia and the student body.

Any significant escalation, or any form of military intervention against the students, would have damaged not only the credibility of the Yugoslav authorities, who had cast themselves as practising a form of enlightened and non-totalitarian communism, but the global reputation of the Yugoslav state—the de facto leader of the Non-Aligned Movement. So a way had to be found to stem any growing discontent, and Tito's intervention, in which he acknowledged the concerns of the students as legitimate, brought the crisis to an end. But though his speech to students did much to assuage their apprehensions, his promises brought little in the way of substantive change. Though the SKJ committed to reforms based on the student demands, these amounted to little in the longer term. Subsequent purges sought to neutralise those students and *Praxis* academics deemed to be 'negative influences' on the student body and mitigate ideological challenges to the authority of the SKJ. The 'June Events' may have shaken the party for a short time, but it soon regained control. Future demonstrations, such as those in Kosovo in late November 1968 and in Croatia in 1971, the so-called *Hrvatsko proljeće* (Croatian Spring), were of a different and, for the SKJ, far more dangerous nationalist character.

Notes

1. For a detailed analysis of the Tito-Stalin split and its consequences, see I. Banac, *With Stalin against Tito: Cominformist Splits in Yugoslav Communism* (Ithaca, NY and London, 1988). For an overview of findings on this issue since 1990, see L. Gibianski, 'The Soviet-Yugoslav Split', in K. McDermott and M. Stibbe (eds), *Revolution and Resistance in Eastern Europe: Challenges to Communist Rule* (Oxford, 2006), pp. 17–36.
2. For further details, see J.V. Starić, 'Stalinist and Anti-Stalinist Repression in Yugoslavia, 1944–1953', in K. McDermott and M. Stibbe (eds), *Stalinist Terror in Eastern Europe: Elite Purges and Mass Repression* (Manchester, 2010), pp. 160–79.
3. See R. Vučetić, 'Violence Against the Anti-War Demonstrations of 1965–1968 in Yugoslavia: Political Balancing between East and West', *European History Quarterly*, vol. 45, no. 2 (2015), pp. 255–74 (here p. 257).
4. See M. Fichter, 'Yugoslav Protest: Student Rebellion in Belgrade, Zagreb and Sarajevo', *Slavic Review*, vol. 75, no. 1 (2016), pp. 99–121 (here p. 105); and B. Kanzleiter, 'Yugoslavia', in M. Klimke and J. Scharloth (eds), *1968 in Europe: A History of Protest and Activism, 1956–1977* (Basingstoke, 2008), pp. 219–28 (here p. 223).
5. M. Petrović, 'Students' Movements of 1968: Unfinished Revolution', *Facta Universitas: Law and Politics*, vol. 5, no. 1 (2017), pp. 1–23 (here p. 16).
6. Petrović, 'Students' Movements of 1968', p. 17.
7. Kanzleiter, 'Yugoslavia', p. 219.
8. In the 1950's, Milovan Djilas—first in a series of articles in *Borba* and later in his book *The New Class*—argued that the Yugoslav party bureaucracy (and those in other communist states) had essentially become a new ruling elite. See M. Djilas, *The New Class: An Analysis of the Communist System* (New York, 1957).

9. Kanzleiter, 'Yugoslavia', p. 221.
10. For a detailed account of the formation, activities and demise of the *Praxis* group, see G.S. Sher, *Praxis: Marxist Criticism and Dissent in Socialist Yugoslavia* (Bloomington, IN and London, 1977).
11. For the structure of elites in Yugoslavia, see L.J. Cohen, *The Socialist Pyramid: Elites and Power in Yugoslavia* (London, 1989).
12. D. Rusinow, *Yugoslavia: Oblique Insights and Observations* (Pittsburgh, PA, 2008), pp. 71–2.
13. Miller suggests that there were additional economic issues underpinning student dissatisfaction. Belgrade University 'had grown enormously in the preceding two decades, offered stipends to only 14% of them in 1965 (down from 25% five years earlier); the percentage of working-class students declined from 15–12% between 1962 and 1967'. See N. Miller, 'Yugoslavia's 1968: The Great Surrender', in V. Tismaneanu (ed.), *Promises of 1968: Crisis, Illusion, and Utopia* (Budapest, 2010), pp. 227–40 (here p. 228, n. 1).
14. Writing in the immediate wake of the protests, Milovan Djilas maintained that 'Although the demonstrations broke out more or less spontaneously, as a revolt against police actions, there had been noted earlier a certain discontent among students and non-conformist academics'. This was evidenced, he claimed, by the fact that 'Opposition trends had appeared in theoretical periodicals'. See M. Djilas, *The Unperfect Society: Beyond the New Class* (London, 1969), p. 169. For a discussion of student politics in Yugoslavia in 1967 and early 1968, see Rusinow, *Yugoslavia*, pp. 71–4.
15. Rusinow, *Yugoslavia*, p. 72.
16. Ž. Žilnik, 'Yugoslavia: Down with the Red Bourgeoisie', in P. Gassert and M. Klimke (eds), *1968: Memories and Legacies of a Global Revolt, Bulletin of the German Historical Institute* (Washington, DC, 2009), pp. 181–7 (here p. 185). Žilnik made a film about the 1968 student demonstrations entitled *Lipanjska gibanja* (June Movement), depicting the events and the numerous speeches by student leaders in the courtyard of the Faculty of Philosophy building.
17. According to Kemal Kurspahić, at that time one of the editors of the *Student* weekly newspaper, 'That year, student protests raged in the streets of Paris and other European cities, and there was a "feeling in the air" that something might happen in Belgrade too ... *Student's* editorial staff took their traditional three-month summer break, focusing on the upcoming June exams and—along with the whole country—celebrating Yugoslavia's soccer victory over England and our team's advancement to the final round of the European championship in Italy; so student protests at Belgrade University caught me, even as a *Student* editor, by surprise'. See K. Kurspahić, *Prime Time Crime: Balkan Media in War and Peace* (Washington, DC, 2003), p. 18.

18. The building of Student City in New Belgrade began in 1949 and was completed in 1955. The 'city' comprised of four blocks and housed, in 1965, over 5000 students. For a fascinating history of its construction, see B. Le Normand, *Designing Tito's Capital: Urban Planning, Modernism and Socialism in Belgrade* (Pittsburgh, PA, 2014).
19. Petrović, 'Students' Movements of 1968', p. 17.
20. R. Pervan, *Tito and the Students: The University and the University Student in Self-Managing Yugoslavia* (Nedlands, 1978), p. 19.
21. N. Popov, *Društveni sukobi—izavov sociologiji: 'Beogradski jun' 1968* (Belgrade, 2008), p. 36. See also *Borba* (Belgrade), 3 June 1968, p. 7.
22. *Borba*, 4 June 1968, p. 2. See also *Politika* (Belgrade), 4 June 1968, pp. 4–5.
23. B. Jakovljević, 'Human Resources: June 1968, "Hair" and the Beginning of Yugoslavia's End', *Grey Room*, no. 30 (2008), pp. 38–53 (here p. 41).
24. Pervan, *Tito and the Students*, p. 20. According to Dennison Rusinow, who witnessed the demonstrations, the students had valid grievances over their living standards. 'Even though tuition is free', he said, 'those without scholarships must pay for their room and board, books and other necessities. Dormitory living is subsidized and cheap—although crowded and uncomfortable, with poor food—but because of overcrowding a growing proportion of students must live in private lodgings. With housing scarce and rents high, university education is out of the question for many young people from low-income families'. See Rusinow, *Yugoslavia*, p. 75.
25. *Politika*, 4 June 1968, p. 5.
26. Petrović, 'Students' Movements of 1968', p. 18.
27. *Borba*, 4 June 1968, p. 7. See also Rusinow, *Yugoslavia*, p. 66.
28. See Kanzleiter, 'Yugoslavia', p. 219.
29. Pervan, *Tito and the Students*, p. 19.
30. *Borba*, 4 June 1968, p. 7.
31. Rusinow, *Yugoslavia*, p. 66. Soon after, Minić defended the rights of the students to protest and described them as 'part of the fight for social reform'. See *Borba*, 7 June 1968, p. 4.
32. See *Politika*, 4 June 1968, p. 6.
33. See Rusinow, *Yugoslavia*, p. 67.
34. Fichter, 'Yugoslav Protest', p. 107. For an analysis of the role of popular music in the context of the 1968 Yugoslav student demonstrations, see M. Vasiljević, 'Popularna muzika kao anticipacija, "uokviravanje" i konstrukcija generacijskog sećanja na studenski bunt 1968. godine u Jugoslaviji', *Muzikologija*, no. 14 (2013), pp. 117–33.
35. The celebrated Yugoslav-American performance artist, Marina Abramović, was part of the demonstrations and was 'literally prepared to die for the cause'. For her account of the 1968 events in Belgrade, see M. Abramović, *Walk Through Walls: A Memoir* (London, 2016), p. 40.

36. Rusinow, *Yugoslavia*, p. 69.
37. Popov, *Društveni sukobi*, p. 45.
38. Ž. Pavlović, *Ispljuvak pun krvi: Dnevnik'68* (Belgrade, 2008), p. 29.
39. *Borba*, 6 June 1968, p. 7.
40. Jakovljević, 'Human Resources', p. 42.
41. Kurspahić, *Prime Time Crime*, pp. 19–20.
42. See *Pobjeda* (Podgorica), 6 June 1968, p. 1 and *Politika*, 6 June 1968, p. 7. Also Popov, *Društveni sukobi*, pp. 76–9.
43. Petrović, 'Students' Movements of 1968', p. 18.
44. Pervan, *Tito and the Students*, p. 23. On the relationship between students and workers in Hungary in 1956, see M. Pittaway, *The Workers' State: Industrial Labor and the Making of Socialist Hungary, 1944–1958* (Pittsburgh, PA, 2012), pp. 204–5.
45. Rusinow, *Yugoslavia*, p. 69.
46. Fichter, 'Yugoslav Protest', p. 19.
47. Rusinow, *Yugoslavia*, p. 72.
48. Pervan, *Tito and the Students*, p. 23.
49. R. Donia, *Radovan Karadžić: Architect of the Bosnian Genocide* (Cambridge, 2015), p. 31. Donia notes that: 'Partly owing to his participation in the demonstrations, Karadžić first came into contact with intellectuals in the humanities, and he embraced their critique of socialist Yugoslavia. That critique began with grievances against nationalism, but in the later years of late socialism its proponents in Bosnia gradually fragmented along national lines. Their critiques subtly shifted to blaming other ethnonational groups for communism's failings. A number of the 1968 critics of communism emerged in the 1990s as leaders of various nationalist movements in Yugoslavia'. See ibid., p. 32.
50. Pervan, *Tito and the Students*, p. 23.
51. *Politika*, 10 July 1968, p. 6.
52. *Borba*, 10 June 1968, p. 1.
53. Jakovljević, 'Human Resources', p. 45.
54. See *Borba*, 10 June 1968, p. 5. For a report on how Tito's speech was greeted by students in Zagreb, Skopje, Sarajevo and Niš, see *Borba*, 11 June 1968, p. 6. Also Pavlović, *Ispljuvak pun krvi*, pp. 106–7.
55. *Politika*, 10 June 1968, p. 7.
56. Rusinow, *Yugoslavia*, p. 80.
57. Pervan, *Tito and the Students*, p. 33.
58. Fichter, 'Yugoslav Protest', p. 119.
59. Fichter, 'Yugoslav Protest', p. 113.
60. The 'Belgrade Eight' were Zagorka Pešić-Golubović, Trivo Inđić, Mihailo Marković, Dragoljub Mićunović, Nebojša Popov, Svetozar Stojanović, Ljubomir Tadić and Miladin Životić.

61. Fichter, 'Yugoslav Protest', p. 118.
62. Kurspahić, *Prime Time Crime*, p. 20.
63. See K. Dawisha, *The Kremlin and the Prague Spring* (Berkeley, CA, 1984), p. 276.
64. For details on the Kosovo protests, see "1968: The Prague Spring and the Albanian 'Castle'", by Ana Lalaj, in this volume.

1968: The Prague Spring and the Albanian 'Castle'

Ana Lalaj

Albanians have, literally and metaphorically, lived in a locked-up state. The castle is one of their symbols. In 1912, they were the last European subjects of the Ottoman Empire to proclaim their independence, but were the only peoples in the region whose claim to sovereign nationhood was sacrificed during the Great Power negotiatons that ended the two Balkan Wars in 1912–13. Although Albania did not take part in World War I, its lands turned into a battlefield between the belligerent forces, and became the source of both agreements and conflicts among the Powers. In World War II, Albania joined the Allies but liberated itself from the Italian fascist and Nazi yoke without outside assistance. After the war, due to its fragile international and diplomatic position, Albania—led by Enver Hoxha's communist partisan revolutionaries—was not permitted to become a member of the Cominform, the Soviet-led organisation of major European communist parties set up in September 1947.[1] For the same reason, Moscow initially left Albania under Yugoslav tutelage. However, in 1948 after the Stalin-Tito split, Albania, hitherto a virtual satellite of Belgrade, switched to the Kremlin's direct orbit.

A. Lalaj (✉)
Institute of History, Tirana, Albania

Thereafter, the country was geo-politically surrounded by non-friendly states. This situation could be termed the 'first siege'. In June 1960, the Albanian leadership chose not to support Moscow in its disagreement with the Chinese communists, whereupon Nikita Khrushchev announced a blockade of Tirana. Hoxha defiantly replied: 'we will eat grass, but we will not violate our principles'.[2] In the wake of this new rupture, relations with the members of the Soviet bloc deteriorated, and economic and diplomatic links were dramatically curtailed. These historical references remind us that the closed nature of Albania became decisive in its attitudes towards the outside world and help to explain the reactions of the Albanian communist leaders to the Prague Spring of 1968.

News from Prague

In 1922, Czechoslovakia was among the first states to establish diplomatic relations with independent Albania and by the 1930s Czechoslovakia was second only to Italy in its exports to the country.[3] After World War II, trade was maintained at fairly bouyant levels and even in the 1960s, when political and cultural exchanges between the two 'allies' were in sharp decline, economic ties were kept alive. In the interest of these mutually beneficial transactions, Tirana maintained a certain reserve in its public criticism of the Czechoslovak party. Nevertheless, by the late 1960s, as the winds of change were beginning to affect Czechoslovakia, the Albanian public was permitted only scarce information about what was happening in Prague, not least because the hard-line leadership in Tirana perceived events there as highly dangerous and threatening.

As tensions mounted in Czechoslovakia in the second half of 1967, Albanian diplomats in Prague endeavoured to keep their superiors in Tirana abreast of developments. For example, on 8 November a radiogram from the Albanian Embassy in Prague announced that on 31 October about five thousand students had demonstrated for several hours in the streets of the city under the slogan 'we want light, we want heating'. It was also reported that some university professors had turned their lectures on socialist political economy into extended and open debates on economic reform in the West, especially in West Germany and the USA.[4] That the students went beyond the 'light and heating' requirements soon became known. On 11 December, the embassy noted that the student committee had issued an appeal condemning police violence.[5]

On 25 December, the Albanian government informed all its diplomatic missions abroad about the tense situation in Prague, which, according to Tirana, was caused by dissatisfaction among the people, notably writers and students. The radiogram mentioned that Leonid Brezhnev, the Soviet leader, had visited Prague.[6] The first public information about events in Czechoslovakia was provided only on 7 January 1968, when the Albanian Telegraphic Agency, quoting the Czechoslovak news service, curtly announced the departure of Antonín Novotný as First Secretary of the Communist Party of Czechoslovakia (KSČ) and his replacement by Alexander Dubček. Albanian news broadcasts spoke vaguely of disagreements among rival groups in the Czechoslovak party, but gave no details.[7]

News from Czechoslovakia was censored for the next two months, until on 10 March an Albanian newspaper speculated—correctly as it turned out—that Novotný would be removed as President of the country.[8] From then on, coverage of developments in Prague was relatively dense, for a while reports appearing almost daily. In this way, Albanian citizens learnt of the main events in the Czechoslovak capital. However, the most interested person was Hoxha himself, leader of the governing Labour Party of Albania (*Partia e Punës e Shqipërisë*—PPSH). It seems he did not attach much importance to the news of Novotný's downfall, but he did take careful note of Dubček's statements, starting from day one when the new KSČ leader pledged quick steps to liberalise the regime, both economically and politically.[9]

Messages from Tirana: People, Be Vigilant!

On 24 March, the day after Novotný's second resignation, the Albanian party organ *Zëri i popullit* ('Voice of the People') published an incendiary article calling on the working classes of the 'revisionist' East European states to go on the offensive. The prime reason for this invective was undoubtedly the recent turmoil in Czechoslovakia, but the entire Soviet bloc, above all Hungary, Poland and the USSR itself, was implicated in the crisis. High-powered editorials in authoritative journals, plus numerous archival records, are testament to the fact that not only Hoxha, but also most other communist dignitaries were anxiously following events in Prague. Excluding Tito (and possibly Nicolae Ceauşescu in Romania), all communist leaders regarded the Czechoslovak innovations as a threat to their respective power positions. In Hoxha's opinion, the Prague Spring represented the culmination of Moscow's entire conciliatory political course since the early 1960s, confirmation that counter-revolution had already occurred in the countries of the Soviet bloc of which the Czechoslovak reforms were merely the ultimate proof. There, 'the counter-revolution has triumphed within the counter-revolution'.[10] Hoxha's message was clear: the East European leaders themselves had prepared the Prague debacle and they would soon be haunted by it in their own backyards. Moreover, they would pay for their 'revisionism' by being forced from power, not by the students, hooligans and reactionary intelligentsia, but by a workers' revolution!

On 9 April 1968, the KSČ released its 'Action Programme' entitled 'The Czechoslovak Road to Socialism'. In response, Hoxha penned a hostile article 'Where is Czechoslovakia Going?', published on 21 April in *Zëri i popullit*. For his subtitle, Hoxha chose to adapt Julius Fučík's well-known rallying cry: 'Mankind, be vigilant!' In Hoxha's view, Dubček's programme was nothing other than a platform to undermine the existing political system in Czechoslovakia. However, he believed that 'new Gottwalds and Fučíks will emerge on the battlefield… and they will lead the struggle of the Czechoslovak working class'.[11] These writings formed an essential component of the propaganda war that raged in 1968. For foreign audiences, selected materials from the Albanian media were translated into different languages and broadcast on the radio. Albanian diplomats, the majority of whom were senior communists with experience in clandestine activities since 1945, played a key role in the propaganda offensive, not least by distributing ideological and political tracts in the countries in which they served. Such activities regularly resulted in the expulsion of Albanian representatives, as occurred in Poland, Hungary and Cuba in the course of the 1960s.[12]

The case of Czechoslovakia in 1968 was one of the most controversial. It appears that the Albanian embassy in Prague prioritised the distribution of the vitriolic articles of 24 March and 21 April. On 11 April, the embassy telegrammed the Ministry of Foreign Affairs in Tirana to say that one hundred thousand personal and institutional addresses had been located in the phone books as potential recipients. It was suggested that the materials from Tirana should be rapidly disseminated as Dubček had not yet stabilised the situation.[13] Although the Albanian embassy was under surveillance by the Czechoslovak authorities, it acted as a clandestine centre that established links with many hard-line agitational groups in Prague and elsewhere, until in mid-May Czechoslovak television reported that tracts and leaflets from Albania, which had entered the country via the diplomatic mail, had been discovered.[14] The problem was so worrisome for the Czechs that the Ministry of the Interior created a Special Commission to investigate the multiplication and dissemination of the materials. On 22 May, the *chargé d'affaires* at the Albanian embassy, Kujtim Myzyri, notified his superiors in Tirana that the chair of the Special Commission had asserted on Prague television that the contents of the tracts were identical to the articles in *Zëri i popullit*. The chairman had even provided details about the letters, envelopes and typewriters.[15] However, it seems that the Czechoslovak authorities could not identify exactly where the materials were produced or from where they were distributed. Subsequent reports stated that in June Myzyri was summoned to the Czechoslovak Foreign Ministry, but the official dealing with the affair did not raise serious complaints about the conduct of embassy staff.[16]

Party Sponsored 'Popular' Movements

The history of communism in postwar Eastern Europe has all too vividly shown that the occasional moments of liberalisation were all crushed or circumvented. The first test came soon after Khrushchev's famous 'secret speech' at the Twentieth Congress of the Soviet party in February 1956. It is not widely recognised that Albania was among the first countries in the bloc to experience the effects of what would become known as 'de-Stalinisation'.[17] On 11 April at an important party conference, a large number of communists, mostly intellectuals and officials in central institutions, initiated a wave of criticism of the top leadership of the Labour Party of Albania. At the time, Hoxha managed to defeat his opponents who were portrayed at home and abroad as 'conspirators' within the party. This muted attempt at reform was followed by the more dramatic events of 1956: the Poznań workers' uprising in June, the 'Polish October' which brought the hitherto outcast Władysław Gomułka back to power in Warsaw, and the violently suppressed Hungarian Revolution of October–November.

By 1968, things had changed. Khrushchev had been ousted from the Kremlin and Stalin's shadow was partially restored. In Tirana, Hoxha had overcome the consequences of the split with Moscow thanks to the new relationship with Beijing. Archival records, memoires, diaries and many other historical sources indicate that the second half of the 1960s was the period when Hoxha was able to strengthen his power base without any serious obstruction. For example, in 1966 he proclaimed a series of significant political directives and reforms on behalf of the party. The first herald of the expected reforms was the 'Open Letter' of 4 March 1966, sent by the PPSH Central Committee to all communists, workers, employees, soldiers and officers.[18] Ostensibly, the missive was an invitation for citizens to participate in the governance of the country. In reality, it represented just the latest attempt to bolster party control over the whole of society, in particular the military. Up to the mid-1960s, the army had enjoyed a measure of autonomy and in order to overcome this undue 'liberalism' the 'Open Letter' stipulated the creation of political commissars alongside the post of commander and a centralised line of control directly linking basic party organisations and committees in the military to the Central Committee in Tirana. It was also decided to remove all ranks in the military hierarchy. That Hoxha did not entirely trust the army was evident in the Politburo discussions on the Letter prior to its publication. 'Our army', he said, 'is not an army of castes, marshals, generals and colonels, an army of putschists' and he ominously raised the example of Marshal Georgy Zhukov, the former Soviet Defence Minister, who had crossed swords with the Central Committee and was removed from office by Khrushchev in October 1957 for, *inter alia*, his burgeoning personality cult.[19]

The major event of 1966 was the Fifth PPSH congress convened in November. Hoxha had every reason to be optimistic as two economic agreements had been signed with China, one in May and the other a month later. With these concordats, Beijing assured the Albanian leadership that it would support Tirana's programme of industrialisation of the country. On this basis, an ambitious five-year economic plan was drafted for the period 1966–70, the mainstay of which was the construction of thirty-four large-scale enterprises. In these circumstances of relative economic security, Hoxha was eager to press on with the reforms earmarked in his March 'Open Letter' and in the weeks immediately after the PPSH congress he delivered several speeches outlining his ideas. In terms of content and purpose, they were overwhelmingly political measures suffused with militaristic terminology—war against bureaucracy, war against old customs, war against foreign 'bourgeois-revisionist' influences. A distinct strain of populism was discernible in the methods to be used: mass gatherings of 'volunteer' youth and student brigades, workers', women and war veterans' groups, and 'solidarity' rallies. For Hoxha, paradoxical as it may seem, popular support was important and he did his best to secure it, in many cases successfully.

It is evident that in the mid-to-late 1960s, the Albanian experiment with radical mass movements in many ways replicated the contemporaneous Cultural Revolution in China, for which Hoxha expressed open support: 'such methods of work as practiced by the Chinese Communist Party are the only fundamental Marxist–Leninist means of healing'.[20] The Chinese experience appears to have inspired the so-called 'revolutionary movements' in Albania starting in 1967. In January, high school students in Durrës announced to the Central Committee that they had occupied a church on the outskirts of the city. This was treated as a spontaneous youth initiative 'from below'. In fact, it was soon understood that it was a party directive 'from above'. In imitation of the Durrës pupils, large groups of young people sprang up everywhere with pick-axes in their hands. The pressure was so great that the leaders of local religious communities one after another informed the Central Committee that they were resigning their functions. Within five months, 740 mosques and 765 Orthodox and Catholic churches were closed and turned into cultural centres, warehouses or stables, although a few buildings were preserved because of their cultural and historic value.[21] In Shkodra, the city where the Catholic clergy had suffered the fiercest persecution, an exhibition was opened on the 'reactionary role of religion'. It later took the name 'Atheist Museum', the only one of its kind. In 1976, under the new constitution, Albania became the first country in the world to proclaim itself officially atheist.[22]

The contradictions in these approaches were rife. For example, it would appear that Hoxha was increasingly motivated in his projects to build a society where everyone controlled everyone and everyone was in turn controlled by the party. In a famous speech on 6 February 1967, he bloodcurdlingly exhorted 'the entire … country [to] stand up, burn off their backward habits and decapitate anyone who misuses the sacred law of the party'. But in the same breath, Hoxha called more positively for 'the protection of the rights of women and girls'.[23] Indeed, documents and press articles of the time describe many meetings, especially in villages mostly in the north of the country, where young girls publicly denounced their early-age engagements and declared them null and void. These kinds of movements in Albania were not few and in one way or another were aimed at all social groups and ages, from children to the elderly. As for comparisons with the Chinese experience, the archival record suggests that the problems of the two countries were essentially dissimilar, although the same political orientation unified the solutions. For Mao Zedong, the mid-1960s were a troubled period following the failure of the 'Great Leap Forward' and it was widely recognised that the mission of the Red Guards during the Cultural Revolution was to purge the Chinese party of 'bourgeois elements' and Mao's opponents and thereby bolster his leadership cult. In Albania it was different; the 'revolutionary movements' had no cleansing goals, but an affirmative mission to strengthen the party's leading role. Unlike Mao, Hoxha was not under pressure, but like Mao, Hoxha was a dictator and he used these 'popular' movements as a means of elevating both the cult of the PPSH and, through it, the cult of his own personality.

WRITERS IN LINE

Whenever there were major socio-political upheavals in the communist world, it was often the intellectuals—writers, journalists, artists and film-makers—who initiated and stood in the forefront of change. As Eduard Goldstücker, an active protagonist in the Prague Spring, intimated, when a writer in a totalitarian system pens a subversive word the audience takes it up as an 'event'.[24] Why? Because dictatorships fear the power of the 'word' like death, and yet they need it like air. This truism is exemplified by the Polish leader, Gomułka, who noted in March 1968 that the uprisings of 1956 in his country and in Hungary started with the intellectuals, and it was the same in Czechoslovakia in 1968.[25] Indeed, it is well-known that in the summer of 1967 several Czechoslovak writers had spoken out against censorship and state control over literature, and had paid the price of expulsion from the party.[26] After January 1968, it remained to be seen whether the new First Secretary, Dubček, was on the intellectuals' side as the protector of freedom of speech.

To understand the state of literature and the arts in Albania, it might be helpful to have a short retrospective chronicle. After World War II, the infant communist regime took care to create a new proletarian culture. For literature, the model was Soviet-style 'socialist realism', although the works of prominent foreign authors of the realist tradition were also translated. For example, from Czech literature the most popular novel was Jaroslav Hašek's *The Good Soldier Švejk*. Fučík's *Reports Written under the Noose* was also widely read, and even entered the school curriculum. Indigenous literature of the 1950s was not particularly impressive. Most writers had cut their spurs during the war, while pre-war authors found it difficult to adapt and for this reason many kept silent. A few courageous writers opposed the socialist realist template with its typecast scheme of 'good', 'bad' and 'rectified' characters. As a sign of revolt, some abandoned the official Writers' League and others like Kasem Trebeshina, a communist who emerged during the war but whose impulsive temperament clashed with Marxist–Leninist discipline, resigned from the party. 'In my poems, revolt and protest are visible', he wrote to Hoxha when announcing his departure from the party, 'but for this I take no responsibility. The responsibility belongs to those who inspire me'.[27]

In the early 1960s, following the rift with the USSR, Soviet art and culture ceased to be the model in Tirana and scarcely any works were translated from Soviet and East European literature. However, literary and other art forms in Albania were gaining a certain creative maturity. A group of young writers, among them Ismail Kadare, Dritëro Agolli and Fatos Arapi, freshly returned from study abroad, published books that differed greatly from the dominant artistic canon. In 1961, their creativity became a *cause célèbre* among writers, sparking intense public debate about tradition and innovativeness. Many older writers upheld the line of traditional poetic standards, while younger writers sought to rejuvenate literary and stylistic means of expression. This discussion was abruptly terminated in July 1961 when at a meeting with writers Hoxha basically supported the young renegades, but demanded that tradition and innovation should not be seen as mutually exclusive.[28]

Later in the decade, as the world was galvanised by numerous social movements, the spirit of which in one way or another penetrated even the walls of the Albanian 'castle', cultural life there experienced a limited liberalisation. In cinema, a few neo-realist films, mainly Italian movies, appeared as did foreign historical productions. In Tirana, regular television broadcasts started late, only in 1971. Before this time, there were no programmes in the Albanian language, although Italian channels, such as *Radiotelevisione italiana* (RAI), were widely available and those few Albanians who had TV screens in their homes turned their rooms into impromptu 'cinema halls' to follow the Italian broadcasts. Radio programmes such as *Canzonissima*, *Hit Parade* and *San Remo Festival* were extremely popular, especially among the youth. This optimistic atmosphere was also felt in literature, which expanded its content to include everyday themes from the life of young people.

It should be emphasised that the 'foreign', both in ideology and lifestyle, was always censored in communist Albania. Even so, there were times when it was not fought *in extremis*, as in the 1960s. At that time, Hoxha's main concern was the struggle against the old, the conservative, the regressive. Writers and artists were armed with this militant spirit and in 1966 they 'went to' the workers and peasants to find subjects for their creative work. But this was no simple task either, as demonstrated by the case of the talented writer, Dhimitër Xhuvani, who wrote a novel based on the construction of a hydro-electric power plant. Readers generally welcomed the book, but Prime Minister Mehmet Shehu ordered the author to return to the plant, this time not with his pencil and notebook, but with a pick-axe. The reason was that the novel told the unpalatable truth about the difficult life of the Albanian working class and it cost Xhuvani five years of hard labour. In general, with the involvement of writers and other cultural figures in the revolutionary 'popular' movements, the party was able to manipulate the creative intelligentsia for political ends, keep them broadly under control and largely stifle their creative activity. As a result, Albanian art overflowed with stylised plaque paintings, sculptures with muscular workers, martial songs, literary heroes delivering interminable speeches, daughters denouncing fathers and other glossy 'realities'.

These tropes dominated the artistic milieu in 1968, when intellectuals, even the best, paid tribute to political engagement. Early in that year, Albanian writers felt constrained to postpone their congress because local party luminaries in Tirana feared possible ideological 'deviation' under the influence of developments abroad, especially from Czechoslovakia. Although Hoxha rebuked his subordinates for their distrust towards the writers, he did not openly support the convocation of the congress.[29] And things were not about to improve. In late 1969, perhaps again in response to the perceived dangers of the Prague Spring, the first signals were given that the frontal battle against conservatism would shift to the fight against liberal manifestations. Specifically, Hoxha decided that a prize-winning play, *Njollat e murme* ('Dark Stains'), was insulting to society,[30] whereupon critics decried its 'erroneous' message about the powerlessness of humans to remedy evil and its implication that social 'stains' were ever-present. Two years later, when the 'revolutionary movements' were at their height, writers were top of the list for political persecution. Both the play's author, Minush Jero, and director, Mihallaq Luarasi, were imprisoned. But an interview in 2001 with the actor who starred in the drama, Vangjush

Furrxhi, revealed an interesting subplot. According to him, 'Dark Stains' paralleled that of a work written by Bertolt Brecht, 'The Spy', which deals with a German family at the time of Hitler's rise to power. The parents were critical of the Nazi regime and were therefore anxious that their son might disclose outside the house what he heard within it. In the case of 'Dark Stains', the parents likewise kept their son within the confines of the house, because he was keen on Western lifestyles and his behaviour outside the home might risk the security of the family.[31] There was no mention of this by the author or director at the time and hence we do not know if this dangerous subtext was intentional or not, just as we do not know if the dictator himself had any inkling of it.

The Albanian Denunciation of Soviet Aggression and the Warsaw Treaty

In the Albanian consciousness, Prague is remembered not so much for its 'Spring' as for its 'Winter'. On 21 August 1968, approximately 500,000 soldiers of the Warsaw Pact member states, excluding Albania and Romania, invaded Czechoslovakia. The next day, the PPSH and the Albanian government in a joint statement condemned the aggression, calling it a 'fascist type' action.[32] There followed in rapid succession meetings of the PPSH Politburo on 3 September and the Central Committee on 5 September.[33] Tirana's opposition to the Soviet-led occupation undoubtedly bolstered the reputation of the Albanian political leadership, both domestically and internationally. Internally, World War II veterans' associations, worker and peasant groups, youth and women organisations, schoolchildren and soldiers among many others sent numerous messages of gratitude to the party, indignantly condemning the Soviet aggressors and voicing solidarity with the Czechoslovak people. There were likewise hyperbolic pronouncements about the Great Leader: 'Enver Hoxha is the Skanderbeg of today, who fights not only for the freedom and independence of his country, but also for the liberation and honour of the peoples of Europe'.[34] Support for the Albanian stance was also received from abroad, especially Czechoslovakia. Reports from the Albanian embassy there state, somewhat exaggeratedly one suspects, that not only in Prague, but throughout the country clandestine Czech and Slovak radio stations repeatedly broadcast declarations and editorials from Albania, without mentioning that Radio Tirana's Czech language service covered the entire country.[35]

However, the most important outcome for Albania of the Soviet action in Czechoslovakia was its decision to formally withdraw from the Warsaw Pact. As Mark Kramer has observed: 'Albania, which had been only a nominal member of the alliance since 1961, protested the intervention by severing its last remaining ties with the Pact and aligning itself ever more firmly with China'.[36] Throughout the 1960s, Albania's relations with the Warsaw Treaty states had been distinctly strained. Tensions began in March 1961, when the Pact's Political Committee stipulated that naval vessels in the Bay of Vlorë should be commanded solely by Soviet officers.[37] Unsurprisingly, the Albanian government rejected this decision and at the end of turbulent bilateral discussions eight out of twelve submarines, as well as a Soviet sailing vessel, departed Vlorë on 26 May. This event was followed by another incident in August 1961, when Ramiz Alia, Hoxha's messenger, was asked to leave a high-level Political Committee meeting on the pretext that he did not possess the appropriate credentials.[38] Thereafter, Tirana was no longer represented at the Warsaw Treaty table. Thus, from 1961 Albania was de facto out of the Warsaw Pact and for several years sought a propitious moment to realise it *de jure*. The crushing of the Prague Spring proved to be the perfect opportunity. On 13 September 1968, the People's Assembly in Tirana adopted the 'Law on the Denunciation of the Warsaw Pact', which foresaw the 'liberation of the Republic of Albania from any obligation deriving from this Treaty'.[39] The next day, Poland's *chargé d'affaires* in Tirana, Piotr Głowacki, was summoned to the Foreign Ministry and handed a memorandum conveying this message to his government in Warsaw, where the ratification documents of the Treaty were deposited. The Polish diplomat refused to accept the note. It was then sent by courier to the Polish Embassy, but an hour later it was returned.[40] We do not know whether the responsible office at Warsaw Pact headquarters reacted to the Albanian denunciation or not, but we do know that Tirana was not invited to sign the act of dissolution of the Pact twenty-three years later in February and July 1991.

Hoxha's denunciation of Soviet aggression against Czechoslovakia may have boosted his popularity ratings at home, but it also represented a potential challenge to the Kremlin. Beyond his exaggerated statements calling for acts of 'manhood' and 'bravery', a characteristic Albanian weakness, it can be seen that Hoxha was attentive to developments. The dangers of a military confrontation had come back on the agenda. In order to shore up its vulnerable position, the Albanian government utilised the Treaty of Friendship and Mutual Cooperation with Bulgaria signed in December 1947. It sent Sofia a note, according to which the Albanian authorities had uncontested data on large concentrations of Soviet military forces in Bulgaria. The memorandum required that the Bulgarian government should not only refrain from any activity against the People's Republic of Albania, but also that Soviet forces should leave Bulgaria as soon as possible.[41] A similar letter, formulated in more restrained language, was despatched on the same day to President Gamal Abdel Nasser of Egypt.[42] Predictably, both governments insisted that there were no foreign military bases on their territories. It appears, however, that Tirana did not stand entirely alone. In the archives of the Albanian Foreign Ministry there are dozens of reports from diplomatic representatives abroad expressing solidarity with Tirana, not least from two noteworthy neighbours, Yugoslavia and Italy. The Foreign Affairs Secretariat in Belgrade welcomed the Albanian decision to leave the Warsaw Pact and offered to improve relations between the two countries, an act which would have had major positive implications for the Balkans,[43] and the message from Rome, at least as interpreted by the Albanian ambassador, was that the Italian government would not stand idly by if Albania were attacked.[44]

Much more significant were the comradely messages arriving from Beijing. A letter signed by Mao Zedong, Lin Biao and Zhou Enlai sent to Tirana on 17 September contained the oft-repeated statement that if the Americans or Soviets dared to touch 'even a hair of Albania, they could expect nothing but complete, shameful and inevitable defeat'.[45] This declaration was celebrated at hundreds of rallies in Albanian towns and villages culminating in a mass demonstration of 100,000 citizens in Tirana.[46] Of course, Mao's commitment to Albania was politically motivated and essentially propagandistic. Indeed, Beijing had made it clear as early as September 1963 that Albania's geographical location made it impossible for China to offer timely military aid in the event of actual war.[47] But this did not preclude the sale of Chinese arms to Albania, especially as putting the country on a high degree of readiness in the autumn of 1968, as we have seen, raised tensions in the region. The Albanian Defence Minister, Beqir Balluku, travelled to Beijing in late September with a list of demands for armaments, primarily heavy land weapons, aircraft artillery and tanks. Arms supply talks were held with Zhou Enlai and Chief of Staff Huan Jun Shen on the night of 6 and 7 October at which Tirana's requests were partially accepted.

According to a list preserved in the Central State Archive, Albania received an additional 110,000 light weapons, including 10,000 machine guns, 2000 75 mm cannons, 180 double gauge 187 mm cannons, 2000 82 mm mortars, 2500 anti-aircraft machine guns and 65 million shells, together with 500 million shells expected to come under the terms of a previous agreement.[48] Hence, Chinese military support was absolutely vital to Albanian security.

THE KOSOVO DEMONSTRATIONS

On 27 November 1968, news agencies reported major protests in the autonomous Yugoslav province of Kosovo, home to a large majority of ethnic Albanians. In the capital city, Pristina, and other towns such as Ferizaj, Gjilan and Podujevë students and high school pupils of Albanian nationality had demonstrated, waving the national flag and calling for self-determination, even a separate republic. In Pristina, the protest had begun peacefully, but had degenerated into clashes with the police, some of whom resorted to firearms. A 16-year-old boy lost his life and many others were injured. Tirana was one of the few capitals in Europe, perhaps the only one, that did not broadcast the news. Only on 30 November did the Albanian Foreign Minister ask the *chargé d'affairs* in Belgrade for details of the events.[49] Reports were submitted to the minister on 3 and 4 December from which we learn that the demonstrations had been scheduled in different cities of Kosovo for 28 November, the Albanian national holiday, but the Yugoslav authorities had taken strong obstructive measures and the protests were banned. Rumours were also doing the rounds that students and teachers were being arrested, although at a press conference Tito had requested that the demonstrations in Pristina should not be dramatised and given greater importance than they deserved.[50]

The cause of the disturbances in Kosovo was national resentment, 'an old virus that twenty years of authoritarian communism had been able to keep under wraps, but not eradicate'.[51] The protests occurred in November 1968, but the embryo had existed since at least July 1966, when the Yugoslav Interior Minister, Alexander Ranković, was fired from all functions. Ranković's demise was the signal for significant change in Yugoslav society. At the end of March 1967, Tito visited Kosovo and promised the modernisation of the province.[52] Most important, one month later citizens were invited to participate in constitutional reform, an entirely new proposition for them. After a year of discussion at the provincial level, it was agreed that greater autonomy in the economic, administrative and judicial spheres should be granted, as well as more open use of national symbols. The most intractable and divisive issue was the status of the province. One group, mainly officials in provincial or federal bodies, advocated extensive autonomy for Kosovo. Another cohort, mostly intellectuals, argued that Kosovo should be detached from Serbia as a separate republic, albeit within Yugoslavia. Meanwhile a third group, active representatives of Serb ethnicity together with adherents of Ranković, supported the preservation of the status quo.[53]

Nevertheless, voices in support of a republic were growing. Political meetings held in Gjakova, Peja, Deçan, Gjilan, Podujeva and Prizren in late August 1968 come out strongly in favour of this option.[54] It appears that leading political actors in the Yugoslav Federation and in the Kosovo Provincial Committee, not to mention the republic of Serbia, were totally unprepared for these maximal demands. Thus in October, Tito received a delegation from Kosovo and in a prudent speech he told his guests that 'a republic would not solve all your problems'.[55] This pronouncement foreclosed any legal route to an autonomous republic, whereupon students, as well as many other citizens, spilled out on to the streets. Although the protests were not completely in vain, and even resulted in certain concessions from Belgrade, they did show that the Albanians of Kosovo had a long way to go in their quest for greater self-governance.[56]

A key question remains: did the Prague Spring in any way influence the Pristina demonstrations? In general, the movements of 1968 were not directly related to each other, but they were the product of similar circumstances. The crushing of the Prague Spring in August elicited a wave of solidarity for the Czechoslovak people throughout Yugoslavia, including Kosovo. Tito himself had followed Dubček's reforms with sympathy and his denunciation of the Soviet-led invasion was undoubtedly sincere. For example, at the time of the intervention there were about 45,000 Czech and Slovak tourists in Yugoslavia and the Belgrade government took special care to cover their expenses until the situation calmed down.[57] However, three months after the occupation, when the demonstrations took place in Pristina, acts of solidarity with the Czechoslovaks were already beginning to dissipate. Popular indignation against Soviet aggression was still in evidence, but the overwhelming cause of the Kosovan protests was precisely the old issue of Albanian national reassertion.

It is important to ascertain whether the People's Republic of Albania played any role in the Pristina events. In the post-disorder analysis, especially that of Serbian republican bodies, it was often claimed that one of the key factors was incitement from Albania, but this version is debatable. Hoxha, it appears, felt extremely anxious about the prospect of a Kosovan republic. Already in August 1966, one month after Ranković's fall, he confided in his diary: 'This so-called Albanian foreign republic designed by the Titoists might become the centre of Kosovar reaction, fascist fugitives and Albanian war criminals ... for the fight against the People's Republic of Albania'.[58] Moreover, records preserved in the archive of the Albanian Foreign Ministry confirm that Hoxha's concerns of 1966 remained valid two years later. On 19 September 1968, at the height of the discussions about constitutional amendment and just two months before the protests, the Albanian embassy in Belgrade requested instructions from Tirana on how to react to Kosovan demands that Albania support their proclamation of a republic.[59] The ministry's categorical response came in a report dated 30 September. Paragraphs 1 and 2 read:

1. Our position on Yugoslavia and the issue of Kosovo has not changed. We advise Kosovars to struggle to gain maximum rights, aiming for the same rights as other nationalities in Yugoslavia.
2. On the issue of whether a republic or an autonomous province should be formed, you have instructions. We repeat that we do not support the creation of a republic because it would not solve the problem.[60]

It seems clear that the Albanian government did not incite the protests in Kosovo and did not even inform its citizens about the events. It remains an open question whether Hoxha's leadership opposed the demonstrations because of their explosive content or because they could engender turmoil among Albania's neighbours, further complicating an already delicate situation—most likely both. However, if Tirana was not directly implicated, were the protests somehow inspired by Albania? It is true that for Kosovar Albanians, the homeland has always been a great inspiration. But such sentiments had been suppressed for many years, until propitious conditions were created for them to re-emerge. The decisive moment came in late 1967 with the onset of cultural exchange between

Tirana and Pristina. On 2 December, four well-known pedagogues and researchers from Pristina visited Albania. In their meetings with scholars from the University of Tirana, they demanded that lecturers from Albania should give classes and attend scientific conferences in Kosovo: 'You will see how our youth will welcome you, how they will gather from all sides! Send the best experts, let the Serbs see that we are a progressive nation'.[61] They were right. 1968 marked the 500th anniversary of the death of Skanderbeg, the Albanian national hero. In January, a scientific colloquium was held in Tirana and four months later a major Skanderbeg Symposium was convened in Pristina, which Kosovar Albanian youth turned into a political and national manifestation. The same thing occurred when Albanian artistic groups or sports teams were warmly received in Kosovo. These occasions surely stirred the emotions of the Kosovar Albanians, emboldening them to demand greater national rights from the Yugoslav authorities.

Conclusion

In Albania, the Prague Spring of 1968 was undoubtedly perceived as a threat to Hoxha's power, while the Soviet-led invasion of Czechoslovakia in August was regarded as a useful opportunity to boost the country's increasingly inward-looking, ultra-leftist course since 1961 by making a final break with the Warsaw Pact alliance. In order to pre-empt the seepage of the Czechoslovak 'disease' into the country, the ruling Party of Labour oversaw the creation of mass 'popular' revolutionary movements composed of detachments of workers, villagers, women, students, soldiers and officers as ready-made militant agitation structures against the winds of change blowing from Prague. After the Hungarian Revolution of 1956, as scholars have noted, the occupation of Czechoslovakia prolonged the life of the Soviet bloc in Eastern Europe for another twenty years.[62] This was the case for Albania too. There, the PPSH and government denounced the Warsaw Pact invasion, but the party with Hoxha at its helm was the prime beneficiary of the aggression. For if the Prague Spring reforms had been allowed to continue, sooner or later their spirit would have penetrated the walls of the Albanian 'castle'. Thus, paradoxically, Soviet tanks in Czechoslovakia afforded Hoxha a measure of political and ideological security just as his denunciation of the intervention gave him a measure of popular legitimacy.

Notes

1. G. Procacci et al. (eds), *The Cominform: Minutes of the Three Conferences 1947/1948/1949* (Milan, 1994), pp. 601 and 603.
2. 'Fjala e Enver Hoxhës në 20 vjetorin e Partisë së Punës të Shqipërisë', *Zëri i popullit*, 8 November 1961.
3. *Vjetari statistikor i RPSH, 1965* (Tirana, 1965), p. 314.
4. Arkivi i Ministrisë së Punëve të Jashtme (Archive of the Ministry of Foreign Affairs—AMPJ), fondi i përkohshëm, v. 1967, d. 17, pp. 70–2. Radiogram from the Albanian embassy in Prague to the Ministry of Foreign Affairs (MPJ) in Tirana, no. 14641–14643, 8 November 1967.
5. AMPJ, v. 1967, d. 17, pp. 128–30. Radiogram from the Albanian embassy in Prague to the MPJ, no. 15990, 11 December 1967.
6. AMPJ, v. 1967, d. 17, pp. 22–2/1. Radiogram from the MPJ to Albanian diplomatic missions abroad, no. 3982–3983, 25 December 1967.
7. 'Ndryshime në udhëheqjen e Partisë Komuniste të Çekosllovakisë', *Zëri i popullit*, 7 January 1968.
8. 'Në Çekosllovaki vazhdon lufta për pushtet', *Bashkimi*, 10 March 1968.
9. E. Hoxha, 'Këmbim shërbëtorësh në udhëheqjen revizioniste të Çekosllovakisë', 5 January 1968, in *Ditar për çështje ndërkombëtare, 1968–1969* (Tirana, 1982), p. 16.
10. 'Klasa punëtore në vendet revizioniste duhet të zbresë në fushën e betejës dhe të rivendosë diktaturën e proletariatit', *Zëri i popullit*, 24 March 1968.
11. 'Ku poshkon Çekosllovakia?', *Zëri i popullit*, 21 April 1968. Julius Fučík was a prominent Czechoslovak communist journalist and activist executed by the Nazis in September 1943. Klement Gottwald was the Stalinist leader of the KSČ from 1929 to his death in March 1953.
12. For details, see AMPJ, v. 1962, d. 405; v. 1965, d. 329; v. 1967, d. 261; v. 1968, d. 108 and d. 279.
13. AMPJ, v. 1968, d. 26. pp. 56–7. Radiogram from the Albanian embassy in Prague to the MPJ, 11 April 1968.
14. AMPJ, v. 1968, d. 25, pp. 57–9. Radiogram from the MPJ to the Albanian embassy in Prague, 14 May 1968.
15. AMPJ, v. 1968, d. 25, pp. 44–6. Radiogram nr. 6678–6680, 22 May 1968.
16. AMPJ, v. 1968, d. 25, pp. 90–2. Radiogram nr. 531–537, 6 June 1968.
17. For details, see E. Mëhilli, 'Defying De-Stalinization: Albania's 1956', *Journal of Cold War Studies*, vol. 13, no. 4 (2011), pp. 4–56.
18. Arkivi Qendror i Shtetit (Central State Archive—AQSH), f. 14/AP-OU, v. 1966, d. 2, pp. 34–62. 'Open Letter of the PPSH Central Committee', 4 March 1966.

19. AQSH, f. 14/AP-OU, v. 1966, d. 10, pp. 158–70. PPSH Politburo Meeting, 23 February 1966.
20. AQSH, f. 14/AP—MPKK, v. 1966, d. 13, pp. 104–6. Meetings between the Chinese party delegation chaired by Zhou Enlai and the Albanian delegation chaired by Enver Hoxha in Tirana, 24–28 June 1966.
21. Ç. Hoxha, 'Marrëdhëniet e besimeve fetare gjatë regjimit komunist në Shqipëri, krahasuar me regjimet komuniste të Evropës Lindore 1960–1967', in S. Boçi and L. Dushku (eds), *Kërkime të reja për historinë e Shqiptarëve* (Tirana, 2017), pp. 157–75.
22. 'Kushtetuta e RPSSH, 28 dhjetor 1976', in *Përmbledhës i Përgjithshëm i Legjislacionit në Fuqi në Republikën Popullore Socialiste të Shqipërisë, 1945–79*, vol. 1 (Tirana, 1986), p. 18.
23. E. Hoxha, 'Revolucionarizimi i mëtejshëm i partisë dhe i pushtetit', 6 February 1967, *Vepra*, vol. 35 (Tirana, 1982), p. 4.
24. https://nsarchive2.gwu.edu/coldwar/interviews/episode-6/gold-stucker22.html, 'Interview with Professor Eduard Goldstücker', from *Episode 6: Reds*.
25. For details, see '"To Hell with Sovereignty!": Poland and the Prague Spring", by Tony Kemp-Welch, in this volume.
26. AQSH, f.14/AP-Strukturë, v. 1968, d. 333, pp. 1–25. Report of the Albanian embassy in Prague for the MPJ, 28 July 1968.
27. AQSH, f. 14/AP-Strukturë, v. 1953, d. 7, pp. 76–7. Letter from Kasem Trebeshina to Enver Hoxha, 19 September 1953.
28. E. Hoxha, 'Populli ynë ka trashëguar një kulturë të madhe me tradita përparimtare', *Vepra*, vol. 21 (Tirana, 1976), p. 374.
29. AQSH, f. 14/AP-Strukturë, d. 271, p. 1. Handwritten note by Hoxha on a report of the Tirana party committee, 19 February 1968.
30. AQSH, f. 14/AP-OU, v. 1969, d. 10, pp. 89–94. PPSH Politburo Meeting, 3 November 1969.
31. www.mapo.al/2016/01 (last accessed on 10 September 2017). V. Murati, 'Drama e ndaluar 'Njollat e murme'", MAPO, 16 January 2016.
32. 'Deklaratë e KQ të PPSH dhe Këshillit të Ministrave të RPSH për agresionin e revizionistëve sovjetikë dhe satelitëve të tyre kundër RSÇ dhe popullit çekosllovak', *Zëri i popullit*, 23 August 1968.
33. AQSH, f. 14/AP-OU, v. 1968, d. 10, p. 35. 'Vendim i Byrosë Politike për denoncimin e TV', 3 September 1968; AQSH, f. 14/AP-OU, v. 1968, d. 1, p. 143. 'Vendim i Plenumit PPSH për denoncimin e TV', 5 September 1968.
34. AMPJ, v 1968, d. 25, pp. 49–50. Radiogram from the Albanian embassy in Prague to the MPJ, 19 September 1968.
35. AMPJ, v. 1968, d. 26, pp 5–7. Radiogram from the Albanian embassy in Prague to the MPJ, 7 August 1968.

36. M. Kramer, 'The Czechoslovak Crisis and the Brezhnev Doctrine', in C. Fink et al. (eds), *1968: The World Transformed* (Cambridge, 1998), pp. 111–72 (here p. 164).
37. V. Mastny, *Parallel History Project on NATO and the Warsaw Pact* (*PHP*), available at www.php.isn.ethz.ch (Zurich, 2009), pp. 1–3. Meeting of the Warsaw Treaty Political Consultative Committee in Moscow, 28–29 March 1961.
38. AQSH, f. 14/AP-MPKBS, v. 1961, d. 5, pp. 7–28. Letter of the PPSH Central Committee to the Communist Parties and Members of the Warsaw Pact, 3 September 1961.
39. 'Fjala e shokut Mehmet Shehu "Mbi qëndrimin e RPSH ndaj Traktatit të Varshavës"', *Zëri i popullit*, 14 September 1968.
40. AMPJ, v. 1968, d. 264, p. 183. Memorandum of Reiz Malile, Deputy Foreign Minister, sent to the Albanian embassy in Warsaw, 14 September 1968.
41. 'Notë e qeverisë së Republikës Popullore të Shqipërisë drejtuar qeverisë së Republikës Popullore të Bullgarisë', *Zëri i popullit*, 22 September 1968.
42. AMPJ, v. 1968, d. 154, pp. 47–50. The letter sent to President Nasser, as distinct from the note to the Bulgarian government, was not published in the press. The reason for this was surely the interest of the Chinese government, shared by its Albanian counterpart, in closer relations with Arab countries.
43. Arhiv Jugoslavije (Yugoslav Archive—AJ), Arhiv Centralnog Komiteta Saveza Komunista Jugoslavije, 507.IX, 1.I-395, pp. 6–13. Information from the State Secretariat of Foreign Affairs sent to the Central Committee of the Communist League of Yugoslavia, 14 October 1968.
44. AMPJ, v. 1968, d. 264, pp. 137–42. Telegram of the Albanian ambassador in Italy, Ksenofon Nushi, to MPJ, 18 September 1968.
45. 'Telegram i Mao Ce Dun, Lin Bjao, Çu En Lai për shokun Enver Hoxha dhe shokun Mehmet Shehu', *Zëri i popullit*, 19 September 1968.
46. 'Miqësi e pathyeshme, unitet revolucionar midis popujve shqiptar dhe kinez', *Zëri i popullit*, 22 September 1968.
47. AQSH, f. 14/AP-MPKK, v. 1963, d. 7, pp. 64–91. Verbal report of the meeting between Beqir Balluku and Ten Hsiao Pin in Beijing, 24 September 1963.
48. AQSH, f. 14/AP-MPKK, v. 1968, d. 8, p. 18. Verbal report of conversation between the Albanian delegation headed by Beqir Balluku and the Chinese delegation headed by Zhou Enlai, 6–7 October 1968.
49. AMPJ, v. 1968, d. 360, p. 121. Radiogram from the Albanian Foreign Minister, Nesti Nase, to the Albanian embassy in Belgrade, 30 November 1968.

50. AMPJ, v. 1968, d. 360, pp. 122–9. Radiogram from the Albanian embassy in Belgrade to the MPJ, 3 and 4 December 1968; see also 'Intervista e Kryetarit Tito me gazetarët e vendit dhe të huej', *Rilindja*, 1 December 1968.
51. B. Lory, *Evropa Ballkanike nga 1945 në ditët tona* (Tirana, 1996), p. 115.
52. R. Dedaj (ed.), *Tito në Kosovë* (Pristina, 1975), pp. 50–4.
53. AMPJ, v. 1968, d. 360, pp. 91–4. Radiogram from the Albanian embassy in Belgrade to the MPJ, 23 September 1968.
54. 'Pa vetëvendosje s'ka barabarësi', *Rilindja*, 19 August 1968; 'Krahinës, kompetenca më të mëdha', *Rilindja*, 6 September 1968; 'Vetvendosja e plotë të zgjidhet pa kompromis', *Rilindja*, 8 September 1968.
55. 'Krahina Autonome duhet t'i gëzojëtë gjitha të drejtat që i takojnë', *Rilindja*, 4 November 1968.
56. A. Lalaj, *Kosova: Rruga e gjatë drejt vetëvendosjes, 1948–1981* (Tirana, 2000), p. 367.
57. 'Hungaria lejoi turistët çekosllovakë të kthehen në atdhe', *Rilindja*, 26 August 1968.
58. E. Hoxha, 'Popujt dhe marksistë-leninistët revolucionarë jugosllavë duhet të luftojnë', 1 August 1966, in *Ditar për çështje ndërkombëtare (1966–1967)*, vol. 4 (Tirana, 1982), pp. 146–7.
59. AMPJ, v. 1968, d. 360, pp. 85–90. Radiogram from the Albanian embassy in Belgrade to the MPJ, 20 September 1968.
60. AMPJ, v. 1968. d. 360, pp. 249–50. Report of the IVth Directory of MPJ, 30 September 1968.
61. AQSH, f. 14/AP-Strukturë, v. 1967, d. 255/1, pp. 2–15. Report of the State University of Tirana to the PPSH Central Committee, 28 December 1967.
62. M. Kramer, 'The Kremlin, the Prague Spring, and the Brezhnev Doctrine', accessed from https://archive.org/details/TheKremlinThePragueSpringand theBrezhnevDoctrinebyMarkKramer.

Echoes of the Prague Spring in the Soviet Baltic Republics

Irēna Saleniece and Iveta Šķiņķe

The year 1968 could have been a real jubilee celebration for the peoples of the three Baltic countries—Estonia, Latvia and Lithuania.[1] In that year they might have commemorated the fiftieth anniversary of their statehood as all of them had been founded in 1918 on the ruins of the Russian Tsarist Empire. However, in 1968 the loss of independence of these countries had lasted for twenty eight years. The spheres of influence in the region foreshadowed by the Molotov-Ribbentrop Pact of August 1939 meant that in the course of World War II the Baltic states were occupied first by the Soviet Union and then by National Socialist Germany. Liberation from the Nazi yoke by the Red Army in 1944–45 was accompanied by the restoration of the Soviet occupation and an intense process of 'Sovietisation'.[2] In the Stalinist period, the Communist Parties of Estonia (ECP), Latvia (LCP) and Lithuania were subordinated to the Communist Party of the Soviet Union (CPSU)

I. Saleniece (✉)
Oral History Centre, Daugavpils University, Daugavpils, Latvia
e-mail: irena.saleniece@du.lv

I. Šķiņķe
Ministry of Foreign Affairs, Riga, Latvia

© The Author(s) 2018
K. McDermott and M. Stibbe (eds.), *Eastern Europe in 1968*,
https://doi.org/10.1007/978-3-319-77069-7_12

and all three republics underwent thorough purges of the population—arrests, mass deportations and even murders of 'class enemies'. Anyone who did not fit into the Soviet system was, according to the official terminology, a 'socially hostile element' or a 'bourgeois nationalist' and subject to persecution. Even in the ranks of the three republican communist parties, periodic cleansings were organised with the aim of making local communists reliable supporters of the central authorities in Moscow.[3] All layers of the population thus lived in fear.

The exposure of the crimes of Stalinism by Nikita Khrushchev at the Twentieth Congress of the CPSU in February 1956 and the subsequent 'Thaw' into the early 1960s gave hope for a measured liberalisation, but the power monopoly of the communist *nomenklatura* still remained the cornerstone of the system. Those who reasoned and tried to act irrespective of the line laid down by the party were liable to suppression, though not in such a severe form as under Stalinism. For instance, the notorious case of the Latvian 'national communists' in the late 1950s and early 1960s[4] shows that attempts by local communist leaders to find their own variant of building communism were used in the power struggles within both the LCP and the Central Committee of the CPSU, arousing Khrushchev's fierce anger.[5] By the mid-1960s, then, the populations of the Baltic republics had survived the process of forced sovietisation (purges, total collectivisation, rapid industrialisation), but nevertheless refrained from public manifestations of their true attitude towards the regime in order not to provoke any negative reactions. At the same time, a generation whose social awareness had been formed in the years of Khrushchev's 'de-Stalinisation' entered active public life. While the younger generation partially adopted the Soviet style of thinking and believed that progress in the framework of the existing system was possible, many of them did not approve of key aspects of Soviet reality.

We know relatively little about what was going on in Latvia, Lithuania and Estonia in 1968. How were the events in Czechoslovakia reflected in people's thoughts and feelings? Did the reformist strivings in Prague facilitate the growth of oppositional moods and the organisation of anti-Soviet resistance? Conversely, how far did local communist officials and publics support the anti-reformist stance of the Kremlin? Before the restoration of Baltic statehood in the early 1990s this topic was under-explored in the historiography.[6] The censored press of the 1960s is of little avail as the media dutifully endorsed the position of the central Soviet authorities. Therefore, in this chapter we have undertaken a careful examination of relevant archival sources and used oral history methodology to reconstruct the response of the Baltic communist leaderships and populations to the Prague Spring. We endeavour to identify commonalities and peculiarities related to the historical experience of Latvia, Lithuania and Estonia, but conclude that the reactions of elites, intellectuals and citizens were broadly comparable in all three republics: forms of immediate protest (and compliance) were interspersed with non-violent resistance and nuanced developments in the cultural field.

REACTIONS OF THE BALTIC COMMUNIST PARTIES TO THE PRAGUE SPRING

In the spring of 1968, the leaderships of the Estonian, Latvian and Lithuanian Communist Parties began, under Moscow's urgings, to pay closer attention to the events in Czechoslovakia. There was a real and growing concern that the population of the Baltic republics might prove receptive to the Dubčekites' reformist agenda. Until August 1968, purely preventive measures had been put in place, but after the Soviet-led invasion the local authorities, demonstrating unconditional support for the general line of the CPSU, strove to eradicate the slightest sign of dissent and pro-Dubček sentiment.

Hence, in Latvia the party Central Committee (CC) began to inform lower-level organisations about the situation in Czechoslovakia immediately after the Soviet Politburo ratified the document 'Regarding the Events in Czechoslovakia' on 25 March. The next day, the Latvian CC bureau met and discussed ways of preventing the winds of change from Prague adversely influencing local culture. The leadership of Soviet Estonia also reckoned with the possibility that Czechoslovak developments might create tension in the Baltics. Therefore, in April 1968 the ECP CC confirmed a plan of operative measures to pre-empt and eliminate any mass disorders in Tallinn. The plan envisaged the foundation of a special headquarters designed to forestall insurgency by means of locating its organisers, activating internal troops of the Estonian branch of the Committee for State Security (KGB), and tightening the security of strategically important sites and the state border. It was likewise deemed essential to identify and strictly monitor all 'anti-Soviet elements' and to apprehend foreigners who incited local citizens to protest. In addition, a few days after the August invasion the ECP CC adopted the resolution 'On Supplying the Population under Wartime Conditions'. It was planned to stock up on reserves, ration supplies to the population and issue food vouchers.[7]

The Baltic communist party leaders also focused on ideological issues and propaganda. From the spring of 1968, the periodical of the LCP CC, *Cīņa* ('Fight'), frequently mentioned Czechoslovakia. Readers were familiarised not only with the successes of the Czechoslovak machine-building industry and cultural life, but also with political developments in the country. Surprisingly, the information was generally positive, without any editorial criticism. Even in the early summer of 1968 a neutral tone was sustained. However, from 22 August articles on Czechoslovakia started to assume a far more negative and categorical character: 'No one will ever be allowed to extract a section from the commonwealth of socialist states'.[8] After the invasion, Latvian communist publications basically reprinted statements of the official Soviet press agency (TASS), articles from *Pravda* and news about the reaction of Moscow workers to the 'urgent aid in defence of the achievements of socialism'. Small items signed by representatives of the Latvian working class and creative intelligentsia also expressed unanimous support for the introduction of troops into Czechoslovakia. Hence, a worker at the Riga Carriage Works wrote: 'I am constantly following the course of events. And only now, frankly speaking, do I feel calm: I know that the armed forces of the Warsaw Pact are so strong that they will never permit reactionaries, instigated by imperialists, to execute their foul black deeds. The Czechoslovak working people will be defended'.[9]

The local Latvian press, for example the city newspaper *Krasnoe znamia* ('Red Banner') published in Daugavpils,[10] followed a similar pattern of information supply. In the spring, occasional news about the success of building socialism in Czechoslovakia was the norm, by the summer there was restrained official unease, but after 16 August events in Czechoslovakia hit the headlines. The floor was given to local working people. Hence, an article on a meeting at the synthetic fibre plant informed its readers that employees welcomed the outcomes of the talks at Čierna nad Tisou and Bratislava and expressed ardent support for the decisions about 'unyielding fidelity to Marxism-Leninism' and 'educating the masses in the spirit of an unrelenting fight against all anti-socialist forces'.[11] A gathering of workers at the furniture factory used the self-same terminology and pledged to fulfil the party's decisions 'not only in words but also by self-denying labour'.[12] By 23–24 August, the Daugavpils newspaper was boiling with the raw emotions of the local proletariat: 'anger and indignation at the black reactionary forces', 'deep compassion' for the Czechoslovak proletariat, and 'solid backing' for the armed fraternal assistance. Such sentiments were forthcoming from veterans of the Great Patriotic War, young people and labourers, both Russian and Latvian. All were absolutely unanimous: 'The reactionary forces must be resisted!' The participants of the meetings promised to work 'for the benefit of the might of our homeland',[13] as well as 'to produce surplus to the planned tasks, thus making our contribution to the undermining of imperialist aspirations'.[14]

On 26 November 1968, the Central Committee of the Latvian party held its ninth plenum entitled 'Regarding the Foreign Policy of the CPSU CC Politburo'. The appearance was created that throughout the republic people were united in condemning the actions of the Czechoslovak leaders. Hence, on behalf of communists and all residents of Liepāja a speech was given by Jānis Vagris, the First Secretary of the local party committee. He stated that socialism was threatened by the onset of an internal counter-revolution in Czechoslovakia and fully endorsed the correct and timely assistance provided by the Soviet military.[15]

Not quite everyone, however, was prepared to toe the party line. At mass meetings and rallies organised by the Latvian leadership a few party members spoke out openly against the Warsaw Pact invasion of Czechoslovakia. For example, in late August 1968 a doctor at Riga Hospital No. 1, Vilen Tolpezhnikov, described Soviet actions in Czechoslovakia as an occupation.[16] The secretary of the primary party organisation at the Jelgava Signaling and Communications Division of Baltic Railways, Vladimir Slushnyi, criticised the use of military force in Czechoslovakia at a meeting on 5 September 1968. Slushnyi accused the Soviet leaders of refusing to recognise the legitimacy of the Czechoslovak party's Fourteenth Congress, held clandestinely in a Prague factory on 22 August, and of isolating the country's representatives. Although all other party members at the Jelgava session voted to accept a resolution supporting the foreign policy of the CPSU, Slushnyi abstained.[17] Both he and Tolpezhnikov were expelled from the party for their 'politically harmful' positions and were thereafter debarred from work in their respective professions. These cases, of course, were never mentioned in the official media.

In Estonia, expressions of oppositional moods drew a rapid response from the party hierarchy, informed and supported by the KGB. A meeting of the Tallinn city party committee on 31 October 1968 unanimously condemned the administration of Tallinn Polytechnic for allowing its students to commit a range of anti-Soviet acts during a torchlight procession marking the foundation of the Young Communist League (*Komsomol*).[18] At a gathering of the Tartu city committee on the same day the organisers of the so-called 'Student Days' at Tartu University were called to account and a few days later, on 5 November, the ECP CC bureau criticised the Student Days as 'unhealthy, nationalistic, anti-socialist hooligan manifestations',[19] noting in addition the weak integration of Russian-speaking students. The *Komsomol* organiser at Tartu University was dismissed from his post and other persons were punished for neglecting the dangerous moods of the youth. The Department of Science and Culture of the ECP CC was given the task of instigating criminal action against the guilty activists. This was followed by exmatriculations and greater efforts to improve ideological and political educational work among the student body.[20]

Neither did Latvia escape student unrest. Of particular note were the disturbances at Christmas 1968 in Riga, during which demonstrators shouted provocative political slogans, and the attempted self-immolation of Ilya Rips on 13 April 1969 to which we will return later.[21] In June 1969, the Central Committee of the Latvian party reported that many instances of disrespectful behaviour and politically harmful moods had been observed at Stučka State University in Riga. Five months later, on 11 November, the head of the Latvian KGB Longins Avdjukevics stated: 'Current international tensions and the ever-increasing anti-communist propaganda of the imperialist countries against our nation encourage the bourgeois nationalist activities of local Latvians. They are able to entice unstable youths to undertake various anti-social activities and crimes against the state'.[22] Even schoolchildren were not immune to the allure of the 'enemy'. A meeting of the LCP CC bureau on 2 December 1969 condemned the formation of anti-Soviet groups among pupils in several Latvian schools and reprimanded teachers for permitting children to discuss events in Czechoslovakia freely, without staff interference.[23]

BALTIC PUBLIC OPINION ON THE PRAGUE SPRING

Echoes of the Prague Spring reached the Baltic republics at a time of ideological and socio-economic contradiction. On the one hand, citizens were subject to pervasive censorship and other external limitations, power-holders were widely distrusted and a sense of alienation was endemic. On the other, standards of living had been slowly improving during the 1960s, welfare provision grew and the remnants of the 'Thaw', particularly the economic reforms mooted by Soviet Prime Minister Alexei

Kosygin, gave rise to certain hopes for a liberalisation of the system. These factors mitigated the atmosphere of fear aroused by the Stalinist repressions. Nevertheless, in general the harsh realities of post-war Soviet existence engendered an aura of nihilism, double standards and divergence between word and deed.

Oral history sources make it possible to trace the parallel lives lived by the Baltic peoples in their public and private spheres. The repetition of stock communist phrases in public by no means bore witness to citizens' inner convictions. In 1961, 'The Moral Code of the Builder of Communism' was adopted at the Twenty-Second Congress of the CPSU as part of the new Party Programme. As one witness (born 1931) recalls, a vast propaganda campaign was launched: 'All communists cited the Moral Code; there was a fashionable magazine *Ogonek* [Spark] ... Everyone was crazy about communism then, it was so trendy'. But solemn declarations and promises did not translate into concrete progress in society and people's everyday lives: 'Khrushchev strongly condemned Stalin. But he didn't last long, that Khrushchev, so there was no great breakthrough. From those times I remember dark grey bread in the shops for which I queued up in a terribly long line ... You know, we heard that things had become [better], but was that true?'[24] The trumpeting of communism seemed absurd in the context of 'real' life. A Latvian teacher (born 1921) remembered: 'I was looking at the children and telling them about life under communism ... [how] by 1980 we will have reached communism ... A girl was squinting at me and slightly smirking ... She said nothing, but when the awakening began [in the 1990s], we met and she told me: "I realised then that you were lying. When you told us about communism, I knew you were lying to us"'.[25]

The chasm between the hardships of everyday life and the visions of a better world aroused disillusionment among many young people, a sense of alienation that often underlay their opposition. The modest living standards in the USSR together with the government's disregard for citizens' rights clashed with the 'bright socialist future' glorified everywhere. Neither the human nor national rights of the population were observed. Estonians, Latvians and Lithuanians had 'lost' their nation. Values and views belonging to the inter-war years had to be renounced and the whole history of independent statehood had to be presented only through negative comparisons as 'reactionary', 'backward' and 'fascist'. In order to fit into the unaccustomed socio-political order after World War II, Latvians born in the 1920s and 1930s had to replace their 'love for the state of Latvia' cultivated at the time of Prime Minister Kārlis Ulmanis[26] by amorphous 'love for the socialist Motherland and for the socialist countries'. Unwritten rules prevented Baltic citizens from taking certain jobs and they were discriminated against in the distribution of apartments.

It was in these circumstances that the population of the Baltic republics learned about events in Czechoslovakia. Balts culled information from various sources: mainly the Soviet mass media, but also the 'Voice of America' and other Western radio stations. In addition, Estonians had access to Finnish television programmes. According to one interviewee: 'My father was very fond of politics and was constantly listening to "Radio Free Europe". There was a lot of interference [because of the 'jamming'], and it was hard to hear... In 1968, during the Prague Spring when Dubček became First Secretary, then I was listening'. The narrator (born in 1948) was a history student and therefore aware of contemporary developments and they stuck well in his memory:

> Soviet, German and Polish forces attacked Dubček, his revolution ... [he] wanted socialism - humane socialism ... so that it was not so rigid, so that there was more democracy and people could elect [whom they liked]. What kind of elections did we have [in the USSR] - all the time 99.99%, no matter if you voted or not. [But the Czechoslovaks] wanted the people to rule the country, not just the party *nomenklatura* and communists. Yes, tanks were brought in and that's it, they were destroyed, and then the pro-Moscow Husák ... became First Secretary.[27]

Fragmentary information about the reformist strivings of the Czechoslovak communists seeped into the Baltic republics and this, enhanced by the existing social malaise, aroused positive feelings for the initiators of the Prague Spring. Sympathy for the Czechoslovak 'rebels' grew, especially after the Warsaw Pact invasion on 20–21 August 1968. According to the Estonian historian, Magnus Ilmjärv, 'Western' lifestyles in Estonia, Latvia and Lithuania made these republics more likely to be infected by the ideals of the Prague Spring,[28] but there is no trustworthy official information on the way people in the Baltics reacted to events in Czechoslovakia. Minutes of party meetings, KGB officer reports and the censored mass media yield contradictory results. Open discussion and exchange of opinion could not take place at that time. Therefore, the most fruitful method of addressing the contentious issue of 'public opinion' is, we believe, post-factum oral interviewing and sociological surveys.[29] Of course, this methodology runs the risk of memory loss, the tendency to modify one's views in light of the contemporary *zeitgeist* and the 'loaded' nature of the questions asked.[30] As Ilmjärv notes, in twenty-first-century Estonia it is customary to write about 'student opposition to the communist regime' under the impact of the Prague Spring.[31] However, given that at the end of the 1960s the overwhelming majority of Baltic students were *Komsomol* members it would appear more accurate to conclude that in Estonia the Prague Spring did indeed activate a measure of *Komsomol* non-conformity, but in the belief that the Soviet system could be reformed from within.

Protest: From Anonymous Leaflets to Self-immolation

As we have seen, regardless of the efforts of party administrative bodies to ration and sift the flow of information, news of the events in Czechoslovakia filtered into Soviet society eliciting reactions both from individuals and social groups. Though there were no major disturbances in the Baltic republics, KGB officials were on high alert throughout the second half of 1968 and beginning of 1969 and it is on the basis of their top-secret reports that we can begin to assess the extent of the impact of the Prague Spring on the Baltic republics. According to data provided by the Lithuanian KGB, 197 'anti-Soviet and nationalist manifestations' were registered in 1968 and in the years 1968–70 103 persons were sentenced for anti-Soviet activities and 375 preventive interviews were carried out.[32] The historian Kristina Burinskaitė agrees that there was no serious insurgency in Lithuania, the protests being of a local character and concentrated in certain towns (Kaunas, Šiauliai), where anti-Soviet inscriptions, anonymous leaflets and letters appeared periodically, accompanied by the tearing down of Soviet flags. The most active participants in the protests were young people, as well as so-called 'nationalist elements'—members of the intelligentsia, former deportees and political convicts.[33]

In Estonia, the most conspicuous disorders were the above-mentioned 'Student Days' in Tartu on 19–20 October 1968 and the torchlight procession in Tallinn dedicated to the fiftieth anniversary of the *Komsomol*. These events were officially treated as anti-Soviet acts in protest against the Kremlin's policies in both Czechoslovakia and Estonia. In addition, there are vague accounts of 'ideological discussions' among the intelligentsia and, as in Lithuania, anti-Soviet inscriptions were daubed on buildings from time to time, leaflets were circulated and protest petitions prepared.[34]

In Latvia, support for the ideas of the Prague Spring and opposition to Soviet policies were expressed in more direct and dramatic forms. The most noteworthy is that of Ilya Rips, a student at the State University, who on 13 April 1969, possibly in conscious imitation of the Czech student Jan Palach who had set fire to himself in Prague on 16 January, tried to commit suicide in similar fashion near the Freedom Monument in Riga.[35] Rips rejected the existing order and Moscow's aggressive foreign and domestic policies. In his opinion, it was unacceptable that people kept silent. He held a poster with the words: 'I am protesting against the occupation of Czechoslovakia'. After the flames had been extinguished, Rips was rushed to the chambers of the KGB. News of his self-immolation reached the Western media and on 13 June 1969 the KGB decided to bring a criminal case against him. Following an investigation, Rips was charged and the court sentenced him to forced psychiatric treatment. Neither was he allowed to finish his studies at the university.[36] A second self-immolation occurred on 9 May 1969, again in Riga. This time P. N. Mizherov died, but the details of the affair are still unknown.[37] The greatest response—youth and worker demonstrations and many arrests—was aroused by the self-immolation of the university student Romas Kalanta in Kaunas on 14 May 1972, but these events were not directly connected to the Prague Spring.[38]

The main Latvian oppositionist to protest against the occupation of Czechoslovakia was Ivan Yahimovich, who had become a dissident even before the Prague Spring.[39] By the late 1960s, Yahimovich had convinced himself that Soviet policies were in reality far removed from socialist ideals. He defended human rights in the USSR and in October 1968 composed a statement condemning the occupation of Czechoslovakia: '"Anyone can make mistakes, but only an idiot persists in his error" (Cicero). Due to his illegal and barbaric actions against the freedom-loving people of Czechoslovakia, Brezhnev and his government are directly responsible for the shame inflicted upon our people'.[40] Sympathetic Soviet dissidents illegally copied and distributed Yahimovich's declaration and it is clear that he spoke not only for himself, but for other defenders of human rights in the USSR when he demanded:

> We repeat: Come to your senses!
> We repeat: Hands off the ČSSR! [Czechoslovakia]
> We repeat: Freedom for political prisoners!
> We repeat: Yes to Leninism, no to Stalinism![41]

In early 1969, Yahimovich, together with the well-known Moscow dissident Piotr Grigorenko, wrote an appeal in support of the Czechoslovak Socialist Republic on which the 'Voice of America' reported (in Latvian) on 7 March 1969. Yahimovich followed this with his address 'To the Citizens of the Soviet Union', published in the 28 February 1969 issue of the illegal publication *Chronicle of Current Events*:

> The greatness of a nation is not dependent on the strength of its military, which has attacked a small freedom-loving nation, but on its spiritual might. Are we really going to stand back and watch in silence as our brothers perish?... We appeal to all Soviet citizens to be careful and cautious and to use all legal means available to facilitate the removal of Soviet military forces from Czechoslovakia and to cease the Soviet Union's interference in Czechoslovakia's internal affairs! That is the only way to renew the friendship between our countries.[42]

Shortly before his arrest on 24 March, Yahimovich's *samizdat* essay 'In Place of the Final Word' was illegally disseminated by Soviet dissidents. In it, he turned to Dubček personally: 'Be strong! The sun will rise!'[43]

Protest in Latvia, however, was not limited to a handful of brave individuals. At the end of 1968 and beginning of 1969 graffiti decrying the Warsaw Pact invasion of Czechoslovakia appeared in Riga and the town of Sigulda, but the republican security forces could not find the perpetrator(s). Finally, on 16 June 1969 the KGB decided to bring a criminal case against Aldis Cilinskis, a worker at a print shop in Riga. Between August 1968 and May 1969, he had painted more than nineteen inscriptions on various buildings, fences, bridges and road surfaces critical of the occupation of Czechoslovakia and expressing support for Dubček's policies. More than this, Cilinskis's inscriptions also attacked the occupation of Latvia and bid the aggressors to leave both Czechoslovakia and Latvia. He put blood red paint on the hands and feet of the monument to Soviet soldiers and also splashed red paint on slogans glorifying the USSR. Cilinskis attested his loyalty to his country in a written public invitation to commemorate 18 November, the day the independent

Republic of Latvia was proclaimed in 1918. On 12 August 1969, the Latvian KGB decided to send Cilinskis's case to court with the intention of sentencing the young man to forced psychiatric treatment.[44] The Latvian government also cleansed public institutions of those people sceptical of the military action against Czechoslovakia. Thus, for example, several employees of the Ministry of Culture were fired in 1969, among them Lidija Lasmane (Doroņina), who had objected to the occupation of Czechoslovakia in a conversation at work.[45] In sum, we can say that overt mass protests against the invasion did not take place in any of the Baltic republics, but both KGB documents and oral testimonies indicate that local people quietly dissented, albeit not in great numbers.

Youth Resistance and the Cultural Sphere

In response to the events in Czechoslovakia, several resistance groups were established in Latvia's technical and secondary schools. The youths involved in these clandestine networks condemned the domination of the CPSU and demanded freedom of speech and the preservation of Latvian folk traditions. Laimonis Markāns and Valērijs Akks, both members of a youth resistance group, prepared leaflets with the slogans: 'Down with Communist Propaganda!', 'Freedom of Speech and of the Press!' and 'Don't Interfere in the Affairs of Other Countries!' The leaflets were located outside the Jēkabpils Economics Technical College on the night of 7 November 1969, and Markāns and Akks were convicted on 4 February 1970 of anti-Soviet agitation and propaganda.[46] Shortly after the invasion of Czechoslovakia, Gunārs Ostrovskis established another youth resistance group. Members collected arms and listened to foreign radio broadcasts supporting the Czechoslovak people. Similar to the Markāns and Akks declaration, an appeal from Ostrovskis's cabal demanded: 'Down with Communist Unruliness in Latvia. Freedom of Speech and of the Press. Independence for the Baltic States. Don't Interfere in Events in Czechoslovakia'.[47] Students also established embryonic groups at Riga's Secondary School No. 24 and in Līvāni Secondary School No. 1. Motivated by events in Czechoslovakia, members listened to Western radio news programmes and distributed anti-Soviet leaflets attacking the 'Russification' of the Latvian republic.[48]

Another understated, but widespread, expression of non-violent dissent was pretending that one did not understand Russian. Other such forms included the 'inadvertent' use of the national colours in various quotidian circumstances (flower beds, cake decorations); the displaying of national flags in public places; graffiti calling for the departure of the Russians; and cheering opposition sports teams when they were playing Soviet opponents.[49] Baltic people also demonstrated their dislike of their position in the USSR by adorning the graves of important pre-Soviet historical figures. For instance, in November 1967 approximately 70,000 people descended on Riga's main cemetery to lay wreaths at the tombs of statesmen from the time of Latvia's independence. The communist authorities and local KGB did everything possible to prevent something similar from happening on 18 November 1968, the fiftieth anniversary of the proclamation of the Republic of Latvia. However, on 24 November KGB agents again encountered people lighting candles on the graves of the first President of Latvia, Jānis Čakste. The candles were red, white and red and arranged in the order of the colours of the Latvian flag. As a result, at least thirteen youths were subjected to 're-education' and two were expelled from Riga's Polytechnic Institute.[50] Nevertheless, throughout the Soviet era citizens took the risk and placed flowers and lighted candles on Čakste's grave. Hence, we can see that non-violent resistance existed before the Prague Spring, but after 1968 the regime tended to conflate all expressions of protest with the Czechoslovak events. Party officials likewise associated the works of Latvian playwrights and film-makers with the 'faulty imperialist-imposed ideology of the Czechs' regardless of the fact that their productions made no direct reference to the Prague Spring.[51]

Indeed, a case study of Latvian cultural life in the late 1960s shows how manifestations of creative intellectual freedom frightened the communist leadership. Beginning in the mid-1960s, theatre performance and cinematography became dominated by a new generation of artists who contrasted markedly with their older Stalin-era acolytes. Subtexts in poetry hinted at Latvia's enslavement and Russia's centuries-long imperialistic aspirations in the Baltic region. In an attempt to counter this dangerous trend, the LCP CC decided at its plenum on 26 March 1968 to halt the performance of Laimonis Purs's play *Redzēt jūru* ('To See the Sea') and prohibit various other plays and films. The First Secretary of the Latvian party, Augusts Voss, said at the meeting:

> I consider it good and correct that the discussion about the production of the play 'To See the Sea' turned into a wider debate about the range of ideological sabotage found in the republic. The direction is known ... Yahimovich revealed this in his letter that was published abroad ... This line of thinking is [also] revealed in Priede's play *Smaržo sēnes* ('The Smell of Mushrooms'),

the play 'To See the Sea' and in the films *Tēvs* ('Father') and *Četri balti krekli* ('Four White Shirts'). These are all links in the same chain... [which] comes from the imperialist world and is the fruit of imperialist propaganda.[52]

Jānis Kalnbērziņš, Chair of the Presidium of the Latvian Supreme Soviet, likewise stated:

> It's characteristic that this play ['To See the Sea'] is anti-Soviet and directed against the friendship of nations and against the Russian people. It is no coincidence. Just as in previous years, it is connected to what is happening beyond the borders of the USSR [which] influence our most unstable authors and playwrights ... The play has been performed nine or ten times and performances will continue. Each occasion ends in a demonstration in the theatre. All we need is for a demonstration to spill out onto the streets.[53]

In his speech Nikolajs Beluha, the second secretary of the LCP, emphasised that 'this play ['To See the Sea'] is not only anti-Soviet. It is also glaringly nationalistic and does great harm to the friendship of nations'.[54] Party secretary Jurijs Rubenis said: 'I think we all understand quite well that these occurrences are not accidental. They are to a certain extent related to the events in Poland and Czechoslovakia. They are also the result of echoes from the "Voice of America"'.[55] Pēteris Strautmanis, vice-chairman of the Latvian Council of Ministers, critically evaluated the film 'Four White Shirts': '[the idea of the film is] to show that the comrades sitting up there in control are all a bunch of idiots. We are not against criticising fools, if there are fools in key organisations ... But one cannot criticise the entire foundation of the Soviet state. Then it becomes simply terrible'.[56] Clearly, a scapegoat had to be found and the unlucky victim was Vladimirs Kaupužs, the Minister of Culture, who was reprimanded for countenancing the production of the 'ideologically harmful' play 'To See the Sea' at the Academic Drama Theatre. The CC LCP also demanded tighter supervision of the theatre by the Ministry of Culture. As a result of this decision, the above-mentioned plays and films were cancelled or banned.[57]

Other Latvian literary figures reacted to the Prague Spring. One of the most active was Alberts Bels, who at a writers' meeting on 9 December 1968, attended by party members, went so far as to propose the abolition of censorship. He said: 'I believe censorship is a very harmful institution. It is like serfdom for writers ... I think that the state will not fall apart if censorship were to be abolished in the Latvian Republic forty years before it is abolished in Russia, just as serfdom was abolished in Latvia forty years before ... Russia'.[58] Four months after Bels's 'politically harmful' speech, the bureau of the LCP CC deemed him ideologically immature and therefore suspended his studies in the scriptwriters' advanced course in Moscow sponsored by the Soviet Council of Ministers Cinematography Committee.[59]

The Latvian party often detected echoes of the events in Czechoslovakia in literary works.[60] Thus Roberts Ķīsis, director of the CC Party Commission, considered the 1969 collection of poetry *Gadu gredzeni* ('Annual Rings') by Vizma Belševica to be based on the Prague Spring, even though her poems placed the tragic situation of the Latvians in the distant past. Consequently, Belševica was prohibited from publishing her works for several years. In the debate at the general meeting of the CC LCP on 11 June 1969, Ķīsis opined:

> Belševica's poems are an example of Aesopean language, in which words are chosen in order to lead the people from clear thinking into the fog of guessing ... This sorcery with the Livonian motif began in 1968, as the poet herself has admitted. We know that the battle between the socialist and bourgeois ideologies, between proletarian internationalism and bourgeois nationalism, intensified that same year. The events in Czechoslovakia aggravated this battle; counter-revolutionary laments filled the air and historical analogies were sought out to portray the introduction of armed forces into Czechoslovakia as a foreign invasion and a loss of Czech and Slovak freedom. And our poet chooses precisely this time to take up the theme of the Livonian Chronicle. With past and future verbs she wrote her damnation of the foreigners.[61]

Thus, the Latvian, as well as the Estonian and Lithuanian Communist Parties, turned against those writers, poets and other creative intellectuals broadly admired by the people. They were tarnished as 'anti-Soviet elements' and 'bourgeois nationalists'. But the existing powers were only able to offer propagandistic ideology and the mass media against the day-to-day vernacular of citizens.

Conclusion

The impact of the Prague Spring on the Baltic republics was twofold. First, the administrative and ideological functionaries of the Estonian, Latvian and Lithuanian communist parties, as well as the state security bodies, treated the events in Czechoslovakia as an alarm signal and hence carried out extremely effective preventive measures in order to stop 'disorder' seeping into the region. Though the mass social base of resistance had been eradicated under Stalinism, the 'Thaw' fostered a new generation who had not experienced widescale repression and cleansings and who tended to favour reform of the existing system from within. Hence, there were no mass actions in the Baltic republics in support of the Czechoslovaks. This relative quiescence was also certainly due to the efficiency of the political and security forces and to limited access to accurate and timely information. Second, in these circumstances whenever the populations of Estonia, Latvia and Lithuania *did* react to the events of the Prague Spring it was generally by way of isolated protest in the spirit of non-violent dissent. Individuals from different sections of the population—students, school youth, intellectuals, even some party members—were inspired by the Czech example and expressed dissatisfaction with Soviet actions, not only in Czechoslovakia but also in the Baltic republics. The main content of non-violent resistance was the call for freedom, both personal and national. Often this demand was grounded in the historical experience of Estonia, Latvia and Lithuania, including disillusionment with the contemporary policy of Russification.

In the public space of the Baltic republics divergence between 'us' (communists, working people) and 'them' (imperialists and their henchmen) was drawn along ideological lines. Communist officials feared that the awakening of 'bourgeois nationalism' could lure the Baltic peoples into anti-social activity and crimes against the Soviet state. To counteract this appeal they expounded 'proletarian internationalism' and extolled 'heroic labour' in the name of the victory of communism. But it proved impossible to manipulate the notion of 'Slavic kinship', not only because the Slavic population at that time was in a minority, but also because of the Balts' deep resentment of the forced Russification that followed the incorporation of the former independent states into the USSR.

The suppression of the Prague Spring left an ambivalent legacy in the Baltic republics and the Soviet Union as a whole. On the one hand, it demonstrated that in the near future there was little hope of meaningful liberalisation. The Kremlin had made it abundantly clear that in case of a threat to its interests, it would not hesitate to use force. Hence, it became apparent that the only reliable route in the struggle for reform was non-violent resistance to the regime. As such, there is a dominant interpretation in contemporary Baltic historiography that the crushing of the Czechoslovak innovations acted as a major impulse for the emergence of the dissident movement both in the USSR and the Baltics.[62]

On the other hand, events in Czechoslovakia gave the Baltic states, at least in the longer term, a measure of hope. On 23 August 1979, more than forty oppositionists signed the Baltic Charter,[63] named thus in honour of Charter 77, the human rights initiative launched by Václav Havel and other prominent 'dissidents' in Prague on 1 January 1977. The Baltic Charter was an appeal to the USSR, West Germany, East Germany, the signatories of the Atlantic Charter and the UN Secretary-General to annul the Molotov-Ribbentrop Pact of 23 August 1939 and do away with its consequences. Considering themselves representatives of occupied nations, the authors also included a key political demand: the right for the Baltic peoples to decide their own fate and statehood. In this way, the Czechoslovak Charter 77, itself an offspring of the Prague Spring, inspired the Baltic Charter's insistence on the renewal of Estonian, Latvian and Lithuanian independence.

NOTES

1. A. Plakans, 'Celebrating Origins: Reflection of Latvia's Ninetieth Birthday', in D.J. Smith et al. (eds), *From Recognition to Restoration: Latvia's History as a Nation-State* (Amsterdam, 2010), pp. 14–15.
2. A. Plakans, *A Concise History of the Baltic States* (New York, 2011), pp. 299–307, 336–86.
3. For details, see A. Purs, 'Soviet in Form, Local in Content: Elite Repression and Mass Terror in the Baltic States, 1940–1953', in K. McDermott and M. Stibbe (eds), *Stalinist Terror in Eastern Europe: Elite Purges and Mass Repression* (Manchester, 2010), pp. 19–38. Also A. Purs, *Baltic Facades: Estonia, Latvia and Lithuania since 1945* (London, 2012), p. 69.
4. W.D. Prigge, 'Power, Popular Opinion, and the Latvian National Communists', *Journal of Baltic Studies*, vol. 45, no. 3 (2014), pp. 305–19; M. Loader, 'The Death of "Socialism with a Latvian Face": The Purge of the Latvian National Communists, July 1959–1962', *Journal of Baltic Studies*, vol. 48, no. 2 (2017), pp. 161–81.
5. G. Swain; '"Come on Latvians, Join the Party—We'll Forgive You Everything". Ideological Struggle during the National Communism Affair, Summer 1959', in D.J. Smith (ed.), *Latvia: A Work in Progress? 100 Years of State- and Nation-Building* (Stuttgart, 2017), pp. 107–21.
6. The first scholarly publications on reactions to the Prague Spring in the Soviet Baltics, and other republics of the USSR, appeared in the 2000s: A.O. Chubarian et al. (eds), *'Prazhskaia vesna' 1968 goda i sovetskie*

respubliki: reaktsiia vlasti i obshchestva. Sbornik nauchnykh statei (Moscow, 2009); N.G. Tomilina et al. (eds), '*Prazhskaia vesna*' *i mezhdunarodnyi krizis 1968 goda. Dokumenty* (Moscow, 2010); N.G. Tomilina et al. (eds), '*Prazhskaia vesna*' *i mezhdunarodnyi krizis 1968 goda. Statii, issledovaniia, vospominaniia* (Moscow, 2010); G. Murashko et al. (eds), *Debaty: 1968 god: 'Prazhskaia vesna': Istoricheskaia retrospektiva. Sbornik statei* (Moscow, 2010). A virtual exhibition 'The Aftermath of the Prague Spring and Charter 77 in Latvia/the Baltics' (authors: Ritvars Jansons and Iveta Šķiņķe) was prepared by the Latvian State Archives (http://www.lvarhivs.gov.lv/Praga68/index.php?id=1003) on the occasion of the 40th anniversary of the Czechoslovak events.

7. Estonian National Archive (ERA), (F) 1-5-108, pp. 2–7; 1-5-109, pp. 1–5, cited in M. Ilmjärv, 'Chekhoslovatskii krizis 1968 goda i estonskoe obshchestvo', in Chubarian et al. (eds), '*Prazhskaia vesna*' *1968 goda*, pp. 6–23.
8. *Cīņa*, 23 August 1968.
9. L. Līnis, 'Citādi nedrīkst!', *Cīņa*, 22 August 1968.
10. Daugavpils is the second largest city in Latvia. After World War II, the majority of its population was Russian-speaking. In Soviet times, the local newspaper was published only in Russian.
11. B. Egorkin, 'Za edinstvo stran sotsializma', *Krasnoe znamia*, 16 August 1968.
12. I. Galitskaia, 'Vernost' marksizmu-leninizmu', *Krasnoe znamia*, 17 August 1968.
13. M. Porfiriev, 'My s vami, chekhoslovatskie druzia', *Krasnoe znamia*, 23 August 1968.
14. V. Shmakov, 'Proiski imperialistov budut sorvany', *Krasnoe znamia*, 24 August 1968.
15. The State Archives of Latvia (LNA LVA), PA-101-32-6, p. 101.
16. LNA LVA, PA-109-43-813, p. 37.
17. LNA LVA, PA-101-33-46, pp. 228–9.
18. ERA, (F) 1-5-110, pp. 19–20. *Komsomol* Day was celebrated in the USSR on 29 October.
19. ERA, (F) 1-5-110, pp. 15–29.
20. ERA, (F) 1-5-110, pp. 24–8.
21. LNA LVA, PA-101-33-5134, p. 93.
22. LNA LVA, PA-101-33-57, p. 64.
23. LNA LVA, PA-101-33-30, pp. 7–8.
24. Renāte Pudāne's life-story, interview undertaken by Zane Stapķeviča, in Vabole parish of Daugavpils district, 4 July 2003, 106 minutes, in Latvian, DU MV: no. 110.

25. Olga Spūle's life-story, interview undertaken by Gints Kokins, in Eglaine parish of Daugavpils district, 10 April 2003, 120 minutes, in Latvian, DU MV: no. 28.
26. 'Likums par tautas izglītību' (The Law of People's Education), 1934.
27. Zbignev Androloic's life-story, interview undertaken by Līva Irbe and Ludmila Rožukalne, in Medininkai (Lithuania), 3 August 2016, 91 minute, in Russian, DU MV: 1088.
28. Ilmjärv, 'Chekhoslovatskii krizis 1968 goda', p. 6.
29. None of the respondents (twenty seven people born in the 1930s and 1940s) in a joint Lithuanian-Latvian oral history expedition to Rokiškis (Lithuania) and Subate (Latvia) in the summer of 2017 mentioned the Prague Spring spontaneously. After suggestive questions, narrators would touch on the events of 1968, but the information is insufficient to judge with certainty the direct impact of the Czechoslovak events on local popular opinion. More generally, the collection of sources in the Oral History Centre at Daugavpils University (over 1100 audio recordings; more than 200 transcriptions studied) reveals only one case (DU MV 1088) of a respondent competently and extensively answering the question on the Prague Spring, explaining how people received information about the events.
30. According to the data of a survey carried out in 1993, a quarter of Estonians and more than a half of the Russian-speaking population of Estonia believed the Soviet leaders were right to suppress the Prague Spring. That is, a considerable number of Estonians thought that the Kremlin acted correctly in 1968. However, it would seem that the survey reflects notions formed post-factum. See Ilmjärv, 'Chekhoslovatskii krizis 1968 goda', p. 14.
31. Ilmjärv, 'Chekhoslovatskii krizis 1968 goda', p. 6
32. K. Burinskaitė, 'Otzvuki "Prazhskoi vesny" v Litve v 1968 godu', in Chubarian et al. (eds), *Prazhskaia vesna' 1968 goda*, p. 46.
33. Burinskaitė, 'Otzvuki "Prazhskoi vesny"', p. 44.
34. Ilmjärv, 'Chekhoslovatskii krizis 1968 goda', pp. 8–11.
35. Ilya (Eliyahu) Rips was considered a genius and accepted into the State University of Latvia at the age of fifteen without having to first pass entrance examinations. He studied mathematics but also strove to understand social reality. He wrote in his diary, confiscated in 1969: 'Power belongs to a relatively small group of mid- and higher-level superiors. They select the leading institutions' (LNA LVA, 1986-1-45165-2, p. 175).
36. Rips currently works at the Holon Academic Institute of Technology in Israel. For information, see the documentary film 'Burning', directed by J. Putniņš in 2016, https://www.filmas.lv/movie/3774/.

37. H. Strods, 'Ekho "Prazhskoi vesny" v Latvii', in Chubarian et al. (eds), *'Prazhskaia vesna' 1968 goda*, p. 30.
38. Lithuanian Special Archive (LSA), K-1-3-793, pp. 150–3, quoted from the virtual exhibition 'The Aftermath of the Prague Spring and Charter 77 in Latvia/the Baltics'.
39. Ivan Yahimovich (1931–2014). After graduating from the State University of Latvia, he worked as a history teacher and later as director of a collective farm. In 1968 he was expelled from the CPSU and fired from his job. Yahimovich was arrested on 24 March 1969 and was forced to undergo psychiatric treatment. In the late 1980s, he became involved in the mass movement to restore Latvia's independence. He was a board member of the Popular Front (*Tautas fronte*) and a candidate in the Latvian Supreme Council (parliament) elections in 1990.
40. LNA LVA, 1986-2-10997-1, p. 6a.
41. 'Memorial' archive on USSR dissidents, 155.f., Ivan Yahimovich's case, quoted from the virtual exhibition 'The Aftermath of the Prague Spring and Charter 77 in Latvia/the Baltics'.
42. Ibid.
43. Ibid.
44. Cilinskis was released from treatment only on 28 February 1973. He was rehabilitated by the Supreme Court of the Republic of Latvia in 1992 (LNA LVA 1986-1-45172).
45. LNA LVA, PA-798-1-40, p. 112. Lidija Lasmane (Doroņina) was the only Latvian woman sentenced three times for anti-Soviet activities.
46. LNA LVA, 1986-2-45170-1, p. 85.
47. LNA LVA, 1986-1-45175-2, p. 197.
48. LNA LVA, PA-106-39-7, p. 135; LNA LVA, PA-101-33-30, pp. 7–8.
49. Plakans, *A Concise History of the Baltic States*, p. 379.
50. LNA LVA, PA-106-39-9, p. 20.
51. LNA LVA, PA-101-33-4, p. 43.
52. LNA LVA, PA-101-32-43, p. 235.
53. LNA LVA, PA-101-32-43, pp. 229–30.
54. LNA LVA, PA-101-32-43, p. 229.
55. LNA LVA, PA-101-32-43, p. 233.
56. LNA LVA, PA-101-32-43, p. 225.
57. LNA LVA, PA-101-32-43, pp. 191–2.
58. LNA LVA, PA-101-33-47, pp. 49–52.
59. LNA LVA, PA-101-33-35, pp. 14–15.
60. For example, Imants Auziņš's poem *Pļi!* ('Fire!') *1905* and Imants Ziedonis's works. See LNA LVA, PA-101-33-67, pp. 104–6.
61. LNA LVA, PA-101-33-4, pp. 42–3.

62. It is sometimes argued in Lithuanian historiography, however, that dissident activity started before the Prague Spring. In particular, religious opposition developed separately and its activists do not see a link between the resistance of the Catholic Church and the Czechoslovak events. See Burinskaitė, 'Otzvuki "Prazhskoi vesny"', p. 43.
63. The original Baltic Charter was written in Russian. It was translated into Latvian (LNA LVA, 1986-1-45322, p. 13), Lithuanian (LSA, K-1-58-47753/3-10, p. 664) and Estonian (ERA, 130 SM-1-8838-2, pp. 113–14).

'Down with Revisionism and Irredentism': Soviet Moldavia and the Prague Spring, 1968–72

Igor Caşu

The archives of the former Communist Party of Moldavia (CPM) have been open for almost thirty years, but it is only in the last decade or so that local historians have turned their attention to Soviet Moldavia in its internal (USSR) and external (Soviet bloc and Cold War) contexts. Two volumes of documents have been published that deal extensively with the late 1960s, but both focus mainly on Soviet–Romanian relations and the so-called 'Bessarabian question'.[1] As far as the Prague Spring is concerned, if one were to use the relevant documents in these volumes and come to a conclusion, it would be the following: the main impact of the Czechoslovak events on Soviet Moldavia was the ethno-national aspect fuelled by Romania's critique of the Soviet-led invasion of Czechoslovakia. In this chapter, I argue that this interpretation is valid only to a certain extent. The other, neglected, influence the Prague Spring had on the Moldavian Soviet Socialist Republic (MSSR) is that it determined the launch of a series of inter-related propaganda campaigns in 1968 on two

---

I. Caşu (✉)
Center for Study of Totalitarian Regimes & Cold War, Faculty of History and Philosophy, State University of Moldova, Chişinău, Moldova

crucial broader topics: the strengthening of Soviet patriotism and the inculcation of 'socialist internationalism'. The latter was intimately intertwined with the need to combat the perceived revival of Romanian revisionism and irredentism, though it went beyond this. More precisely, the campaigns aimed to address both general and specific issues related to the challenges the Prague Spring raised for communist ideology as a whole, and the Soviet version of socialism in particular: one-party rule, state censorship and, ultimately, the very future of communism and its supposed superiority over the Western model of liberal democracy and capitalism.

The MSSR: A Contested Soviet–Romanian Borderland

The history of the present day Republic of Moldova, the heir of the MSSR, has been closely interlinked with Romanian history, language and culture since the Middle Ages and with Russian/Soviet history in the last two centuries. In terms of geography and statehood, Soviet Moldavia was a Moscow construct created from two distinct historical regions: Bessarabia and Transnistria, the latter, as a small strip of interwar Soviet Ukraine, never having been a part of historical Moldavia. In the aftermath of the Russo-Ottoman War of 1812, just a few weeks before Napoleon's invasion, the Tsarist Empire annexed the eastern part of the Principality of Moldavia, which had existed since the late fourteenth century, and gave it the name Bessarabia. In 1856, following Russia's defeat in the Crimean War, the southern part of Bessarabia was returned to the Principality of Moldavia by the European powers and three years later in 1859 this area united with Wallachia to create the Kingdom of Romania. Since then, though a multi-ethnic and multi-lingual region, the language of inter-ethnic communication in southern Bessarabia has been Romanian, a reality that would endure even after the area's re-annexation by Russia after another Russo-Turkish War in 1877–78. The social status of the Romanian language was reinforced throughout Bessarabia in the inter-war period when the province united with Romania based on the Wilsonian principle of 'national self-determination'. However, the vote of the local parliament to join Romania in March 1918 was not recognised by Soviet Russia. Indeed, Moscow never foreswore its territorial pretensions over Bessarabia and in 1940, as a direct consequence of the Nazi-Soviet Pact, Bessarabia (and Northern Bukovina) was occupied by the Red Army. The USSR lost control of the area after the Nazi invasion in June 1941, which was supported by Romania, and it was only in 1944–45 that the Soviets reoccupied Bessarabia and re-established the MSSR. The republic was run for much of the post-war period by profoundly Russified officials of Moldavian-Romanian ethnicity from Transnistria, Bessarabian Romanians having to wait to the early 1960s to be promoted to upper-level posts in the government. Only in the late 1980s were the real power positions in the KGB, Interior Ministry and Central Committee open to Bessarabian elites.

The Prague Spring, Ceauşescu and the Challenge to Moscow's Hegemony in Eastern Europe

At the time of the Prague Spring in 1968, the First Secretary of the CPM was Ivan Bodiul, a Russian-speaking Moldavian born in the Nikolaev region of Ukraine. He had been an acquaintance of the Soviet leader, Leonid Brezhnev, since the early 1950s when the latter headed the Moldavian party. Thus, Brezhnev himself was aware from direct experience of the Romanian–Soviet competition over Bessarabia and trusted Bodiul to keep the south-western Soviet borderland quiet in the troublesome context of the Prague Spring and Romania's challenge to Moscow's hegemony over the Soviet bloc. It is fair to say that Bodiul was a neo-Stalinist. Promoted to his position in 1961, he was to become one of the longest serving first secretaries in the national republics. Partly because of his loyalty and connections to Brezhnev, but also because of the adroit way he managed to deal with the 1968 crisis in Soviet Moldavia—unlike Petro Shelest in Ukraine—he remained in office till 1980, when he was transferred to Moscow to become Vice-Chairman of the USSR Council of Ministers.

The Prague Spring impacted on Soviet Moldavia primarily through the attitude adopted by neighbouring Romania to the Soviet-led invasion of Czechoslovakia in August 1968.[2] The communist leader of Romania, Nicolae Ceauşescu, became a 'hero' in his country, and to a certain degree in Soviet Moldavia, not because he endorsed the democratic reforms of Alexander Dubček and his team or supported the Czech and Slovak people in their efforts to create 'socialism with a human face'. Rather, it was because of his speech, improvised at the last minute in front of 100,000 people gathered at the Central Committee building in Bucharest on 21 August 1968, in which Ceauşescu dared to criticise the Soviets for meddling in the internal affairs of other communist states. In short, his relative popularity rested on his stance on the highly sensitive issue of national sovereignty.[3] Many observers in the West at the time, and later, were not able to decipher what Ceaușescu actually stood for. In the context of East–West competition, what was important for many Americans and, to a lesser extent, West Europeans was that Ceaușescu had seemingly attacked Moscow, and that in itself was worth admiring and applauding. In reality, Romania's position on the Soviet invasion of Czechoslovakia was not about defending the values of the Prague Spring: reform communism, the end of censorship, free speech and decreasing the prerogatives of the secret police. As would become clear in the next few years, Ceaușescu used his anti-Soviet posture to consolidate personalised power in Romania, emerging as a dictator of almost neo-Stalinist pedigree. According to many experts, he did not even hesitate to use right-wing ideas and personalities, like the wartime Romanian dictator Ion Antonescu, in order to build his 'national-communist' regime.[4]

Hence, in 1968 Romania was a headache for the Kremlin because Ceaușescu's critical attitude undermined the image of the Soviet bloc as a unified and monolithic alliance under Moscow's hegemony. Even though Romania was a member of the Warsaw Pact, it was not summoned to participate in the invasion of Czechoslovakia. Indeed, this outcome was anticipated months in advance by the Soviets, who already in early 1968 declined to invite Romania to Warsaw Pact meetings and other multilateral gatherings.[5] If there was something Ceaușescu *did* endorse in the unofficial agenda of the Prague Spring, it was Czechoslovak territorial pretensions against the Soviet Union. This concerned the Transcarpathian region, which had been an integral component of inter-war Czechoslovakia, was then annexed by Hungary in 1939 after the Nazi liquidation of Czechoslovakia following the Munich Treaty of late September 1938, and ultimately occupied by the USSR and attached to Soviet Ukraine after World War II.[6] As noted above, Romania had its own 'Transcarpathian' issue with the Soviet Union, and it was this highly delicate problem that further complicated Moscow–Bucharest relations after 1968.[7]

Echoes of the Prague Spring in Soviet Moldavia

The political agenda of the Prague Spring not only challenged Soviet influence in Eastern Europe, but also the USSR's monopoly on interpreting communist ideology. For Moscow, this was a threefold threat:

first, as we have seen, to its dominant status in the Eastern bloc; second, to its role in the wider international communist movement; and, finally, at the level of East–West Cold War relations. As events in the late 1980s were to graphically demonstrate, reforms in one state of the region had an immediate and direct impact on the evolution of the internal situation in other countries. But creating a united front of Soviet bloc states was more difficult to implement than to envisage. Yugoslavia in the late 1940s was the initial maverick to break Moscow's monopoly in Eastern Europe, followed later by Albania. To make things worse, Mao's China joined the club of rebels refusing to accept Soviet tutelage, especially after Khrushchev denounced Stalin's crimes in February 1956. Although this facilitated a temporary détente with Tito, after 1960 Albania was definitely under the Chinese grip and Yugoslavia continued its independent course until the collapse of the Soviet bloc in the late 1980s.[8] Thus, for the Kremlin it was imperative, at an absolute minimum, to ensure firm unity at home among the fifteen constituent Soviet republics and given the centralising character of the Soviet state and the monopoly of the CPSU at all levels of cadre policy, this was an easier task to achieve. Nevertheless, in 1968 and beyond each national republic had to struggle with specific dangers unleashed by the Prague Spring. For Soviet Moldavia, the main task was to combat perceived Romanian irredentism, but also to enforce ideological control on the south-western border of the USSR.

In May–June 1968, every party organisation in the Soviet Union was instructed to discuss the international conjuncture based on the resolution adopted at the April Central Committee plenum, 'On Current International Issues and the Struggle of the CPSU to Unite the World Communist Movement'. The wording of the resolution was formulated euphemistically, but it undoubtedly addressed first and foremost the emerging Czechoslovak crisis. Although the reports of these primary meetings were drawn up by local party functionaries, we can discern valuable information beneath the surface of the standard triumphalism and 'solid support' of the Soviet people for the Communist Party. It is true that at first glance the reports were thoroughly loyalist, backing the leadership in its response to the 'bourgeois' offensive in Czechoslovakia and the anti-Soviet 'nationalist' upsurge, especially in Romania and China. This ostensible unanimity is, however, doubtful and one can assume that the reports were censored at the local or regional level before being dispatched to the republican and then all-Union party authorities in Moscow. Moreover, as James C. Scott has argued, people often disguise their opinions and feelings when in the presence of superiors and this behaviour is even more noticeable in authoritarian regimes.[9] Consequently, one should look at other clues in order to grasp what was intentionally hidden by the official discourse.

A useful way of doing this is to pay due attention to the list of questions raised by rank-and-file party members on the international situation as a whole, and on events in Czechoslovakia and Romania in particular. Based on the nature and subject of the queries, one can ascertain the specific issues that concerned various social and ethnic groups. Hence, in urban areas like Chişinău, Bălţi, Tiraspol and Râbniţa, where workers and the technical intelligentsia were represented largely by Russian and Russified minorities including ethnic Moldavian-Romanians, the main questions dealt with the Czechoslovak imbroglio and the threat it posed to the unity of the Soviet bloc, but also other highly topical international problems such as the Vietnam War, Mao's China and Arab–Israeli relations. By way of contrast, in districts dominated by peasants and ethnic Moldavians-Romanians, the vast bulk of questions concerned Romania's position on various issues, including its stance at the Budapest conference of world communist parties held in late February 1968. More specifically, rural inhabitants and representatives of the titular nationality were interested in Romania's attitude towards Bessarabia and the Soviet Union in general. In some instances, the audience was galvanised by internal developments in Romania possibly assuming that Bucharest's nascent anti-Soviet posture would bring economic reform and political liberalisation, which, unfortunately, was not the case. On the contrary, Ceauşescu's Romania was about to embark on a Stalinist version of communism that had been repudiated in the Soviet Union since the mid-1950s. Another observation one can make is that in the border districts, inhabited predominantly by Romanian speakers, interest in the Prague Spring, in Romania's attitude towards it and in Bessarabia was more accentuated than in the Romanian-speaking districts not bordering Romania. This is probably explained by the fact that Romanian radio broadcasting was stronger in the frontier districts and, inversely, Soviet radio did not cover all these areas.[10]

On 18 October 1968, First Secretary Bodiul delivered a 140-minute speech to a meeting of propagandists in the Moldavian capital, Chişinău. In it, he addressed in exhaustive detail the feedback from the May–June primary MSSR party meetings. The seemingly endless peroration was formally dedicated to the preparations for the hundredth anniversary of Lenin's birth to be celebrated in 1970 and corresponding ideological tasks in the MSSR. But in the background was the challenge posed by the Prague Spring and its global reverberations. Bodiul started his monologue by saying that the decision of the CPSU to commemorate Lenin's centenary came at a difficult international conjuncture when:

> the aggressiveness of imperialism and the aspiration of peoples to socialism demand the intensification of propaganda, a profound study of the theory and practice of revolutionary struggle, a class approach of assessing social phenomena, intolerance to opportunism, revisionism and sectarianism, and the need to preserve and consolidate the unity of the working people and their organisations.[11]

He stressed the fact that the current situation was a result of the upsurge of anti-communist campaigns initiated by the 'imperialist states', which involved a myriad of official and unofficial Western bodies. Among them was the US Central Intelligence Agency (CIA), the State Department, the Pentagon and other government structures that were 'supported by 124 propagandistic, spying and academic institutions dealing with the Soviet Union and other socialist states'.[12] In West Germany alone, there were, according to Bodiul, 'more than one hundred anti-Soviet centres, research institutes and special organisations focused on planning and conducting ideological diversion'. These associations were eager to employ ever more actively the methods of 'psychological war to fight the communist countries with the aim of seizing people's minds and undermining their faith [*vera*] in communist ideology'.[13]

Bodiul went on to claim that in the framework of this 'psychological war' the enemy used 'various means of ideological influence—the social sciences, press, radio, TV, fiction, art, school, Church, cultural and economic relations, tourism and advertising'. One of the most tactically astute methods devised for this new type of war was the doctrine of 'building bridges' between East and West, which was designed to 'drive a wedge into the unity of the socialist countries, especially the member states of the Warsaw Treaty'. Bodiul was convinced that 'these stratagems were applied by imperialist circles to Czechoslovakia' and they were effective because 'emphasis was laid on human emotions, on escalating anxiety and fear, suspicion and exaggeration, speculating on the limitations of the socialist countries, all of this in order to deprive people of their ability to think soberly, to consciously approach events'.[14] The Moldavian supremo was insistent that 'nowadays the right as well as left opportunists, were trying to substitute the doctrine of class struggle and dictatorship of the proletariat with relations between various social groups based on race, ethnicity, age, occupation and culture'. More exactly, it was about imagining the revolutionary process as a 'set of clashes between white and coloured people, parents and children, intellectuals and masses'. This conviction was based on the assumption that the working class in the West had lost interest in the revolutionary struggle because it had won higher salaries, received access to social security and improvements in housing conditions.[15]

Here, Bodiul was upbraiding Herbert Marcuse, the leading Western leftist intellectual associated (from the Soviet viewpoint) with revisionist and 'pseudo-Marxist' ideas. Marcuse was attacked because he failed to understand that the degree of revolutionary consciousness is not dependent on material well-being and that starvation and deprivation are not obligatory preconditions for attracting the working class to the revolutionary struggle. In support of his point, Bodiul made reference to the May 1968 *événements* in France in which some of the most active protesters were well-paid workers from the Renault car plant.[16] He then turned increasingly to Czechoslovak developments. The political agenda of the Prague Spring, he said, was dangerous because, founded as it was on revisionist principles, it combatted 'real socialism' and thus represented nothing more than a Western-inspired ideological diversion against the Soviet bloc. According to Bodiul, the 'improved model' of 'democratic socialism' in Czechoslovakia was merely a strategy to revisit Marxist-Leninist doctrine. Moreover, political revisionism was inevitably closely tied to economic reform, Bodiul adding that 'the economic basis of the Czechoslovak model of socialism, preached for many years, was the multi-subjective household; that is, the market economy with its spontaneous laws and competitiveness, which envisage the acceptance of private and foreign investments'.[17]

As Rasma Karklins has argued in relation to Mikhail Gorbachev's *perestroika* (reconstruction) in the late 1980s, control of the media in a totalitarian state is quintessential for maintaining monopoly one-party rule. If censorship of the press is rescinded, the other institutions of the state, such as the secret police, subsequently lose their grip on society.[18] Bodiul excoriated the Prague Spring reforms precisely on the grounds that the Czechoslovak party had forfeited its tight control of the press, either consciously or out of ignorance, without comprehending the perils that this process entailed. In this way, 'demagogically using the slogan of "freedom of the press", the anti-socialist forces in Czechoslovakia succeeded in transforming the organs of information into an instrument of counter-revolution. Newspapers, radio and TV became the mouthpiece of a slanderous campaign against the party, against socialism, and created an atmosphere of uncertainty, petit-bourgeois anarchy and anti-communist hysteria'.[19]

The Prague Spring not only reactivated fears that communist ideology could lose its influence and dynamism; it also struck at the heart of the Soviet conviction, and indeed pride, that no matter what the temporary difficulties and limitations in the building of communism, the socialist regime remained superior to capitalism and would outlive it in the mortal struggles that lay ahead. Two specific achievements in the social welfare domain largely accounted for this Soviet pride: health insurance and housing policy. While reluctantly acknowledging that workers received higher salaries in the West and many commodity goods were better and cheaper, the Soviets—in this case represented by Bodiul—attempted to minimise the benefits of capitalism by stressing the not inconsiderable costs Western citizens had to pay for health and housing. In comparison, under socialism the state covered full health insurance and housing; that is, the main expenses needed for a decent standard of living.[20] The Soviets could also have added that education was free in the USSR and its satellite countries, but interestingly they did not include this aspect in the dispute on the superiority of communism over capitalism. This oversight was probably deliberate, as students were among the most unreliable social category in the party's fight against so-called Western ideological diversion. The Prague Spring brought this potent issue once again to the fore: the youth problem reflected the insurmountable difficulty of the regime, evident since the immediate post-war years, to reproduce its values among the younger generation.[21]

The Prague Spring and the Nationality Question

The Czechoslovak reforms raised another spectre that Soviet propaganda always tried hard to counter: the nationality question. Although in his meetings with Shelest, the Ukrainian party leader, Dubček consistently denied that his country sought the return of Transcarpathia, a region that belonged to Czechoslovakia before World War II, certain Czechoslovak officials (according to Shelest) could be accused of complicity in stirring up this territorial dispute with the Soviets.[22] As noted above, Romania had its own 'Transcarpathian issue' with the USSR and it was even more complicated given the fact that the majority of the population of Bessarabia and Northern Bukovina, occupied by the Soviets in 1940 and again in 1944, was ethnically and linguistically Romanian and belonged historically to the medieval Principality of Moldavia. The Bessarabia question did not become paramount in Soviet–Romanian relations during the Prague Spring, but it did play a pivotal role in the growing unease between Moscow and Bucharest. Initially, in the first decade-and-a-half after World War II Romania did not dwell on the issue of the 'lost territories' and seemed resigned to the Soviet notion that Bessarabia was inhabited by a different nation that spoke a different language to Romanian, namely Moldavian. However, after the withdrawal of Soviet troops from Romania in 1958, the then General Secretary of the ruling Romanian Workers' Party, Gheorghe Gheorghiu-Dej, started to become more assertive in defence of the country's national interests. Hence, in April 1964 the party adopted the so-called 'declaration of independence', which stipulated that Romania did not accept a supranational economic plan inside Comecon and would not agree to become a mere agricultural producer to the detriment of industrial development, as the Soviets seemed tempted to propose to Romania in the so-called Valev plan.[23] Dej's successor after 1965, Ceaușescu, continued his predecessor's foreign policy, if anything adopting a firmer stance on the eastern provinces annexed by the Soviets. The whole problem was exacerbated by the publication in Romania in 1964 of an incendiary text, attributed to Karl Marx, in which it was mentioned that Tsarist Russia had occupied Romanian Bessarabia in 1812.[24]

Romanian revisionism towards the Soviet Union reached its climax on 21 August 1968 with Ceaușescu's public criticism of the Warsaw Pact invasion of Czechoslovakia. Bucharest's negative standpoint convinced many Romanians that Ceaușescu was preparing to officially request the return of Bessarabia. The same thought occurred to certain intellectual circles in Soviet Moldavia, although they would soon be disillusioned over the extent to which the Romanian leader could afford to alienate the Kremlin (see below on the case of the Usatiuc-Ghimpu group). But shortly thereafter, starting in autumn 1968, Ceaușescu was obliged to revise his anti-Soviet bravado, one of the reasons being a growing perception that the Soviets could invade the country.[25] In 1976, Ceaușescu visited Chișinău and formally acknowledged the existence of the MSSR.

But he did not renounce his conviction that Bessarabia was Romanian, even though he understood it was impossible for Moscow to agree to its reunification with Romania. One of the most memorable moments came during a meeting with Brezhnev in the Crimea in August 1977. The Soviet leader asked Ceaușescu to ensure that the Romanian press, academic journals and textbooks cease their insistence that Bessarabia's unification with Romania in 1918 was based on the principle of national self-determination. Ceaușescu replied that he had no territorial designs on the USSR, and he could not accept that there was just one 'historical truth': that Bessarabia was occupied by Tsarist Russia in 1812 and a century later [in 1918] it became a part of the Romanian unified state.[26] The most common scholarly assessment of the motivations for Ceaușescu's irredentism is that he sought to instrumentalise ethno-nationalism in order to consolidate his regime.[27] It seems, however, that it was something more than this, given that in 1977 his rule went essentially unchallenged both internally and externally, and yet he still insisted on his point of view. In other words, it would appear that for Ceaușescu the 'Bessarabia issue' was not only an instrument to 'blackmail' the Soviets, but he believed it his duty to express his awareness about the ex-Romanian province of Bessarabia still inhabited at that time by a majority of Romanian speakers.

Romanian Tourism to Soviet Moldavia in 1968

In the aftermath of the invasion of Czechoslovakia, the growing tensions between Moscow and Bucharest were reflected in the reports of Romanian tourists visiting Moldavia. In light of the near breakdown in Soviet–Romanian relations by late August 1968, Soviet tourist guides, under close KGB supervision, were extremely keen to extract as much information as possible from Romanian visitors to the USSR, especially to Soviet Moldavia. Previously, interest had been rather prosaic, pertaining largely to how Romanians perceived socio-economic conditions in Soviet Moldavia in terms of prosperity, living standards, nationality policy and the like, but by late August the Soviets were paying far more attention to specific political issues. Above all, they wanted to know what Romanian citizens thought about the Warsaw Pact 'fraternal assistance' to Czechoslovakia and what, if any, preparations were taking place in Romania in the wake of the Soviet response to its maverick ally. According to Soviet guide reports, attitudes towards Ceaușescu were divided and some Romanian tourists were anxious about the future. For instance, Marcela Celea from Craiova was fearful that Ceaușescu's speech on 21 August was a prologue to war, given that in her home town workers from industrial enterprises were armed and ready for war with the USSR to break out at any time. Celea wished Romania and the Soviet Union had the same stance on events in Czechoslovakia. Another Romanian tourist, a certain Pleșa from Râmnicu Sărat, was confused about what was happening and did not know who to believe, Ceaușescu or Brezhnev.[28]

Other tourists, however, viewed the situation more positively, asserting their self-dignity as Romanian citizens.[29] One Ștrengaru, a former secret police (Securitate) officer from Oradea, spoke of his pride as he listened to Radio Free Europe and described Romania as the protector of Czechoslovak sovereignty. He believed that his country was morally obliged to support Czechoslovakia since Romania was next on the list of Soviet-led invasions together with Hungary, Bulgaria and Poland. Ștrengaru was convinced that the Soviets were responsible for the near crisis atmosphere as it was a predictable outcome of their economic policy of exploiting Romania, and the other socialist states, through so-called joint ventures (*sovroms* in Romanian). Even citizens with no direct relations with the Romanian political police were prepared to make bold statements. Vlad Babiac, an electrician, was outraged at the invasion of Czechoslovakia, cursing the Soviets: 'You will regret what you did in Czechoslovakia. You do not let people decide their own fate'.[30]

Neither was it easy being a Soviet tourist in Romania in late August 1968; in fact, it was probably worse. No-one bothered what they thought about the dramatic events in Czechoslovakia, probably because their answers were more or less predictable. After returning home, Soviet tourists complained about the bad treatment they had received from their hosts. First, nobody was waiting to greet them at the border as was the rule. Then, on arriving in Constanța and embarking on a tour of the city, the guide did not utter a word about the Red Army liberation of Romania in August 1944. As if that were not enough, the food and service in the hotels were poor and Romanians daubed Soviet tourist buses with unfriendly inscriptions. One shouted: 'Occupiers, go home!'[31]

The Campaign Against Local Nationalism

Long before the Prague Spring, the Moldavian republican leadership had been concerned about what it called the rise of local nationalism. In the late Stalinist era, the drive for Russification was paramount, but under

The Ministry of Culture endeavoured to limit the band's repertoire, but they refused to stick to the officially approved range of songs. Hence, in July 1970, after a concert in Odessa, the Ukrainian port city close to the border with Moldavia, NOROC was disbanded on the grounds that the group performed tunes that had not been formally sanctioned.[39] This kind of band was dangerous for the regime given their 'bad' influence on the youth both in terms of national content (singing in Romanian heightened the social prestige of the Romanian language in Soviet Moldavia) as well as their 'rotten bourgeois' Western oeuvre, above all rock'n'roll, which was viewed as a weapon in the psychological war against the USSR and its satellites.

The KGB Against Pro-Union Moldavians

As Romania expressed its anti-Soviet position on the invasion of Czechoslovakia, certain nationally inclined intellectual circles in Soviet Moldavia came to believe that a solution to the Bessarabia question would soon follow. To this end, a political organisation, informally known as the Usatiuc-Ghimpu group but more formally called the National Patriotic Front (NPF), began to plead the case for the union of Bessarabia and Northern Bukovina with Romania. The circle, established in 1967, advocated the observance of the Moldavians' rights to freedom, liberation from Soviet occupation and unification with Romania. The principal founder of the NPF was Alexandru Usatiuc, born in 1915 in the village of Ivancea, Orhei District. When he was arrested in December 1971, he was head of a department for the sale of goods at the 'Moldobuvtorg' enterprise; hence, he was a minor member of the *nomenklatura*. The other founder-member of the NPF was Gheorghe Ghimpu, born in 1937 in the village of Colonița, Criuleni District (now in Chișinău municipality). According to KGB interrogations, Ghimpu was an ardent supporter of Usatiuc's ideas and closely cooperated with him in drafting the most important NPF programme documents. The ideological sources of the Front originated from textbooks on Romanian history published before 1940: the volume by Ștefan Ciobanu *106 Years under the Russian Yoke* and the aforementioned work by Marx, 'Notes on the Romanians', published in Bucharest in 1964. But the main influence on the Front was the Prague Spring and Romania's stance against the Soviet-led invasion of Czechoslovakia. Both Usatiuc and Ghimpu were convinced that as a result of Ceaușescu's publicly expressed position on the afternoon of 21 August 1968, Bucharest had irredeemably broken its ties with Moscow, and the latter was responsible for the impasse. Thus, the ball was firmly in the Soviet court and the only way to improve relations between the two countries was to return Bessarabia and Northern Bukovina to Romania, especially as Romania was at that time—unlike in the inter-war period—a communist country.

Usatiuc conceived the idea of sending a comprehensive written statement to Ceauşescu. Initially, he sent the declaration via the Romanian postal service on 29 March 1969, while on a visit to Romania. Doubting that his message had reached its destination, Usatiuc travelled to Bucharest, where on 12 June 1971 he asked for a meeting with Ceauşescu in person. The latter refused and Usatiuc left the six-page document at the chancellery of the Romanian Council of State. Consequently, on 30 June the head of the Romanian Security Service, Ion Stănescu, informed the then KGB head, Yuri Andropov, about Usatiuc's visit to Bucharest. Stănescu also sent 'big brother' in Moscow a copy of the statement that Usatiuc had intended for Ceauşescu. The Romanian point of view on this controversial episode, supported by present-day Romanian historians, is that Ceauşescu was fearful that the group was a set-up by the KGB to verify his loyalty to the Soviet Union following his 21 August speech condemning the invasion of Czechoslovakia.

As a result, the KGB arrested Usatiuc, Ghimpu and several other leading NFP members and associates. The Moldavian Supreme Court of Justice completed the hearing of the case on 13 July 1972, sentencing the main 'culprit', Usatiuc, to seven years in a high-security labour correction colony in Perm' and a five-year exile in the city of Tyumen'. Ghimpu and another defendant, Alexandru Şoltoianu, received six years in a high-security labour correction colony, while Valeriu Graur was handed down four years.[40] With that the campaign against so-called 'Moldo-Romanian' nationalism, which had started in 1968 in the framework of the Prague Spring, effectively came to an end. For the next fifteen years until Gorbachev's *perestroika*, there was no important nationalist group or organisation that put in danger the 'friendship of the peoples' or threatened ideological purity in Soviet Moldavia. This ostensible conformity was the outcome of the specific hard-line 'normalisation' the Moscow authorities pursued in their western borderlands, and in the MSSR in particular, in the aftermath of the intervention in Czechoslovakia.[41]

Conclusion

The Prague Spring and the Romanian response to the Soviet-led invasion had a profound impact on Soviet Moldavia in subsequent years. The leadership of Moldavia launched several campaigns in order to safeguard the ideological rigidity of the regime aimed at demonstrating the superiority of communism over capitalism. Because of Romania's political position, a special drive was directed against 'Moldo-Romanian' nationalism. Consequently, the regime established tighter ideological control in various domains such as literature and the arts. Censorship became more severe and publications from Romania were drastically limited. The campaign, designed to inculcate Soviet patriotism and socialist internationalism, did not only entail propaganda, but also drastic measures including political repression on a scale unknown since Stalin's death. The last important organisations supporting greater linguistic and cultural rights for the titular nationality, as well as those backing the union of Soviet Moldavia with Romania, were liquidated and their members condemned to the Gulag. This was the specificity of the 'normalisation' policies pursued by Moscow and Chișinău in the Soviet borderlands.

The Prague Spring and Romania's anti-Soviet stance in 1968 were perceived multifariously in Moldavian society. Ethnic Romanians, largely inhabiting the rural areas, appeared more interested in the events in Czechoslovakia and to some extent in Romania. That did not, however, translate into a general enthusiasm for the Prague Spring or Ceaușescu's vituperations against Moscow. By contrast, urban citizens, overwhelmingly Russian or heavily Russified, were manifestly more critical of the Czechoslovak reforms and some even appealed to the Soviet authorities to militarily crush the Prague Spring weeks before the actual invasion took place. The Russians of Soviet Moldavia were also more worried than the Romanian-speaking population about Bucharest's territorial pretensions against the USSR resuscitated in 1968 as never before. This is explained by the fact that the Romanian- and non-Romanian speaking populations were in varying degrees critical or supportive of their status in Soviet Moldavia. At the same time, their different perceptions of the Prague Spring, and particularly Romania's anti-Soviet posture, were framed by different memories of the inter-war period to 1940 and the years 1941–44 when Bessarabia was part of the modern Romanian state and, implicitly, of the French-inspired anti-Soviet *cordon sanitaire* stretching from the Baltic Sea in the north to the Black Sea in the south. Last but not least, it is evident from Soviet sources, especially those reflecting the views of Romanian tourists visiting Soviet Moldavia in late August 1968, that representatives of various social strata were divided in their attitudes on Ceaușescu's critique of Soviet actions in Czechoslovakia.

Notes

1. Gh. E. Cojocaru (ed.), *Confruntarea sovieto-română pe frontul ideologic din RSS Moldovenească, 1968–1979. Studiu și documente* (Iași, 2011); E. Negru and Gh. Negru (eds), *'Cursul deosebit' al României și supărarea Moscovei. Disputa sovieto-română și campaniile propagandistice anti-românești din RSSM, 1965–1989*, vol. I, 1965–1975 (Chișinău, 2013).
2. See I. Cașu and M. Sandle, 'Discontent and Uncertainty in the Borderlands: Soviet Moldavia and the Secret Speech, 1956–1957', *Europe-Asia Studies*, vol. 66, no. 4 (2014), pp. 613–44.
3. For details on Ceaușescu's speech and the impact of the Prague Spring on Romania, see Calin Goina's chapter in this volume. Also D. Cătănuș (ed.), *România și 'Primăvara de la Praga'* (Bucharest, 2005). For a documentary history, see M. Berindei et al. (eds), *Istoria Comunismului în România. Nicolae Ceaușescu, 1965–1971* (Bucharest, 2012).
4. See K. Verdery, *National Ideology under Communism: Identity and Cultural Politics in Ceaușescu's Romania* (Berkeley, CA, 1995); V. Tismaneanu, *Stalinism for All Seasons: A History of Romanian Communism* (Berkeley, CA, 2003); E. Copilaș, *Națiunea Socialistă. Politica Identității în Epoca de Aur* (Iași, 2015).
5. R. G. Pikhoia, *Sovetskii Soiuz: Istoriia vlasti, 1945–1991* (Novosibirsk, 2000), p. 273.
6. A. Weiner, 'Déjà Vu All over Again: Prague Spring, Romanian Summer and Soviet Autumn on the Soviet Western Frontier', *Contemporary European History*, vol. 15, no. 2 (2006), pp. 171–2.
7. The 'Transcarpathian' issue concerns Bessarabia and Northern Bukovina, annexed by the Soviet Union on 28 June 1940 under the terms of the Nazi-Soviet Pact of 23 August 1939.
8. See R. Service, *Comrades! A History of World Communism* (New York, 2010); D. Priestland, *Red Flag: A History of Communism* (New York, 2010).
9. J.C. Scott, *Domination and the Arts of Resistance: Hidden Transcripts* (New Haven, 1990), pp. 37–44.
10. Archive of Social-Political Organisations of the Republic of Moldova, (former archive of the Central Committee of the Communist Party of Moldavia, hereafter AOSPRM), f. 51, op. 29, d. 164, ll. 15, 19–20,

24–8, 30–5, 38–9, 44–5, 52–3, 58, 59, 61–2, 96; d. 133, ll. 2, 6, 8, 17, 22, 25, 33, 36, 38–9, 40, 44, 52, 65–70, 71, 73, 80, 83, 85, 87–8, 90–1, 93; see also T.A. Pokivailova and A.S. Stykalin, 'Iz istorii sovetsko-rumynskikh otnoshenii v epokhu sotsializma', *Slavianskii al'manakh*, no. 3–4 (2010), pp. 183–95.
11. AOSPRM, f. 51, op. 29, d. 95, l. 3.
12. AOSPRM, f. 51, op. 29, d. 95, l. 5.
13. AOSPRM, f. 51, op. 29, d. 95, l. 6.
14. AOSPRM, f. 51, op. 29, d. 95, ll. 6–7.
15. AOSPRM, f. 51, op. 29, d. 95, l. 8.
16. AOSPRM, f. 51, op. 29, d. 95, ll. 9–10.
17. AOSPRM, f. 51, op. 29, d. 95, l. 11.
18. R. Karklins, 'Explaining Regime Change in the Soviet Union', *Europe-Asia Studies*, vol. 46, no. 1 (1994), pp. 29–45.
19. AOSPRM, f. 51, op. 29, d. 95, ll. 49–50.
20. AOSPRM, f. 51, op. 29, d. 95, l. 9, 54.
21. AOSPRM, f. 51, op. 29, d. 45, ll. 5–6. For more details on the failure of the Soviet regime to instill communist ideology and discipline among the youth, see B. Firsov, *Raznomyslie v SSSR, 1940-e–1960-e gody* (St. Petersburg, 2008), pp. 31–8. For the immediate post-war youth issue, see J. Fürst, *Stalin's Last Generation: Soviet Postwar Youth and the Emergence of Mature Socialism* (Oxford, 2010).
22. Weiner, 'Déjà Vu All over Again', pp. 71–2.
23. For more details, see M. Anton, *Ieşirea din cerc. Politica externă a regimului Ceauşescu* (Bucharest, 2007), p. 140; Tismaneanu, *Stalinism for All Seasons*, pp. 216, 341 (cited from the Romanian edition, Iaşi, 2005). Comecon was the Soviet-led council that oversaw the macro-planning of East European economies.
24. For more details, see I. Constantin, *Problema Basarabiei în relaţiile româno-sovietice din timpul Războiului Rece, 1945–1989* (Bucharest, 2015), pp. 58–96; V. Buga, *Pe muchie de cuţit. Relaţiile româno-sovietice, 1965–1989* (Bucharest, 2013), pp. 17–59; Pokivailova and Stykalin, 'Iz istorii sovetsko-rumynskikh otnoshenii', pp. 183–95.
25. Buga, *Pe muchie de cuţit*, pp. 78–82.
26. The minutes of Brezhnev and Ceauşescu's discussion on Bessarabia that took place in the Crimea on 5 August 1977 are available in English translation at the Cold War Digital Archive, Woodrow Wilson Center, Washington, DC: http://digitalarchive.wilsoncenter.org/document/114142 (last accessed 24 October 2017).
27. 'Ethno-nationalism' in the sense used by W. Connor, *Ethnonationalism: A Quest for Understanding* (Princeton, NJ, 1994).
28. AOSPRM, f. 51, op. 29, d. 102, l. 45.

29. AOSPRM, f. 51, op. 29, d. 102, l. 48.
30. AOSPRM, f. 51, op. 29, d. 102, l. 57.
31. AOSPRM, f. 51, op. 29, d. 102, l. 61.
32. I. Cașu, '"The Quiet Revolution": Revisiting the National Identity Issue in Soviet Moldavia at the Height of Khrushchev's Thaw (1956)', *Euxeinos*, vol. 15–16, (2014), pp. 77–91.
33. AOSPRM, f. 51, op. 25, d. 25, ll. 18, 22.
34. A. S. Stykalin, 'Mezhdunarodnyi krizis 1968 g. i situatsiia na sovetsko-rumynskoi granitse posle 21 avgusta', in E.S. Uzeneva (ed.), *Slavianskii mir v tret'em tysiachiletii. Obraz Rossii v slavianskikh stranakh* (Moscow, 2012), p. 206; Negru and Negru (eds), '*Cursul deosebit*', pp. 305–9.
35. AOSPRM, f. 51, op. 29, d. 35, ll. 4–223.
36. Negru and Negru (eds), '*Cursul deosebit*', pp. 138–41.
37. M. Ellman, 'The 1947 Soviet Famine and the Entitlement Approach to Famines', *Cambridge Journal of Economics*, vol. 24, no.1 (2000), pp. 612–13. For more details, see I. Cașu, 'Stalinist Terror in Soviet Moldavia, 1940–1953', in K. McDermott and M. Stibbe (eds), *Stalinist Terror in Eastern Europe: Elite Purges and Mass Repression* (Manchester, 2010), pp. 43–7.
38. AOSPRM, f. 51, op. 31, d. 93, ll. 105–6.
39. AOSPRM, f. 51, op. 29, d. 141, ll. 15–16; op. 31, d. 197, ll. 21–4. On NOROC, see M.Ș. Poiată, *Mihai Dolgan. De ce au plâns ghitarele?* (Chișinău, 2017).
40. The Usatiuc-Ghimpu file is preserved in the KGB archive in Chișinău, nowadays the Archive of the Service for Information and Security of the Republic of Moldova. See ASISRM-KGB, fond 'Politically Repressed Persons', personal file Usatiuc-Ghimpu, vols. 1–11. For a summary of the files, see I. Cașu, 'Political Repressions in Soviet Moldavia after 1956: A Typology Based on KGB Files', in *Dystopia. Journal of Totalitarian Ideologies and Regimes*, vol. 1, no. 1–2 (2012), pp. 118–22.
41. For developments in Soviet Ukraine, see "The Impact of the Prague Spring on the USSR", by Zbigniew Wojnowski, in this volume.

Index

A
Action Programme (April 1968), 5–6, 13, 17, 87, 103, 116, 132–3
Akks, Valērijs, 268
Albania
  art and culture, 242–5
  and Bulgaria, 247
  and China, 185, 239, 240–2, 247–8, 283
  government response to the Prague Spring, 236–9, 245, 251
  Hoxha's Open Letter, 240
  isolation, 235–6
  and the Kosovo demonstrations, 229, 248–51
  state patriotism, 15
  withdrawal from Warsaw Pact, 2, 10, 246, 251
Alia, Ramiz, 246
Andropov, Yuri, 74, 131
Andrzejewski, Jerzy, 141
anti-communism
  in Czechoslovakia, 7, 45–6, 48–9, 53–5, 60–1
  in Latvia, 199
  in Romania, 199, 292
  and West Germany, 101, 285
  see also dissent
anti-reformism
  breakdown of the reformist consensus, 58–9
  multiple strands, 46–7, 53, 59–64
  and the USSR, 56, 72–3, 82, 258
  see also neo-Stalinism
anti-Semitism
  and Bulgaria, 172–3
  in Czechoslovakia, 6, 48, 50–2, 58
  in Poland, 2, 84, 129–31, 142
  and the USSR, 15, 78, 80, 138
anti-war activism, 1, 217–18
  see also student activism; youth culture
armed forces
  Albanian, 240, 247–8
  in the Balkans, 183–4
  Bulgarian, 177–81, 186
  composition of invasion force, 9, 138, 156
  Czechoslovak, 6, 108–9, 133
  East German, 104, 111, 113, 156
  Hungarian, 157–8, 160
  Polish, 140

Romanian, 184, 197, 203
Soviet, 11, 60, 83, 201–2
see also 'Šumava' manoeuvres
Aurelia (Romanian villager), 204–5
Austria, 78–9, 98, 197

B

Babiac, Vlad (Romanian tourist), 290
Bacílek, Karol, 53–4
Balluku, Beqir, 185, 247
Baltic States
  acts of resistance, 268–72
  Baltic Charter, 273
  loss of independence, 257–8, 263–4, 272–3
  public opinion on the Prague Spring, 262–3, 264–8
  see also Estonia; Latvia; Lithuania
Beater, Bruno, 104, 108
Beatles, 109, 176
Bels, Alberts, 270–1
Belševica, Vizma, 271
Beluha, Nikolajs, 270
Beránek, Bohumír, 54
Berlinguer, Enrico, 186
Berlin Wall, 15, 100, 116
Berthold, Erika, 113
Bessarabia, 280–1, 284, 288–9, 291, 293–4, 295–6
Biafra, 1–2, 17
Biermann, Wolf, 116
Bil'ak, Vasil, 6, 47, 54, 60, 63, 173–4
Bismarck, Otto von, 98–9, 117
Bodiul, Ivan, 281, 284–7, 291, 292
Bohemia, 52, 56, 98–9, 101
Bower, Gordon H., 202, 210
Brandt, Willy, 101, 173
Brasch, Thomas, 113
Bratislava meeting, 8, 106, 137–8, 139, 154

Brecht, Bertolt, 245
Brezhnev Doctrine, 12–13, 16–17, 137, 159–60, 163–4, 175, 186, 194
Brezhnev, Leonid
  and Bulgaria, 170, 171–2, 185–6
  and the Czech neo-Stalinists, 57
  and dissent, 84–5, 87
  Gomułka and Dubček, 130, 131, 136, 138–9
  invasion of Czechoslovakia, 8, 76, 106, 156
  Kádár and Dubček, 151–5
  and Moldavia, 281, 289
  on the Prague Spring, 5, 6
  and reform, 71–2, 73, 74–5, 126
Brovják, Jaromír, 47, 59–60, 62
Brzezinski, Zbigniew, 130, 137
Bulgaria
  and Albania, 247
  foreign policy, 151
  government response to the Prague Spring, 10, 106, 153, 169–70, 172–6
  Ninth World Youth and Student Festival, 176–7
  participation of troops in invasion, 138, 156, 177–81
  political control and censorship, 182, 186
  popular response to the Prague Spring, 11, 181–2
  post-invasion repercussions in Balkans, 183–5, 186
Bulgarian Communist Party (BCP), 170–5, 181–2, 186
The Burden of Our Goodness (Druţă), 292

C

Castro, Fidel, 3

Catholic Church, 80, 89, 126, 150, 241
Ceaușescu, Nicolae
  autonomy, 10, 140, 195–6, 281–2
  and Bessarabia, 288–9, 294
  condemnation of invasion of Czechoslovakia, 12, 160, 193–4, 210–11, 296
  and Dubček, 134, 196
  fear of Soviet invasion of Romania, 197–8, 288
  intellectuals' response, 198–200
  relations with Warsaw Pact allies, 183–4
Celea, Marcela (Romanian tourist), 289–90
censorship
  abolition, 6, 56, 135
  in Albania, 237, 244–5
  in the Baltic states, 262, 270–1
  in Bulgaria, 182
  and the GDR, 102, 104
  in Moldavia, 292–3, 295
  in Poland, 16, 127–8
  restoration, 9
  and totalitarianism, 242, 286–7
  and the USSR, 71, 72–3, 75–6, 84–6
  in Yugoslavia, 228
  see also media
Central Europe, 78, 117, 141, 151
Černík, Oldřich, 51, 54, 111–12, 139, 153, 154
Četri balti krekli (film), 270
Charles University, Prague, 25, 62
Charter 77, 25, 38–9, 164, 273
Chervonenko, Stepan, 57
China
  and Albania, 185, 239, 240–2, 246, 247–8
  Cultural Revolution, 1, 242
  reaction to invasion of Czechoslovakia, 13, 184–5
  and the USSR, 79–80, 246, 283
Chonkov, Yancho, 182
The Chronicle of Current Events (Khronika tekushchikh sobytyi) (*samizdat* periodical), 85–6, 267
Čierna nad Tisou meeting, 8, 57, 74, 137, 138, 139, 154
Cilinskis, Aldis, 267–8
Ciobanu, Ștefan, 293
The Citizen, Law and Democracy (Občan, právo a demokracie) (Lakatoš), 28–30
civil society
  as employed by Lakatoš, 30–2
  participation, 33–5, 86
  and the Prague Spring, 4, 6, 24, 45
  and 'socialist legality', 37–9
Cominform, 140, 216, 235
Communist Party of Czechoslovakia (KSČ)
  anti-communist terror, 53–4
  and democratisation, 4–7, 153–4
  disunity, 52–3
  and East Germany, 102–4
  loss of leading role, 55–6
  neo-Stalinism, 15, 45–7, 50–1, 57–8
  normalisation, 63–4
  and social democracy, 136, 139
  and West Germany, 100
  see also Action Programme; Dubček
Communist Party of Moldavia (CPM), 279, 291
Communist Party of the Soviet Union (CPSU), 74, 134, 171–2, 174, 257–8, 263, 283
Considerations on the Values of Democracy (Úvahy o hodnotách demokracie) (Lakatoš), 24–5, 30–4
Corbyn, Jeremy, 3

'The Counter-Revolution Shall Not Succeed' (*Kontrrevoliutsiia ne proidet*) (film), 79, 83
Czechoslovakia
 and Albania, 236–9
 foreign policy, 151
 Ninth World Youth and Student Festival delegation, 176–7
 normalisation, 9, 46, 159
 strategic importance, 132, 134, 137–40, 171–2, 175–6
 see also Dubček

D

Danton's Death (Büchner), 222–3
Dawisha, Karen, 132–3
Delchev, Delcho, 182
Demichev, Petr, 80
democracy
 and dissent, 86, 107
 managed, 26
 and neo-Stalinism, 50–2, 55
 and oversight, 34–5
 Polish opposition, 132–3, 136
 and socialism, 3–5, 32–3, 264
 Soviet opposition, 73, 76, 126, 159
Der Traum von der Revolte (Wolle), 115
de-Stalinisation
 in Albania, 239
 in the GDR, 103
 in Hungary, 147–8, 151
 in Poland, 128
 and Romania, 195
 in the USSR, 71–3, 89, 125, 258
Deutsche Welle, 82
Die Zeit (newspaper), 107
dissent
 Charter 77, 25, 38–9, 164, 273
 in the GDR, 106–8, 112–16
 March Events (Poland), 2, 127–30

Praxis group, 219, 228, 230
 in the USSR, 11, 81, 84–90, 259, 261–2, 265–73, 292–3
 in the Warsaw Pact states, 11–12, 140–1, 181–2, 242–5, 248–51
 see also intellectuals; student activism
Djilas, Milovan, 228, 230n, 231n
Dresden meeting, 8, 103, 105, 131–2, 152, 172, 195
Druță, Ion, 292
Dubček, Alexander
 attempted political come-back, 14
 and Brezhnev, 8, 85, 130, 131, 136, 138–9
 election, 4, 49, 102
 and Gomułka, 126–7, 131, 134, 137–8
 and Hoxha, 237
 and Kádár, 10, 151–5
 reform communism, 16, 17, 72–3
 removal from office, 9, 111–12
 and the Soviet leadership, 74–5
 and Transcarpathia, 287–8
 and Ulbricht, 104
 and Zhivkov, 170, 173
Dzhurov, Dobri, 173, 178, 180
Dziady (Mickiewicz), 127–8

E

East Germany, *see* German Democratic Republic (GDR)
Eberlein, Werner, 104
Egypt, 13, 129, 247
Engelberg, Ernst, 97–100, 117
Engels, Friedrich, 98
Estonia, 259, 261–2, 264–6
 see also Baltic States
Estonian Communist Party (ECP), 257, 259, 262
ethnicity
 Bessarabia, 280–1, 288

and dissent, 87–8, 89
Magyar, 157–8
and patriotism, 15–16, 73, 90
Romania, 200–1, 206–8, 211, 284, 295
and Soviet public culture, 76–7, 78–83
see also Ukraine
Euro-communism, 13, 185–6

F
Famíra, Emanuel, 60
France, 13, 77, 111, 196, 221, 286
Fučík, Julius, 238
Furrxhi, Vangjush, 244–5

G
Gadu gredzeni (Belševica), 271
Gdańsk Agreement 1980, 142
Geremek, Bronisław, 141
German Democratic Republic (GDR)
 foreign policy, 151
 and the FRG, 97–8, 100–3, 140
 government response to the Prague Spring, 10, 103–6, 110–11, 137
 popular response to the Prague Spring, 11, 17, 111–13
 punishment for dissent, 113–15
 role in Warsaw Pact invasion, 156, 161
 significance of 1968, 115–17
 Stasi report on the Prague Spring, 108–10
 state patriotism, 14–15
 youth policy, 106–8
 see also Socialist Unity Party of Germany (SED)
German Federal Republic (FRG)
 anti-communist propaganda, 285
 and Czechoslovakia, 100, 103, 108–9
 and the GDR, 100, 111, 116–17, 140
 Ostpolitik, 132, 134, 135
 and Soviet state patriotism, 14–15, 78–9, 82
 see also Social Democratic Party, West Germany
Gheorghe (Romanian villager), 209–10
Gheorghiu-Dej, Gheorghe, 195, 288
Ghimpu, Gheorghe, 293–4
glasnost, 4
Głowacki, Piotr, 246
Goldstücker, Eduard, 50, 52, 172–3, 242
Goma, Paul, 198
Gomułka, Władysław
 anti-Semitism, 78, 84, 129–30
 and dissent, 242
 and Dubček, 126–7, 134
 loss of power, 141–2
 and the 'Polish October', 239
 and reform socialism, 10, 125–6, 131, 132–3, 170
 support for invasion of Czechoslovakia, 136–8, 139–40
Gorbachev, Mikhail, 4, 90, 286
Gorbanevskaia, Natalia, 85
Graur, Valeriu, 294
Grechko, Andrei, 75, 156
Grigorenko, Piotr, 267
Gromyko, Andrei, 74, 135

H
Hager, Kurt, 107
Hájek, Jiří, 176
Havel, Václav, 2, 273
Havemann, Frank and Florian, 113
Havemann, Robert, 105, 107, 113

Havlíček, František, 47, 48, 56–7
Hegedüs, András, 162–3
Honecker, Erich, 15, 103, 106, 115, 116
Hoxha, Enver
　art and culture, 243–4
　and China, 185, 247
　and Kosovo, 250
　power and control, 239–42
　response to the Prague Spring, 10, 237–8, 251
　rupture with USSR, 236, 246
human rights, 16, 36–7, 266–7
　see also Charter 77
Hungarian Socialist Workers' Party (HSWP), 153, 161–2, 163
Hungary
　1956 Revolution, 48–9, 103, 131, 155, 242
　de-Stalinisation, 147–8, 151
　foreign policy, 150–1
　freedom of movement and culture, 149
　government response to the Prague Spring, 10, 163–4
　Korčula declaration, 162, 163
　mediation between Prague and Moscow, 151–5, 158–9
　New Economic Mechanism, 149, 151
　popular response to the Prague Spring, 11, 161–3, 164
　present day, 3, 17
　role in Warsaw Pact invasion, 138, 156–8, 160–1
　see also Kádár
Husák, Gustáv, 9, 62, 64, 99

I
Ianoşi, Ion, 199, 208
Illyés, Gyula, 163

Ilmjärv, Magnus, 264, 265
'In Place of the Final Word' (Yahimovich), 267
India, 13
Indra, Alois, 47, 54, 136
intellectuals
　Albanian, 236, 239, 242–5
　in the Baltic states, 259, 269–72
　and neo-Stalinism, 48–51, 61
　Praxis group, 219, 228, 230
　Red Square demonstration, 85–6
　response to Warsaw Pact invasion, 141, 162–3, 164, 181–2, 198–200
　role in the Prague Spring, 6–7, 131
　and the Stasi, 112, 116
　see also Usatiuc-Ghimpu group
irredentism, 15–16, 76, 280, 283, 287–9
Israel, 2, 16–17, 129
　see also anti-Semitism
Italy, 13, 77, 186, 243, 247

J
Jero, Minush, 244
Jičínský, Zdeněk, 24, 39
Jodas, Josef, 47, 48, 49–51, 57, 60–2, 63
Johan (Romanian villager), 209–10
Johnson, Lyndon B., 183
Judt, Tony, 13–14
jurisprudence, see law

K
K-231 (Club of Former Political Prisoners), 7, 54–5, 63
Kádár, János
　on the Action Programme, 133
　and dissent, 163
　political strategy, 148–9, 160–1

role as mediator, 10, 151–5, 158–9, 164, 170–1
Kalanta, Romas, 266
Kalnbērziņš, Jānis, 270
KAN (Club of Committed Non-Party Members), 6–7, 54–5, 63
Kapek, Antonín, 47, 48, 55, 60, 61, 62, 63
Karadžić, Radovan, 16, 226
Karlovy Vary, 74, 104, 105, 108
Karlovy Vary conference 1967, 102, 134
Karner, Stefan, 3
Kati (Romanian villager), 209–10
Kaupužs, Vladimirs, 270
Kersten, Krystyna, 141
KGB (Soviet state security)
  in the Baltic states, 259, 261, 262, 265–8, 269
  and dissent, 83–4, 85, 88
  and the Greek Catholic Church, 80
  in Moldavia, 281, 293, 294
  role in Warsaw Pact invasion, 7, 74–5
Khrushchev, Nikita, 28, 71, 89, 125, 195, 236, 239, 258
Kisielewski, Stefan, 128
Ķīsis, Roberts, 271
Kodaj, Samuel, 182–3
Kolder, Drahomír, 173
Komsomol, 262, 265
Kořalka, Jiří, 100, 117n
Korčula, 162, 163, 219
Kosovo demonstrations, 228–9, 248–51
Kosygin, Alexei, 74, 87, 139, 159, 262–3
Kowalczuk, Ilko-Sascha, 2
Krasnaia zvezda (newspaper), 78
Krasnoe znamia (newspaper), 260–1
Kriegel, František, 50, 138, 172–3
Kuczyński, Rita, 122n

Kuroń, Jacek, 127, 142
Kurspahić, Kemal, 224, 228
Kuznetsov, Marat, 56, 57

L
Labour Party of Albania (PPSH), 240, 242, 245, 251
Lakatoš, Michal, 4, 39
  The Citizen, Law and Democracy, 28–30
  Considerations on the Values of Democracy, 30–4
  early works, 24–8
Latvia
  culture, 269–71
  national communists, 258
  patriotism, 263–4, 269
  popular support for Czechoslovakia, 266–8
  self-immolations, 11, 262, 266
  suppression of dissent, 259–62, 270–1
  see also Baltic States
Latvian Communist Party (LCP), 257, 258, 262, 269–70, 271
law
  and citizen's rights, 28–30, 35–7
  and civil society, 30–4
  and dissent, 38–9
  enduring legal theories, 23–4
  Lakatoš's early writings, 24–8
  'socialist legality', 17, 37–8, 159
Lica (Romanian villager), 208–10
Liliana (Romanian villager), 209–10
Lithuania, 265
  see also Baltic States
Lukács, György, 162–3

M
Magdeburg, 101, 111–12

Mao Zedong, 27, 185, 242, 247
Mara (Romanian villager), 209–10
Marcuse, Herbert, 286
Maria (Romanian villager), 208, 210
Marino, Adrian, 199–200
Markāns, Laimonis, 268
Marx, Karl, 98, 288, 293
Mazurov, Kirill, 76
media
    Albanian, 237, 238–9, 243
    Baltic states, 258, 260–1, 264, 267, 268, 269–70
    Bulgarian, 172, 182
    East German, 101, 111
    in Moldavia, 291, 292
    and Czech neo-Stalinists, 51–2, 56–7, 61
    and public opinion, 33, 35–6, 285
    Romanian, 183–4, 201
    samizdat publications, 85–8
    Soviet propaganda campaign, 8, 78–9
    transnational reach, 72, 77, 90, 109
    Yugoslav, 220, 224
    see also censorship
Michnik, Adam, 128, 142
Mickiewicz, Adam, 127
Mielke, Erich, 104, 110
Minić, Miloš, 221, 222
Mitrokhin, Vasili, 2
Mizherov, P. N., 266
Mladenov, Petar, 170, 177
Mlynář, Zdeněk, 28, 30, 51, 54, 137–8, 139
Modzelewski, Karol, 127, 142
Moldavia
    concerns of ethnic groups, 284, 295
    culture and nationalism, 290–3, 295
    propaganda campaigns, 279–80, 285–6
    and Romania, 283, 288–9, 293–5
    as a Soviet construct, 280–1

Mommsen, Hans, 97–100
'Moral Code of the Builder of Communism', 263
Morávek, Ladislav, 48, 49
Moravia, 52, 56, 101
Moscow meeting (May 1968), 8, 133, 152, 174
Moscow Protocol, 9, 159
Myzyri, Kujtim, 239

N
Nagy, Imre, 155
Naidenov, Dimitar, 180
NATO (North Atlantic Treaty Organisation), 109, 183, 186–7
Nazi Germany, 82, 101, 245
Nedelchev, Stoyan, 172
NEM (New Economic Mechanism), 149, 151, 164
neo-Stalinism
    and anti-communism, 45–6, 48–9, 53–5
    and anti-Semitism, 50–2
    and Ceaușescu, 199, 282
    and consolidation, 62–4
    factions, 46–8
    February 1968 letter, 49–51
    response to Warsaw Pact invasion, 15, 57–62
    and the Soviet Union, 6, 56–7
Neues Deutschland (newspaper), 102, 113
Nicolae (Romanian villager), 207–8
Nikolov, Raiko, 172
Ninth World Youth and Student Festival, 176–7, 202
Njollat e murme (Jero), 244–5
normalisation, 9, 37–8, 46, 47, 62–4, 294–5
NOROC (band), 292–3

'Notes on the Romanians' (Marx), 288, 293
Novotný, Antonín, 4, 6, 55, 86, 102, 237
Nový, Vilém, 47, 55, 61, 62, 63
NPF (National Patriotic Front, Soviet Moldavia), 293–4
NVA (National People's Army, East Germany), 104, 111, 113, 156

O
Ochab, Edward, 130–1
106 Years under the Russian Yoke (Ciobanu), 293
'Operation Danube', 104, 134, 177–8
Ostrava, 59–60, 126, 134
Ostrovskis, Gunārs, 268

P
Palach, Jan, 61, 116
Palestine Liberation Organisation, 2
Paris ('May Events' 1968), 2
patriotism, 14–16, 49, 73, 78–85, 89–90, 115, 198
Pennigerová, Soňa, 61–2
perestroika, 4
Petre (Romanian villager), 203–4
Petrescu, Dragos, 194
Pithart, Petr, 39
Podemos, 3
Podgornyi, Nikolai, 75
Poland
 after the invasion of Czechoslovakia, 141–2
 and Albania, 246
 foreign policy, 151
 government response to the Prague Spring, 10, 132–9, 156
 and Israel, 16–17, 129
 'March Events', 2, 127–30
 'Polish October', 125–6, 155, 239, 242
 popular response to the Prague Spring, 11, 140–1
 present day, 3, 17
 see also Gomułka; Warsaw summit
Polish United Workers' Party (PZPR), 125, 129, 130–1, 136, 139–40
Political Consultative Committee (PCC) of the Warsaw Pact, 171
populism, 3, 16, 17, 240
Pospíšil, Karel, 49
Postwar (Judt), 14
Poznań uprising, 125, 155, 239
Prasolov, Sergei, 56–7
Pravda (newspaper), 12, 60, 127
Praxis group, 162, 219, 228, 230
public opinion
 in the Baltic states, 262–70
 in the GDR, 101, 111–13
 and policy making, 33, 35–6
 on reform politics, 36–7, 58–9
 in Romania, 201–2
 in the USSR, 72–3, 81–5, 90
 see also dissent
Purs, Laimonis, 269

R
Ranković, Aleksander, 218, 248
Rapacki, Adam, 141–2
Red Square demonstration, 11, 85
Redzēt jūru (Purs), 269–70
Resi (Romanian villager), 209–10
responsibility and accountability, 31, 35
Ripka, Hubert, 50
Rips, Ilya, 262, 266
Rolling Stones, 108

308 INDEX

Romania
  autonomy, 195–6, 281–2, 288
  foreign policy, 151
  and the FRG, 102
  government response to the Prague Spring, 10, 12, 134, 160, 196–7
  intellectuals, 198–200
  and Moldavia, 280–1, 284, 288–9, 291–5
  popular support for Ceauşescu, 194, 203–5, 210–11, 289–90, 296
  state patriotism, 15–16
  villager accounts of August 1968, 200–11
  and the Warsaw Pact, 2, 136, 183–5
  see also Ceauşescu
Romanian Communist Party (RCP), 183, 195–6, 198
Rubenis, Jurijs, 270
Rudé právo (newspaper), 50, 51
Rusinow, Dennison, 220, 222, 223, 225, 232n

S
samizdat publications, 85–8, 267
Semerdzhiev, Atanas, 178–9
Shcherbyts'kyi, Volodymyr, 81
Shelest, Petro, 76, 81, 83, 134, 138, 287–8
Šik, Ota, 50, 51, 75, 99, 100, 172
Šimečka, Milan, 63
Šimek, Jan, 47, 48, 55
Simon, Annette, 2
Sino-Soviet split, 13, 27
Six Day War, 2, 80, 129
SKH (Croatian League of Communists), 225, 228
SKJ (Yugoslav League of Communists), 217–19, 221–3, 226–30
Słonimski, Antoni, 128
Slovak National Uprising (1944), 36, 99
Slushnyi, Vladimir, 261
Šmidrkal, Karel, 48, 49
Smrkovský, Josef, 50, 111–12
Social Democratic Party, Czechoslovakia (SDP), 7, 133, 139
Social Democratic Party, West Germany (SPD), 98, 101
'socialism with a human face', 2–7, 16, 36, 45–6, 63, 74
Socialist Unity Party of Germany (SED), 99, 100–6, 110–11, 113–14, 116–17
Solakov, Angel, 172, 173, 176–7, 178
Solidarity (trade union movement), 142
Şoltoianu, Alexandru, 294
sovereignty, 12–13, 15–17, 127, 136–9, 175, 195–6, 281–2
'The Spy' (Brecht), 245
Stalin, Josef, 125, 186, 216–17
Stalinism, 26, 27, 29, 37, 78, 85–6, 126
  see also de-Stalinisation; neo-Stalinism
Stănescu, Ion, 294
Stasi (East German secret police), 101, 106, 107–12, 116
State and Man (Stát a člověk) (Mlynář), 28
StB (Czechoslovak state security), 54
Stefi (Romanian villager), 209–10
Šťovíčková, Věra, 51
Strautmanis, Pēteris, 270
Ştrengaru (Romanian tourist), 290
student activism
  in 1989, 39
  in Albania, 241
  in the Baltic states, 261–2, 265–6, 268–9, 272

in Bulgaria, 181, 182
in Czechoslovakia, 132, 236–7
in the GDR, 17, 107–8, 111, 112, 114–15
Ninth World Youth and Student Festival, 176–7, 202–3
in Poland, 72, 78, 84, 127–30, 141
Strahov demonstration, 34–5, 36
Tito's response, 12, 215–16, 226–8, 229–30
in the USSR, 85, 86
in Western Europe, 2, 219–20
in Yugoslavia, 218–26, 228–9, 248–9
see also dissent; youth culture
Sudetenland, 78, 101, 111
'Šumava' manoeuvres, 8, 59, 134–5, 174
Suslov, Mikhail, 77, 134
Švestka, Oldřich, 51, 61
Svoboda, Jan, 47, 48, 56
Svoboda, Ludvík, 6, 109
Svoboda, Václav, 49
Syriza, 3
Szlajfer, Henryk, 128

T
TASS (Soviet news agency), 79, 138, 260
terror
 anti-communist, 53–5
 in the Baltic states, 258
 in the GDR, 113
 Stalinist, 71, 126
 in Yugoslavia, 217
Testimițanu, Nicolae, 291–2
Thant, U, 150
Tito, Josip Broz
 and Ceaușescu, 183, 197
 and Dubček, 134, 228, 249
 and Hoxha, 185

and Kosovo, 248–9
response to student protests, 12, 215–16, 226–30
and the USSR, 13, 216–17
'To the Citizens of the Soviet Union' (Yahimovich), 267
Todorov, Stanko, 172, 175
Tolpezhnikov, Vilen, 261
Tömpe, András, 163
Toni (Romanian villager), 209–10
Transcarpathia, 73, 76, 82, 83, 282, 287–8
Transnistria, 280, 281
Trebeshina, Kasem, 243
Tribuna (newspaper), 61
Trojan, Jaroslav, 61–2
'Two Thousand Words' manifesto, 7, 52, 107, 135, 137, 175, 176

U
Ukraine
 and Czechoslovakia, 73, 75, 76, 83
 dissent, 86, 87–8
 ethnicity and nationalism, 80, 81, 88–9
 see also Shelest
Ulbricht, Walter
 and Dubček, 131
 and the FRG, 116
 and Novotný, 102
 support for invasion of Czechoslovakia, 103–6, 137–8, 153, 159, 161
ultra-leftist extremism, *see* neo Stalinism
United Nations, 150, 151
United States, 1, 150, 183, 197–8, 217–18, 285
Usatiuc, Alexandru, 293–4
Usatiuc-Ghimpu group, 293–4

USSR
 and Albania, 235–6, 246
 and Bessarabia, 280–1, 288–9, 291
 Brezhnev Doctrine, 12–13, 17, 137, 159–60, 163–4, 174–5
 and China, 185
 'Commission on the Czechoslovak Question', 134–5
 de-Stalinisation, 71–3
 dissent, 85–8, 266–70, 272–3, 292
 domination of communist ideology, 282–4
 and Hungary, 150–1
 identity politics, 79–81, 89–90
 'Moral Code of the Builder of Communism', 263
 normalisation, 294–5
 reasons for invasion of Czechoslovakia, 7–9, 74–6, 138–40
 relations with Eastern Europe, 76–8, 83–4, 90, 155–7, 171–2, 251
 response to 'Two Thousand Words' manifesto, 135–6
 and Romania, 195–8, 201–3, 206, 282, 289–90
 social welfare, 287
 state patriotism, 15–16, 81–3
 troops' reaction to invasion of Czechoslovakia, 11
 and West Germany, 14–15, 78–9, 134
 and Yugoslavia, 216–17
 see also Brezhnev; Ukraine

V
Vaculík, Ludvík, 7, 52, 107, 135
Vagris, Jānis, 261
Valenta, Josef, 47, 48, 56
Valtin (Romanian villager), 205–7

values (Lakatoš), 30–2, 34, 36, 39
Velvet Revolution, 13–14
Vietnam War, 1, 12, 101, 150, 151, 215, 217–18, 284
Vlahović, Veljko, 221–2
Voss, Augusts, 269–70
Vyshinsky, Andrei, 26

W
Warsaw Letter, 106, 137, 175, 176
Warsaw Pact
 Albania's withdrawal from, 10, 246–7, 251
 multi-lateralisation, 155–6
 unity, 10, 11, 13
 and West Germany, 132–3, 134, 139–40
Warsaw summit (July 1968), 8, 106, 136–7, 153, 175
Weigel, Sandra, 113
West Germany, *see* German Federal Republic (FRG)
Western Europe
 building bridges, 285–6
 Euro-communism, 13, 185–6
 health and housing, 287
 populism, 16, 17
 post invasion, 186–7, 197
 relationship with Hungary, 149, 150, 162
 and Romania, 196
 student protests, 2, 215, 219–20
'Where is Czechoslovakia Going?' (Hoxha), 238
Williams, Kieran, 9
Windsor, Philip, 135
Wolle, Stefan, 115

X
xenophobia, 73, 78–84, 207–8

see also patriotism
Xhuvani, Dhimitër, 244

Y
Yahimovich, Ivan, 266–7
youth culture
 anti-invasion sentiment, 11, 112–14, 181, 266, 268
 and communist ideology, 241, 287
 in the GDR, 106, 107–8
 music and nationalism, 292–3
 Ninth World Youth and Student Festival, 176–7, 202–3
 transnational protest movement, 1
 westernised, 63, 109, 182, 243
 see also student activism
Yugoslavia
 and Albania, 235, 247
 ethno-nationalism, 16, 226
 foreign policy, 217–18
 and the FRG, 102
 response to the Prague Spring, 134, 186, 197
 Kosovo demonstrations, 248–51
 legislature, 30
 planned Warsaw Pact intervention, 183–5
 split with USSR, 13, 216–17, 283
 state patriotism, 15
 student protests ('June Events'), 2, 12, 215–16, 218–26, 228–30
 suppression of activism, 227–9

Z
Zëri i popullit (newspaper), 237, 238, 239
Zhivkov, Todor
 and Brezhnev, 171–2, 185, 186
 Dresden meeting, 172
 hard-line attitude to the Prague Spring, 106, 153, 159, 169–71
 Moscow meeting, 174
 order to invade, 178–9
 visit to Czechoslovakia, 173–4
 Warsaw summit, 175–6
Zhou Enlai, 2, 185, 247
Zhukov, Georgy, 240
Žigon, Stevo, 222–3
Zikulov, Vasil, 183
Žilnik, Želimir, 220

Printed in the United States
By Bookmasters